Shifting Boundaries

Ideas, History, and Modern China

Edited by

Ban Wang (*Stanford University*)
Wang Hui (*Tsinghua University*)

VOLUME 35

The titles published in this series are listed at *brill.com/ihmc*

Shifting Boundaries

A Global History of the Monroe Doctrine

By

Zhang Yongle

Translated by

Zheng Huan

BRILL

This project is supported by the National Social Science Fund of China. 本项目获得“中华社会科学基金”资助。English edition licensed by SDX Joint Publishing Co., Ltd.

The Library of Congress Cataloging-in-Publication Data is available online at https://catalog.loc.gov
LC record available at https://lccn.loc.gov/2025029605

Typeface for the Latin, Greek, and Cyrillic scripts: "Brill". See and download: brill.com/brill-typeface.

ISSN 1875-9394
ISBN 978-90-04-74622-0 (hardback)
ISBN 978-90-04-74623-7 (e-book)
DOI 10.1163/9789004746237

This book is printed on acid-free paper and produced in a sustainable manner.

O accomplished Hou-ji,
Thou didst prove thyself the correlate of Heaven;
Thou didst give grain-food to our multitudes; —
The immense gift of thy goodness.
Thou didst confer on us the wheat and the barley,
Which God appointed for the nourishment of all;
And without distinction of territory or boundary,
The rules of social duty were diffused throughout these great regions.

The Book of Songs, Zhou Song, Si Wen

• • •

Asian copper, Asian copper
After beating the drum, we call the heart dancing in the dark the moon.
The moon is mainly composed of you.

HAI ZI, Asian Copper

Contents

Acknowledgements

This book is my first academic monograph published in English. The Chinese version of this book has already been published in the Harvard-Yanching series of SDX Press in 2021. Feng Jinhong, Shu Wei and Zhong Yun, editors of SDX Press, gave me strong support in the process of publication. Professor Zheng Huan presided over the translation of the English version of the book. Professor Sabrina Habich-Sobiegalla from Freie Universität Berlin, Su Jin, and Stacy Mosher oversaw the proofreading the book. Zheng Tao, Li Xu, Wu Yingjuan, Zhao Xiya and other doctoral students participated in the proofreading of the English manuscript. Without their joint efforts, the publication of this English version would have been impossible.

The brewing, writing, and dissemination of this book benefited from many institutions. The Law School of Peking University which I work for has given me plenty of freedom to do research across the three disciplines of law, politics and history; Institut d'études avancées de Nantes provides an inspiring environment for the final production of the manuscript. I would like to especially thank Professor Alain Supiot, the leading soul of the Institute, as well as my colleagues Professor Wang Pu and José Emilio Burucua, who discussed with me frequently in Nantes. The Institute of Humanities and Social Sciences of Peking University generously awarded me the Xingquan Young Scholar Book Award, which is no less encouraging than another award from Ministry of Education—the Second Prize of the 9th Outstanding Achievement Award of Scientific Research in Colleges and Universities (Humanities and Social Sciences).

Some chapters or segments of this book have been shared and discussed at the following Conferences and seminars in 2019 and have received comments from many scholars: the "China's Growth in the Perspective of World Political History" seminar held at the Institute of Humanities and Social Sciences, Peking University on December 14; the 8th "Legal Order and the China Path" Conference held at Chongqing University on August 25–26; the 2nd "Nomos" Summer School held at the Law School of Peking University from July 8 to 12; the International Conference on "Community with Shared Futures for Mankind: Civilizations of China and Europe and the New Global Legal Order" held at the Law School of Beijing Institute of Technology on June 21–22; the "China and the World in Historical Time and Space" Conference held at the Institute of Global Civilization History, Shanghai International Studies University on May 25; the "Monroe vs. Wilson? The Spatial Struggle between Regional

Hegemony and Global Hegemony" symposium held at the Law School of Renmin University of China on May 8, and so on. Among all these events, the most intensive discussion was the seminar on "China's Growth in the Perspective of World Political History" hosted by Professor Liu Xiaofeng. This is a closed-door meeting, with more than thirty scholars conducting a "joint diagnosis" on an earlier version of the manuscript of this book for more than three hours. I am deeply grateful to the scholars who participated in these conferences and seminars.

I would like to express my heartfelt gratitude to Perry Anderson and Carlo Ginzburg for their continuous encouragement over the past two decades. Their guidance has been an invaluable source of inspiration and support throughout my academic journey. In particular, I am deeply indebted to Professor Perry Anderson for his insightful lectures on the "Concert of Great Powers" delivered at Peking University in 2016, which inspired me to delve deeper into the study of international order. Professor Ginzburg's historical research, especially *Cheese and Worms*, have always been my exemplar in research methodology, prompting me to carefully distinguish the texture of history and not to easily leap over the gap between the present and the historical scenes. Professor Ginzburg visited Peking University in the fall of 2019, which brought me another methodological baptism. This book benefited from their teachings, but all the errors and imperfections are due to my own negligence and immaturity.

Here, I would also like to thank Wang Hui, Huang Ping, Gan Yang, Wang Shaoguang, Su Li, Feng Xiang, Liang Zhiping, Cui Zhiyuan, Pan Wei, Zhang Xudong, Huang Xingtao, Guo Shuanglin, Jiang Shigong, Anthony Carty, Daniel A. Bell, Wang Xixin, Chen Duanhong, Takahiro Nakajima, Ishii Tsuyoshi, Wu Chongqing, Yang Lihua, Luo Gang, Li Meng, Ding Yun, Han Chao, Li Fangchun, Wang Xianhua, Ou Shujun, Zhang Guangsheng, Jiang Youfu, Bai Gang, He Jianyu, Wei Nanzhi, Yan Yilong, Jia Jinjing, Wang Weijia, Chen Baifeng, Nie Xin, Zhang Taisu, Yin Zhiguang, Tao Qingmei, Zhang Xiang, Liu Zhong, Tian Lei, Xiao Wu, Chang An, Yu Ming, Chen Ruoying, Pan Nini, Liu Zhuo, Liu Cheng, Yan Tian, Chen Yifeng, Zuo Yilu, Tang Jie, Zhang Huiyu, Wang Yang, Chen Qi, Li Guangyi, Li Sheng, Xu Jian, Li Site, Yang Ang, Wei Leijie, Wei Chun, Li Zhen, Wang Weihua, Guo Shaomin, Lei Shaohua, Sun Feiyu, Jiang Hongsheng, Zan Tao, Qu Jun, Wang Qin, Liu Yang, Liu Chenguang, Kong Yuan, Wang Rui, Pan Dan, Zheng Huan, Ge Xiaohui and other scholars and friends for their long-term encouragement, support and inspiration. I would like to thank Shi Zhiqiang and Zhu Xiaoqi for their help in collecting and reading Japanese literature, and thank Xu Bin, Shao Liuyi, Fu Zheng and other friends in our "Ban Du" (which means "crossing the river halfway") reading group.

I dedicated this little book to my deceased friend Zhang Xiaobo. He once wrote enthusiastic book reviews for my second book *Rivalry of Nations: Kang Youwei and the Decay of the Vienna System* in the *Liberation Daily*. At this moment, he has already fallen asleep underground and could not read my words. However, the major changes in the global order he envisioned during his lifetime are accelerating. If he could see all this, I believe he would feel both worried and gratified, just like me.

Introduction "Monroe Doctrine": the Global Circulation of a Concept of Spatial Politics

> Pacific Ocean! Pacific Ocean! The wind is so strong and the tide is so violent.
>
> LIANG QICHAO, The Song of the 20th Century Pacific[1]

∴

Being human, we live in space. All manifestations of property systems, governance models, and lifestyles are fundamentally rooted in the demarcation, appropriation, and utilization of space. When we live in a specific space with a sense of comfort and use it as a medium to engage in a diverse range of activities, we typically do not perceive the entire space as an object of scrutiny. Instead, it exists as a backdrop to our daily lives, a taken-for-granted environment. However, when the established boundaries of that space are challenged, it is abruptly removed from its intermediary role and thrust into the spotlight as an object of both attention and contestation. In response to this disruption, different groups are compelled to view the space as an entity worthy of examination, seeking to strengthen the link between a particular human collective and a specific spatial domain. This process aims to restore the spatial boundaries to a state that once again provides a sense of relative comfort and security for its inhabitants. When the conflicts around the boundaries of space reach a certain intensity, "spatial politics" occurs. This term encapsulates the complex interplay of power, interests, and identity that unfolds within the context of spatial disputes, highlighting the ways in which space becomes a site of struggle and negotiation in social and political life.

When two primitive tribes quarrel or even engage in combat over the boundaries of their hunting and gathering spheres, the rudimentary form of spatial politics comes into being. In contrast to today's highly sophisticated forms of spatial politics, the conflict among primitive tribes undeniably lacks the diverse array of physical means prevalent in the modern world. Moreover, the proliferation of discourses typical of such conflicts is also absent in

1 Zhang Pinxing 张品兴 ed., *Liang Qichao quan ji* 梁启超全集 [Complete Works of Liang Qichao], (Beijing: Beijing Press, 1999), 5427.

 | DOI:10.1163/9789004746237_002

their case. The unit of spatial politics then was small-scale and its forms were restricted. In the contemporary era, the dynamics and mechanisms of spatial politics have developed and are evident at numerous levels, ranging from the demarcation of national and supranational regional boundaries to the rivalry for global space and even outer space. Novel spatial constructs such as "cyberspace," which exists in a more abstract realm compared to the tangible and geographical space we are accustomed to, have emerged as one of the focal points in contemporary spatial politics.[2] Spatial politics has also produced numerous types of legal norms, which sometimes could settle the disputes, but sometimes directly serve the narrow interests of one party in the conflict and become an instrument of war, thus forming the so-called "lawfare."[3]

In the mainstream historical narratives and social theories in the 19th century Europe, space was gradually rearranged in a position subordinate to time.[4] Within numerous discourses, human history was portrayed as a linear progression through a series of continuous stages. Accordingly, societies situated in various locations across the global space could be aligned along the timeline based on their differing developmental stages and levels of civilization. It was presumed that European civilization occupied such an elevated position that it was deemed entitled to lead, or even dominate, other regions. The 19th century was an era in which European powers coordinated with one another via congresses, conferences, and numerous other diplomatic mechanisms, and sought to subjugate non-European peoples. The conquests and domination were often celebrated as the remarkable accomplishments of European powers in "civilizing" all peoples from a privileged temporal-historical vantage point.

However, in the 20th century, with the escalation of conflicts among European powers, the theoretical significance of space has been rising. Political

---

2 The U.S.-led North Atlantic Treaty Organization officially approved the inclusion of space in its defense field at its London summit on December 3–4, 2019, and listed it as one of the five battlefields alongside land, sea, air and cyberspace. In view of the fact that "war is the continuation of politics" (Krakowitz), this list itself is a list of the fields of spatial politics.

3 On the concept of "lawfare," see Orde F. Kittrie, *Lawfare: Law as a Weapon of War*, (Oxford: Oxford University Press, 2016).

4 This is also the judgment made by Barney Warf and Santa Arias in the book *The Spatial Turn: Interdisciplinary Perspectives*, Barney Warf and Santa Arias ed. *The Spatial Turn: Interdisciplinary Perspectives*, (London & New York: Routledge, 2009), 2–3. I shared their judgment on the mainstream consciousness of the 19th century. However, as to why "space" gained a higher status in the 20th century, I tend to emphasize the interaction of various structural forces rather than the writings of a few scholars.

geography/geopolitics[5] was born in the contexts of regional and global competition among European powers (especially Britain and Germany) with similar "civilizational levels." Because the temporal-historical positioning of the parties to the conflict in the hierarchy of civilization is deemed to be similar, the spatial differences stood out as a significant factor. The two world wars originated from Europe were a heavy blow to the Eurocentric view of linear temporality and hierarchy of civilization, accelerating the decolonization of peoples under colonial domination. One nation after another gained their independence from the colonized status. After that, post-colonial nations' tortuous experience of social and economic development brought a new wave of controversy on the spatial position of the "center" and "periphery."[6]

Within the Eastern bloc, buoyed by a profound sense of self-assurance stemming from its perceived privileged historical-temporal vantage point, Moscow persistently advocated and sought to establish the universal applicability of its own experience. Nevertheless, this dogmatic stance encountered significant resistance in the form of independent explorations undertaken by Communist Parties in numerous countries. Notably, China's strong emphasis on the principle of "tailoring measures to local conditions" in both its revolutionary struggles and subsequent construction efforts was a particularly potent challenge based upon the self-consciousness of spatiality. On the other side of the "Iron Curtain," the U.S. promoted the "modernization theory" with an highly significant temporal-historical implication to compete with Moscow's discourse. Approaching the end of the Cold War, Francis Fukuyama announced "the end of history," which was grounded in the idea of "recognition" and underpinned by a linear historical perspective, and made an earnest attempt to subsume

5 Johan Rudolf Kjellén, a student of Ratzel and a Swedish political scientist, is the connecting link between political geography and geopolitics. See Joe Painter and Alex Jeffery, *Political Geography*, London: Sage, 2009; Colin Flint, *Introduction to Geopolitics*, London: Routledge, 2017.

6 As for the representative works of the theoretical spectrum from the Dependency Theory to the theory of the "world system," see R. Prebisch, *Capitalismo Periferico: crisis y transformación*, México: Fondo de Cultura Económica, 1981; Paul A. Baran, *The Political Economy of Growth*, New York: Monthly Review Press, 1968; Samir Amin, *Accumulation on a world scale: Accumulation on a world scale: a critique of the theory of underdevelopment*, New York, Monthly Review Press (1974); Samir Amin, *Unequal development: An essay on the social formations of peripheral capitalism*, New York, Monthly Review Press, 1976; A.G. Frank, *Dependent Accumulation and Underdevelopment*, New York, Monthly Review Press, 1979, Immanuel Wallerstein, *Modern World-System*, Berkeley, University of California Press, 2011, Giovanni Arrighi, *The Long Twentieth Century: Money, Power and the Origins of Our Time*, London; New York: Verso, 1994.

the vast expanse of the global space within its logical framework.[7] However, after nearly 30 years, even in the North America, many elites are discussing the "divided states of America" or "the coming civil war."[8]

What profound and tangible changes have unfolded across the globe three decades following the conclusion of the Cold War? The concept of "globalization" with strong temporal-historical connotations became popular, which once led to close attention to the spatial concept of "global." In 2005, The famous American journalist Thomas L. Friedman published a best-selling book entitled "The World is Flat."[9] Similarly, many intellectuals in the U.S. or China imagined that the ongoing historical process would bring about an increasingly homogeneous global space in which capital, commodities and technical knowledge should flow freely. This vision seems novel to many of Friedman's audiences because it may weaken the conventional spatial boundaries of the nation-state, but it was worth embracing as the benefits of the impact to people worldwide far outweigh the losses. Three years later, British scholar Mark Leonard published *What Does China Think*? Based on Thomas Friedman's concept of "flat world," the book summarized the imagination of a series of Chinese thinkers interviewed by the author on the world order as "the walled world."[10] This seemed to imply that although China has joined the WTO and become a key participant in the global economy, Chinese thinkers were still more attuned to the order of the nation-state and kept cautious about taking new steps in politics.

However, Mark Leonard probably could not imagine that ten years later, it was the U.S., not China, that became a nation that was most keen on "building walls." U.S. President Donald Trump openly declared that he was a "nationalist" rather than a "globalist."[11] His signature campaign proposition was to build a wall on the border between the U.S. and Mexico to prevent the influx of Latin American refugees/immigrants. In this endeavor, the keenness to construct the universal temporal-historical view in the 20th century have evaporated, leaving only the propaganda of the narrow interests of the majority race within the nation-state. It is also Trump who launched a series of trade wars against

---

7 Francis Fukuyama, *The End of History and the Last Man*, Glencoe, IL: Free Press, 1992.

8 Louis Menand, "Francis Fukuyama Postpones the End of History," 3 September 2018, *New Yorker* at: <https://www.newyorker.com/magazine/2018/09/03/francis-fukuyama-postpones-the-end-of-history>.

9 Thomas L. Friedman, *The World Is Flat: A Brief History of the Twenty-first Century*, New York: Farrar, Straus and Giroux, 2005.

10 Mark Leonard, *What Does China Think?* London: Fourth Estate, 2008.

11 Quint Forgey, "Trump: 'I'm a nationalist,'" 22 October 2018, at: <https://www.politico.com/story/2018/10/22/trump-nationalist-926745> (accessed 25 February 2020).

many countries including U.S. allies, as well as a technological and financial war against China, and withdrew from many international treaties and organizations. The U.S. also used its own financial hegemony[12] to force a series of EU countries to weaken their trade ties with Iran.

The Trump administration openly weaponized economic interdependence to attack the targeted "competitors," and the Biden administration between Trump's two terms succeeded many of these policies. This reminds many other countries of the risk of economic interdependence and forces them to consider adjusting industrial supply chains and building non-U.S. dollar international monetary settlement systems. Against this backdrop of heightened geopolitical and economic tensions, it has become abundantly clear that "the world is not flat." Instead, the spatial fabric of our global existence is undergoing a profound and transformative wave of reconfiguration. Many long-established boundaries and walls are being steadily fortified, and a fresh crop of boundaries and barriers is emerging, reflecting the evolving geopolitical and economic landscapes.

Among the various "wall-building" initiatives, U.S. actions in Latin America are particularly striking. In 2018–2019, the Trump administration adopted a series of foreign policies aimed at reasserting U.S. power in Latin America: reversing the Obama administration's détente with Cuba and pushing for regime change; accusing China's Belt and Road Initiative of creating a "debt trap" for several Latin American countries; accusing Russia of supporting the Maduro regime in Venezuela while fostering political opposition in Venezuela and Bolivia to promote regime change; and, by recalling ambassadors, expressing dissatisfaction with the independent decisions of countries like the Dominican Republic, El Salvador, and Panama to establish diplomatic relations with Beijing. The Trump administration also inserted a "poison pill" clause into the U.S.-Mexico-Canada Trade Agreement (USMCA) signed in October 2018, stipulating that if any member country reached a free trade agreement with a "non-market economy," the other member countries could withdraw from the agreement after six months. This clause effectively limited the foreign trade sovereignty of Canada and Mexico, although the two countries formally agreed to the terms. In early 2025, Trump even astonishingly expresses his territorial interest in Canada, Greenland, and the Panama Canal. Under his pressure,

12 This book uses the word "hegemony" in Gramsci's sense, as the combination of coercion and consent, but in the final analysis the order maintained by hegemony does not necessarily serve the ruled. For the historical evolution of the meaning of the word "hegemony," see Perry Anderson, *The H-Word: The Peripeteia of Hegemony*, (Brooklyn & New York: Verso, 2017).

Panama withdrew from the Belt and Road Initiative. These actions reflect the hegemonic mindset that the Americas, or the Western Hemisphere, should remain the exclusive sphere of U.S. influence.

The Trump administration not only renewed public interference in the internal affairs of Latin American countries but also openly celebrated these actions. On February 1, 2018, then-Secretary of State Rex Tillerson praised the Monroe Doctrine, first articulated by President James Monroe in 1823, as an "obvious success" in a speech in Austin, Texas, arguing that the principle was still as relevant as ever. He also accused China's "state-led model of development" of being a threat to the Western Hemisphere.[13] On March 3, 2019, when CNN host asked then-National Security Advisor John Bolton if it was contradictory for the U.S. to describe Venezuela's Maduro as a "dictator" while supporting other dictatorial regimes around the world, Bolton responded negatively, claiming that because Venezuela was in "our hemisphere," the U.S. was justified in invoking the Monroe Doctrine.[14] On April 17, 2019, when Bolton announced new sanctions against Cuba, Venezuela, and Nicaragua, he remarked, "The Monroe Doctrine is alive and well." The *Economist* commented that this statement was aimed at countering the growing influence of Russia and China in Latin America.[15] In an interview with Fox News in January 2025, Mike Waltz, the National Security Advisor appointed by Trump, undisguisedly called Trump's plan to redraw the map of the Americas "Monroe Doctrine 2.0."[16] Donald Trump, in his inaugural speeches on 20 January, openly evoked the concept "Manifest Destiny," a term invented during the westward expansion on the American continent in the 19th century.[17] James Petras, emeritus professor at Binghamton University, argued that the Trump administration was pursuing a "Neo-Monroe Doctrine," aimed at re-establishing U.S. dominance in Latin

---

13 Robbie Gramer and Keith Johnson, "Tillerson Praises Monroe Doctrine, Warns Latin America of 'Imperial' Chinese Ambulances," 2 February 2018, at: <https://foreignpolicy.com/2018/02/02/tillerson-praises-monroe-doctrine-warns-latin-america-off-imperial-chinese-ambitions-mexico-south-america-nafta-diplomacy-trump-trade-venezuela-maduro/>.

14 Interview with U.S. National Security Advisor John Bolton, 3 March 2019, at: <http://edition.cnn.com/TRANSCRIPTS/1903/03/sotu.01.html>.

15 "John Bolton and the Monroe Doctrine," 9 May 2019, *The Economist* at: <https://www.economist.com/leaders/2019/05/09/John-Bolton-and-the-Monroe-Doctrine>.

16 "Trump Adviser Admits Seizing Greenland Is About Fossil Fuels, Raw Imperialism," Jan 9, 2025, at: <https://alaska-native-news.com/trump-adviser-admits-seizing-greenland-is-about-fossil-fuels-raw-imperialism/77102/>.

17 "The Inaugural Address," 20 January, 2025, at: <https://www.whitehouse.gov/remarks/2025/01/the-inaugural-address/>.

America.[18] This was substantiated by The U.S. 2025 National Security Strategy, which bluntly announced "the Trump Corollary to the Monroe Doctrine."[19]

But is the "Neo-Monroe Doctrine" of Donald Trump really new?[20] Historically, the U.S. has repeatedly used the Monroe Doctrine to justify interference in the internal affairs of other countries. When President James Monroe introduced the doctrine in his 1823 State of the Union Address, the U.S. lacked the capability to interfere in the internal affairs of Latin American countries, but it soon expanded its influence in the region under the guise of resisting foreign interference.

The term "Monroe Doctrine" itself did not emerge until the 1850s and was retrospectively applied to Monroe's diplomatic policy. From its inception, the doctrine was used to set concrete spatial boundaries, and various theories about the legitimacy of these boundaries, including the practice of regional international law, emerged around it.[21] By the 1850s, the U.S. had extended its influence to Central America, where it competed with Britain. By the late 19th century, Britain had recognized U.S. hegemony in the Americas. In the early 20th century, President Theodore Roosevelt expanded the Monroe Doctrine into a justification for U.S. intervention as the "international police" of the Western Hemisphere. Even President Woodrow Wilson, who championed the right of nations to determine their own paths during World War I,

18 James Petras, "Latin America in the Time of Trump: U.S. Domination and The 'Neo-Monroe Doctrine'" 23 April 2018, at: <https://www.globalresearch.ca/Latin-America-in-the-time-of-Trump-us-domination-and-the-neo-Monroe-Doctrine/5637399>.

19 "The 2025 National Security Strategy of the United States of America," 4 December 2025, at <https://www.whitehouse.gov/wp-content/uploads/2025/12/2025-National-Security-Strategy.pdf>.

20 The concept of the "New Monroe Doctrine" or "Neo-Monroe Doctrine" recurred in history. Using ProQuest U.S. Newspapers Database, I found that the following American English newspapers published articles with the words "New Monroe Doctrine" in their titles in the following years: *Bankers' Magazine*, No. 2, 1911; *The Graphic*, No. 1, 1896; *Outlook*, August 27th, 1898, February 11th, 1905; *Advocate of Peace*, No. 2, 1896; *The North American Review*, No. 4, 1905; *The Youth's Companion*, No. 1, 1916; *International Marine Engineering*, No. 5, 1917; *The Living Age*, December 10th, 1921; *The Spectator*, January 25th, 1896, as for the newspaper articles with the words "New Monroe Doctrine" in the text, there are countless more.

21 For the relationship between the Monroe Doctrine and regional international law in Latin America, see Bardo Fassbender and Anne Peters eds., *Oxford Handbook of International Law History*, Oxford, United Kingdom, Oxford University Press, 2012, pp. 553–577.

was supportive of military intervention in Latin America, as were the three Republican presidents who succeeded him.

In the 1930s, President Franklin D. Roosevelt introduced the "Good Neighbor Policy," which sought to reduce direct interference in Latin America. However, during the Cold War, the Monroe Doctrine was revitalized under the guise of eliminating the "communist threat," leading to extensive U.S. interference in Latin American countries, leaving them with lasting historical trauma.[22] As John Bolton aptly noted, the Monroe Doctrine has been "alive and well" from 1823 to the Cold War.

The end of the Cold War made the "communist threat" more or less obsolete as a justification for U.S. intervention. More significantly, the U.S. gained unprecedented confidence in its global empire, viewing Latin America as just one of the regions under its control. Graham Allison, in his article "The New Spheres of Influence," pointed out that American policymakers, after the Cold War, did not recognize other powers' spheres of influence because they considered the entire world to be an American sphere.[23] As the U.S. sought to maintain the appearance of multilateralism to sustain its global hegemony, emphasizing the Monroe Doctrine was no longer a suitable rhetorical strategy.

As a result, post-Cold War U.S. administrations downplayed the Monroe Doctrine. In 1995, Yale historian Gaddis Smith published *The Last Years of the Monroe Doctrine*, suggesting the doctrine had reached its end.[24] The official U.S. announcement came in 2013, when Secretary of State John Kerry declared at the Organization of American States that the era of the Monroe Doctrine had ended and that the U.S. would no longer interfere in the affairs of other American nations.[25] However, just after a few years, the U.S. reasserted its control over Latin America, demonstrating that while the extent and depth of interference under the Monroe Doctrine may vary, the interference itself does not disappear.

U.S. critics have also applied the term "Monroe Doctrine" to political spaces beyond the Western Hemisphere. For instance, China's Belt and Road Initiative has been described as a Chinese version of the Monroe Doctrine, aimed at

22 Gaddis Smith, *The Last Years of the Monroe Doctrine: 1945–1993*, New York: Hill and Wang, 1994.

23 Graham Allison, "The New Spheres of Influence: Sharing the Globe With Other Great Powers," *Foreign Affairs* (March/April 2020).

24 Smith (n. 20).

25 Keith Johnson, "Kerry Makes It Official: 'Era of Monroe Doctrine Is Over,'" *The Wall Street Journal* (18 November 2013).

excluding U.S. influence in relevant regions.[26] In *International Relations and the Origins of the Pacific War* (2016), Japanese scholar Ko Unoki made an interesting comparison between contemporary China and modern Japan, exploring whether China is indeed on a trajectory that might resemble Japan's historical path of adopting a so-called "Asiatic Monroe Doctrine."[27] Notably, many critics view the Monroe Doctrine positively when applied to the U.S., but negatively when applied to China. In this context, the shifting in the meaning of the "Monroe Doctrine" becomes evident. Any serious response to such comparisons must first address the fundamental question: What exactly does the Monroe Doctrine mean?

1 Problems, Approaches and Methods

Answering the question "what is the Monroe Doctrine?" is far more intricate and multi-faceted task than it might initially appear on the surface. From President Monroe's 1823 State of the Union Address to the 21st century, the symbol of the "Monroe Doctrine" has been disseminated globally. It no longer belongs exclusively to the U.S., and its interpretation has undergone tremendous changes, even within the U.S. itself, let alone in various countries and regions where local needs shaped different interpretations. To truly understand what the "Monroe Doctrine" means across different times and spaces, we urgently need a historical account tracing the transformations in the interpretation of Monroe Doctrine discourses and symbols. Such a study would also need to outline the morphological types of "spatial politics" concerning the boundaries of "political space" that underpin these changes. As of now, the existing research lacks a comprehensive monograph of this kind, which provides space for further thinking and discussion.

It is not a profound revelation that the Monroe Doctrine has significantly influenced the modern world. In different languages—Chinese, Japanese, English, and German—numerous books and papers have been written on the history of the Monroe Doctrine in the U.S. There is also concrete research on Carl Schmitt's theory of international order, Japan's "Asianism" discourse,

26 Steven F. Jackson, "Does China Have a Monroe Doctrine? Evidence for Regional Exclusion," *Strategic Studies Quarterly* Vol. 10, No. 4 (Winter 2016), 64–89; Joshua Kurlantzick, *Charm Offensive: How China's Soft Power is Transforming the World*, (New Haven: Yale University Press, 2007), 11.

27 Ko Unoki, *International Relations and the Origins of the Pacific War*, (New York: Palgrave Macmillan, 2016), 177–195.

China's "United Provincial Autonomy" movement, and the Chinese reception of and response to Japan's "Asianism." These works touch on the symbols and concepts of the Monroe Doctrine sporadically. In the U.S., where the Monroe Doctrine originated, the research on its evolution remains particularly vibrant. For example, Dexter Perkins has authored several books detailing the development of the Monroe Doctrine, with particular focus on the periods 1823–1826 and 1867–1907.[28] Jay Sexton's *The Monroe Doctrine: Empire and Nation in Nineteenth-Century America*[29] examines the U.S.'s nation-building and empire-building projects, dividing the evolution of the Monroe Doctrine in the 19th century into distinct stages.

Francis Anthony Boyle's *Foundations of World Order: The Legalist Approach to International Relations (1898–1922)*,[30] Juan Pablo Scarfi's *The Hidden History of International Law in the Americas: Empire and Legal Networks*,[31] and Christopher Rossi's *Whiggish International Law: Elihu Root, the Monroe Doctrine, and International Law in the Americas*[32] focus on the U.S. government's legal strategies and its interactions with Latin American politico-legal elites at the end of the 19th century and the beginning of the 20th century. The latter two works explore "American international law," with particular emphasis on the interpretation of the Monroe Doctrine by Latin American jurists.[33] Scarfi's recent book, *Denaturalizing the Monroe Doctrine: The Rise of Latin American Legal Anti-Imperialism in the Face of the Modern U.S. and Hemispheric Redefinition of the Monroe Doctrine*, examines the anti-imperialist readings of the Monroe Doctrine by Latin American jurists. Boyle's work also demonstrates the continuity between U.S. regional hegemony in Latin America and its later global hegemony.[34] Gretchen Murphy's *Hemispheric*

---

28 Dexter Perkins, *The Monroe Doctrine, 1826–1867*, (Baltimore, Md: The Johns Hopkins University Press, 1933); Dexter Perkins, *The Monroe Doctrine, 1867–1907*, (Baltimore, Md: The Johns Hopkins University Press, 1937); Dexter Perkins, *A History of the Monroe Doctrine*, (Boston: Little, Brown and Co., 1955).

29 Jay Sexton, *The Monroe Doctrine: Empire and Nation in Nineteenth-Century America*, (New York: Hill and Wang, 2011).

30 Francis Anthony Boyle, *Foundations of World Order: The Legalist Approach to International Relations (1898–1922)*, (Durham and London: Duke University Press, 1999).

31 Juan Pablo Scarfi, *The Hidden History of International Law in the Americas: Empire and Legal Networks*, (Oxford & New York: Oxford University Press, 2017).

32 Christopher Rossi, *Whiggish International Law: Elihu Root, the Monroe Doctrine, and International Law in the Americas*, (Leiden & Boston: Brill Nijhoff, 2019).

33 Juan Pablo Scarfi, "Denaturalizing the Monroe Doctrine: The rise of Latin American legal anti-imperialism in the face of the modern U.S. and hemispheric redefinition of the Monroe Doctrine," *Leiden Journal of International Law* Vol. 33, Issue 3, 541–555.

34 Arnulf Becker Lorca, *Mestizo International Law: A Global Intellectual History 1842–1933*, (Cambridge: Cambridge University Press, 2014). Part of this book involves the entanglement between the Monroe Doctrine and international law. The Oxford Handbook of

Imaginings: The Monroe Doctrine and Narratives of U.S. Empire[35] and Grace Livingstone's *America's Backyard: The United States & Latin America from the Monroe Doctrine to the War on Terror*[36] trace the U.S.'s changing relations with Latin America and explore how the Monroe Doctrine has evolved.

In the German-speaking world, Carl Schmitt's analysis of international law and order before World War II provides one of the most influential critiques of the U.S. Monroe Doctrine. Schmitt distinguishes between the original Monroe Doctrine, which he argues was grounded in the true spirit of regional space, and the "distorted" Monroe Doctrine, which transcended regional space to become a tool of global interventionism. Schmitt believed Germany should learn from the original spirit of the Monroe Doctrine to build its own "Großraum" order. This reinterpretation formed an important link in the global dissemination and reception of the Monroe Doctrine in Germany. Adolf Hitler even referred to the "German Monroe Doctrine" in 1939.[37] However, Lothar Gruchmann's *National Socialist Large Space Order: The Construction of "German Monroe Doctrine"* (1962) strongly criticized Hitler's and Schmitt's misappropriation of the Monroe Doctrine, arguing that their interpretations deviated from the doctrine's original spirit. Gruchmann's work reflects the mainstream German political attitude after World War II.[38] It is worth noting that scholars in the U.S. and China, lacking Germany's historical burdens, have been able to analyze German geopolitics and international law between the two world wars more freely than their German counterparts after 1945.

I first encountered Japan's appropriation of the Monroe Doctrine when studying Schmitt's reinterpretation of it. Schmitt's brief but insightful remarks on Japan's "Asiatic Monroe Doctrine" discourse provided crucial clues about Japan's complex diplomatic relations in East Asia after the U.S. extended its influence beyond the Western Hemisphere. Following these clues, I explored relevant literature and discovered that Japan's "Asianism" discourse had a significant interaction with the Monroe Doctrine by the late 19th century, shaping

International Law, co-edited by Fassbender and Peters, briefly mentions the influence of the "Monroe Doctrine" in the discussion of regional international law in Latin America, see Bardo Fassbender and Anne Peters eds., *Oxford Handbook of International Law History*, (Oxford: Oxford University Press, 2012), 553–577.

35 Gretchen Murphy, *Hemispheric Imaginings: The Monroe Doctrine and Narratives of U.S. Empire*, (Durham & London: Duke University Press, 2005).

36 Grace Livingstone, *America's Backyard: The United States & Latin America from the Monroe Doctrine to the War on Terror*, (London & New York: Zed Books, 2009).

37 Alton Frye, *Nazi Germany and the American Hemisphere, 1933–1941*, (New Haven: Yale University Press, 1967).

38 Lothar Gruchmann, *Nationalsozialistische Großraumordnung. Die Konstruktion einer "deutschen Monroe-Doktrin*," (Stuttgart: Deutsche Verlags-Anstalt, 1962).

Japan's international strategy. Japanese intellectuals such as Konoe Atsumaro, Ukita Kazutami, Ōkuma Shigenobu, Kaneko Kentarō, Ishii Kikujiro, Kodera Kenkichi, Tokutomi Sohō, Sawada Ken, Yanagisawa Shinnosuke, Takeuchi Ta, Suehiro Shigeo, Tagawa Daikichirō, Tamura Kosaku, Matsubara Kazuo, Uchida Kōsai, Hirota Kōki, Amō Eiji and Yokota Kisaburō, played key roles in developing the Japanese Monroe Doctrine. During World War II, Schmitt's works on international law and "Großraum" inspired Japanese international law scholars such as Yasui Kaoru, Matsushita Masatoshi, and Tabata Shigejirō, demonstrating that Japan both directly and indirectly adopted and adapted the American Monroe Doctrine, with Germany acting as an intermediary.

My reflection on Japan's "Asianism" is also influenced by Takeuchi Yoshimi's post-war analysis of "Asianism." Takeuchi reveals the ambivalence in Japan's imagination of its "resistance" to the West and its self-definition of "Asia" in relation to this resistance.[39] However, Takeuchi did not systematically explore the relationship between "Asianism" and the "Monroe Doctrine," leaving room for further discussion in this book.

In Chinese literature, research on the history of the Monroe Doctrine is relatively underdeveloped. Professor Guo Shuanglin's work on the relationship between Monroe Doctrine discourse and national identity during the late Qing Dynasty is one of the few comprehensive studies of the doctrine's reception in modern China.[40] His research provides essential clues for understanding how Chinese elites in Japan, especially those involved with *The China Discussion* editorial team, received and transformed the Monroe Doctrine discourse during the late Qing period.

Building on this, I searched for historical materials on how the Provincial spatial politics of the Republic of China era appropriated and adapted the Monroe Doctrine, yielding rich findings. For example, the connection between the "provincial constitution movement" of Hunan province and the Monroe Doctrine discourse has drawn attention in other academic contexts but has yet to be fully integrated into the global history of the Monroe Doctrine. Similarly, the interactions between Chinese intellectuals like Kang Youwei, Liang Qichao,

---

39 Takeuchi Yoshimi 竹内好:「方法としてのアジア」[Asia as a Method],『日本とアジア 竹内好評論集第3巻』[Japan and Asia: Takeuchi Yoshimi's Commentary, vol. 3], (Chikuma Shobō, 1966), 419–420.

40 Guo Shuanglin 郭双林, "Menluo zhuyi yu Qingmoguojiaminzurentong 门罗主义与清末国家民族认同 [The Monroe Doctrine and National Identity in the Late Qing Dynasty]," in *Zhongguo jindaishishang de minzuzhuyi* 中国近代史上的民族主义 [*Nationalism in Modern Chinese History—Proceedings of the Second International Symposium on the History of Modern Chinese Thought*] (Beijing: Shehui kexuewenxian chubanshe, 2006), 346–367.

Sun Yat-Sen, Li Dazhao and Japanese "Asianism" have been well studied, but the influence of Monroe Doctrine discourses on their thought has not been adequately analyzed. These aspects could be re-examined in a thematic study of Monroe Doctrine discourses and symbols. Professor Liu Xiaofeng's *Monroe Doctrine and the Era of Globalization* (2020), which discusses the Monroe Doctrine in the context of key moments in modern Chinese history, also provides insights that inform the fourth chapter of this book.[41]

To sum up, the principal innovation of this book does not reside in the discovery of hitherto unknown historical materials, but in constructing a fresh framework for narrative and analysis. On the one hand, it reintegrates existing research on the Monroe Doctrine discourse from a new perspective; on the other hand, this book builds upon the often-overlooked "peripheries" of other scholars' work, using the concept and discourse of the Monroe Doctrine, which have typically been merely sparingly referenced or cursorily touched upon, as pivotal threads of inquiry. This book traces these clues and attempts to connect scattered fragments of thought, akin to stringing together scattered pearls, to depict the trajectory of the Monroe Doctrine's evolution and the spectrum of its meanings. Based on this approach, this study could offer a new perspective for understanding China's place in the global order since the modern era.

The composition of this book has substantially benefited from the "Empire and International Law" methodological approach within the field of the history of international law. In recent years, many legal scholars and historians have sought to rewrite the history of international law, challenging the "myth of Westphalia" and traditional Eurocentric narratives that link international law exclusively to European sovereign states. Instead, they relate the formation of modern European international law to the expansion of colonial empires. From this view, international law, as disseminated from Europe to the globe, was not created in isolation but was shaped through interactions with the outside world via colonization and imperial expansion. Historically, international law often served as an instrument of imperial expansion and hegemony.[42] The "internationality" of European international law also varied throughout history.[43] This book's study of the global history of the Monroe Doctrine explores the relationship between colonial expansion and international law

41 Liu Xiaofeng 刘小枫, "Menluo zhuyi yu quanqiuhua jiyuan 门罗主义与全球化纪元 [The Monroe Doctrine and the Era of Globalization]," *Xueshu qianyan* 3 (2020).

42 Martti Koskenniemi, Walter Rech and Manuel Jiménez Fonseca ed., *International Law and Empire: Historical Explorations*, (Oxford: Oxford University Press, 2017), 1–20.

43 Jennifer Pitts, *Boundaries of the International: Law and Empire*, (Cambridge & London: Harvard University Press, 2018).

practices. The expansion of the American empire profoundly influenced regional international law in Latin America and later shaped the development of international law globally. For example, Wilsonianism significantly influenced international law under the Versailles-Washington system. However, in the 20th century, the U.S. government refused to recognize the Monroe Doctrine as a principle of international law, to prevent other powers from claiming the right to interpret it. The imperial expansions of Germany and Japan in the 1930s and 1940s frequently invoked the Monroe Doctrine, and their theorists sought to reinterpret it as the foundation for a new version of international law, known as "large space international law"—although this ultimately failed, it left a significant mark on the history of international law.

The writing of this book benefits from the "Empire and International Law" approach in the field of history of international law. In recent years, many legal scholars and historians have devoted themselves to rewriting the history of international law, breaking the "myth of Westphalia" and the traditional Eurocentric narrative that links international law with European sovereign states. Instead, it relates the formation of modern European regional international law with the expansion of colonial empires. In their view, international law disseminating from Europe to the globe was not created in the closed space of Europe but was shaped in its interaction with the outside world through colonization and imperial expansion. Historically, international law often served as an instrument of imperial expansion and hegemony. The "internationality" of European international law also varied with the development of history. The study of the global history of the Monroe Doctrine in this book helps explore the relationship between the expansion of several colonial empires and contemporary international law practices/concepts: the expansion of the American empire has profoundly influenced the regional international law in Latin America, and then influenced the development of international law globally, for example, it is widely recognized that Wilsonianism has exerted significant influence on international law under Versailles-Washington System; however, in the 20th century, the U.S. government refused to admit the Monroe Doctrine as a principle of international law, so as to prevent other forces from sharing the right to interpret the Monroe Doctrine. The imperial expansion of Germany and Japan in 1930s and 1940s frequently resorted to the precedent of the Monroe Doctrine in the Western Hemisphere, and the German and Japanese theorists even attempted to turn the Monroe Doctrine into the basis of a new version of international law. These efforts gave rise to "large space international law," which failed, but left a deep mark in the history of international law.

Although this book engages with the history of international law, its scope extends far beyond this field. To a certain extent, it can also be situated within the emerging research field of "global intellectual history."[44] This field intersects global history with the history of thought. "Global history" as a research approach critiques the narrowness of nation-state-centered historical narratives and challenges Eurocentric assumptions in traditional historiography, emphasizing transnational or global relationships. However, what constitutes "global" can vary in practice. Globality may relate to the idea of "universal history"—the belief that all humanity is part of the same historical process and shares a common future direction. Many contemporary narratives of "globalization" rest on this assumption. Conversely, globality may also mean including as many geographical and cultural traditions as possible in comparative studies, without assuming a reciprocal relationship between the objects of comparison. In this view, "globality" is not only about recognizing uniqueness but also about establishing a shared framework for comparison.[45]

Globality may also exist in the intermediary factors that traverse national, cultural, and even civilizational boundaries—such as tea, sugar, coffee, the slave trade, judicial review, or positivism.[46] These elements acquire "global" implications as they travel across borders. For example, David Armitage's research on the global dissemination of the U.S. Declaration of Independence traces the cross-border influence of a text and a set of related symbols.[47] In this book, the study of the Monroe Doctrine is global, not in the sense of a transcendental universal history, but rather through the cross-border movement of the concept itself. Historical actors across different times and spaces, with

---

44 There have been some introductions to the history of global thought in Chinese academic circles, such as Li Hongtu 李宏图, "Quanqiu sixiangshi: chongsi xiandai quanqiuzhixu de sixiangqiyuan 全球思想史：重思现代全球秩序的思想起源 [History of Global Thought: The Ideological Origin of Re-Modernizing the Global Order]," Huadong Shifandaxue xuebao (Zhexue shehuikexue ban) 5 (2020).

45 Samuel Moyn and Andrew Sartori ed., *Global Intellectual History*, (New York: Columbia University Press, 2013), 5–8.

46 Related works, see Andrew F. Smith, *Sugar: A Global History*, (London: Rational Books, 2015); Helen Saberi, *Tea: A Global History*, (London: Rational Books, 2010); Jonathan Morris, *Coffee: A Global History*, (London: Reaktion Books, 2018); Olivier Pétré-Grenouilleau, *Les Traites Négrières: Essai d'Histoire Globale*, (Paris: Editions Gallimard, 2004); Tom Ginsburg, "The Global Spread of Constitutional Review"; Keith E. Whittington, R. Daniel Kelemen and Gregory A. Caldeira eds., *The Oxford Handbook of Law and Politics*, (Oxford: Oxford University Press, 2008), 81–98.

47 David Armitage, *The Declaration of Independence: A Global History*, (Cambridge, Massachusetts & London: Harvard University Press, 2008).

various spatial-political agendas, have invoked the Monroe Doctrine to express their demands. This makes it possible to use the Monroe Doctrine discourse as a starting point to investigate the local spatial-political conflicts underlying its development. Perry Anderson's *The H-Word: The Peripeteia of Hegemony*[48] offers a model for this book—he examines not only the changing meaning of the term "hegemony" but also the historical and political processes that shaped this change.

To trace the global journey of the Monroe Doctrine discourse, it is essential to remain highly sensitive to both time and space. Conceptually, this book employs a historical approach. However, it does not follow the "unit-idea" method of intellectual history practiced by Arthur O. Lovejoy in *The Great Chain of Being*,[49] where ideas are treated as autonomous entities moving through history. Clearly, the Monroe Doctrine is not a self-moving "unit-idea"; instead, it is a complex of symbols that flows through concrete historical contexts, gaining meaning in practice as different political forces use, reinterpret, and transform it. To capture this process, we must employ perspectives from pragmatics and genealogy. In 1823, President James Monroe could not have imagined that President Woodrow Wilson would use his principles to extend U.S. influence beyond the Western Hemisphere. Likewise, Wilson could not have foreseen that his reinterpretation of the Monroe Doctrine would later be applied to China's provincial autonomy movements. The transmission of concepts is full of unexpected breaks and transformations, largely driven by the richness and diversity of human political practice.

We should avoid observing the spread of the Monroe Doctrine's symbols through an essentialist lens. Some may view President Monroe's articulation of the Monroe Doctrine in 1823 as the most authentic version, with all subsequent interpretations seen as deviations, filled with distortions and misunderstandings. Carl Schmitt's analysis similarly contrasted an "original version" of the Monroe Doctrine against various "distorted" interpretations. However, we must recognize that Schmitt's approach exemplifies his broader "concept of the political," especially his emphasis on the friend/enemy distinction and complementary strategies of action. Schmitt aimed to expose an internal contradiction within the official U.S. Monroe Doctrine discourse, leveraging the authority of the "origin" to justify Germany's appropriation of the Monroe Doctrine in its diplomacy. In contrast, the genealogical perspective adopted in this book intentionally weakens the privileged position of the

48 Perry Anderson, *The H-Word: The Peripeteia of Hegemony*, (London: Verso, 2017).

49 Arthur O. Lovejoy, *The Great Chain of Being*, (Cambridge, Massachusetts: Harvard University Press, 1971).

"origin." It is irrelevant whether historical actors were familiar with Monroe's original 1823 articulation, or whether they understood how their interpretations diverged from the so-called "authentic" version. Particularly in modern China, we observe an isomorphism of concepts like the Monroe Doctrine, federalism, democracy, and autonomy in the writings of many historical actors. It is likely that many of these actors only encountered the Monroe Doctrine concept sporadically, without fully grasping its precise meaning, and instead used it as a convenient tool to express their political stance. The symbols of the "Monroe Doctrine" they invoked may not correspond to any systematic theory.

The gap between later interpretations and the "original version" does not imply that later actors lacked understanding or suffered from a "corruption of conscience." From a historical perspective, it is common for human action to seize upon historical legacies as resources, reshaping them to suit contemporary needs. As researchers of historical experience, our task is to understand and explain how this gap emerges. If a group of people, within the same space and time, coincidentally uses a word in similar ways—whether or not they understand its original meaning—the usage itself can become a phenomenon of interest. By tracing the flow of meaning through these varied usages, we can explore the movements and transformations that occur within political societies.

While tracing the evolution of the meaning of concepts, we need not always strictly follow Reinhart Koselleck, the leading scholar in conceptual history, in emphasizing the ambiguity and fluidity of concepts. In practice, the overlap of meanings often occurs for significant, practical reasons: the conditions of a particular time drive different historical actors to move in similar directions, whether intentionally or unintentionally. In the evolution of the concept "Monroe Doctrine", we might instead use an inductive approach to differentiate between areas where meanings are vague and changeable, and those where meanings are relatively more stable.[50] By doing so, we can explore the historical conditions that made this distribution of meanings possible.

In analyzing the spread of ideas, I have been primarily inspired by Carlo Ginzburg's use of morphology in historical research. Ginzburg often formulates theoretical hypotheses by identifying morphological similarities between two phenomena separated by significant time and space, and then searches for the "intermediary link" to establish a chain of evidence for communication

---

50 This argument benefited from Professor Huang Xingtao. See Huang Xingtao 黄兴涛, "Gainianshi fangfa yu Zhongguo jindaishi yanjiu 概念史方法与中国近代史研究 [Conceptual History Method and Research on Modern Chinese History]," *Shixue yuekan* 9 (2012).

and influence.[51] Chapter 4 of this book heavily draws on this approach to explore the relationship between the "Provincial Monroe Doctrine" in modern China, the U.S. Monroe Doctrine introduced in Japan, and Japan's "Greater Asian Doctrine." Although these discourses are not as distant in time and space as many of Ginzburg's cases, the morphological approach remains central to this book's research process.

For instance, the slogan of the U.S. Monroe Doctrine, "America for the Americans," bears a striking morphological resemblance to the Chinese "Provincial Monroe Doctrine" slogans "Guangdong for the Cantonese" and "Hunan for the Hunanese." This similarity serves as a key starting point for the research in this book. The methodology involves "sticking to both ends," identifying a series of intermediary links with "family resemblance," arranging these links in chronological order, and then investigating the specific channels and mechanisms through which influence was transmitted.

The research process resembles that of a criminal investigation: hypotheses are formulated based on existing clues, and new evidence is sought to either confirm or disprove these hypotheses, ultimately reconstructing a historical narrative. However, due to limited historical sources and my own constraints in data searching and analysis, some aspects of this book offer only probabilistic evidence. It will be up to future researchers to further solidify this chain of evidence.

2 The Monroe Doctrine and the Four Levels of Spatial Politics

After outlining the problem consciousness and research methods of this book, it is necessary to explain its structure and specific content. The book is divided into five chapters. The first three chapters focus on the evolution of Monroe Doctrine discourse in the United States, Germany, and Japan, respectively. The first chapter also briefly touched upon the Latin American response to the Monroe Doctrine. The final two chapters examine the complex relationship between modern China and the Monroe Doctrine discourse.

Throughout the evolution of the Monroe Doctrine discourse, the British Empire has played a significant role as a promoter. However, due to the close connections between this topic and both the U.S. and Germany, the book integrates the content related to Britain into the chapters on the U.S. and Germany. Similarly, the involvement of Spain and France in the Monroe

51 Carlo Ginzburg, Raymond Rosenthal trans., *Ecstasies: Deciphering the Witches' Sabbath*, (Chicago: University of Chicago Press, 1991), 15.

Doctrine discourse is distributed across the relevant chapters, rather than being treated in a concentrated manner.

Let's begin by examining the development and evolution of the Monroe Doctrine in its place of origin, the United States. The term "Monroe Doctrine" itself appeared no earlier than in the 1850s, as a retrospective label for the foreign policy principles advocated by President James Monroe in his 1823 State of the Union address.[52] However, when the term "Monroe Doctrine" first appeared in the 1850s, the American government's interpretation of President Monroe's policy had already diverged from Monroe's original concerns. Since then, the concept of the "Monroe Doctrine" has undergone significant evolution, taking on varied and, at times, unexpected meanings as different political forces have adapted it to suit their own agendas.

The symbolic slogan associated with the Monroe Doctrine in 19th-century America was "America for the Americans," a phrase that originally emerged from the anti-Catholic, xenophobic movements of the 1850s.[53] The Monroe Doctrine was closely tied to a consciousness of the Western Hemisphere, or the New World, as a distinct space unit from its inception. It represented a rebellion against the Vienna system, which had been recently established by European powers and derived its legitimacy from monarchism and dynastic rule. The Monroe Doctrine also rejected the Holy Alliance's interference in the Latin American revolutions, and it made a clear claim to protect the republican system of government in the New World. While people often

52 See Paul Dickson, *Words From the White House: Words and Phrases Coined or Popularized by America's Presidents*, (New York: Walker Books, 2013), 106.

53 John Bassett Moore, "The Monroe Doctrine," *The Annals of the American Academy of Political and Social Science* 96, *The Place of the United States in a World Organization for the Maintenance of Peace* (July 1921), 31–33. As a slogan, "America for the Americans" originated from the Know Nothing Party that opposed Catholic immigrants in the United States in the 1840s and 1850s. In 1854, the leading organization of this movement was reorganized into the "American Party," which shouted the slogan "Americans must rule America" or "America for the Americans" to mobilize local Protestants to oppose Catholic immigrants during the presidential election in 1856. See Robert North Roberts et al., *Presidential Campaigns, Slogans, Issues, and Platforms: The Complete Encyclopedia* Vol. 1, (Santa Barbara, CA: ABC-CLIO, LLC, 2012), 17. Due to the intensification of the struggle around slavery, the party's anti-immigration agenda failed to become the mainstream in the election, and the party's popular basis was also absorbed by the two major political parties in the United States. However, the slogan "America for the Americans" has been passed down and used in the scene of advocating the "Monroe Doctrine." The Irish nationalist slogan "Ireland for the Irish, " which appeared in the early 1840s, also contributed to making the correlation. In 1845, some British authors have summarized the aspiration underlying the American claim to Oregon as the phrase "America for the Americans," drawing a parallel between this anti-British sentiment and Irish nationalism, but emphasizing the American endeavor to spread republicanism on the continent. See "American Relations," *The Spectator* Vol. 18, No. 912, (December 20, 1845), 1213.

associate the 19th-century Monroe Doctrine with "isolationism," being "isolated" from European affairs did not equate to restraining U.S. expansion in the Western Hemisphere. In 1823, the American frontier was still expanding westward. When President Monroe delivered his address, Secretary of State John Quincy Adams was already looking toward Texas and Cuba, attempting to leave room for future U.S. expansion into these regions.[54] Within the space of the "Americas" or the "Western Hemisphere," the Monroe Doctrine became a potent tool for expanding U.S. hegemonic power. It stoked fear among other nations in the region by highlighting the presence of "external threats," and then used this fear to establish U.S. dominance over them. In some cases, the Doctrine was even used to justify the absorption or division of their territories under the pretext of excluding external interference.

The potential for U.S. expansion is reflected even in its name and form of government. In its full name, "the United States of America," "America" signifies the country's geographical location on the American continent, while "United States" points to its federal structure, which provides great flexibility for expansion. The U.S. can annex new territories by first establishing them as independent states and then admitting them as new members under the federal constitution. This allows newly joined political units to retain a significant degree of autonomy. Originally, the U.S. consisted of 13 states, but new "states" were established and admitted as the country expanded westward. Theoretically, this expansion could continue indefinitely across North and South America, encompassing the entire continent without contradicting the literal meaning of its name.[55]

From the first half of the 19th century to the early 20th century, as U.S. territory and power expanded dramatically, the meaning of the Monroe Doctrine's slogan "America for the Americans" shifted. Initially understood as "the American continent for the Americans," it gradually evolved into "the American continent for the U.S." During the 19th century, as the U.S. competed with Britain in Latin America, it significantly learned from Britain's practice of managing an "informal empire." This approach involved gaining profits through trade and financial power backed by military strength, rather than acquiring new territory. Since Jay's Treaty between Britain and the U.S. in 1794, the U.S. had used mediation to resolve conflicts with Britain, eventually

54 Charles Francis Adams ed., *Memoires of John Quincy Adams, Comprising Portions of His Diary from 1795 to 1848* Vol. 6, (Philadelphia: J.B. Lippincott & Co., 1875), 177–178.

55 From the perspective of the country name, the most thorough "de-regionalization" is represented by the Soviet Union, whose full name is "the Union of Soviet Socialist Republics." The Soviet Union refers to an ideal, not the name of a region or a nation. Theoretically, even Cuba in the Western Hemisphere can apply to become a member of the Soviet Union.

developing this mechanism into arbitration and extending it to resolve disputes among American nations.

In this framework, politics and economics were carefully distinguished, with economic power viewed as neutral and expanding through voluntary cooperation. By the end of the 19th century, U.S. capital had reached across the Pacific Ocean to pursue the Open Door Policy in China. In President Theodore Roosevelt's view, the two policies were closely aligned: just as the Monroe Doctrine sought to prevent European powers from acquiring new territory in the Americas, the Open Door Policy aimed to prevent European powers from doing the same in China.[56] As William A. Williams put it, the Open Door Policy represented a form of imperial anti-colonialism.[57]

In 1903, during his stay in the U.S., Liang Qichao read President Theodore Roosevelt's speech on the Monroe Doctrine in Chicago and keenly observed that the Monroe Doctrine was evolving toward "the whole world for the U.S."[58] In practice, the Monroe Doctrine had been reinterpreted to justify expansion and interference beyond the Western Hemisphere. During World War I, President Woodrow Wilson took a step further, interpreting the Monroe Doctrine as a global political principle without regional boundaries, thus legitimizing U.S. global intervention. In his reinterpretation, Wilson appeared to position the autonomy of other countries and nations as the core of the doctrine. However, he was also a president deeply committed to military intervention. How can these seemingly contradictory positions be reconciled? Wilsonian interventionism, in its rhetoric, typically did not openly appeal to U.S. self-interest. Instead, it was framed as protecting and restoring the autonomy of nations and peoples threatened by external forces—or internal forces acting as proxies for external powers. This logic of "vicarial autonomy"—representing the "autonomy" of others—proved to be more delicate and intricate than Theodore Roosevelt's interpretation, which was based on the blatant "hierarchy of civilizations." While Wilson claimed to respect the equal status of other nations, his rhetorical mechanism of excluding external interference and restoring autonomy enabled the U.S. to justify its hegemony over other countries. The argument that the U.S. was responsible for safeguarding the autonomy of other nations implied that the U.S. could act globally without being restricted to the

56 Gregory Moore, *Defining and Defending the Open Door Policy: Theodore Roosevelt and China, 1901–1909*, (Lanham: Lexington Books, 2015), 45.

57 William Appleman Williams, *The Tragedy of American Diplomacy*, (New York: Norton & Company, 1972), 19–57.

58 Liang Qichao 梁启超, "Xindalu youji jielu 新大陆游记节录 [Excerpts from Travel Notes in the New World]," in *Liangqichao quanji* 梁启超全集 [*Complete Works of Liang Qichao*], ed. Zhang Pinxing (Beijing: Beijing Press, 1999): 1155.

boundaries of the Western Hemisphere. By the end of World War I, the Monroe Doctrine had undergone three stages of evolution: from "the American continent for the Americans" to "the American continent for the U.S.," and finally to "the whole world for the U.S."

Despite these evolving interpretations, the Monroe Doctrine retained a consistent discursive structure: it defined a supranational regional space, identified external threats, and expanded U.S. national interests in the name of resisting these threats. American elites held a strong belief in American exceptionalism, emphasizing that "empire" was an outdated form of power embraced by the old European powers, which the U.S. disdained. Some admitted, albeit reluctantly, that while the U.S. had indeed become an empire, it ruled in a unique and superior way compared to the old European powers and Japan, the newly emerging non-Western power. U.S. ruling elites often portrayed the expansion of American territory or interests as acts of self-defense or the protection of the shared values and interests of other countries in the region. Even after the U.S. became a colonial territorial empire following the Spanish-American War, many American elites continued to verbally oppose colonialism and imperialism, instead framing their rule over the Philippines and Puerto Rico as part of a "civilizing mission."[59]

The discourse of "civilizing missions" was not unique to the U.S., but shared by many colonial empires. What sets the U.S. apart, perhaps, is its negative form of discourse based on spatial division: the U.S. portrayed itself as the embodiment of a Western Civilization reborn in the "New World," one that was more upright and more vibrant than the corrupt old Europe. The U.S. claimed to defend the Western Hemisphere from European powers while counterbalancing them in East Asia through the Open Door Policy. Following the same logic, the U.S. later targeted non-European powers for exclusion. For example, in 1956, W. Mallory Browne, the U.S. Consul General in Dakar, Senegal, proposed to the State Department that the U.S. declare a "European Monroe Doctrine for Africa" to counter Communist forces from the Soviet Union and Asia.[60] All these efforts aimed to redefine the boundaries of homogeneity within the political spaces they sought to dominate, particularly by identifying and rejecting heterogeneous elements. This allowed for the continuous reproduction of homogeneity in the political space, while forcing identified enemies to bear the burden of proving their innocence. The evolution of the

59 See Daniel Immer Wahr, *How to Hide an Empire: A History of the Greater United States*, (New York: Farrar, Straus and Giroux, 2019).

60 Stanley Shaloff ed., *Foreign Relations of the United States, 1955–1957, Vol. XVIII: Africa*, (Washington: United States Government Printing Office, 1989), 164–165.

Monroe Doctrine's discourse reflects the U.S.'s ongoing attempts to distinguish between friends and enemies within the framework of international order.

As the Monroe Doctrine spread to other countries, it became deeply intertwined with local spatial politics, resulting in various new interpretations. For example, after World War I, advocates of pan-Europeanism adopted the slogan "Europe for the Europeans," while Carl Schmitt formulated the "Großraum" theory to justify Germany's expansion in Central Europe. Japanese theorists developed the "Asiatic Monroe Doctrine" or "East Asian Monroe Doctrine" to legitimize Japan's expansion into Korea, China, and Southeast Asia. Italy similarly proposed its own version of the Monroe Doctrine in the Balkans, which Chinese newspapers referred to as the "Balkan Monroe Doctrine."[61] In the Soviet Union, Leon Trotsky once criticized the idea of "Socialism in One Country" (социали́зм в отде́льно взя́той стране́) as the "Socialist Monroe Doctrine."[62] In the 1880s, before Australia became a dominion within the British Empire, it proposed its own version of the Monroe Doctrine for the South Pacific.[63] Similarly, Jawaharlal Nehru, the first Prime Minister of India, advocated for an "Indian Monroe Doctrine" for the South Asian subcontinent and the Indian Ocean.[64] In Africa, Marcus Garvey, the black nationalist and pan-Africanist from Jamaica, imitated the Monroe Doctrine with his call for "Africa for the Africans."[65] In the 1960s, Charles de Gaulle's foreign policy toward former French colonies in Central and West Africa was often referred to as the "French Monroe Doctrine."[66] In modern China, alongside many comments on the American and Japanese versions of the Monroe Doctrine, slogans such as "China for the Chinese," "Guangdong for the Cantonese," and "Hunan for the

61 "Yidali ye chang Menluozhuyi 意大利也倡门罗主义 [Italy also advocates Monroe Doctrine]," *Zhongyang zhoukan* 26 (1928).

62 Richard B. Day, *Leon Trotsky and the Politics of Economic Isolation*, (Cambridge & New York: Cambridge University Press, 1973), 167.

63 Neville Meaney, *The Search for Security in the Pacific, 1901–1914*, (Sydney University Press, 2009), 16; Merze Tate, "The Australasian Monroe Doctrine," *Political Science Quarterly* Vol. 76 No. 2 (Jun. 1961): 264–284; Cait Storr, "'Imperium in Imperio': Sub-Imperialism and the Formation of Australia as a Subject of International Law," *Melbourne Journal of International Law* Vol. 19, No. 1 (2018), 335–368.

64 James R. Holmes and Toshi Yoshihara, "India's 'Monroe Doctrine' and the Gulf"; Jefferey R. Macris and Saul Kelly, *Imperial Crossroads: The Great Powers and the Persian Gulf*, (Annapolis: Naval Institute Press, 2012), 147–166.

65 Robert A. Hill ed., *The Marcus Garvey and Universal Negro Improvement Association Papers, Vol. IX: Africa for the Africans, 1921–1922*, (Berkeley & Los Angeles: University of California Press, 1995), 115.

66 Walter Feichtinger, *Sorting Out the Mess: Wars, Conflicts, and Conflict Management in West Africa*, (Wien: Landesverteidigungsakademie, 2007), 50.

Hunanese" emerged, bearing a certain resemblance to the Monroe Doctrine discourse that originated in the Western Hemisphere. These examples demonstrate how the Monroe Doctrine has played a significant role in shaping political boundaries across different levels of political space.

The conceptual cornerstone of the modern international order is the sovereign state, defined by clear territorial boundaries. Using this as an anchor point, we can divide political space into three levels: national, supra-national, and sub-national. If we further differentiate between "global" and "regional" levels within the supra-national category, we could identify four levels of political space. The typical Monroe Doctrine sentence pattern—"X for the Xans"—can be applied across all these levels, with spatial consciousness on each level often inspiring and reinforcing the others. However, generally speaking, the Monroe Doctrine discourse is most commonly used at the supra-national and sub-national levels.

In historical documents, slogans such as "Deutschland den Deutschen" and "La France aux Français" are typically not classified as expression of the Monroe Doctrine. This is because, at the national level, there was already a strong discourse of sovereignty long before the emergence of the Monroe Doctrine, which served to define the boundaries of state political space and exclude external interference. The discourse of sovereignty arose in Europe through the historical process of kingdoms struggling against the universal jurisdiction of the Holy Roman Empire and the Catholic Church.[67] The concept of sovereignty negates the overlapping jurisdictions typical of the feudal order, supporting the central government's establishment of unified and exclusive control over a defined territory. After the Thirty Years' War in Europe in the 17th century, sovereign states became widely accepted as the basic units of international law. Subsequently, the traditional view of the state as the *dominium* of monarchs—handed down from the feudal era—was strongly challenged by the French Revolution and the Revolutions of 1848. As a result, monarchs sought to rebuild the legitimacy of their rule based on national identity, rather than divine right or succession through noble bloodlines. Thus, slogans like "Deutschland den Deutschen" and "La France aux Français" became expressions of national consciousness. Since the state already possessed the powerful symbol of sovereignty, there was no need for additional symbols to justify resistance to external forces encroaching on territorial boundaries.

67 Walter Ullmann, "The Development of the Medieval Idea of Sovereignty," *English Historical Review* 64 (1949), 1–33.

However, disputes arise when cultural and political boundaries do not align: do ethnic groups who disagree with existing state boundaries have the right to form their own sovereign state, or to join a neighboring sovereign state ruled by people of the same ethnic origins? In the 19th century, with the decline of monarchical legitimacy defended by the Holy Alliance and the rising legitimacy of nationalism, the tension between national boundaries and state boundaries became increasingly significant. For example, after Poland was partitioned by Prussia, Austria, and Russia, could the Poles declare "Poland for the Poles" and expel their Prussian, Austrian, and Russian rulers? Could German-speaking populations in the Czech lands and Poland break away and join Germany? Should Germany and Austria, both of German origin, unite into a single state? In these cases, advocates of boundary changes would still invoke the concept of sovereignty, but with the nation as the ultimate bearer of sovereignty or constituent power, they argued that state territorial boundaries should be adjusted to reflect the boundaries where the nation resides.

European classical international law, with "sovereignty" as its foundational concept, spread globally and became the standard for reorganizing the political space. From this perspective, non-Western nations needed only to adopt the concept of sovereignty and apply it to their own territorial claims. By doing so, they could legitimately exclude external forces from their territorial space without needing to develop new theories. Thus, since the 19th century, spatial struggles where the Monroe Doctrine symbol has been applicable have primarily unfolded on two levels: the "supra-national" level, which could further divide into regional or even global contexts, and the sub-national or provincial level.[68] Political and cultural elites in Germany and Japan primarily employed Monroe Doctrine discourses to advance their own spatial politics at the regional level. In modern China, there was a dual response: on one hand, some political and cultural elites engaged with Monroe Doctrine discourses from other countries at regional and global levels; on the other hand, China had a unique

68 However, it is worth pointing out that the "Monroe Doctrine" discourse at the "supra-national" or "sub-national" levels is not isolated from the discourse of "sovereignty." To a great extent, the discourse of "sovereignty" is the reference point of the discourse of "Monroe Doctrine." The classic modern public international law produced in Europe takes the sovereign state as the basic unit, "Sovereignty" implies internal dominance and external repulsion, which is widely recognized by European powers and enjoys high legitimacy. In this way, the discourse and practice of "sovereignty" at the national level can provide an example for other space units to strive for autonomy-through expansion, "supra-national" regions may be integrated into a sovereign state. And through the separatist movement, provinces may also become new countries.

historical experience. The symbols of the Monroe Doctrine, "descending" from the supra-national level, were widely applied in provincial-level spatial politics, forming what became known as the "provincial Monroe Doctrine" discourse.

After World War I, despite President Wilson's failure to secure U.S. membership in the League of Nations and the Permanent Court of International Justice, the vast power of the U.S. in Europe and Asia was already an objective reality. European and Asian powers faced the pressure of U.S. interference. For those seeking regional hegemony in Europe and Asia, the evolution of the Monroe Doctrine in the U.S. not only offered a powerful model for developing regional dominance but also provided a rhetorical framework for defending themselves against U.S. influence. In Germany, Carl Schmitt dedicated himself to theorizing Germany's revival. He reinterpreted the Monroe Doctrine, distinguishing between its initial phase, which focused on rejecting extraterritorial intervention, and a later imperialist-interventionist phase that, in his view, deviated from the "original" Monroe Doctrine.

From the perspective of Carl Schmitt's political theology, the power that dominates the interpretation of the Monroe Doctrine has undergone a transformation—from "the one who withholds" (ὁ κατέχων), as mentioned by Saint Paul in the Second Epistle to the Thessalonians, to "the lawless one" (ὁ ἄνομος) or the "Anti-Christ."[69] Schmitt called on Germany to learn from the original Monroe Doctrine and to play the role of the Katechon, a force that restrains chaos, to counter the prevailing imperialist-interventionist tendencies. On this basis, he developed his "Großraum" theory, interpreting the Western Hemisphere or Americas as the *Großraum* of the U.S., where the U.S., as a leading power (Reich), applied its own political principles. Schmitt proposed that Germany should seek a similar position in Europe and exclude foreign interference. In his view, when the time was ripe, the world could be reorganized into several large spaces, and international law based on sovereign states would be transformed into a new system based on these Großraum regions.

Japan was influenced by the Monroe Doctrine even earlier than Germany. In 1872, the Japanese Ministry of Foreign Affairs hired Charles Le Gendre, a former U.S. consul in Amoy (Xiamen), China, as a diplomatic advisor. Le Gendre introduced Japan's ruling elites to the U.S. experience with the Monroe Doctrine, encouraging Japan to establish its own sphere of influence in Asia under the guise of "civilizing barbarians." By the end of the 19th century,

69 For the interpretation of Schmitt's concept of "Katechon" in domestic academic circles, see Xu Jian 徐戬, "Shimite yu 'Zulanzhe' xueshuo 施米特与 '阻拦者' 学说 [Schmitt and the Theory of 'Katechon']," *Hainan Daxue xuebao* (*renwenshehuikexue ban*) 1 (2020).

Japanese political elites advocating for "Greater Asianism" explicitly linked their own Asianism to the Monroe Doctrine discourse, seeking to establish Japan's sphere of influence in East Asia. A common theme in their rhetoric was the "struggle between the yellow and white races," which was expected to culminate in "Asian liberation" led by Japan. However, Japan's national strength lagged far behind that of the European powers and the U.S. In 1902, Japan joined the Anglo-Japanese Alliance and pursued a foreign policy of cooperation with Western powers for a long time, making it difficult for Japanese officials to adopt a confrontational Japanese Monroe Doctrine.

To a certain extent, Japan's diplomatic doctrine of concert with Western powers also supported its claims for a sphere of influence in East Asia. By acknowledging that Europe and the U.S. were leading in terms of the "degree of civilization," Japan argued that its alliance with Britain demonstrated that it had reached an equal level of civilization. This, in turn, positioned Japan as a coordinator between Eastern and Western civilizations. The Russo-Japanese War of 1904–1905 further bolstered Japan's claim to progress in civilization and accelerated its annexation of Korea.

After the outbreak of World War I, Japan's ruling elites took advantage of Europe's distraction to implement parts of their "East Asian Monroe Doctrine" as actual policy. They pressured Yuan Shikai to sign the "Twenty-One Demands" in 1915 and later influenced the Beiyang government through the Nishihara Loans in 1917. The White House's policy toward Japan also allowed Japan to draw analogies to the U.S. Monroe Doctrine in advancing its domination over China. However, during the post-war Washington Conference, Japan's grip on China was weakened by pressure from the European powers and the U.S., forcing Japan to scale back its Monroe Doctrine ambitions. After the Mukden Incident in 1931, Japan revived its Monroe Doctrine aspirations. Rebuffed by Britain, the U.S., and other power, Japan withdrew from the League of Nations in March 1933 and pursued domination over China more openly. During World War II, Japan expanded its ambitions from "East Asia" to the "Greater East Asia Co-Prosperity Sphere," including Southeast Asia and the South Pacific. Japanese international jurists drew inspiration from Carl Schmitt's idea of "Großraum" and developed theories about the relationship between countries within this "large space." However, with the defeat of Germany and Japan by the Allies, the attempt by regional hegemonies in Eurasia to reorganize the global order—mirroring the U.S. Monroe Doctrine—came to an end.

There were notable differences between how Germany and Japan used the Monroe Doctrine and how the U.S. employed it. In the U.S., the Monroe Doctrine was often used from a perspective of hegemony in the Gramscian sense. The U.S. sought to win consent in several ways: first, whether in the

Western Hemisphere or globally, U.S. elites consistently emphasized their defense of "democracy," even though their actions often diverged from their rhetoric. Second, although the Monroe Doctrine began at the regional level and eventually extended to global considerations, the discourse of "sovereignty" at the national level never completely disappeared from U.S. Monroe Doctrine discourse.

A significant example is the speech "The Real Monroe Doctrine" delivered in 1914 at the eighth annual meeting of the American Society of International Law by Elihu Root, a senior Republican statesman who had served as Secretary of State under President Theodore Roosevelt and was then a member of the Senate Judiciary Committee. In his speech, Root stated that the Monroe Doctrine was not a principle of international law but was instead based on the right of self-protection recognized by international law—an ethical implication of national sovereignty. He emphasized that the Monroe Doctrine's purpose was to ensure a secure external environment for the U.S., and it was not intended to damage or control the sovereignty of other countries in the Americas.[70]

According to Root's explanation, European powers' interference in Latin American internal affairs was not only a violation of the sovereignty of Latin American countries but also a violation of the U.S.'s right of self-protection, as implied by the concept of national sovereignty. This can be seen as an expansive interpretation of "sovereignty," originally developed in Europe. It suggests that U.S. ruling elites, while basing their notion of sovereignty on territorial borders, did not confine their understanding of defense to their own borders. Instead, they believed they had the right to intervene in other countries in the name of "self-defense," effectively hollowing out the sovereignty of those countries without outright denying it. For the U.S., this concept of sovereignty could not be generalized: if other countries were to claim similar rights, regional conflicts would become inevitable. Nonetheless, it is clear that U.S. ruling elites had not abandoned the notion of "sovereignty." They live with this concept and appropriate it for their own interests.

70 Instead of discussing Roosevelt's Inference in 1904 directly, Root quoted Roosevelt's speech in the Congress on December 3rd, 1906, which tried to argue that the Monroe Doctrine did not mean the superiority of the United States or the exercise of the U.S. guardianship of American countries. In view of Roosevelt's saying "Speak softly and carry a big stick." It can be understood as part of Roosevelt's "soft speech." Elihu Root, "The Real Monroe Doctrine," *The American Journal of International Law* Vol. 8 No. 3 (Jul. 1914), 427–442.

The concept of "empire" was historically tied not only to the degree of homogenization within a political body but also to the monarchical system. Since U.S. elites emphasized the defense of a "hemisphere" composed of republics, they often associated "empire" with the powers of the Old Continent and were cautious about using the term to describe themselves. When the word "empire" was used, it was often qualified, emphasizing that the U.S.'s way of governance was fundamentally different from that of the European powers. The American approach was portrayed as benevolent and liberal, concerned with cultivating autonomy and fostering social progress in its territories, with the Philippines and Puerto Rico frequently cited as examples. This exceptionalist argument, however, overlooks the contradictory policies the U.S. pursued in other colonies (e.g., Guam, Samoa) and ignores the British government's efforts to project a similar benevolent image after assuming direct rule over India.[71] Despite its shaky factual foundation, this argument persisted at a discursive level. U.S. ruling elites were more introverted about the "empire" discourse and remained cautious about replacing the concept of "sovereignty" with that of "empire."

In contrast, Germany's and Japan's appropriation of the Monroe Doctrine discourse greatly simplified the complex relationship between rhetoric and practice. First, the rhetoric of "protecting democratic (or republican) government" was abandoned, as the form of government was not central to the regional homogeneity envisioned by German and Japanese elites. Second, in the 19th century, the most significant competition the U.S. faced in the Western Hemisphere came from Britain's "informal empire"—a model that separated political domination from economic penetration. Against this backdrop, the U.S. implementation of the Monroe Doctrine increasingly reflected a political/economic dichotomy based on the principles of the free-market economy, treating the cross-border flow of capital as a neutral phenomenon. This distinction was weakened in the German and Japanese discussions of *Lebensraum* and *Großraum*. In these contexts, the integration of raw material production, consumption markets, and industrial chains within a region emphasized the political importance of securing "survival." Closely tied to this, German and Japanese theorists explicitly argued for the weakening of national sovereignty and the restructuring of international law around the concept of Großraum. In this scenario, the discourse of empire and colonial expansion took center stage with far less pretense.

---

71 Julian Go refuted the "American exceptionalism" by comparing the British Empire with the American Empire in a thought-provoking manner. Julian Go, *Patterns of Empire: The British and American Empires, 1688 to the Present*, (New York: Cambridge University Press, 2011), 67–102.

This reinterpretation of the Monroe Doctrine was clearly more candid and less hypocritical than the U.S. version. However, we may recall the motto of French proverb writer François de La Rochefoucauld: "Hypocrisy is a tribute vice pays to virtue."[72] Criticism of hypocrisy can stem from the pursuit of true virtue, but it can also reflect a deeper skepticism about the very existence of virtue.

Finally, let us turn to China. Historically, China viewed itself as the center of a long-lasting Asian regional order. In the latter half of the 19th century, Qing government diplomats attempted to preserve the existing tributary system by appealing to the discourse of Asian identity. However, the encroachment of Western powers and Japan's expansion during the Meiji period gradually dismantled the tributary system, and China became a semi-colony, co-dominated by Eastern and Western powers. The situation deteriorated to the point where even China's status as a "semi-civilized state" within the international system was in jeopardy. Given this, China's political and cultural elites found it difficult to envision a larger regional sphere of influence for China, although a few theorists entertained such a possibility. Thus, the dissemination and application of the Monroe Doctrine in China took two distinct directions:

The first direction involved applying the Monroe Doctrine to the sub-national political space, particularly the provinces. At the turn of the century, the editorial team of *The China Discussion* (清议报), led by Liang Qichao, closely followed the U.S. conquest of the Philippines and introduced discussions of the Monroe Doctrine in the U.S., along with reports on the Philippine national independence movement. The slogan "X for the Xans" was used by the editorial team at the supra-national, national, and sub-national levels. Notably, Ou Jujia's *New Guangdong* advocated for anti-Manchu slogans such as "China for the Chinese" and "Guangdong for the Cantonese," which deeply influenced anti-Manchu rhetoric in other provinces, such as Hunan.

Shortly after the outbreak of the 1911 Revolution, several provinces declared independence from the Qing court. However, this revolutionary path weakened the central government. In many provinces, the "provincial Monroe Doctrine" transitioned from being a slogan to becoming an institutional reality, as local magnates took control of military, financial, and personnel powers, seeking to maintain their high level of autonomy from the new central government. Yuan Shikai attempted to reassert Beijing's control over local military, financial, and administrative affairs. His efforts to rebuild state institutions between 1912 and 1915 were ultimately thwarted by local magnates' rebellions against his

72 La Rochefoucauld, John Heard Jr. trans., *La Rochefoucauld Maxims*, (Mineola, New York: Dover Publications, 2006), 27.

self-declared monarchy. After Yuan Shikai's death in 1916, the Beiyang Clique further fragmented. In 1917, following the "dispute between the president and the premier" and Zhang Xun's monarchical restoration attempt, Duan Qirui (段祺瑞) refused to restore the 1912 Provisional Constitution. Sun Yat-sen then moved south to Guangzhou to establish a military government claiming to protect the 1912 Provisional Constitution. As a result, the constitutional order of the Republic of China splintered, and both the Northern and Southern governments claimed to be the legitimate central authority. Reunifying the North and South became a highly contentious issue once again.

During World War I, the United States established the Committee on Public Information, an official wartime propaganda organization, and set up a branch in China to promote a positive image of the U.S. and President Wilson's ideas. This initiative significantly influenced public opinion in China. Although Wilson's disappointing performance at the Paris Peace Conference damaged his reputation in China, the Monroe Doctrine remained largely viewed in a positive light by many Chinese intellectuals. Like "federalism," it was associated with ideals such as "democracy," "autonomy," and even "national self-determination." In the early 1920s, the movement for "United Provincial Autonomy" emerged in the confrontation between the Beiyang government and Sun Yat-sen's government. Several provinces in central China sought to formulate their own constitutions, promote autonomy, and declared their intent to eventually form a new central government. Many future revolutionaries participated in this movement for "United Provincial Autonomy." In 1936, during an interview with U.S. journalist Edgar Snow, Mao Zedong mentioned that in 1920, he had been a supporter of both the Open Door Policy and the Monroe Doctrine.[73]

For President Wilson, the Monroe Doctrine and the Open Door Policy shared the same spirit, as both were aimed at removing obstacles to U.S. expansion—first beyond the Western Hemisphere, and later requiring other countries to open up to U.S. capital and goods. However, Wilson's 1917 interpretation of the Monroe Doctrine indirectly stimulated an emphasis on provincial spatial boundaries in China. The "provincial Monroe Doctrine" was often articulated in opposition to the spirit of the Open Door Policy. Young reformers who sought to promote mass political participation through the provincial Monroe Doctrine quickly realized that the real manipulators of this discourse were warlords and bureaucrats. These figures often appropriated the slogan

73 Liu Peng 刘朋 ed., *Zhonggong dangshi koushu shilu* 中共党史口述实录 [*Oral Record of the History of the Communist Party of China*], Vol. 1, (Beijing: Zhongguo guji chubanshe, 2010), 3.

of "autonomy" to undermine substantive national unity, leaving little room for genuine participatory democracy. As the Kuomintang and the Communist Party embarked on their campaigns to unify the nation through the Nationalist Revolution in the 1920s, the reputation of the "provincial Monroe Doctrine" increasingly turned negative. It became associated with warlord separatism, parochialism, and resistance to reunification. The Mukden Incident and Japan's subsequent appropriation of the Monroe Doctrine to justify its full-scale invasion of China further tarnished the image of the provincial Monroe Doctrine.

The second direction of development involved responding to the U.S. and Japanese versions of the Monroe Doctrine, particularly Japan's "Asian Monroe Doctrine" following the U.S. example. Many Chinese elites who had spent time in Japan were initially attracted to the Japanese Monroe Doctrine, only to become disillusioned for various reasons. When Kang Youwei fled to Japan after the 1898 reform, he attempted to gain support from the Japanese government through "Asianism" rhetoric, but made little progress and soon left Japan under various pressures. Kang Youwei's student, Liang Qichao, was drawn to the "Asianism" discourse for a longer period. However, the U.S. conquest of the Philippines at the turn of the century shifted Liang's focus toward imperialism, and he soon recognized that both the U.S. and Japanese versions of the Monroe Doctrine were imperialist in nature. In contrast, Sun Yat-sen sought support from the Japanese government and public during the 1911 Revolution, the Second Revolution, and the proposed Third Revolution. It took a longer and more complex process for him to distance himself from the discourse of the Japanese Monroe Doctrine. During Sun Yat-sen's Constitution Protection Movement, the Japanese government aligned itself with the Beiyang government, ultimately pushing Sun Yat-sen to oppose Japan. In 1924, Sun delivered a speech in Kobe on "Greater Asianism," in which he finally rejected Japan's mainstream interpretation of the "Asiatic Monroe Doctrine."

After the start of the War of Resistance against Japanese Invasion, in response to Japan's "Asian Monroe Doctrine," some commentators, such as Chiang Kai-shek, invoked the principle of "balance of power" and sought to use U.S. influence to counter Japan. In an effort to gain U.S. support, Chiang Kai-shek went as far as distinguishing the U.S. Monroe Doctrine from Japan's version, glorifying the former while condemning the latter. Meanwhile, authors from the Statist School of the Warring States drew on Oswald Spengler's cultural morphology and the historical experiences of China's Spring and Autumn as well as Warring States Periods, labeling the present era as a "Neo-Warring States Period." They predicted that the future would likely see the unification of various regions of the world, the rise of several great powers as regional hegemons, and eventually the global unification of these powers. Hong Si-qi shared this vision, hoping that China would achieve the integration of its former tributary states through an "Asian federation," thus reviving the old system in a modern form.[74]

Among all these Chinese commentators, Li Dazhao stands out as the most remarkable. Before studying in Japan, Li was a sharp critic of the Japanese Monroe Doctrine. Japan's aggressive policies toward China during World War I further solidified his critical stance. Unlike the Revolutionary Alliance, which had long been based in Japan, the Communist Party of China never sought financial support from Japan, maintaining a high degree of autonomy from the start. In this sense, the divergent policies of the Kuomintang and the Communist Party towards Japan in the 1930s and 1940s are unsurprising—"Rome was not built in a day." More importantly, even before Li Dazhao became a Marxist, he had developed a deep understanding and critique of hegemonism. The new Asia he envisioned was neither one dominated by Japan nor a revival of the tributary system. Instead, it was a political entity reconstructed on the basis of liberation and equality for all nations. The world he envisioned similarly rested on the principles of liberation and equality. Today, the two slogans—"Long Live the People's Republic of China" and "Long Live the Great Solidarity of the People of the World"—displayed on Tiananmen Gate continue to reflect Li Dazhao's spirit.

Historical researchers, with a magnifying glass, may find traces of the Monroe Doctrine in the Manifesto of the Ministry of National Defense of the People's Republic of China to Taiwan Compatriots, drafted by Mao Zedong on October 6, 1958, and published under the name of Peng Dehuai. The manifesto criticized U.S. interference in China's reunification efforts, stating: "Why did a country in the Eastern Pacific come to the Western Pacific? The Western Pacific is for the people of the Western Pacific, just as the Eastern Pacific is for the people of the Eastern Pacific."[75] The phrase "The Western Pacific for the Western Pacific people" adopted the typical Monroe Doctrine sentence pattern of "X for the Xans." However, the focus of this declaration was to exclude U.S. imperialist interference in China's sovereignty. On March 18 of the following year, during a meeting with Japanese Socialist Party Secretary Asanuma Inajirō 浅沼稲次郎, Mao Zedong further clarified this position by stating, "The

74 "Zhanguoce 战国策 [Strategies of the Warring States] 10 (15 August 1940)," quoted from Cao Yinglong and Guo Na 曹颖龙、郭娜 eds., *Zhanguocepai* 战国策派 [*The Strategies of the Warring States School*], (Changchun: Changchun chubanshe, 2013), 359.

75 Literature Research Office of the CPC Central Committee eds., *Mao Zedong wenji* 毛泽东文集 [*Selected Works of Mao Zedong*], Vol. 7, (Beijing: Renmin chubanshe, 1999), 421.

Western Pacific Ocean should be managed by the countries of the Western Pacific itself."[76] The purpose of this statement was to advocate for cooperation between the Chinese and Japanese people in rejecting U.S. occupation and intervention in regional affairs.

Although the structure of "the Western Pacific for the people of the Western Pacific" resembles the famous American slogan "America for the Americans" and Japan's "Asia for the Asians," its focus was not on delineating a "sphere of influence" for any particular country. Instead, it called for the countries in the region to collectively oppose imperialist oppression. The concept of the "Western Pacific" did not imply the formation of a regionalism akin to "Asianism" or the revival of the suzerain-vassal relationship under the tributary system. At the time, China's strategic decision-makers embedded the "Western Pacific" or "Asia" discourse within the broader framework of "Asia, Africa, and Latin America," representing a global anti-imperialist alliance. The primary focus was not on the contradiction between a specific region and foreign intervention, but rather on the global struggle between imperialism and its potential adversaries—the "people of Asia, Africa, and Latin America"—and even the "people of the world." Further evidence of this can be seen in Premier Zhou Enlai's remarks on April 6, 1960, during a meeting with Chilean guests from cultural and educational backgrounds. Zhou commented on U.S. policy regarding Taiwan and suggested, "The U.S. has the Monroe Doctrine, and you in Latin America should have a new Latin American Monroe Doctrine. Do not allow others to interfere. Unite yourselves to form a strong economic power."[77] Zhou's "Latin American Monroe Doctrine" emphasized the importance of Latin American countries creating a shared economic system, conducting independent economic exchanges, and asserting autonomy from U.S. dominance. This reflected China's efforts to align with progressive forces in Latin America in their resistance against imperialism.

This book uses the dissemination and interpretation of the Monroe Doctrine as a fundamental thread to reexamine the course of modern history, offering readers a fresh perspective on conventional historical narratives. For example, since the U.S. participated in the anti-Fascist camp during World War II and made significant contributions, U.S. narratives often framed the divide

76 The Ministry of Foreign Affairs of the People's Republic of China and the Literature Research Office of the CPC Central Committee eds., *Mao Zedong waijiao wenxuan* 毛泽东外交文选 [Selected Works of Mao Zedong's Diplomacy], (Beijing: Zhongyang wenxian chubanshe, 1994), 371.

77 Literature Research Office of the CPC Central Committee eds., *Zhou Enlai nianpu (1949–1976)* 周恩来年谱（1949 - 1976）[Chronicle of Zhou Enlai (1949–1976)], (Beijing: Zhongyang wenxian chubanshe, 2007), 302.

between the U.S. and the Axis powers as a clear opposition between light and darkness. This "black or white" narrative has had a far-reaching influence but obscures an important fact: both Germany and Japan admired America's application of the Monroe Doctrine in Latin America and sought to emulate it during their rise. Carl Schmitt is a prime example of this viewpoint. In the late 1930s, Schmitt criticized the U.S. for "kicking away the ladder" after climbing it. He argued that while the U.S. had started with the Monroe Doctrine in the Western Hemisphere, it evolved into a universal imperial power, intervening in various global regions under the guise of "universal interests." At the same time, it forbade other countries from adopting a similar practice of excluding external intervention, as the U.S. had done in the 19th century. This critique sheds light on the transition from regional to global hegemony and helps us move beyond the "Whig history" narrative that we may have unconsciously accepted.

Schmitt's affirmation and praise of the Monroe Doctrine in the Western Hemisphere show that his *Großraum* theory offered an alternative to the global unipolar hegemonic order, which can be summarized as the coexistence of several regional hegemonic powers. Schmitt's criticism of universal imperialism carries profound implications, especially in its exposure of the gap between hegemonic practice and its self-proclaimed universalism. This critique has the potential to pierce the illusion of universal imperialism and awaken its audience from blind faith in such narratives. However, Germany after the First World War did not experience the same steep decline as China since the 19th century. Chinese literati-bureaucrats, who had witnessed China's fall, often sympathized with the oppressed and annexed countries such as Korea, Annan (Vietnam), India, and Poland. Schmitt, in contrast, did not express similar sympathy. In an effort to justify Germany's pursuit of a regional sphere of influence, he even regarded Japan's "Asian Monroe Doctrine" as a potential ally in the 1930s.[78]

The historical narrations and theoretical discussions in several chapters of this book are related to Schmitt's theories of international order/international law and political theology. At present, no matter in Western or Chinese academia, there is more or less a "witch-hunting" mentality: whoever quotes or discusses Schmitt is Schmitt's sympathizer and even admirer with a desire to become a "Nazi Jurist." This "witch-hunting" mentality is certainly ridiculous. But in order to avoid unnecessary misunderstanding and contention, it is necessary to state my theoretical position here: Firstly, Schmitt is a theorist

78 Carl Schmitt, "Großraum gegen Universalismus (1939)," in *Positionen und Begriffe im Kampf mit Weimar-Genf-Versailles 1923–1939*, 9 (Berlin: Duncker & Humblot, 2014): 339.

fed on Germany's historical experience of "regional hegemony." From this position, he criticized the global-universal imperialism profoundly, but after all, his mentality is inherently hegemonic. In particular, Schmitt used "Poland is not a state" to justify the division of Poland by Russia, Poland and Austria in the 18th century. In 1939, the "Großraum" he expected included the part of Poland taken by Nazi Germany. In *Theorie des Partisanen*, Schmitt mistakenly finds in Mao Zedong's poem Niannujiao-Kunlun 念奴娇·昆仑 a picture of independent and non-interfering "Großraum." However, what Mao wrote was a picture of allied global opposition to imperialism, while the "world revolution" was fundamentally rejected and opposed by Schmitt. In modern times, China was the target of oppression by global hegemony and regional hegemony at the same time in the global order, which produced more thorough anti-imperialist and anti-hegemonic thoughts. Secondly, temporality is a fundamental dimension for understanding the Chinese revolution in the 20th century and the Chinese constitution established from it. One need to read Marx, Engels, Lenin and Mao Zedong instead of Schmitt to understand this consciousness of temporality. Based upon his political theology, from the very beginning, Schmitt regarded both the international communist movement and the universal imperialism of the United States as "Anti-Christ," and he even regarded the Soviet regime of proletariat dictatorship as based upon "aristocratic constituent power." The reason is that his theoretical logic is in conflict with the concepts of "progressiveness" and "vanguard." If the dimension of temporaty is stripped off, of course, we can only see the superficial phenomenon that revolutionary activists only account for a minority in the national population, and we can't discuss their representatives for the future, the fundamental interests and long-term interests of the nation and the people. If Schmitt's theory can be used to explain the Chinese revolution in the 20th century, at most, it can only partially explain the anti-imperialist and anti-colonial nature as well as the nationalist dimension of this revolution, but will inevitably question the legitimacy of the socialist revolution and its relationship with the world revolution. Thirdly, based on historical evidence, Schmitt was quickly marginalized after a brief honeymoon with the Nazi Party. However, his "Großraum" theory echoed with the external expansion of the Third Reich. Nor should we forget that, in the late 1930s, Schmitt was inspired by Japanese imperialism which advocated the "Asiatic Monroe Doctrine," and stood against the Chinese soldiers and civilians who fought hard against Japanese imperialism. Japanese international jurists during World War II also used Schmitt's "Großraum" theory to make legal arguments for the "Greater East Asia Co-Prosperity Sphere."

The earlier discussion of the Monroe Doctrine in the U.S., Germany, and Japan offers deeper insights into modern China's position in the global order. The traditional narrative of Chinese revolutionary history states that since

1840, China was reduced to a semi-feudal, semi-colonial society, exploited and oppressed by imperialism. However, through the lens of the Monroe Doctrine and the spatial politics it represents, we can add that China was once a prey to both global and regional hegemons. Many of China's political elites of the time, from Li Hongzhang to Chiang Kai-shek, consciously attempted to leverage the global hegemon of their era to prevent Japan, the regional hegemon of East Asia, from encroaching on or annexing China. This strategy occasionally succeeded and mostly failed. When it did succeed, it was not because China had the strength to resist aggression on its own, but rather because the global powers had a vested interest in balancing each other's influence.

Since the mid-19th century, the political authority of the Qing imperial court had been in decline. In China, the Monroe Doctrine discourse did not inspire ambitions for supra-national regional hegemony, but rather fueled calls for provincial autonomy. Historically, Chinese governance has seen a persistent tension between "feudalism" (feng jian) and the "system of prefectures and counties" (jun xian). As the authority of the Qing court weakened, the balance momentarily tilted toward "feudalism." However, in its discursive form, this shift cannot be simply viewed as a return to traditional "feudalism."

Many Chinese elites, influenced by their observations of Western domestic governance, recognized that local autonomy could lead to more effective governance, stimulate grassroots vitality, and promote competition among regions—factors that could contribute to the prosperity of the entire nation. At the end of the Qing Dynasty and the beginning of the Republic of China, both Kang Youwei, representing the constitutional monarchists, and Sun Yat-sen, representing the anti-Manchu revolutionaries, held high hopes for local autonomy. Kang Youwei argued that the "competition between small countries" in Europe had led to advancements in transportation, political enlightenment, and a general trend of nations learning from one another.[79] He believed that China, by fostering local autonomy while preserving national unity, could promote state-building. Sun Yat-sen saw local autonomy as a crucial means for people to learn to exercise their political rights and become masters of their own affairs.[80]

---

79 Kang Youwei 康有为, "Deguo youji 德国游记 [Travel Notes in Germany]," in *Kang Youwei quanji* 康有为全集 [*Complete Works of Kang Youwei*], Vol. 7, ed. Jiang Yihua and Zhang Ronghua (Beijing: Renmin daxue chubanshe, 2007), 433.

80 Sun Yat-Sen 孙中山, "Jianguo fanglve 建国方略 [The General Strategy of Founding a Country]," in *Sun Yat-Sen quanji* 孙中山全集 [*Complete Works of Sun Yat-Sen*], Vol. 6, ed. Zhongguo shehuikexueyuan jindaishi yanjiusuo zhonghuaminguoshi yanjiushi deng 中国社会科学院近代史研究所中华民国史研究室等 [History Research Office of the Republic of China, Institute of Modern History, Chinese Academy of Social Sciences, etc.] (Beijing: Zhonghua shuju, 1982), 204–205.

However, the local autonomy of the late Qing Dynasty and the Republic of China emerged in a context where the central government was in decline, and great powers were watching with predatory intent. With the weakening of the Beiyang Clique, many advocates of local autonomy soon realized that China was caught in a cycle of warlord separatism and infighting. Local autonomy often became a pretext for local warlords to entrench their control over society, while genuine grassroots participation in public affairs remained a distant ideal. This fragmentation further weakened China's ability to respond to external oppression. A new historical process of re-integration through politico-social revolution began in the 1920s and achieved significant results by the mid-20th century. The Chinese people's struggle against Japan's "Asian Monroe Doctrine" was an important aspect of this process of national renewal. The "Yan'an Road," which came to maturity during the War of Resistance against Japanese Invasion, aimed at remaking both the domestic and international order simultaneously.

3 Multipolarization and Uncertain Prospects for Global Order

In the first half of the 20th century, a plethora of discourses on the Monroe Doctrine sprang up in both Europe and Asia. This book endeavors to collate and analyze these exemplary discourses, emphasizing that the symbols of the Monroe Doctrine were wielded as discursive instruments by emerging regional powers to counter the U.S.'s inclination towards a universal empire, drawing on the U.S.'s own history as a regional hegemon. Certainly, such utilization of Monroe Doctrine discourse signals a conception of a multipolar global order. Its defining characteristic is the concurrent existence of multiple regional hegemonic powers, each possessing its own cohesive sphere of influence.

Nearly 30 years after the end of the Cold War, U.S. unipolar hegemony has been in decline, and the multipolarization of the world order has become increasingly apparent. We have seen German theorists advocating for greater German leadership within the European Union and calling for enhancing "strategic autonomy" within the U.S.-led transatlantic alliance.[81] French President Emmanuel Macron has called for strengthening "European sovereignty,"[82] even though the EU is not a sovereign state. Meanwhile, Russian theorists

81 Herfried Münkler, *Macht in der Mitte: Dieneuen Aufgaben Deutschlands in Europa*, (Hamburg: Edition Körber-Stiftung, 2015).

82 Emmanuel Macron, "Initiative for Europe" 26 September 2017, Sorbonne Speech at: <http://international.blogs.ouest-france.fr/archive/2017/09/29/macron-sorbonne-verbatim-europe-18583.html>.

have embraced "Eurasianism" and sought connections between "Eurasia" and China's Belt and Road Initiative.[83] All these trends have been watched closely by the White House. Finally, Marco Rubio, Secretary of State of the Trump administration, openly admitted in early 2025 that unipolarity was an anomaly, a product of the end of the Cold War, "but eventually you were going to reach back to a point where you had a multipolar world, multi-great powers in different parts of the planet."[84] In this context, the question of "what kind of multipolarization" has become more urgent than ever, and historical experience offers valuable references and lessons for the present.

In the past decade, China's contemporary vision of a multipolar world order has significantly challenged U.S. unipolar hegemony, provoking a backlash. Some commentators in the Western world have used the term "Monroe Doctrine" to describe China's policies, particularly referring to The Belt and Road Initiative as an example of a "Chinese Monroe Doctrine."[85] This comparison suggests that China's multipolarization proposition is no different from the regional hegemony pursued by Germany and Japan in the past. However, this interpretation is misleading both historically and in contemporary practice.

Taking the Belt and Road Initiative (BRI) as an example, the historical "Silk Road" has always been a route for the interconnection of diverse peoples and civilizations. Even at its peak, the Chinese dynasties in the Central Plains could only exert influence over parts of Central Asia. It would be historically inaccurate to consider the entire Silk Road as the "sphere of influence" of these Chinese dynasties. In fact, the term "Silk Road" was not a Chinese invention; it was coined by the 19th-century German geographer Carl Ritter.[86] Interestingly, as early as 2011, the U.S. State Department proposed a "New Silk Road" regional

83 On the afternoon of December 12th, 2018, Russian scholar Alexander Dukin gave a speech entitled *The Belt and Road Initiative in the Geopolitical Context of Europe and Asia* at Peking University, which covered this topic. Summary of lecture content: <https://www.youtube.com/watch?v=jOv1EYDFSck>.

84 "Interview: Secretary Marco Rubio with Megyn Kelly of The Megyn Kelly Show," 30 January, 2025, at: <https://www.state.gov/secretary-marco-rubio-with-megyn-kelly-of-the-megyn-kelly-show/>.

85 See Steven F. Jackson, "Does China have a Monroe Doctrine? Evidence for Regional Exclusion," *Strategic Studies Quarterly*, Vol. 10, No. 4 (2016): 64–89; Changhoon CHA, "China's Westward March: Strategic Views of One Belt, One Road," *The Korean Journal of International Studies*, Vol. 15, No. 3 (December 2017): 483–500. Another criticism is that China's South China Sea policy reflects the Chinese-style "Monroe Doctrine," see Christopher Rossi, *Whiggish International Law: Elihu Root, the Monroe Doctrine, and International Law in the Americas*, (Leiden & Boston: Brill Nijhoff, 2019), 196–200.

86 Matthias Mertens, "Did Richthofen Really Coin 'the Silk Road'?" *The Silk Road* 17 (2019): 1–9.

cooperation program, particularly in response to the situation in Afghanistan.[87] However, this initiative did not become a priority in U.S. national strategy. Soon after, China introduced the Belt and Road Initiative to carry forward the concept of the Silk Road. The space related to the Belt and Road Initiative is fundamentally different from regions like the Americas, which have clear, defined boundaries. The BRI uses concepts like "road," "belt," "corridor" and "bridge," all focusing on openness, connectivity, and communication based upon heterogeneity rather than closed, exclusive control on a homogeneous space. China's role in the Belt and Road Initiative is better understood as that of an "initiator" rather than a dominator seeking to control the entire region from above.

Indeed, some of the regions connected by the Belt and Road Initiative (BRI) are sensitive areas for certain regional powers. For instance, many Eurasianists in Russia have long regarded Central Asia as Russia's exclusive "sphere of influence." If the BRI were truly a "Chinese Monroe Doctrine," China and Russia would inevitably compete for exclusive dominance in Central Asia. This obviously did not happen. The two countries co-ordinate with each other bilaterally as well as using multi-lateral platforms like Shanghai Cooperation Organization and BRICS. China develops its relationship with Central Asian Countries without challenging Russian influence in this area. For example, the project of the China-Kyrgyzstan-Uzbekistan railway was launched with the consent of Russia. Moreover, China's eastern and southeastern borders are surrounded by a network of U.S. military bases, from Yokosuka and Ryukyu to Changi. The U.S. military dominance in these areas is evident, yet the BRI does not directly challenge or question the U.S. military presence in Asia under the banner of "Asia."

Although within the realm of international discussions, there has been no instance of anyone drawing a parallel between the Belt and Road Initiative and the spatial thinking that characterized the British Empire at the zenith of its power, it is nonetheless prudent and timely to proactively engage with and address the very notion of such a comparison. In the early 20th century, particularly during the drafting and signing of the Kellogg-Briand Pact in 1928, the British Empire introduced its own version of the Monroe Doctrine, known as the "British Monroe Doctrine." Unlike the U.S. Monroe Doctrine, which focused on territorial boundaries like those of the Americas, the British Monroe Doctrine emphasized control over key maritime transport hubs, such as the Suez Canal, the Strait of Malacca, the Bosporus, and the Dardanelles. The

---

87 Lynne M. Tracy, "The United States and the New Silk Road," 25 October 2013, at: <https://2009-2017.state.gov/p/sca/rls/rmks/2013/215906.htm>.

British navy's dominance over these hubs was critical to ensuring the safety of the British Empire.[88] As a result, Britain is sensitive to any action that threatens its navy's control over these hubs. The question then arises: Does the Belt and Road Initiative share this same mentality? This analogy seems groundless. After the decline of Britain's maritime empire, the U.S. became its only successor, with military bases dominating most major global maritime transportation hubs. We can ask: which maritime hub can China exclusively control under the Belt and Road Initiative?

In more abstract forms of spatial politics, China continues to appeal to the defensive principle of sovereignty, rather than the expansionary logic of the Monroe Doctrine. For example, in cyberspace, China invokes "internet sovereignty" to counter the U.S.'s global dominance in network information, establishing a "firewall" and requiring the localized storage of data.[89] In judicial matters, China criticizes the imperial "extraterritorial jurisdiction" of U.S. courts by emphasizing "judicial sovereignty." These are defensive positions rooted in the traditional concept of sovereignty, rather than attempts at global or regional expansion.

In the global financial arena, two of the most important financial communication network systems—SWIFT and CHIPS—are dominated by the U.S. For foreign enterprises settling international trade in U.S. dollars, it is difficult to bypass these systems, which have long been tools for the U.S. to establish "long-arm jurisdiction" over other countries' financial and trade activities. In response to these limitations, in early 2019, Germany, France, and Britain initiated the Instrument in Support of Trade Exchanges (INSTEX) to circumvent U.S. sanctions on Iran. Similarly, in October 2015, China launched the Cross-Border Interbank Payment System (CIPS) to maintain the autonomy of RMB cross-border payment settlements. These are defensive efforts aimed at safeguarding national financial sovereignty against U.S. financial hegemony. Unlike geographical space, financial networks are not constrained by fixed

88 Of course, as George Curzon, who served as the governor of India in the British Empire, pointed out at the beginning of the 20th century, Britain was not only the strongest maritime country in the world at that time, but also the largest land power in the world with the widest land territory boundary. "The Romanes Lecture, 1907. Frontiers." By the Right Hon. Lord Curzon of Kedleston, D.c.n., LL.D., F.R.S., Chancellor of the University. (Oxford: Clarendon Press, 1907). However, the maritime nature of the British Empire still comes first, focusing on the connection between different land territories.

89 See Liu Han 刘晗, "Yuming xitong, Wangluo Zhuquan yu Hulianwang zhili lishi fansi jiqi dangdai qishi 域名系统、网络主权与互联网治理历史反思及其当代启示 [Historical Reflection on Domain Name System, Internet Sovereignty and Internet Governance and Its Contemporary Enlightenment]," *Zhongwai faxue* 2 (2016).

limits; they are flexible. This allows many countries to develop their own independent settlement mechanisms based on their own currencies, offering a range of options for international financial and trade practitioners.

Many observers have noted that the Trump administration often expressed opposition to "globalism" and "globalization," instead emphasizing "sovereignty." For example, in his speech at the 72nd UN General Assembly on September 19, 2017, Donald Trump mentioned the word "sovereign" 21 times.[90] However, Trump's interpretation of sovereignty includes the imperial extraterritorial jurisdiction that the U.S. has established over the past two centuries. The use of domestic law to govern international affairs has long been a standard American legal practice. Therefore, Trump's sovereignty discourse does not have the implication of the "equality of sovereignty." Instead, its actual intent is to use the concept of sovereignty to exclude foreign influence and shed the numerous international obligations the U.S. has undertaken in the past without diminishing the many privileges the U.S. enjoys within the international system. Trump's lip service to "sovereignty" did not prevent him from expressing blatantly his interest in annexing Greenland and Canada. From the perspective of Antonio Gramsci, a classic theorist of the concept "hegemony," this suggests that the element of "consent" in U.S. global hegemony is weakening, while the dimension of "coercion" is becoming more prominent.[91]

What merits our further comprehension is that a multitude of discourses which level accusations against China of purportedly pursuing the Monroe Doctrine actually serve as a vivid manifestation of the very logic inherent in the Monroe Doctrine that has long been employed by the ruling elites of the United States. This logic involves identifying certain elements that are considered heterogenous and then attempting to expel them from what is regarded as a homogeneous spatial and geopolitical framework. In the eyes of these commentators, China's political, economic and social mode within its own sovereign territory has already interfered with the homogeneous order that the U.S. is trying to establish globally. If China dares to draw a supranational regional space and promote its own political, economic and social practice different from that of the U.S., this will further prove that China is a saboteur in the global space. This accusation requires China to bear the burden of proof to defend herself. This type of "preemptive" strategy of verbal attack has always been a part of the U.S. foreign policy tradition.

---

90 Remarks by President Trump to the 72nd Session of the United Nations General Assembly, at: <https://www.whitehouse.gov/briefings-statements/remarks-president-trump-72nd-session-united-nations-general-assembly/>.

91 Perry Anderson, *The H-Word: The Peripeteia of Hegemony*, (London: Verso, 2017), 19–23, 108–116.

However, based on this historical research into the discursive lineage of the Monroe Doctrine, one can easily judge: it is the U.S., not China, that currently advocates a hegemonic "Neo-Monroe Doctrine." With the U.S. government's announcement of the "Trump Corollary" to the Monroe Doctrine in its new nationary strategy, this has become even more evident than ever. In contrast, what China advocates today is the concept of a "Community of Shared Future for Mankind." While the specific meaning of this concept is still evolving, its current practice is markedly different from imperialist interventionism. On the other hand, this position is unlike those who claim to represent the universal interests of mankind or the "international community"—often designating certain nations as the "public enemies" of humanity; on the other hand, it is also distinct from the Monroe Doctrine's notion of "sphere of influence."

China's contemporary vision for international order is rooted in its ancient historical experience and is an extension of the country's revolutionary path and development since the 20th century. Protected by oceans, mountains, and deserts, the geographical space China is located today is largely self-contained. Throughout history, the Central Plains Dynasty—based on agriculture—often had the advantage in strength over its surrounding regions. As long as internal order was maintained, China enjoyed a strong sense of psychological security and did not exhibit the deep-rooted suspicion or the "preemptive" behavior that characterizes the U.S. Monroe Doctrine, which emerged in the context of inter-state rivalry in Europe and Americas.

In the 19th century, China was thrust into an international system of intense geopolitical competition and quickly fell to the bottom, weakening its sense of geopolitical security. After the collapse of the tributary system, China's semi-colonial status made it difficult to imagine dominating a supranational region. However, the experience of becoming a semi-colony enabled China to resonate deeply with the plight of oppressed nations within the international system, cultivating a sensitivity to the logic of regional and global hegemony.

In the 20th century, China underwent a long process of revolution, established strong national sovereignty, and then opened to the Western world on this basis. With its autonomy, China could control the degree and pace of this opening, avoiding dependency on other great powers. This is key to what Professor Wang Hui refers to as China's historical experience of "autonomous opening."[92] Grounded in the Confucian axiom, "do not do to others what you do not want them to do to you," China promotes the equal sovereignty of all

92 Wang Hui 汪晖, "Zhongguo jueqi de jingyan jiqi mianlin de tiaozhan 中国崛起的经验及其面临的挑战 [The Experience of China's Rise and the Challenges it Faces]," *Wenhua zongheng* 2 (2010).

nations, advocating for mutual opening, inter-connectivity, and mutual learning between civilizations. The concept of the "Community of Shared Future for Mankind" acknowledges that every nation, large or small, exerts influence within a certain region, but this influence is mutual, creating a "symbiotic" relationship among nations. For China, the exercise of influence must respect the sovereignty of other nations. It is essential to remain vigilant against any illegal unilateral sanctions and "long-arm jurisdiction" that lack a basis in international law.

Grounding itself in the principles of equality and voluntariness, regional integration holds the potential to make substantial and positive contributions to the realization of the "Community of Shared Future for Mankind." Due to the increasing complexity of industrial supply chains and the rising costs of scientific and technological innovation, many countries are unable to build a complete industrial system on their own. It has become essential to create cooperative industrial systems and develop scientific research collaborations through regional integration. For example, Airbus is a product of cooperation between France, Germany, Spain, and Britain, as no single country could establish the full industrial chain for large aircraft production. Similarly, during the COVID-19 pandemic, EU decision-makers realized the shortcomings of their manufacturing sectors, further highlighting the importance of regional integration. However, there is also the risk that regional alliances may transform into new instruments of a Monroe Doctrine, where regional powers impose their will on others, restricting their relationships with countries outside the region. It is an inherent challenge of regional integration to make sure that regional alliances remain voluntary, equal, and mutually beneficial.

If the previous analysis seems less appealing to realists in international relations, now we can switch to a more realist perspective. There is an inherent asymmetry between the economic and military-political strength of both China and the U.S. Today, China is not in a realistic position to desire the U.S.'s unipolar hegemony. While China's economic strength ranks among the top two globally, with its manufacturing sector surpassing that of the U.S., Japan, and Germany combined, there remains a significant gap in military-political power. China is still a country that has not fully reunified its territory, is surrounded by U.S. military bases, and is frequently attacked by U.S. funded media for its political system and mode of development.

In contrast, the U.S., despite experiencing deterioration of its manufacturing sector, still wields formidable military and political power. Faced with its the decline of its industrial capacity, the U.S. is likely to rely on extra-economic means to bolster its economy, and some of its allies may be pressured to follow suit. Under such conditions, Chinese enterprises operating abroad may face interference from the U.S. and its allies under the pretext of national security or political values—as seen with ZTE, Huawei, and TikTok. If China were to respond with similar extra-economic coercion, it could provoke resistance and be counterproductive.

China's centralized political and social system, characterized by compactness rather than expansive flexibility often seen in other models, not only allows the country to mobilize effectively in the face of major crises like the pandemic or earthquake, but also imposes restrictions on capital and individual entrepreneurs, making it difficult for unscrupulous adventurers to expand by appropriating state power like British Indian Company did in history. This compactness extends to China's industrial structure. While *Autarky* (economic self-sufficiency) is no longer realistic for most countries, including China, the nation's ability to maintain "internal circulation" of its economy is stronger than that of most other nations in the world. Since the 1950s, China has built an all-encompassing industrial system that spans across every sector, making it the sole nation to possess all industrial categories as defined by the United Nations industrial classification.

The trade, financial, and technology wars launched by the Trump administration—and continued under Biden—have further de-Americanized China's economy, forcing China to develop internal circulation domestically and external circulation internationally with more non-American partners. During the COVID-19 pandemic in 2020, China's economy demonstrated considerable resilience in extreme conditions, proving its capacity for internal circulation. Given its comprehensive industrial system, China is uniquely positioned to cooperate with both developed and developing countries, and even often act as a mediator between them. Focusing on continued growth and equal, mutually beneficial cooperation with other nations is the most effective path forward for China. However, this realist perspective cannot fully capture the profound impact of historical experience and memory on shaping a country's behavior.

The evolution of the global order is shaped by the interaction of various forces, and no single country can unilaterally dictate its course. Today, the form of spatial politics is constantly evolving. Emerging spatial political struggles are linked, but not limited, to issues like "Cyber Sovereignty." This struggle centers on the control of data and technical standards. In the coming era of the "Internet of Things," data control will become an increasingly critical source of power. In this new landscape, a handful of transnational corporations possess more data than most governments, which significantly undermines the traditional monopoly that national governments have over legitimate violence within their own territories. This shift threatens to create a form of "Digital Feudalism,"[93] an insurmountable challenge for most governments around the world. As nominal sovereignty over physical territory becomes increasingly hollow, the few governments capable of integrating these multinational companies into a military-industrial complex will have significant advantages in the spatial political struggle. However, even governments with the capacity to form such complexes will face the critical issue of "who controls" within these power structures.

At the same time, in an era when industrial chains are becoming longer and the interdependence between products is growing, technical standards have increasingly become the "admission ticket" to market space. Different and mutually exclusive technical standards can shape the division not only of market space but also of political space. If friendly cooperation is the prevailing mode, the possibility for convergence and compatibility between different technical standards can be possible. However, the right to set technical standards for key infrastructure is closely tied to the future of technological and economic hegemony, which inevitably triggers political anxieties. For example, since 2019, China's large-scale rollout of 5G technology has alarmed many in the U.S., who believed the control of standards for such key infrastructure can pave the way for establishing leadership in the future industrial ecosystem built upon that infrastructure. The U.S. ruling elites lobbied globally to prevent countries from adopting Huawei's products and technologies, and pressured chip foundries worldwide to halt production for the company. This unprecedented campaign reflects a genuine anxiety—the importance of technical standards lies in their "low reversibility." Once a standard is established, economic and social exchanges, as well as industrial chains, are built upon it, and reversing these standards incurs significant economic costs. As a result, while alliances formed through formal international treaties have traditionally shaped geopolitics, today's technical standards can quietly redraw these boundaries, making the legal forms of alliances themselves less significant.

The technicalization of politics also leads to the politicization of technology. The struggle over technical standards has become a crucial entry point for understanding contemporary spatial politics. The significance of the trans-national dimension of the global order has been rising while traditional

93 Sascha D. Meinrath, James W. Losey and Victor W. Picard, "Digital Feudalism: Enclosures and Erasures from Digital Rights Management to the Digital Divide," *Advances in Computers* 81 (2011): 237–287. See also Wang Shaoguang 王绍光, "Xinjishu geming yu guojia lilun 新技术革命与国家理论 [New Technological Revolution and State Theory]," *Zhongyang shehuizhuyi xueyuan xuebao* 5 (2019).

geopolitics, which takes place mainly on the inter-state dimension, remains significant. In this context, we will see increasingly abstract boundaries drawn by different technical standards, which may overlap or diverge from traditional distinctions between "us" and "them" in public opinion. Once these boundaries are established, they possess great stability and may even shape collective identity. At the level of international order, the key question is whether a unipolar hegemony will continue to set technical standards and control data, or whether a multipolar world with intercommunicating platforms and collaborative innovation will emerge. This will be the defining struggle of the future.

Of course, there are key differences between a bipolar order and a multipolar order. On September 24, 2019, during the UN General Assembly, UN Secretary-General António Guterres warned of the looming risk of the world splitting into two, with the United States and China creating rival internets, currencies, trade systems, financial rules, and adopting zero-sum geopolitical and military strategies.[94] Guterres' concept of space is undoubtedly more comprehensive and realistic than the traditional geopolitical perspective. Compared to the first half of the 20th century, today's spatial politics has become more multidimensional and pervasive. The power of the internet, finance, and the industrial systems that consist of global supply chains may no longer align with the physical boundaries of sovereign states. The U.S. in the 20th century has already demonstrated how a hegemonic power can substantially influence—and even dominate—the political, economic, and cultural life of other nations without altering their geographical borders. After World War II, the humanity witnessed a polarized world order. However, in the 1970s, China promoted the theory of "three worlds" and became a key force in pushing the bipolar order to its end. In the subsequent international system, China experienced rapid development with no incentive to establish a new bipolar order—which would undoubtedly impose more pressure on China than a multipolar order. Additionally, in a bipolar world, when countries are forced to choose sides between two opposing powers, the diversity of the world is significantly diminished. In such a system, addressing global challenges like climate change, epidemic prevention and control, anti-terrorism, and nuclear non-proliferation—all of which require the coordination of multiple global powers—becomes far more difficult.

However, there are structural factors that limit "decoupling" and "polarization." During the Cold War, the two blocs were not only ideologically opposed

94 "UN chief warns of a world divided between U.S. and China," at: <https://apnews.com/general-news-ef7a57b2a31b42efbb81acbdbbe6910f?utm_source=copy&utm_medium=share> (accessed 23 February 2024).

but also lacked significant economic interaction. In contrast, contemporary China holds a large amount of U.S. debt, while U.S. capital has significant investments in China. China has become the world's largest single consumer market and the only country with a full industrial chain. Many U.S. corporations rely on both China's consumer market and its manufacturing and industrial support capacities. During the global COVID-19 pandemic in 2020, many Chinese factories delayed production due to strict epidemic prevention policies, causing shocks to the global supply chain. When Western governments eventually had to confront their own outbreaks—after initially "watching the fire from afar"—they found themselves facing shortages of strategic materials. At this critical moment, China became a "safety island," accelerating its industrial production and supplying essential materials to countries worldwide. Amid the global economic turbulence, more countries began to recognize the stabilizing role China's manufacturing industry plays in the global economy.

During the pandemic, the so-called over-reliance on Chinese imports became a topic of public debate in many countries. In the post-pandemic world, some nations may reconsider the fragility of their international supply chains and attempt to rebuild industries that produce strategic materials domestically. However, as these countries face economic and social instability, there will be pressure to restore their economies as quickly as possible. Completely abandoning established supply chains and starting anew are not realistic. Governments would need to offer substantial compensation to persuade multinational corporations—many of which have "gone global"—to forsake the 1.4 billion-person Chinese market in favor of narrowly defined national interests. More importantly, such a shift would require strong state power to direct the flow of private capital. In political systems where politicians depend on big business for campaign contributions to win competitive elections, this kind of redirection may succeed in certain industries, but achieving overall success would be highly difficult. Donald Trump's endeavor to build comprehensive supply chains in the U.S. will be proved to be an illusion.

The signing of the Regional Comprehensive Economic Partnership (RCEP) in November 2020, involving 10 ASEAN countries, along with China, Japan, South Korea, Australia, and New Zealand, highlights the fact that despite political and military alliances with the U.S., many countries lack the economic motivation to decouple from China. RCEP makes it even less likely that Western Pacific countries will sever their economic ties with China. This is not to suggest that the U.S. "new cold war" initiative will evaporate naturally—throughout the pandemic, the U.S. ruling elite's "contain China" stance remained unwavering. While China prepares for the worst-case scenario, it should also recognize that favorable factors for "multipolarization" and "multilateralism" are still increasing. Marco Rubio's recognition of the uniplar world order as an anomaly is the further sign of the American elites moving toward "multipolarization." Effectively combining and applying these resources can help reduce the likelihood of slipping into a new cold war and continue promoting the evolution of the global order towards multipolarization.

When the concept of "multipolarity" itself is no longer considered a heretical idea, what we need to further explore is precisely what kind of multipolarity we actually require. In the 1930s, Germany and Japan, in an attempt to mirror the United States' hegemonic dominance in the Western Hemisphere, proposed the establishment of an international order in which several great powers would possess and mutually recognize each other's spheres of influence. Should such an order be resurrected in the contemporary era, it would incontrovertibly mark the utter failure of the United Nations order that was instituted in 1945, which aimed to promote a more just and equitable international system. If the Monroe Doctrine is to be repudiated as a global hegemonic project, its function as a regional hegemonic vehicle must be equally challenged.

4 Concluding Remarks

The exploration of the dissemination and reception of the Monroe Doctrine in this book is not simply a study of spatial politics and its discursive forms (including legal discourse) but also a reflection on the relationship between the United States and the world since the 19th century. Human history is filled with examples where practices of boundary delineation have given rise to discourses expressing the consciousness of exclusive domination over a space. The Monroe Doctrine, originating in the U.S., is just one of many such spatial political discourses. However, since the 19th century, the international influence of the Monroe Doctrine has dramatically escalated, spreading globally. The remarkable historical phenomenon of the doctrine being appropriated by so many political forces is worthy of in-depth study.

Behind this process lies the U.S.'s transformation from regional hegemony in the Western Hemisphere to global hegemony. The U.S.'s influence in various regions—at least as a potential audience—motivated cultural-political elites in these regions to frame their spatial political demands through the lens of the Monroe Doctrine, thereby increasing visibility in a space with a U.S. audience. Given that the U.S. has not entirely lost its unipolar hegemonic position in the international system, we can predict that the Monroe Doctrine will continue to be disseminated, giving rise to new responses in spatial politics.

Today, we live in an era of uncertainty. Since the fall of the Berlin Wall, optimism about the prospects of globalization has grown, with the cross-border flow of capital seen as a neutral process, divorced from politics. However, the world has not become a flat playing field. The highly uneven distribution of benefits among countries and different social classes within nation-states, has triggered backlashes against post-Cold War globalization. Ironically, the most dramatic backlash has occurred in the U.S. political arena rather than elsewhere. If, under the Bush administration, Neo-conservatives sought to spread American values and control vast global spaces through a temporal-historical vision, by the time of the Trump administration, Washington had lost that confidence. What remained was a defensive mentality—using U.S. military-political hegemony to maintain its vested interest around the world.

One manifestation of this conservatism is how the Trump administration weakened the "political/economic" dichotomy that was implicit in the expansionary Monroe Doctrine discourses of the Roosevelt-Wilson era. In a defensive manner, Trump emphasized that the economic activities of other countries might threaten U.S. political interests. Yet, the Trump administration did not allow other countries to make similar claims and still expected the world to remain "undefended" to U.S. capital. In his first presidential term, Trump essentially acted as a "switchman," steering subsequent U.S. administrations toward the explicit politicization of the economy.

In 2020, the world was shaken by the COVID-19 pandemic. Unsurprisingly, the global financial and commercial networks that expanded during the post-Cold War era also facilitated the rapid spread of the virus—although no one could have predicted the pandemic's alarming intensity. The COVID-19 crisis connected the world through fear, while simultaneously reactivating many boundaries that had been weakened by globalization. As people became stationary, the flow of capital slowed down as well. From the fall of the Berlin Wall to the 2020 pandemic, the post-Cold War globalization championed by the U.S. appears to have reached the end of its life cycle.

After the pandemic, many countries and regional organizations will likely focus more on de-risking strategies. For example, some may rebuild industries locally that do not align with the theory of comparative advantage to ensure the supply of strategic materials. In certain areas of social policy, the free market principle may be restricted, and the emphasis on de-risking for societal stability will grow. As a result, the voices advocating for national and regional spatial autonomy will continue to rise, creating more space for Monroe Doctrine-like discourses such as "X for the Xans." In 2020, European Union statesmen placed unprecedented emphasis on "European sovereignty," and several Western

Pacific countries signed the Regional Comprehensive Economic Partnership (RCEP) to strengthen regional economic integration. It has become increasingly clear that in a world shaped by capital and military forces, the diversity and richness of human culture and ways of life are fragile. Moreover, the upper limits imposed by global hegemonic power undermine the potential excellence that nations and individuals subjected to this hegemony could otherwise achieve.

However, the turbulent and violent history of the first half of the 20th century reminds us that there are different paths to "multipolarization." A strict division of borders, high walls, and competing regional hegemonic powers suppressing weaker nations are one possible—yet undesirable—path. This path, characterized by regional hegemony, is not conducive to the peaceful and prosperous human civilization we aspire to build. In the early 20th century, German and Japanese theorists—imitating the Monroe Doctrine—proposed that different regions be ruled by different hegemonic powers. If such a vision were realized, it would mean the end of global coordination mechanisms like the United Nations. Yet this vision is inherently unstable. The vicissitudes of the U.S. Monroe Doctrine demonstrate that regional hegemonic powers often emphasize regional autonomy in a defensive posture when confronting global hegemony. However, when given the opportunity to assume global hegemony themselves, they tend to abandon the regional limit on expansion. A similar opportunism was evident in the warlord politics of China, where local powers also invoked the Monroe Doctrine discourse opportunistically. An order based on the division of the world by several regional hegemonic powers can hardly address the major risks facing humanity in the 21st century—such as climate change, pandemics, terrorism, and nuclear proliferation.

Therefore, it is more important to discuss the concrete forms of multipolarization rather than simply advocating for it. While international organizations and mechanisms for coordination can be exploited by hegemonic states, this is not a reason to abandon them. The post-war coordination mechanisms—centered around the United Nations—were established as a response to the failures of Wilson and the League of Nations. They are a hard-won institutional achievement. As the Trump administration pursued "America First" policies, tensions between the U.S. and the United Nations intensified. It becomes increasingly important to strengthen the UN's coordinating and leading role and to promote the political influence of developing countries. This approach aligns with the direction of multipolarization. In the new historical context, the "pseudo-universalism" of hegemonic powers, which prioritizes capital appreciation as the main objective, should be overcome.

New forms of internationalism that recognize cultural and political diversity while strengthening cooperation to improve global well-being in the face of humanity's common challenges should be explored.

In a rapidly changing world, we need to constantly rethink spatial politics, particularly the role of boundaries. Boundaries can separate peoples and protect a political community's sovereignty and control over its destiny, including managing cross-border health threats. Yet boundaries can also be "contact zones" that promote communication, cooperation, and co-evolution—a "moral zone" for internationalism. On the brink of a multipolar era, we hope the world will not repeat the mistakes of the past, shaped by hegemonic logic and a "sphere of influence" mentality. We hope that the boundaries between states, nations, and civilizations will become golden lines—preserving differences and diversity while promoting intercommunication. Whether this hope is realizable depends on how effectively the contemporary era navigates the interplay between traditional and novel spatial politics.

CHAPTER 1

Beyond the Western Hemisphere: the Evolution of American Discourse on the Monroe Doctrine

> Ah! Ah, the Atlantic Ocean! Morning! The Atlantic Ocean!
> Morning! The new continent by the Atlantic Ocean!
> Morning! The tomb of Washington! The Tomb of Lincoln! The Tomb of Whitman!
> Ah! Oh, Whitman! Oh, Whitman! the Pacific Ocean-like Whitman!
> Ah! The Pacific Ocean! Morning! The Pacific Ocean! Islands in the Pacific Ocean!
>
> GUO MORUO, Good Morning[95]

∴

On January 7, 1919, U.S. President Woodrow Wilson returned to Paris after a three-week lecture tour across continental Europe. During this tour, he was greeted with near-cult-like adoration in major European cities, where people hoped his vision would bring peace to a continent ravaged by war.[96] When Wilson entered the Palace of Versailles for the Paris Peace Conference, it was undeniably a "Wilsonian moment," with the U.S. at the center of the world stage.[97]

---

95 Guo Moruo 郭沫若, *Nüshen* 女神 [*Goddess*], (Shanghai: Taidong tushuju, 1921), 95–96.

96 As John Maynard Keynes, an economist who participated in the Paris Peace Conference, pointed out: "When President Wilson left Washington he enjoyed a prestige and a moral influence throughout the world unequalled in history. His bold and measured words carried to the peoples of Europe above and beyond the voices of their own politicians. The people of the enemy states trusted that he could carry out the compact he had made with them; and the people of the Entente states acknowledged him not only as a victor but almost as a prophet. In addition to this moral influence, the realities of power were in his hands." John Maynard Keynes, *The Economic Consequences of the Peace*, (New York: Harcourt, Brace and Howe, 1920), p. 42.

97 Of course, what we can't ignore is that Wilson's Fourteen-point Peace Plan, to a large extent, was a response to Lenin—it aimed to stop the Bolshevik's "world revolution" by imitating some part of Lenin's ideas. In this sense, Wilson lived in the shadow of Lenin. Lenin's proposition of "Self-determination" was far more thorough than Wilson's. In fact,

 | DOI:10.1163/9789004746237_003

Wilson presented an idealistic vision of world order, sharply criticizing long-standing European practices such as the balance of power, secret diplomacy, trade barriers, and the arms race. He believed the world should embrace new principles and practices based on international law, collective security, open diplomacy, free trade, freedom of the seas, and arms reduction. Among these, his most striking idea was the establishment of a League of Nations—a global alliance of nations that would serve as a collective security mechanism to resolve disputes through peaceful means. This vision, disseminated through Wilson's Committee on Public Information and embraced by Chinese intellectuals who admired the U.S., inspired enthusiastic responses from China's political and cultural elites.[98] Kang Youwei even hailed this moment as the dawn of what he called "the great harmony."[99]

However, Wilson's "highlight moment" did not last long. The European powers and Japan exploited his eagerness to establish the League of Nations by inducing him to make concessions on other key issues. Wilson accepted France's proposal to punish and weaken Germany economically, militarily, and territorially. He also agreed to acknowledge Britain's special interests on the issue of freedom of the seas. To appease Japan and secure their withdrawal of the racial equality proposal, Wilson consented to transferring Germany's privileges in Shandong, China to Japan. At the same time, he showed great indifference to the demands for self-determination from many oppressed nations under the control of the victorious powers of World War I. This severely disillusioned global expectations of Wilson's vision. As the peace conference progressed, Wilson's prestige sharply declined.

---

the latter never really got rid of racist prejudice and the imperialist-colonial notion of the hierarchy of civilization.

98 For the publicity of and response to Wilsonianism in China, see Ma Jianbiao 马建标, "Suzao jiushizhu: 'Yizhan' houqi 'weierxun' zhuyi zaizhongguo de chuanbo 塑造救世主：'一战'后期'威尔逊'主义在中国的传播 [Shaping the Savior: The Spread of Wilsonianism in China in the Late Period of World War I]," *Xueshu yuekan* 6, (2017); Ren Yi 任一, "Huanshi dumei: Wusi qianxi meiguo zaihua xuanchuan yu zhongguo dui xinguojia shenfen de zhuiqiu '寰世独美'：五四前夕美国在华宣传与中国对新国家身份的追求 [The Only Beauty in the World: American Propaganda in China on the Eve of the May 4th Movement and China's Pursuit of New National Identity]," *Shixue jikan* 1 (2016).

99 In January 1919, Kang Youwei wrote a letter to Lu Zhengxiang, Gu Weijun, Wang Zhengting, Shi Zhaoji and Wei Chen, saying: "the current U.S. President Wilson's proposal of the League of Nations seeks world peace, which will bring equality and freedom to all countries in the world, big or small. This is the real practice of great peace and will lay the foundation of great harmony." Kang Youwei 康有为, *Kang Youwei quanji* 康有为全集 [*Complete Works of Kang Youwei*], Vol. 11, (Beijing: Renmin daxue chubanshe, 2007), 99.

The Treaty of Versailles, which contained the Covenant of the League of Nations, was signed on June 28, 1919. Wilson had formally realized his core project, but when he returned to the U.S. to seek Congress's approval of the Covenant, he encountered his personal Waterloo. Despite being the League's strongest advocate, the U.S. never became a member. This was a significant blow to the international prestige of the United States. In 1919, the U.S. had shone brilliantly at the center of the world stage, only to soon retreat to the sidelines, exerting influence in global affairs through indirect and circuitous means until the outbreak of World War II.

Nevertheless, this "Wilsonian moment" left a lasting historical impact. Wilson demonstrated the trajectory through which a new Republic in North America grew from regional hegemony into a nation with global influence. However, there was much debate at the time—both at home and abroad—over whether Wilson's "leap" from Washington to Paris represented the natural development of U.S. international strategy in the 19th century, or a deviation from the diplomatic tradition of the Monroe Doctrine. Wilson and his allies emphasized that this shift from the Monroe Doctrine to Wilsonianism was a sign of historical progress, not a decline or departure. However, in U.S. domestic politics, Wilson's rivals argued that his League of Nations project represented a deviation from the Monroe Doctrine, which could allow a European-led League to interfere in U.S. and American affairs, leading to potential losses rather than gains. Ultimately, the U.S. Senate rejected the Covenant of the League of Nations, and the backlash to Wilson's "leap" continued to influence U.S. politics for years, even constraining President Franklin Roosevelt's decisions during World War II.

In Europe and Asia, great powers pressured by the U.S. after World War I were also dissatisfied with Wilsonianism. Both Germany and Japan responded by drawing on the Monroe Doctrine's 19th-century example in the U.S., constructing it as a universal model to justify their own expansion and regional influence. Discursively, this strategy involved using the past of the U.S. against its present—emphasizing that President Monroe's principles were universal, legitimate, and worthy of imitation, while contrasting this with Wilson's new interpretation. They argued that U.S. global hegemony denied other powers their legitimate spheres of influence, accusing the U.S. of "removing the ladder after climbing it" and "burning bridges after crossing them." German jurist Carl Schmitt reflected on the U.S. Monroe Doctrine and showed great interest in Japan's "Asian Monroe Doctrine." His work significantly influenced Japanese international law scholars' theoretical interpretations of Japan's Monroe Doctrine during World War II.

Therefore, both at home and abroad, the "Wilsonian Moment" raised significant questions about the relationship between the Monroe Doctrine and Wilsonianism. Whether U.S. foreign policy under Wilson had betrayed its own past became a key issue for discussion, sparking new theoretical thinking that persisted even after World War II. In China, a series of studies on the evolution of U.S. foreign policy during the Wilson administration have emerged, typically framing the conflict of Wilson's era as a struggle between isolationism and internationalism.[100] However, this chapter seeks to move beyond simply labeling these two -isms and instead explores the core concepts and symbols that these ideologies relied on. The Monroe Doctrine held a central position in the U.S. diplomatic tradition of the 19th century—both cognitively and emotionally. For Wilson to justify his shift toward active participation in world affairs, he needed to reinterpret this tradition. In contrast, Wilson's domestic and international political opponents needed to offer different interpretations to effectively challenge his innovations. Despite the relevance of this conflict, the current literature in China has not yet given it sufficient attention. Building on previous studies, this chapter aims to trace the development of the Monroe Doctrine and its evolving meanings, providing material for further theoretical reflection on the symbolic and conceptual shifts in U.S. foreign policy.

1 From the "Monroe Doctrine" to Wilsonianism: Continuity or Discontinuity?

The years 1821–1823 marked a crucial moment for U.S. foreign policy, as the country faced new challenges both in the East and West. In the West, in 1821, Tsarist Russia, which had already occupied Alaska, announced that it would

100 For example, Han Li 韩莉, *Xin waijiao, jiu shijie: Wuluode weierxun yu guoji lianmeng* 新外交，旧世界：伍德罗·威尔逊与国际联盟 [*New Diplomacy, Old World: Woodrow Wilson and League of Nations*], (Beijing: Tongxin chubanshe, 2002); Qin Shan 秦珊, *Meiguo Weierxun zhegnfu duihua zhengce yanjiu* 美国威尔逊政府对华政策研究 [*A Study of the American Wilson Administration's China Policy*], (Beijing: Zhongguo shehuikexue chubanshe, 2005); Wang Xiaode 王晓德, *Mengxiang yu xianshi: Weierxun "lixiang zhuyi" waijiao yanjiu* 梦想与现实：威尔逊"理想主义"外交研究 [*Dreams and Reality: A Study of Wilson's Idealism Diplomacy*], (Beijing: Zhongguo shehuikexue chubanshe, 1995); Ren Liming 任李明, *Weierxun zhuyi yanjiu* 威尔逊主义研究 [*Wilson Studies*], (Beijing: Zhongguo shehuikexue chubanshe, 2013); Deng Shusheng 邓蜀生, *Wudeluo Weierxun* 伍德罗·威尔逊 [*Woodrow Wilson*], (Shanghai: Shanghai renmin chubanshe, 1982); Gao Hongzhi 高鸿志, *Weierxun yu beiyang junfa zhengfu* 威尔逊与北洋军阀政府 [*Wilson and the Northern Warlords Government*], (Beijing: Renmin chubanshe, 2015).

expand its territorial waters in North America southward to the 51st parallel north. Although this did not directly infringe on U.S. territory, it was perceived as a challenge to the principle of "freedom of navigation" advocated by the U.S. Meanwhile, across the Atlantic, in 1822, the Congress of Verona, held by the European dynastic monarchies, resulted in an agreement between Russia, Austria, Prussia, and France, authorizing Bourbon France to intervene in the Spanish Revolution under the banner of the Holy Alliance. France restored Bourbon rule in Spain through military intervention and then sought support from other European powers to intervene in the Spanish American wars of independence. This posed a potential threat to the balance of power in continental Europe, which Britain opposed. In 1823, British Foreign Minister George Canning approached the U.S. through Richard Rush, the U.S. minister to Britain, with a proposal for a joint British-U.S. statement opposing Spanish efforts to regain control of its American colonies, many of which were already independent. Canning emphasized that neither Britain nor the U.S. sought control over these colonies but would not stand by and watch them fall into the hands of other powers.

John Quincy Adams, the U.S. Secretary of State, responded to this proposal. At a cabinet meeting on November 7, 1823, Adams argued that a joint statement with Britain would be both unprofitable and self-limiting for the U.S. With an eye toward future U.S. expansion, Adams pointed out that while the U.S. had no immediate plans to seize Texas or Cuba, it was important to remain open to the possibility that the people of those regions might someday seek to unite with the U.S. Issuing a joint statement with Britain, he argued, would give Britain an excuse to interfere, thereby depriving the U.S. of its initiative in such situations.[101] However, Adams also asserted that the U.S. needed to make a claim on Latin American affairs[102]—first, to prevent Britain from joining the Holy Alliance to divide Latin America, and second, to prevent Britain

101 Charles Francis Adams ed., *Memoires of John Quincy Adams, Comprising Portions of His Diary from 1795 to 1848*, Vol. 6, (Philadelphia: J.B. Lippincott & Co., 1875), 177–178.

102 John Quincy Adams pointed to the geographical space now called "Latin America," but did not use the word "Latin America." In fact, the term "Latin America" did not exist in the 1820s. The origin of this term can be traced back to the 1830s, especially the French author Saint-Simon Michel Chevalier, who believed that the residents of Central America and South America belong to the Latin race, so they could stand with Latin Europe and fight against Teutonic Europe, Anglo-Saxon America and Slavic Europe. See Walter Migno, *The Idea of Latin America*, (Oxford: Wiley-Blackwell, 2005), 77–80. Napoléon III supported Maximiliano I, a member of the Habsburg family, to be the emperor of Mexico, and the term "Latin America" just met his need to emphasize the role of France in America. See John Charles Chasteen, *Born in Blood and Fire: A Concur History of Latin America*, (New York: W.W. Norton, 2001), 156.

from monopolizing the region after defeating the Holy Alliance.[103] These ideas were adopted by President James Monroe, shaping what would soon become known as the Monroe Doctrine.

Another factor, though less frequently mentioned, is no less important: while the United States had passed the Act Prohibiting Importation of Slaves in 1807, many U.S. elites continued to use Cuba as a transit point for smuggling enslaved Africans, even as the British navy patrolled the Atlantic to intercept and punish slave-trading ships. For many U.S. elites at the time, Britain posed as much of a threat—if not more—than the Holy Alliance. This deep sense of alienation and hostility toward Britain discouraged U.S. elites from issuing a joint statement with the United Kingdom, as they viewed British intervention with suspicion.[104]

On December 2, 1823, President James Monroe delivered his State of the Union address to the U.S. Congress, outlining three core propositions concerning U.S. foreign policy that would become known as the Monroe Doctrine.

1. Opposition to New Colonization by European Powers in the Americas: Monroe asserted that the American continents, having assumed and maintained their free and independent status, were no longer open to future colonization by European powers. He declared, "*the American continents, by the free and independent condition which they have assumed and maintain, are henceforth not to be considered as subjects for future colonization by any European powers.*"
2. Opposition to European Interference in Independent American Countries: Monroe also warned European powers against interfering in the affairs of newly independent American nations, especially by attempting to impose their political systems. He stated, "*We owe it, therefore, to candor and to the amicable relations existing between the United States and those powers to declare that we should consider any attempt on their part to extend their system to any portion of this hemisphere as dangerous to our peace and safety. With the existing colonies or dependencies of any European power we have not interfered and shall not interfere. But with the Governments who have declared their independence and maintained it, and whose independence we have, on great consideration and on just principles, acknowledged, we could not view any interposition for the purpose of oppressing them, or controlling in any other manner their destiny,*

103 Adams (n. 101), 207–208.

104 Stephen Chambers, *No God But Gain: The Untold Story of Cuban Slavery, the Monroe Doctrine, and the Making of the United States*, (London: Verso, 2017).

by any European power in any other light than as the manifestation of an unfriendly disposition toward the United States."[105]

3. Non-Interference in European Affairs: Finally, Monroe reaffirmed that the U.S. would not involve itself in the internal affairs or wars of European nations, emphasizing that U.S. policy had always been to refrain from interfering in European matters. He remarked, "*In the wars of the European powers in matters relating to themselves we have never taken any part, nor does it comport with our policy so to do. Our policy in regard to Europe, which was adopted at an early stage of the wars which have so long agitated that quarter of the globe, nevertheless remains the same, which is, not to interfere in the internal concerns of any of its powers; to consider the government de facto as the legitimate government for us; to cultivate friendly relations with it, and to preserve those relations by a frank, firm, and manly policy, meeting in all instances the just claims of every power, submitting to injuries from none.*"[106]

Among these three propositions, the third—non-interference in European affairs—was often associated with the principle of isolationism. Suspicion and fear of

Old Europe were deeply ingrained among the founding elites of the United States. In 1776, Thomas Paine advocated for non-intervention in European affairs in his famous work Common Sense. Similarly, George Washington, the first U.S. president, warned against foreign influence in his Farewell Address in 1796, stating that "*foreign influence is one of the most baneful foes of republican government*," and that "*the great rule of conduct for us in regard to foreign nations is, in extending our commercial relations, to have with them as little political connection as possible.*" Washington's words reflected a deep-seated mistrust of foreign governments, particularly those of Europe.[107] Thomas Jefferson further emphasized this separation by advocating for the division of

---

105 Ironically, in the Malvinas War between Britain and Argentina in 1982, the United States sided with Britain, a European state, and opposed Argentina, an American state. It not only passed a resolution on arms embargo against Argentina in the United Nations, but also supported Britain logistically.

106 Wang Shengzu, He Chunchao and Wu Shimin 王绳祖、何春超、吴世民, eds., *Guoji guanxishi ziliao xanbian: 17 shiji zhongye–1945* 国际关系史资料选编 [*Selected Materials of the History of International Relations: Mid-17th Century–1945*], (Beijing: Falü chubanshe, 1988), 91–93.

107 George Washington, *Washington's Farewell Address to the People of the United States*, (Trenton: Printed by George Sherman, 1812), 29–33.

the two hemispheres, arguing that the United States and the Americas should remain distanced from the corrupt and despotic systems of Old Europe.[108]

President Monroe's statement reflected the misgivings of the founding fathers—Washington and Jefferson—about Old Europe, but this "isolationism" was by no means a purely non-expansionist policy. As mentioned earlier, when Secretary of State John Quincy Adams was drafting Monroe's 1823 State of the Union address, he was already contemplating the prospect of Texas or Cuba eventually joining the United States. His mindset was more expansionary than conservative. The U.S. political system itself provided the framework for further territorial expansion in the Americas. As a republic, the U.S. did not follow the dynastic principles of the Holy Alliance in Europe and instead shared common political ideals with the newly independent Latin American republics. Additionally, as a federal state, the U.S. offered flexibility in its institutional structure, allowing new states to join the union, creating ample space for expansion.[109]

The "America" defined by President Monroe in his 1823 address, which sought to exclude European interference, was primarily a political concept. At the time, its spatial scope did not include Canada, which remained part of the British Empire and adhered to monarchic principles, nor did it encompass the various European colonies that had not yet gained independence. However, Monroe's statement was intentionally flexible: once these colonies gained independence and established republican regimes, they could be incorporated into this political space that excluded European powers. The concept of "America" was closely tied to republicanism, in contrast to the dynastic legitimacy promoted by the Holy Alliance. Monroe's address also explicitly invoked the term "hemisphere," referring to the Western Hemisphere. Yet, this concept of the Western Hemisphere was political in nature, with its boundaries shaped by the strategic interests of the United States. From a purely geographical

108 Joyce Appleby and Terence Ball eds., *Jefferson: Political Writings*, (Cambridge: Cambridge University Press, 1999), 193, 405.

109 As Robert Kagan pointed out, from the colonial era, the North American colonists were ambitious expansionists instead of isolationists. The important reason of the American War of Independence was precisely that the British Empire hindered the expansion of the North American colonists. See Robert Kagan, *Dangerous Nation: America's Place in the World from its Earliest Days to the Dawn of the Twentieth Century*, New York: Knopf, 2006. For a long time after the founding, the United States was fledgling, busy with the expansion to the west of North America and internal integration, and it was not cost-effective for it to intervene in the disputes among European powers. However, with the strength of the United States growing to a certain extent, it not only firmly grasped regional hegemony, but also got involved in European affairs, which has become an inherent need of American national interests.

perspective, the "Western Hemisphere" was larger than the Americas, encompassing regions such as Greenland, parts of Britain, Iceland, and even parts of West Africa. However, in the political sense, these regions were not considered part of the Western Hemisphere as defined by the Monroe Doctrine.

In the 19th century and much of the time leading up to World War II, the U.S. government used the concepts of "America" and the "Western Hemisphere" in a somewhat vague manner. However, President Franklin Roosevelt provided a more precise definition of the Western Hemisphere as a means of guarding against potential threats from Germany and Japan. In 1938, the U.S. extended its protection to the entire territories of South America and North America, including Canada. By the spring of 1939, this protection was expanded to include the Galápagos Islands, with Japan seen as a potential threat.

In 1940, Greenland was also brought under U.S. protection. At the start of World War II, Iceland—then part of a composite monarchy with Denmark—became a point of concern for the U.S. government when Nazi Germany occupied Denmark. Fearing that Hitler would use Iceland as a strategic base for westward attacks, the Icelandic government officially requested U.S. protection under the Monroe Doctrine. In July 1941, the U.S. sent military forces to Iceland, marking its formal inclusion in the Western Hemisphere under American protection.[110] Roosevelt even contemplated extending the Monroe Doctrine to parts of West Africa to prevent a German occupation. However, after discussions with his advisors, he gave up applying the Monroe Doctrine to West Africa.[111]

The foreign policy framework set by President Monroe's 1823 address officially became known as the Monroe Doctrine in the 1850s.[112] Over the course of the 19th century, it was reinterpreted, shifting from a principle of protection from external interference to one of actively seeking regional hegemony.

At the time of Monroe's declaration, the United States was still relatively weak, and it was unlikely to pose a strategic threat to European powers. The U.S. had limited ability to prevent European colonization or interference in the Americas, as its naval strength was inferior to that of France and Russia. While the U.S. may have had some chance of success in the Gulf of Mexico, its overall military power was insufficient to enforce the doctrine. For instance,

110 Michael T. Corgan, "Franklin D. Roosevelt and the Occupation of Iceland," *Naval War College Review* 45 (1992), 34–52.

111 Gaddis Smith, *The Last Years of the Monroe Doctrine: 1945–1993*, (New York: Hill and Wang, 1994), 38–39.

112 See Paul Dickson, *Words From the White House: Words and Phrases Coined or Popularized by America's Presidents*, (New York: Walker Books, 2013), 106.

shortly after Monroe's address, when Colombia requested U.S. military support to defend its independence in line with the spirit of the Monroe Doctrine, the U.S. government chose to ignore the plea. In reality, it was not Monroe's statement that restrained the Holy Alliance from intervening in the Americas, but rather the strength of the British Royal Navy and the mutual suspicions among the European powers.[113] In 1943, Walter Lippmann's work, *U.S. Foreign Policy: Shield of the Republic*, highlighted that the United States inadvertently benefited from Britain's confrontation with other European powers. According to Lippmann, this experience of "getting something for nothing" led U.S. elites to the illusion that they could prevent European interference in the Americas without needing to rely on alliances.[114]

At the time, the true significance of the Monroe Doctrine was, first and foremost, a moderate response to Britain's initiative to use the U.S. as leverage to balance the European powers. This strategy reduced potential conflict between Britain and the United States, while also presenting a moral stance to win over the new Latin American republics. In doing so, the U.S. could secure a favorable international environment for its own development and potentially gain new overseas markets to stimulate its economic growth.[115]

In the first half of the 19th century, the Monroe Doctrine primarily served to escort the U.S.'s westward expansion across North America. In June 1845, French historian François Guizot, then foreign minister under the July Monarchy in France, expressed his concern over the U.S.'s expansion, arguing that France should actively work to maintain the balance of power in the Americas. On December 2, 1845, in his annual State of the Union address, President James Polk responded directly to Guizot's argument:

> We must ever maintain the principle that the people of this continent alone have the right to decide their own destiny. Should any portion of them, constituting an independent state, propose to unite themselves with our Confederacy, this will be a question for them and us to determine without any foreign interposition. We can never consent that European powers shall interfere to prevent such a union because it might disturb the 'balance of power' which they may desire to maintain upon this continent.

---

113 Nicholas Spykman, Wang Shan and Guo Xinyu trans., *America's Strategy in World Politics: The United States and the Balance of Power*, (Shanghai: Shanghai renmin chubanshe, 2018), 73.

114 Walter Lippmann, *U.S. Foreign Policy: Shield of the Republic*, (New York: H. Wolff, 1943), 31.

115 On the specific measures to develop business relations between the United States and the new American Republic, see A.P. Whitake, *The United States and the Independence of Latin America, 1800–1830*, (New York: Russell & Russell, 1962), 546–563.

He further declared: "The American continents, by the free and independent condition which they have assumed and maintain, are henceforth not to be considered as subjects for colonization by any European powers."[116]

In the context of the U.S.'s ambition to seize Texas and fully annex Oregon, which was partially occupied by Britain, the realistic policy implications of President Polk's statements were clear. While he invoked the Monroe Doctrine under the banner of opposing external interference, it was, in fact, used to further the U.S. territorial expansion westward. Before Texas officially joined the Union on December 29, 1845, there were rumors, fueled by its cotton trade with Britain, that Britain might consider Texas a colony. Polk's statements served as a warning to Britain, indicating that the U.S. would not tolerate any European interference in what it considered its rightful sphere.

As the U.S. expanded westward and accumulated more power through the Westward Movement, the focus of the Monroe Doctrine shifted from protecting against European interference to actively weakening European influence on the American continent. A key development in this direction was the signing of the Clayton-Bulwer Treaty in 1850 between Britain and the U.S., which symbolized a non-violent method to curtail British influence in Central America. Both nations agreed to jointly control Central America, especially regarding maritime traffic lines. It was also during this time that President Monroe's policy began to be widely referred to as the "Monroe Doctrine."

In 1862, during the American Civil War, Emperor Napoleon III of France's Second Empire sent troops to overthrow the Mexican Republican government under the pretext of "debt collection." Backed by France, Maximilian I, a member of the Habsburg dynasty, was installed as Emperor of Mexico, thus promoting the concept of "Amérique latine."[117] This development alarmed U.S. elites, as it realized a long-feared scenario of European powers establishing monarchies in the Americas. Since the Latin American revolutions, U.S. elites had often speculated about this potential threat, but now it was a reality. Even during the Civil War, many Northern elites had debated how to defend the Republican system in Mexico, but the U.S. was too preoccupied to intervene. Once the American Civil War ended, the U.S. immediately sent troops to support Mexican Republicans in regaining control of Mexico City in 1867, leading to the execution of Maximilian I. In this sense, the U.S. fulfilled its

116 Wang Shengzu 王绳祖 et al. eds., *Guoji guanxishi ziliao xuanbian* 国际关系史资料选编 [*Selected Materials of International Relations History*] (Volume I), (Wuhan: Wuhan daxue chubanshe, 1983), 68–69.

117 John Leddy Phelan, "Pan-Latinism, French Intervention in Mexico (1861–1867) and the Genesis of the Idea of Latin America," in Juan A. Ortega y Medina ed., *Conciencia y autenticidad históricas: Escritos en homenaje a Edmundo O'Gorman*, (Mexico City: UNAM, 1968), 279–298.

Monroe Doctrine promise, expelling European-backed monarchic rule from the Americas. However, this victory also brought Mexico more deeply into the U.S. sphere of influence, ensuring American dominance in the region.

President Ulysses S. Grant introduced the "Grant Corollary" to the Monroe Doctrine in his 1870 State of the Union address, advocating for the annexation of the Dominican Republic by the United States. He stated that "no territory on this continent shall be regarded as subject to transfer to a European power,"[118] aiming to block any European power from acquiring new territories in the Americas. The real intention behind this policy was to eliminate potential competitors for the U.S. annexation of Dominica. This "Grant Corollary" went further than Polk's 1845 declaration by prohibiting even voluntary territorial transfers to European powers. However, this annexation effort was blocked in Congress due to concerns among racists over the racial composition of the Dominican population. As a result, the U.S. was unable to expand its territory in the Caribbean through this initiative.

A crucial aspect of the U.S. regional hegemony strategy in the late 19th century was the promotion of a Pan-American system. This began with Simón Bolívar's initiative in 1826, when the Republic of Colombia hosted the first joint conference of newly independent Spanish American countries in Panama. Bolívar extended an invitation to the U.S., but due to opposition from politicians in slave-holding states, the U.S. did not actively participate. One U.S. representative died on the way to the conference, and the other arrived after it had concluded. This early attempt at creating a regional alliance failed to hold subsequent conferences and fell apart. However, with the rapid growth of U.S. national strength after the Civil War, the idea of a Pan-American system under U.S. leadership was revived. In 1890, James G. Blaine, then U.S. Secretary of State, organized the first International Conference of American States in Washington, D.C., with 18 states from the Americas participating. The aim was to create mechanisms for resolving disputes among American nations. Subsequent conferences took place in Mexico City (1901), Rio de Janeiro (1906), and Buenos Aires (1910).

One of the key outcomes of these Pan-American conferences was the effort to establish an arbitration mechanism for resolving disputes among the American states. This was an extension of the practice of mediation that had been formalized between the U.S. and Britain with the Jay's Treaty in 1794. Arbitration represented a further legal development, where disputes could be settled peacefully through a formal process. The U.S. strongly advocated

118 Dexter Perkins, *A History of the Monroe Doctrine*, (Boston: Little, Brown and Co., 1955), 158–159.

for this approach, as it had repeatedly used mediation to settle disputes with Britain. The idea of arbitration, however, was not widely embraced by European powers, despite efforts at the Hague Peace Conferences in 1899 and 1907 to promote it. The U.S., nonetheless, viewed arbitration as an essential tool for maintaining stability and peace in the Western Hemisphere.

At the first International Conference of American States in 1890, a significant discussion centered on proposals from Argentina and Brazil to formally declare aggression as a violation of American public law. The conference ultimately adopted a scheme that combined compulsory arbitration with the prohibition of aggression. This agreement stipulated that: Any territorial cession made under the threat of war or the presence of armed forces would be invalid during the arbitration treaty's duration. Any waiver of arbitration rights made under duress, such as the threat of war or military pressure, would be considered null and void.[119] Although this scheme failed to lead to an effective international treaty, it articulated the basic U.S. approach to dominating the Americas: rather than relying on the balance of power method familiar to European powers, the United States could secure its dominant position in the region through an arbitration mechanism. Given the disparity in strength between the U.S. and other American nations, arbitration was a strategic tool to assert U.S. hegemony without resorting to the principle of "balance of power" that European powers were accustomed to.[120]

At subsequent International Conferences of American States, the establishment of an arbitration mechanism remained a key issue. Although the United States did not successfully create a pan-American international court of justice, on December 20, 1907, it brokered a significant treaty between five Central American countries—El Salvador, Costa Rica, Guatemala, Nicaragua, and Honduras—to establish the Central American Court of Justice in Washington. This marked the creation of the first international court in modern history.

119 Francis Anthony Boyle, *Foundations of World Order: The Legalist Approach to International Relations (1898–1922)*, (Durham & London: Duke University Press, 1999), 104–107.

120 It is worth pointing out that even the Harrison regime, which planned the first Pan-American Conference, was not interested in applying arbitration when the United States had disputes with other American countries. In 1891, the pro-U.S. José Manuel Balmaceda regime in Chile was overthrown, which caused great dissatisfaction of the U.S. government. In Valparaiso, Chile, locals attacked a group of American sailors from Baltimore, causing casualties, and the relationship between the United States and Chile deteriorated sharply. Instead of arbitration, Harrison's government sent an ultimatum to the Chilean government, forcing the latter to apologize and compensate. Jay Sexton, *The Monroe Doctrine: Empire and Nation in Nineteenth-Century America*, (New York: Hill and Wang, 2011), 196–197.

The court was granted jurisdiction over disputes between the member states and also allowed citizens to bring cases after exhausting domestic remedies. The treaty came into force on March 11, 1908, and the court began operations in Cartago, Costa Rica's largest city, on March 25. Each of the five countries appointed a judge to form a collegiate panel. The court continued to operate until the treaty expired on March 12, 1918.

The First International Conference of American States in 1890 also promoted the establishment of the International Union of American Republics and its permanent institution, the Commercial Bureau of the American Republics. The Bureau's primary function was to facilitate the exchange of economic and technical information among its member states.[121] In 1901, the Second International Conference of American States decided to reorganize the Commercial Bureau into the International Bureau of the American Republics. Later, in 1910, the Fourth International Conference of American States passed a resolution to rename the League of American Republics as the Pan-American Union. The Council of this newly renamed organization was chaired by the U.S. Secretary of State.[122]

In the last decade of the 19th century, the United States was committed to weakening the influence of Britain and Spain in the Americas, thereby establishing its own regional hegemony. In 1895, when the U.S. intervened in the border dispute between British Guiana and Venezuela, U.S. Secretary of State Richard Olney sent a note to the British government, boldly asserting that the U.S. and the American states, "by geographical proximity, natural sympathy, and similarity of governmental constitutions," formed an alliance to protect all states in the Western Hemisphere according to the Monroe Doctrine. Olney even went as far as to declare, "Today the United States is practically sovereign on this continent, and its fiat is law upon the subjects to which it confines its

121 Boyle (n. 119), 108.

122 Wu Tingfang once commented on the Monroe Doctrine and the Bureau of International Affairs of American States in his English book *America, Through the Spectacles of an Oriental Diplomat* published in 1914, saying that Monroe Doctrine was the main factor to protect the territorial integrity of all states in the American continent, and the United States played the role of the guardian of America. It was also considered that the Bureau of International Affairs of American States had strengthened the status of the United States, and tried to make the American Republic form a closer friendship. Wu Tingfang, *America, Through the Spectacles of an Oriental Diplomat*, (New York: Frederick A. Stokes Company, 1914), 11.

interposition."[123] Since Grover Cleveland was president at the time, some critics referred to Olney's claims as the "Cleveland Doctrine."[124]

The U.S. government invoked the Monroe Doctrine and urged the British government to submit the border dispute to arbitration. This raised the question of whether the Monroe Doctrine was recognized as a principle of international law. Robert Arthur Talbot Gascoyne-Cecil, 3rd Marquess of Salisbury, who served as both British Prime Minister and Foreign Secretary, responded: "International law is founded on the general consent of nations, and no statesman, however eminent, and no nation, however powerful, are competent to insert into the code of international law a novel principle which was never recognized before, and which has not since been recognized by the government of any other country."[125] President Cleveland countered, "The Monroe Doctrine finds its recognition in those principles of international law which are based upon the theory that every nation shall have its rights protected and its just claims enforced."[126]

As rising Germany posed a greater threat to Britain, the British government had no interest in wasting resources on a conflict with the U.S. and thus accepted the arbitration proposal. On October 3, 1899, an arbitration tribunal composed of two U.S. Supreme Court judges, two British jurists, and a Russian jurist elected by both parties delivered a final judgment in Paris, which was largely favorable to Britain. However, the mere fact that Britain agreed to arbitration was politically significant, as it signaled Britain's recognition of U.S. political superiority in the Western Hemisphere. Public opinion in both Britain and the U.S. hailed this cooperation as a symbol of the unity of the English-speaking Anglo-Saxon race in jointly guarding against the German threat.

As for Canada, a part of the British Empire on the American continent, it had been defensive towards the U.S. during the conflict between Britain and the U.S. However, after Britain recognized the U.S. as the hegemon in the Americas, Canada's attitude toward the U.S. softened. In 1902, Canadian Prime Minister Wilfrid Laurier acknowledged that the Monroe Doctrine was

123 United States Department of State, *Foreign Relations of United States*, (Washington: Government Printing Office, 1895), 558.

124 C.K. Adams, "The Monroe Doctrine and the Cleveland Doctrine," *The Independent*, 49 (18 February 1897).

125 Arthur Irwin Street, "Salisbury's First Note," in, *Handbook of the Venezuelan Question and the Monroe Doctrine*, (Denver: The Times Publishing Co., 1895): 32.

126 "President Cleveland's Message," Ibid., 4.

a security guarantee for Canada.[127] That same year, the U.S. leveraged the pressure Britain was facing due to the Boer War in Africa to induce Britain to sign the Hay-Pauncefote Treaty, replacing the Clayton-Bulwer Treaty of 1850. The U.S. secured the right to construct an isthmus canal in Central America and obtained exclusive control over it. Subsequently, the U.S. supported Panama's secession from Colombia and led the construction and operation of the Panama Canal.

In the 19th century, U.S. political elites consistently maintained vigilance and suspicion regarding European affairs. They viewed the world as divided into distinct political spaces with different ways of political life, not as a homogeneous whole. Although there was the possibility of republican revolutions in old Europe, as seen when the Hungarians established a republic during the revolution of 1848 and when the Irish launched a nationalist movement against the British Empire, the mainstream opinion in the U.S. Congress still favored "non-interference," despite debates over whether the U.S. should support these republican movements.[128]

However, as U.S. capital and military-political forces expanded, the spatial boundaries of the Americas began to feel constraining. In 1893, historian Frederick Jackson Turner published *The Significance of the Frontier in American History* at the American Historical Society's annual meeting, lamenting that the frontier was disappearing with the completion of the westward movement.[129] Yet, a new vision of the frontier was emerging. Alfred Thayer Mahan, a professor at the U.S. Naval Academy, argued in his book *The Influence of Sea Power upon History* that the U.S. needed a strong navy to seize sea power and protect its expanding trade.[130]

Mahan's strategic thinking was well-timed for the U.S. exploration of a "new frontier," significantly impacting U.S. naval construction. In the 1890s, the U.S. invested heavily in naval expansion, and by 1898, these efforts bore fruit with

127 Charles P. Stacey, *The Military Problems of Canada*, (Toronto: Ryerson Press, 1940), 68. But it was not until 1938 that the U.S. government explicitly included Canada under the coverage of the Monroe Doctrine.

128 Mary Minors Engle Bright, *Congress and the Monroe Doctrine, 1850–1860*, (Chicago: The University of Chicago, 1942).

129 Zhang Shiming 张世明 et al. eds., *Kongjian, falü yu xueshu huayu: Xifang bianjiang lilun jingdian wenxian* 空间，法律与学术话语：西方边疆理论经典文献 [*Space, Law and Academic Discourse: Classical Literature of Western Frontier Theory*], (Harbin: Heilongjiang jiaoyu chubanshe, 2014), 93.

130 A.T. Mahan, An Changrong and Cheng Zhongqin 安常容、成忠勤 trans., *Haiquan dui lishi de yingxiang* 海权对历史的影响 [*The Influence of Sea Power on History: 1660–1783*], (Beijing: Jiefangjun chubanshe, 2006).

the U.S. victory in the Spanish-American War, further weakening Spanish influence in the Americas. The U.S. gained control of Puerto Rico and turned newly independent Cuba into a protectorate through the Platt Amendment, consolidating its dominance in the Western Hemisphere. The U.S. also gained control of territories beyond the Americas, such as Guam, Wake Island, and the Philippines, extending its influence to the western Pacific.[131]

U.S. Congress members were deeply divided over whether annexing the Philippines and Hawaii violated the Monroe Doctrine.[132] Some believed that annexing the Philippines contradicted the spirit of the Monroe Doctrine by allowing the U.S. to engage in colonial actions in Asia that it had prohibited European powers from undertaking in the Americas. These members argued that allowing the Philippines to form its own government would better align with U.S. principles. Others, like Congressman Jacob H. Bromwell of Ohio, argued that the Monroe Doctrine should no longer be confined to "America for Americans" but should extend to protect American commerce and influence globally.[133] A third group of Congress members acknowledged that annexing the Philippines might violate the Monroe Doctrine but proposed measures to mitigate this, such as selling the Philippines to another country or exchanging it for British colonies in the Americas.[134] In 1899, when the Senate voted on the Spanish-American treaty annexing the Philippines, the vote was 57-27, with just two votes above the threshold for approval.[135]

On the question of annexing Hawaii, Congress was similarly divided. Some argued that the Monroe Doctrine prohibited the acquisition of overseas territories, while others claimed that Hawaii, though distant from the American mainland, was part of the Western Hemisphere. They argued that if the U.S. did not annex Hawaii, it might fall into the hands of European powers or Japan, which would directly contradict the Monroe Doctrine.[136]

---

131 This change has caused some opposition in the United States. For example, Senator Geroge Frisbie Hoar warned that if the United States acquired a colony in the other hemisphere, it could not deny that European powers had the right to acquire colonies in America. Dexter Perkins, *Monroe Doctrine, 1867–1907*, (Baltimore, Md: The Johns Hopkins University Press, 1937), 282–283.

132 Lillie Cornelia Porterfield, *Congress And The Monroe Doctrine: 1895–1905*, (Ph.D. Dissertation, The University of Chicago, 1942).

133 Ibid., 29.

134 Ibid., 33.

135 U.S. Congress, *Executive Journal*, Vol. XXI, Part II, (Washington D.C.: Government Printing Office, 1909), 1234.

136 Porterfield (n. 134), 40–50.

In the 1900 presidential election, debates over the Monroe Doctrine and imperial policy played a central role. The Republican Party platform declared adherence to the Monroe Doctrine, while the Democratic Party accused Republicans of using the Monroe Doctrine deceptively, opposing their "imperialist" expansionist policies.[137] This debate highlighted that the geographical limits of the Monroe Doctrine were still a key point of contention.

However, U.S. expansion in Asia did not stop with the Philippines. In 1899 and 1900, the U.S. issued two Open Door Policy notes advocating for equal trade access to China and opposing monopolization by other powers. The relationship between the Open Door Policy and the Monroe Doctrine remained unclear in U.S. theoretical discussions. A March 1899 *North American Review* article suggested that the China issue called for a more significant revision of the Monroe Doctrine than the Philippine question.[138] U.S. theorists worked hard to adapt the Monroe Doctrine to the new reality of imperialist expansion. For instance, Yale University professor Edward Gaylord Bourne argued in his 1907 book *The Discovery, Conquest, and Early History of the Philippine Islands* that the Philippines had long been connected to the Americas through the Spanish Empire and thus fell within the Monroe Doctrine's scope.[139] After his death, this argument was used to justify the application of the Monroe Doctrine to the Philippines.[140] President Theodore Roosevelt contributed to this discussion, arguing in a letter to German diplomat Hermann Speck von Sternberg in 1901 that the Monroe Doctrine and the Open Door Policy were fundamentally similar, with the former serving as the "Open Door" policy of South America.[141] Such discussions on whether the Monroe Doctrine could be applied outside the Western Hemisphere continued throughout the early 20th century.

---

137 "The Democratic Platform," *Outlook*, 65 (14 Jul 1900), 635–637.

138 George Smyth et al., *The Crisis in China*, (New York & London: Harper & Brothers Publishers, 1900), 218.

139 Edward Gaylord Bourne, *The Discovery, Conquest, and Early Histories of the Philippine Islands*, (Cleveland, Ohio: The Authur H. Clark Company, 1907), 21–22.

140 Charles Francis Adams, James Ford Rhodes, Samuel A. Green et al. "March Meeting, 1908. Tribute to Charles Henry Dalton; History of the Forged Mather Letter; Conditions in the South," *Proceedings of the Massachusetts Historical Society*, Third Series, Vol. 1, [Vol. 41 of continuous numbering] (1907–1908), 403. Albert Bushnell Hart, "Pacific and Asiatic Doctrines Akin to the Monroe Doctrine," *The American Journal of International Law*, 9, (Oct. 1915), 803.

141 Donald J. Davidson ed., *The Wisdom of Theodore Roosevelt*, (New York: Citadel Press, 2003), 50–51.

Owen Lattimore, a U.S. diplomat who once served as an adviser to Chiang Kai-shek, called the Open Door Policy a doctrine of "me too." He explained, "Since the U.S., though now vigorous enough to take part in almost any economic competition, was not yet sure what American activities would become most important, it was desirable to ensure that no country should acquire interests which would later enable it to block the entry or development of American interests."[142] However, the primary goal of the Open Door Policy was not to revoke the spheres of influence that other foreign powers had already established but rather to prevent further expansion of those spheres. Lattimore also pointed out that the first draft of the Open Door Policy notes was not the work of the U.S. State Department, but of an Englishman named A.E. Hippisley.[143] On the issue of China, there was cooperation rather than hostility between Britain and the U.S. In fact, throughout the 19th century, despite some major conflicts of interest between Britain and the U.S. in the Americas, Britain's influence on the U.S. remained profound. While other European powers focused on acquiring territory, Britain shifted its colonialism toward an "informal empire," using economic power to exert control.[144] Britain supported the independence of several colonies in the Americas from Spain, Portugal, and France, including persuading the Portuguese royal family to accept Brazil's independence. It also advocated for the abolition of slavery, while the U.S. South stubbornly maintained the institution of slavery for much longer. These actions maximized Britain's stable economic benefits in those regions.

Thus, despite being a hereditary monarchy, Britain's foreign policy during the Latin American revolutions differed from that of other European powers. One could even argue that President Monroe's 1823 address was an unintended consequence of Britain's challenge to the Holy Alliance. By 1897, British investment in Latin America was more than twice that of France and six times that of the U.S. Britain extracted sugar from Guyana and the West Indies, meat and wheat from Argentina, and rubber and coffee from Brazil. As the U.S. rose to compete with Britain for influence in Latin America, it learned from Britain's "informal empire" approach.[145]

---

142 Owen Lattimore, Cao Weifeng 曹未风 et al. trans., Yazhou de juece 亚洲的决策 [*Solution in Asia*], (Beijing: Shangwu yinshuguan, 1962), 9–11.

143 Owen Lattimore and Eleanor Holgate Lattimore, *The Making of Modern China: A Short History*, (London: G. Allen & Unwin, 1945), 122.

144 See Gregory A. Barton, *Informal Empire and the Rise of One World Culture*, (London: Palgrave Macmillan, 2014), 10–21.

145 Jill Hills, *The Struggle for Control of Global Communication, The Formative Century*, (Champaign, Illinois: University of Illinois Press, 2002), 153–177.

The U.S. adopted some of Britain's strategies, but its rhetoric had its own distinctive features. By the turn of the 20th century, the U.S. had effectively become a territorial colonial empire, with formal colonies and protectorates in Latin America and Asia. Yet, in official discourse, the U.S. continued to present itself as an anti-colonial power. It used negative rhetoric, defining its rivals as invaders or alien elements in the political space while positioning itself as the defender of that space—fitting its own expansionist ambitions.

Once the U.S. had successfully diminished British and Spanish influence in the Western Hemisphere, Germany became a new threat for U.S. elites, and the Monroe Doctrine was increasingly applied to counter Germany's growing presence. Like the U.S., Germany had rapidly industrialized during the Second Industrial Revolution. Under Kaiser Wilhelm II, Germany strengthened its economic and trade ties with Latin America, sold arms, sent military advisors to Chile, Argentina, and Brazil, and founded the South American Colonial Association to purchase land and encourage immigration.[146] During the Spanish-American War, Germany sought to acquire territories in the Caribbean. Between 1902 and 1903, Germany, Britain, and Italy blockaded Venezuela over debt disputes. U.S. and German naval forces nearly clashed during this incident, but eventually, the three European powers accepted arbitration under U.S. insistence, and Venezuela agreed to repay part of its debts.

Rumors soon spread that Britain and Germany planned to intervene in the internal affairs of the Dominican Republic under the pretext of debt collection. In response, President Theodore Roosevelt introduced the "Roosevelt Corollary" to the Monroe Doctrine in his State of the Union Address on December 6, 1904. This corollary took the Monroe Doctrine to a new level: "Chronic wrongdoing, or an impotence which results in a general loosening of the ties of civilized society, may in America, as elsewhere, ultimately require intervention by some civilized nation. In the Western Hemisphere, the adherence of the United States to the Monroe Doctrine may force the United States, however reluctantly, in flagrant cases of such wrongdoing or impotence, to exercise an international police power."[147]

---

146 Moritz Julius Bonn, a German economist, published an article in the United States in 1916 to defend Germany, arguing that Germany had no ambition to covet South America, and that Germany at that time could not send enough immigrants. M.J. Bonn, "Germany and the Monroe Doctrine," *The Annals of the American Academy of Political and Social Science, Vol. 66, Preparedness and America's International Program* (Jul. 1916), 102–105.

147 Wang Zu, He Chunchao and Wu Shimin 王绳祖、何春超、吴世民 eds., *Guoji guanxi-shi ziliao xuanbian: 17 shiji zhongye–1945* 国际关系史资料选编：17世纪中叶–1945 [*Selected Materials of the History of International Relations: Mid-17th Century–1945*], (Beijing: Falü chubanshe, 1988), 316.

The theoretical core of the "Roosevelt Corollary" was the 19th-century concept of the "hierarchy of civilization," which held that the U.S., as a more "civilized" nation, had a responsibility to guide less "civilized" nations in the Americas. This was to prevent European powers from intervening or conquering these nations. Under this corollary, the U.S. could intervene in other American countries even when European powers were not immediately involved. The Roosevelt Corollary transformed the Monroe Doctrine into a proactive principle of regional hegemony, representing a significant leap from the doctrine's original formulation. Alfred Thayer Mahan, the naval strategist, wrote in 1903 that the U.S. "does not find the true complement of the Monroe Doctrine in an undefined control over [Latin] American states, exercised by her and denied to Europe." Roosevelt's new interpretation pushed this position further, and by 1908, Mahan reconciled the two stances, arguing that the Monroe Doctrine was a "living, growing, and changing" entity, adapting to the times.[148]

The Roosevelt Corollary laid the foundation for "dollar diplomacy" in Latin America. By the early 20th century, the U.S. was the world's largest industrial power with significant surplus capital to invest abroad. Many Central American and Caribbean countries owed substantial debts to European powers, and the U.S. government feared this might lead to European intervention. To safeguard the Americas, the U.S. provided loans to these countries to pay off their debts to Europe. Once the U.S. became the creditor, it sought to control these countries' customs and financial systems, often toppling local governments through military interventions to ensure the repayment of its investments. Nicaragua, Haiti, the Dominican Republic, and Honduras were among the victims of this "dollar diplomacy."[149]

Believing it necessary to control Latin American countries economically, the U.S. government was unwilling to limit its options on key issues. From 1902 to 1903, Britain, Germany, and Italy pressured Venezuela to pay its debts by force, causing panic in many Latin American countries. On December 29, 1902, Argentine Foreign Minister Luis María Drago sent a note to the U.S. government on behalf of Argentina. He argued that in the Americas, the collection of public debt should not justify armed intervention, and the territories of American countries should never be occupied by European powers. Drago believed that debt collection by force violated the spirit of the U.S. Monroe

148 Seager Robert, *Alfred Thayer Mahan: The Man and His Letters*, (Annapolis: Naval Institute Press, 1977), 493–494.

149 Cyrus Veeser, *A World Safe for Capitalism: Dollar Diplomacy and America's Rise to Global Power*, (New York: Columbia University Press, 2002).

Doctrine and hoped the U.S. would support this view. This proposal to prohibit armed intervention for debt collection became known as the "Drago Doctrine."

The "Drago Doctrine" was narrower in scope than the earlier "Calvo Doctrine," proposed by Carlos Calvo, a renowned international jurist and former Argentine foreign minister. In his 1868 work *Derecho Internacional Teórico y Práctico de Europa y América*, Calvo argued that once foreigners enter the jurisdiction of a sovereign state, they should not expect more protection than the state's citizens. If harmed, they should rely on local legal remedies, and their home government should not demand monetary compensation. Calvo not only rejected foreign governments' use of force to collect debts for their nationals but also denied the legitimacy of diplomatic protection for private compensation claims.[150] This doctrine challenged the hegemonic role of the U.S. in Latin America. While the U.S. generally adhered to "non-intervention" in cases of contractual disputes involving its citizens, it reserved the right to intervene if foreign governments refused justice. However, the U.S. was reluctant to limit its options in cases involving foreign government bonds.[151] Although the Drago Doctrine was milder than Calvo's, it still conflicted with U.S. practices.

On August 22, 1906, the Third International Conference of American States discussed the Drago Doctrine but reached no substantive conclusions. The issue was later addressed at the Second Hague Peace Conference in 1907, where the U.S. played a prominent role. The final resolution adopted at The Hague opposed the use of force to collect debts in contractual disputes, except when the debtor government refused arbitration or failed to comply with arbitration decisions. However, the resolution did not address Drago's concerns regarding government bond disputes. By 1914, only 17 of the 45 participating states had signed the resolution, with several making reservations on key points.[152] While the Argentine government succeeded in promoting its ideas, Drago's effort to add new content to the Monroe Doctrine ultimately failed.

In the early 20th century, the U.S. not only consolidated its hegemonic position in the Americas but also gained strength to expand globally. In 1905, President Theodore Roosevelt broke with the U.S. tradition of non-interference in European affairs by mediating both the Russo-Japanese

150 Amos S. Hershey, "The Calvo and Drago Doctrines," (1907) Maurer Faculty Paper 1961 at: <http://www.repository.law.indiana.edu/facpub/1961>.

151 Luis M. Drago and H. Edward Nettles, "The Drago Doctrine in International Law and Politics," *The Hispanic American Historical Review* 8 (May 1928), 217.

152 T.S. Woolsey, "Drago and the Drago Doctrine," *The American Journal of International Law* 15 (July 1921), 558–559.

War in the Far East and the Moroccan crises between France and Germany. However, Roosevelt did not offer a systematic theory to justify U.S. involvement in European affairs, and his involvement was selective, avoiding long-term commitments. At the time, U.S. diplomatic elites recognized that American colonial expansion might provoke European criticism by invoking the U.S.'s own Monroe Doctrine. In June 1903, Whitelaw Reid, a diplomat who served during the Spanish-American War, speculated on an "Asian-style Monroe Doctrine" in a speech at Yale Law School. He argued that if autocratic Russia and China united to impose despotism in Asia, U.S. expansion in the Philippines would face major challenges. Reid also imagined a "European Monroe Doctrine," in which European constitutional monarchies like Britain, Belgium, and Germany would ask the U.S. to cease supporting the Republic of Liberia on the grounds that Africa should remain under monarchical rule.[153]

Reid's concerns reflected the tension between three different regional orders based on distinct forms of government. Fortunately for the U.S., this scenario did not materialize. The Concert of Europe, the post-Napoleonic system of legitimism, had long been in decline, and the European powers were too divided to form a united front against republicanism.

Despite its calls for an "Open Door" policy in China at the start of the 20th century, the U.S. remained highly wary of Asian immigration. The Chinese Exclusion Act of 1882 was the first U.S. immigration law targeting a specific ethnic group. On April 27, 1904, Congress renewed the act indefinitely. After the Russo-Japanese War (1904–1905), Japan's economic struggles led to large-scale Japanese emigration to Hawaii and the U.S. Pacific coast, prompting backlash from xenophobic forces in the U.S. In 1906, San Francisco passed a law requiring all Asian students to attend segregated "Oriental Schools," sparking anti-American sentiment in Japan. President Roosevelt intervened personally, asking San Francisco to repeal the segregation law while simultaneously negotiating the "Gentlemen's Agreement" of 1907, in which Japan agreed to limit the emigration of its citizens to the U.S.

This crisis sparked a strong reaction from Alfred Thayer Mahan, author of *The Influence of Sea Power Upon History, 1660–1783*, who believed: "Asiatic immigration is against the spirit of the Monroe Doctrine because, as they don't assimilate, they colonize, and virtually annex."[154] Similar sentiments resurfaced after World War I, leading to the passage of the Japanese Exclusion Act in

---

153 Reid used the term "European Monroe Doctrine" explicitly. Whitelaw Reid, "The Monroe Doctrine; The Polk Doctrine; Anarchism," *Yale Law Journal* 13 (1903).

154 Robert (n. 148), 479.

1924. This, in turn, fueled a surge of anti-American sentiment in Japan, which further bolstered the discourse of Asianism within the country.

World War I propelled the Monroe Doctrine to a new phase. At the start of Woodrow Wilson's presidency in 1912, his policy was primarily focused on domestic affairs. After the war broke out, the U.S. maintained neutrality, profiting from the sale of arms and other goods to both sides. However, as the war progressed, Wilson realized that without abandoning neutrality, the U.S. could encourage European nations to negotiate a peace settlement mediated by the U.S., and in doing so, establish a collective security mechanism through an international organization of sovereign states. This could enhance the U.S.'s international standing and bring greater benefits, but it would inevitably mean intervening in European affairs. To justify this shift, Wilson needed to reinterpret the political tradition established by George Washington and continued by President Monroe. In a speech delivered in Omaha on October 5, 1916, Wilson reinterpreted Washington's Farewell Address: "You know that we have always remembered and revered the advice of the great Washington, who advised us to avoid foreign entanglements. By that, I understand him to mean avoid being entangled in the ambitions and the national purposes of other nations."[155] This redefined Washington's warning, allowing the U.S. to engage in European affairs that did not involve "ambitions and national purposes."

On January 22nd, 1917, Wilson delivered a speech later called "Peace Without Victory" in the Senate, reinterpreting the Monroe Doctrine:

> I am proposing, as it were, that the nations should with one accord adopt the doctrine of President Monroe as the doctrine of the world: that no nation should seek to extend its polity over any other nation or people, but that every people should be left free to determine its own polity, its own way of development—unhindered, unthreatened, unafraid, the little along with the great and powerful.[156]

In this interpretation, Wilson broke through the spatial limitation of the "Western Hemisphere" or "Americas" and expanded the Monroe Doctrine to suggest that each country or nation should have the right to determine its own political system and path of development. This expansion implied that

155 Woodrow Wilson, *War and Peace: Presidential Messages, Addresses, and Public Papers (1917–1924)*, Vol. 2, (Honolulu: University Press of the Pacific, 2002), 346–347.

156 President Woodrow Wilson, "Peace without Victory" Speech, 22 January 1917. 64th Cong., 23 Sess., Senate Document No. 685: "A League for Peace."

the doctrine could potentially be applied anywhere on Earth. However, there was clear tension between Wilson's interpretation and the Roosevelt Corollary. In 1904, Theodore Roosevelt argued that, in the name of "civilization," the U.S. had the right to exercise international police power over American countries, limiting their freedom to choose their own political systems. While Wilson proclaimed that every nation had the right to choose its own political system, he did not imply that all regimes would be treated equally. He certainly did not accept that some nations could freely choose systems opposed to the democratic model championed by the U.S. Wilson assumed that once a nation was free to choose, it would naturally gravitate toward democracy.[157] Therefore, Latin American countries were not free to turn to monarchy without risking U.S. intervention.

In practice, Wilson did not hesitate to interfere in the internal affairs of Latin American countries. In fact, he intensified such interventions. During his presidency, the U.S. invaded and controlled Haiti's internal affairs in 1915, launched "Pershing's Expedition" to Mexico in 1916, and occupied the Dominican Republic the same year. For those who understood the Monroe Doctrine's original practice, Wilson's explanation of it ran counter to U.S. actions in Latin America. How can we reconcile Wilson's rhetoric with his actions? The key lies in the U.S. belief that it had the right and responsibility to judge which countries faced obstacles and threats to their own political systems. The U.S. claimed the authority to intervene to eliminate such threats, representing the "autonomy" of other nations. In this logic of "vicarial autonomy," the judgment of the U.S. was superior because other nations might be under external pressures and unable to express their will freely. Through this reasoning, Wilson could justify U.S. interference in the domestic politics of any country. The geographic limitation of the "Western Hemisphere" had been lifted from the Monroe Doctrine's interpretation.

In his speech, Wilson also proposed the idea of establishing universal international cooperation, which became the embryo of a collective security mechanism. However, Wilson emphasized that such cooperation should be voluntary, not a binding alliance. This reflected the 19th-century American diplomatic tradition of avoiding international obligations beyond the Americas. Wilson's ideal vision was for the U.S. to lead the world based on goodwill, without bearing rigid global responsibilities.

---

157 Gaddis Smith, *The Last Years of the Monroe Doctrine: 1945–1993*, (New York: Hill and Wang, 1994), 29.

In April 1917, the U.S. abandoned neutrality and declared war on Germany and Austria. Wilson argued that U.S. involvement was necessary to "make the world safe for democracy"[158] while adhering to the principle of "peace without victory." However, after the Bolshevik Revolution of October 1917, the new Bolshevik government withdrew Russia from World War I and published secret diplomatic agreements signed by the previous regime. To counter the appeal of Bolshevism in Europe, Wilson was forced to present his own vision of the post-war international order. On January 8, 1918, Wilson introduced his "Fourteen Points" to Congress, which included principles like the abolition of secret diplomacy, freedom of navigation, equal trade conditions, arms reduction, fair treatment of colonial peoples, and the establishment of the League of Nations. However, Wilson's Fourteen Points did not endorse Lenin's version of "national self-determination."[159]

Wilson's vision fundamentally differed from Lenin's. In the "Fourteen Points," Wilson supported the independence of certain nations, primarily to weaken the defeated powers. The nations he deemed eligible for independence were mostly white, rather than people of color. Having grown up in the racially segregated South, Wilson never transcended the ideology of white supremacy. He promoted racial segregation in the federal government and opposed interracial marriages between Asians and white Americans.[160] It was not his intention for the colonized non-European peoples of European or American territories to immediately receive "self-determination." Even in the Philippines, Wilson claimed that "they are children and we are men in these deep matters of government and justice," arguing that Filipinos needed to develop self-governance under U.S. tutelage before achieving statehood.[161] While Wilson did not exclude non-European peoples from the scope of "self-determination," he believed they needed to achieve "autonomy" under the mandate of a more civilized power. This thinking became the ideological foundation for the League of Nations' "mandate" system, which had little in common with Lenin's call for immediate self-determination.[162]

---

158 Woodrow Wilson, "An Address to a Joint Session of Congress" (lecture, Washington, D.C., 2 April 1917), in *The Papers of Woodrow Wilson* 41, (Princeton: Princeton University Press, 1983): 525.

159 Wang, He and Wu (n. 147), 448–452.

160 Ko Unoki, *International Relations and the Origins of the Pacific War*, (New York: Palgrave Macmillan, 2016), 98.

161 Woodrow Wilson, *The Papers of Woodrow Wilson*, 12, (Princeton: Princeton University Press, 1972), 223.

162 N. Gordon Levin, *Woodrow Wilson and World Politics: America's Response to War and Revolution*, (New York: Oxford University Press, 1968), 237, 247–248. A more detailed

At the Paris Peace Conference, Wilson rejected Japan's proposal for "racial equality," fearing its impact on U.S. domestic racial policies. However, his newly formed Committee on Public Information[163] promoted Wilson's ideas on national autonomy, and when European and Asian newspapers conflated them with Lenin's "self-determination," Wilson did not clarify the distinction. As a result, many elites in colonies and semi-colonies—such as Egypt, India, China, Korea, and Annam—who hoped for independence, initially held high expectations of Wilson. When he failed to meet those expectations, his reputation collapsed.

In conclusion, President Monroe's 1823 State of the Union address maintained Washington's suspicion of European affairs. While the U.S. acted in the name of "America" or the "Western Hemisphere," the underlying goal was to secure a favorable international environment for U.S. security and development. As U.S. power grew, the Monroe Doctrine shifted from opposing European interference in the Americas to establishing U.S. dominance over American affairs under the guise of rejecting foreign influence, effectively making the U.S. an "international policeman" in the Western Hemisphere. Wilson's plan to solve global order problems built on the U.S. hegemony in the hemisphere, while reinterpreting Washington's Farewell Address and the Monroe Doctrine to expand their geographic application. Wilson's project diminished the hemisphere's division once maintained by the Monroe Doctrine, bringing the U.S. to directly face global responsibilities on an unprecedented scale.

In the late 19th century and early 20th century, the U.S. government promoted regional organizations in Latin America to expand its influence through multilateralism, particularly in the field of international law. In 1912, James Brown Scott, an American jurist, and Alejandro Álvarez, a Chilean jurist, founded the American Institute of International Law, with financial backing from the Carnegie Endowment for International Peace. This established a Pan-American international law research network aimed at promoting the concept of so-called "American international law."

However, disagreements persisted between U.S. and Latin American jurists regarding the interpretation of the Monroe Doctrine, particularly around issues of sovereign equality and non-interference. U.S. jurists generally advocated for formal sovereign equality but opposed the absolute non-interference

---

analysis, See Erez Manela, *The Wilsonian Moment: Self-Determination and the International Origins of Anti-colonial Nationalism*, (New York: Oxford University Press, 2009), 25, 61.

163 See Richard L. Hughes, "Propaganda: Wilson and the Committee on Public Information," in *A Companion to Woodrow Wilson*, ed. Ross A. Kennedy (Malden, Oxford & Chichester: John Wiley & Sons Ltd, 2015): 308–322.

claim of Latin American jurists, seeking to preserve legal space for U.S. intervention in the internal affairs of American countries. James Brown Scott, who had worked for the U.S. State Department and presided over the Carnegie Endowment for a long time, used the American Institute of International Law to promote American values. For instance, in 1916, the American Institute of International Law issued a declaration on the rights and duties of nations in the Americas, drawing from U.S. court rulings and authoritative expositions by American jurists.[164] The U.S. actively disseminated its legal culture in Latin America but showed little interest in incorporating ideas from Latin American countries.

Latin American elites held divergent views on whether the Monroe Doctrine could be considered a principle of international law. Saenz Peña, who represented Argentina at the first International Conference of American States in 1889, criticized the Monroe Doctrine as merely an expression of U.S. hegemony over other American countries. In contrast, his fellow Argentine jurist, Drago, sought to reinterpret the Monroe Doctrine as an egalitarian legal principle specific to the Western Hemisphere.[165] During the Venezuela Crisis of 1895, President Cleveland declared that "the Monroe Doctrine finds its recognition in those principles of international law which are based upon the theory that every nation shall have its rights protected and its just claims enforced."[166] However, with Britain's acceptance of U.S. hegemony in the Western Hemisphere, it became questionable whether this explanation still served U.S. interests.

On April 2, 1903, President Theodore Roosevelt delivered a speech in Chicago, arguing that "the Monroe Doctrine is not international law, and though I think one day it may become such, this is not necessary as long as it remains the cardinal feature of our foreign policy and as long as we possess both the will and strength to make it effective."[167] A month later, Samuel

164 Elihu Root, "The Declaration of the Rights and Duties of Nations Adopted by the American Institute of International Law," *The American Journal of International Law* 10 (Apr. 1916), 211–221.

165 Juan Pablo Scarfi, *The Hidden History of International law in the Americas: Empire and Legal Networks*, (Oxford & New York: Oxford University Press, 2017), 71.

166 Street (n. 126), 4.

167 Theodore Roosevelt, "The Monroe Doctrine," Speech at Chicago, Illinois (2 April 1903). Liang Qichao noticed in his *Travels to the New World* that the second half of this speech talked a lot about the naval construction of the United States, and made the following comments: "If the Monroe Doctrine only means 'America for the Americans,' why the U.S. needs naval power? The Monroe Doctrine was often understood as conservative and defensive. Therefore, it might appeal to other states. Now the Monroe Doctrine is used against others. I don't understand what it means." Liang Qichao 梁启超, "Xindalu

Herrick wrote *The Monroe Doctrine as a Principle of International Law*, attempting to prove that the Monroe Doctrine was already a principle of international law in five aspects.[168] However, the U.S. government did not adopt his argument. On April 22, 1914, at the 8th annual conference of the American Institute of International Law, historian and international relations scholar William I. Hull, who had participated in the Second Hague Peace Conference in 1907, asserted that the Monroe Doctrine was evolving towards international recognition and should be further internationalized.[169]

Proponents of upgrading the Monroe Doctrine to a principle of public international law emphasized that doing so would enhance U.S. international prestige. However, U.S. elites remained cautious. The U.S. government made reservations to both the 1899 and 1907 Conventions for the Pacific Settlement of International Disputes, stating that "nothing contained in the above convention can be interpreted as implying that the U.S. of America has given up her traditional attitude towards purely American issues."[170] At the 8th annual meeting of the American Institute of International Law in 1914, Elihu Root, a prominent Republican statesman and former Secretary of State under President Roosevelt, delivered a speech titled "The Real Monroe Doctrine." Root argued that the Monroe Doctrine was not a principle of international law but was based on the right of self-defense inherent in national sovereignty, which was recognized by international law. He claimed that the Monroe Doctrine aimed to maintain an external environment for U.S. security without infringing on the sovereignty of other American countries.[171]

---

youji jielu 新大陆游记节录 [Travel to the New World (excerpt)]," in *Liang Qichao quanji* 梁启超全集 [*Complete Works of Liang Qichao*], ed. Zhang Pinxing 张品兴 (Beijing Press, 1999), 1156.

168 Samuel Herrick, "The Monroe Doctrine as a Principle of International Law," *4 Brief* 360 (1903).

169 William Hull, "The Monroe Doctrine: National or International," *Proceedings of the American Society of International Law at Its Annual Meeting* (1907–1917) 8 (22–25 April 1914), 155–170.

170 James Scott ed., *The Hague Court Reports, 1916*, (New York: Oxford University Press, 1916), civ, cvi. It is worth mentioning that at the Hague International Peace Conference in 1899, Alfred Thayer Mahan, the representative of the United States, who advocated the "sea power theory," strongly advocated that the jurisdiction of the Permanent Court of International Arbitration should not be extended to those "purely American" issues. Robert (n. 148), 394.

171 Instead of discussing the Roosevelt Corollary in 1904 directly, Root quoted Roosevelt's speech in Congress on December 3rd, 1906, which said that the Monroe Doctrine did not mean the superiority of the United States or the exercise of protective rights to American countries. In view of Roosevelt's famous saying "Speak softly and carry a big stick," Root

In 1906, Root had given a speech in Rio de Janeiro, Brazil, where he characterized the Monroe Doctrine as a symbol of fraternal unity and shared purpose among countries in the Western Hemisphere. His 1914 speech clearly reversed the spirit of that earlier address. He also asserted that the Monroe Doctrine did not entail U.S. expansionism or interference in the internal affairs of other American countries, responding to critics in both Latin America and the U.S.[172]

In 1923, Charles Evans Hughes, Secretary of State under President Harding and a noted international jurist, further elaborated that "as the policy embodied in the Monroe Doctrine is distinctively the policy of the United States, the Government of the United States reserves to itself its definition, interpretation, and application." Despite being a Republican strongly opposed to Wilson, Hughes quoted former President Wilson to support his argument: "The Monroe Doctrine was proclaimed by the United States on her own authority. It always has been maintained and always will be maintained upon her own responsibility."[173] As mentioned earlier, Wilson's interpretation of the Monroe Doctrine was quite radical, but in practice, it did not diminish the U.S. government's power to unilaterally define and apply it. Therefore, Hughes's statement reflected a long-standing U.S. foreign policy tradition that neither political party had significantly altered.

There was a very pragmatic reason why American ruling elites insisted that the Monroe Doctrine was a foreign policy principle rather than a principle of international law. The U.S. government advocated for compulsory arbitration and other peaceful dispute resolution methods to replace the force and conquest often used by European powers. However, it did not want international arbitration or adjudication to bring Monroe Doctrine-related issues under their jurisdiction, thereby limiting its own freedom of action. If the U.S. government acknowledged the Monroe Doctrine as international law, international arbitration institutions and jurists could begin interpreting it independently, removing the U.S. government's monopoly over the doctrine's interpretation.[174]

---

quoted this speech to show Roosevelt's "soft speech." Elihu Root, "The Real Monroe Doctrine," *The American Journal of International Law* 8 (Jul. 1914), 427–442.

172 Christopher R. Rossi, *Whiggish International Law: Elihu Root, the Monroe Doctrine, and International Law in the Americas*, (Leiden and Boston: Brill), 2.

173 Charles Hughes, "Observations on the Monroe Doctrine," *American Bar Association Journal* 9 (1923), 561.

174 See Editorial Comment, "The Monroe Doctrine Again," *American Journal of International Law* 5 (1911), 729–735.

Francis Anthony Boyle, a contemporary U.S. historian of international law, explained why many U.S. international lawyers supported the government's stance: at the time, war had not been declared illegal, and national self-defense was guaranteed not by arbitration or adjudication, but by military power. Therefore, U.S. international lawyers felt that submitting Monroe Doctrine issues to arbitration or adjudication would effectively give up the right to self-defense through force, which was deemed dangerous for the U.S.[175] However, Boyle's analysis did not address the "double standards" of the U.S. ruling elites—while the U.S. reserved the unilateral right to use force, it sought to limit the corresponding rights of Latin American countries. Defenders of this position could argue that the U.S., acting as a protector in a world governed by power politics, should not weaken its protective capacity. Yet from a more critical perspective, this so-called protector role restricted Latin American countries' ability to choose their own development paths, revealing a form of regional hegemonism.

2 Return from Wilson to Monroe?

At the 1919 Paris Peace Conference, President Wilson faced many difficult issues but held high hopes for the League of Nations. He made concessions on other matters to secure support from foreign powers for his League of Nations plan. At the same time, Wilson had to contend with a Republican-led Congress that largely opposed taking on additional international obligations. Thus, his strategy was to demonstrate that the U.S. could gain greater global influence without incurring too many international commitments—an approach aligning with the Chinese proverb, "Make incremental reforms without disturbing the existing structure."

To increase the likelihood of Congress approving the League of Nations Covenant, Wilson emphasized Article 21: "Nothing in this Covenant shall be deemed to affect the validity of international engagements, such as treaties of arbitration or regional understandings like the Monroe Doctrine, for securing the maintenance of peace."[176] This clause excluded American issues from

175 Boyle (n. 119), 88.

176 Wilson tried to define Monroe Doctrine as a kind of "regional understanding," but met his Waterloo later in Senate's approval process. As mentioned earlier, the official statement of the U.S. government is that the Monroe Doctrine is a foreign policy of the U.S. government, which is neither a principle of international law nor a "regional understanding."

the League's jurisdiction, preserving the U.S.'s ability to uphold the Monroe Doctrine in the Americas. This exclusion was not Wilson's invention; in both the 1899 and 1907 Hague Peace Conferences, the U.S. had made similar reservations regarding the Monroe Doctrine.[177] The most significant obligation in the Covenant was Article 10, which stated: "The Members of the League undertake to respect and preserve as against external aggression the territorial integrity and existing political independence of all Members of the League. In case of any such aggression or threat, the Council shall advise on how this obligation should be fulfilled."[178] The core debate around these two articles was whether the U.S. would control the League of Nations or be controlled by it.

The path dependence of U.S. foreign policy, rooted in the Monroe Doctrine, meant that most American elites sought to maintain regional hegemony in the Western Hemisphere while avoiding excessive international obligations, particularly in European affairs. When Wilson returned to the U.S. to secure congressional approval for the League Covenant, many Republicans were discontented, believing it undermined U.S. diplomatic traditions. They called for amendments. On June 23, 1920, Henry Cabot Lodge, Chairman of the Senate Foreign Relations Committee, presented three reservations proposed by Elihu Root: first, rejecting Article 10 because its obligations were vague and overly broad, which could restrict U.S. freedom of action; second, opposing the withdrawal clause that required two years' notice, asserting that the U.S. should decide on its obligations independently; and third, excluding all "purely American issues" (including those related to the Monroe Doctrine and immigration) from League jurisdiction, ensuring mutual non-interference between Europe and the U.S.

Charles Evans Hughes, a jurist and Wilson's Republican opponent in the 1916 presidential election, also supported these strong reservations, in line with Root's stance. He saw Article 10 as problematic, arguing that the U.S. should bear no legal or moral responsibility for defending other League members, and that the article should be removed.[179] Regarding Article 21, Hughes believed two points should be clarified: first, that foreign states could not acquire American territory or adjacent islands by conquest, purchase, or any other means; and

---

177 Carnegie Endowment for International Peace. Division of Intercourse and Education ed., *American Foreign Policy: Based Upon Statements of Presidents and Secretaries of State of the United States and of Publicists of the American Republics*, (Washington D.C., 1920), 29, 60, 83.

178 World Knowledge Press ed., *International Treaty Collection* (1917–1923), (Beijing: World Knowledge Press, 1961), 274.

179 Lloyd E. Ambrosius, *Woodrow Wilson and the American Diplomatic Tradition: The Treaty Fight in Perspective*, (Cambridge & New York: Cambridge University Press, 1987), 155.

second, that purely American issues should be resolved by American countries themselves, without European interference unless requested by an American nation.[180]

Mild reservationists in the Republican Party did not seek the abolition of Article 10 of the League of Nations Covenant but advocated for placing more restrictions on it. For instance, former President William Howard Taft suggested that the obligations of Article 10 be limited to ten years, after which the president and a two-thirds majority of the Senate could decide whether to extend them.

Another faction within the Republican Party, led by William Borah, was entirely opposed to joining the League of Nations. Following Wilson's "Peace Without Victory" speech in January 1917, Borah introduced a motion in Congress to reaffirm the foreign policies of Washington, Jefferson, and Monroe. During the 1919 debate, Borah argued that Article 10 would entangle the U.S. in European affairs and enable foreign powers to control American actions. He noted that since Canada, Australia, New Zealand, South Africa, and India had seats in the League, Britain, not the U.S., would dominate decision-making. Borah believed this would violate the Monroe Doctrine's tradition of rejecting European interference in the Americas. He wanted the U.S. to retain unilateral control over its foreign policy, free from European influence.[181]

On August 19, 1920, President Wilson invited the Senate Foreign Relations Committee to the White House to persuade them to accept his proposal. He argued that the League's unanimous votes were merely suggestions and that U.S. obligations to the League were moral rather than legal. However, critics believed Article 10 would legally bind the U.S. to League decisions. Wilson also sidestepped the issue of the British Empire having six votes in the League.[182] Wilson's claim that the U.S. could announce universal principles without being bound by them, and could retreat to a position of control at any time, sounded too good to be true to his political opponents. This meeting deepened the divide between the White House and the Senate. After failing to convince the senators, Wilson launched a nationwide speaking tour but suffered a stroke during the journey, severely limiting his ability to work and communicate with the Senate.

---

180 "The Proposed Covenant for a League of Nations," Address of Charles E. Hughes, 26 March 1919, *Charles Evans Hughes Papers*, Box 172, Library of Congress at: <http://dla.library.upenn.edu/dla/print/detail.html?Id=print_9959262683503681> (accessed 12 February 2019).

181 Ambrosius (n. 179), 90.

182 Ibid., 164.

Meanwhile, Senator Lodge continued efforts to win over moderate conservatives. On September 5, he proposed four new reservations to the Senate Foreign Affairs Committee: (1) the U.S. could withdraw from the League of Nations unconditionally; (2) the U.S. would not take on international obligations under Article 10 unless approved by Congress; (3) the League would not interfere in U.S. domestic affairs, with the U.S. defining what constitutes a "domestic affair"; and (4) the Monroe Doctrine would be interpreted exclusively by the U.S., and would not fall under League jurisdiction:

> The United States will not submit to arbitration or to inquiry by the Assembly or by the Council of the League of Nations, provided for in said treaty of peace, any questions which in the judgment of the United States depend upon or relate to its long-established policy, commonly known as the Monroe Doctrine; said doctrine is to be interpreted by the United States alone and is hereby declared to be wholly outside the jurisdiction of said League of Nations and entirely unaffected by any provision contained in the said treaty of peace with Germany.[183]

Wilson received Lodge's bill on November 3 and strongly criticized the Article 10 reservation, arguing it undermined the covenant's core, and refused to make concessions.

As tensions between the White House and Senate persisted, the presidential campaign approached. Wilson, hoping for a third term, was not nominated. Instead, James M. Cox, a Democrat loyal to Wilson's foreign policy, defended Article 10 during his campaign, arguing it extended the Monroe Doctrine's principles from Latin America to the entire world. Cox declared that ratifying the Treaty of Versailles would be his first priority if elected.[184] Republican candidate Warren G. Harding tied Cox to Wilson's unpopular foreign policy. Wilson called the election a "solemn referendum" on U.S. foreign policy, but his unpopularity led to a landslide victory for Harding, who won by 26.2% more votes than Cox. Republicans also gained control of the Senate, marking the beginning of over a decade of Republican leadership until Franklin Roosevelt took office in 1933.

The Republican administration rejected Wilson's League of Nations. However, as a major creditor with extensive overseas investments, the U.S. could not retreat entirely from international affairs. The Senate's stance toward different international agreements during this period reflects this balancing

183 Ibid., 173–174.

184 Ibid., 274.

act. In November 1921, the U.S. hosted the Washington Conference, resulting in the Four-Power Pact with Britain, Japan, France, and the U.S., effectively terminating the Anglo-Japanese Alliance. The Senate ratified the treaty after adding an amendment that clarified it imposed no obligations regarding the use of force, alliances, or common defense. Similarly, the Five-Power Naval Limitation Treaty and the Nine-Power Treaty, reached at the same conference, were ratified easily, as they did not impose strict legal obligations on the U.S.

After witnessing Wilson's failure, the subsequent Republican administrations took a very cautious approach to international affairs outside the Western Hemisphere. On the one hand, they worked to advance U.S. national interests by recovering loans in Europe and preventing Japan from expanding too much in China. On the other hand, they avoided joining the League of Nations or entering into any bilateral alliances. This stance was essentially a compromise between the 19th-century "Monroe Doctrine" and the more interventionist Wilsonianism.

In 1928, U.S. Secretary of State Frank B. Kellogg initiated the Kellogg-Briand Pact (also known as the Pact of Paris). Article 1 of the pact declared: "The High Contracting Parties solemnly declare in the names of their respective peoples that they condemn recourse to war for the solution of international controversies and renounce it as an instrument of national policy in their relations with one another."[185] The U.S. Senate passed the treaty almost unanimously. The appeal lay in its flexibility: the U.S. could influence other countries in peacetime but still remain neutral if war erupted. The U.S. incorporated its concerns about the Monroe Doctrine into the pact's interpretation. For example, on July 14, 1928, France responded to the pact by pointing out that states retain the right to self-defense, with each state deciding if a war is defensive. Britain echoed this, arguing that its right to self-defense included protecting certain regions of special interest to British security. Meanwhile, the U.S. maintained that the Monroe Doctrine was foundational to its own right of self-defense.[186]

Although the U.S. did not join the League of Nations, it did not entirely stay away from the League's activities. The Harding and Coolidge administrations sent "unofficial observers" to League of Nations meetings, where they protected U.S. interests without taking responsibility for League decisions. Since many Latin American states were members of the League, the U.S. could exert influence indirectly. In this way, the U.S. could interfere in League matters while avoiding binding commitments. The U.S. was also a major creditor to many

185 Wang, He and Wu (n. 147), 630.

186 Hersch Lauterpacht ed., *Oppenheim International Law* (Part II), (Beijing: Commercial Press, 1989), 137, Note 1.

European nations after World War I, and this financial leverage—exemplified by the Dawes Plan for Germany—allowed the U.S. to shape international affairs without taking on rigid political and military obligations. Capital, seemingly apolitical, strengthened U.S. political influence.

Despite not joining the League, the Harding administration considered joining the Permanent Court of International Justice (PCIJ), which was closely associated with the League. In 1923, the White House made several reservations to the PCIJ, including rejecting the rule that only League members could elect judges and exempting the U.S. from compulsory court rulings in disputes. These reservations weakened the court's authority, and U.S. senators feared that joining the PCIJ would draw the U.S. into the League of Nations. Heated debates led to further demands for special privileges. However, these U.S. demands angered other powers, and the League of Nations Council proposed further negotiations, which the White House declined, wary of Senate backlash.[187] Before World War II, the U.S. generally maintained a cautious stance toward international affairs outside the Americas—seeking to expand its interests while avoiding entanglement in European conflicts.

Since Theodore Roosevelt's presidency, the U.S. had repeatedly intervened in Latin America, creating widespread resentment. In April 1920, Uruguayan President Baltasar Brum criticized the U.S. for establishing a "protection system" through the Monroe Doctrine to serve its own interests. Brum argued that Latin American nations needed to break free from the Monroe Doctrine and form an alliance to protect their territorial integrity. At the Fifth Pan-American Conference in 1923, Uruguay openly proposed establishing the League of American States, directly challenging the Monroe Doctrine. By the Sixth Pan-American Conference in 1928, non-interference in domestic affairs had become a major issue, and the U.S. faced growing diplomatic pressure.

In response, the Republican administration sought strategic adjustments. On December 17, 1928, Deputy Secretary of State J. Reuben Clark drafted a memorandum that clarified the U.S. right to intervene militarily in Latin America. Published under the Hoover administration in 1930, the Clark Memorandum did not advocate for limiting U.S. military intervention but redefined its legal justification. The memo argued that the Monroe Doctrine was meant to protect Latin American states from European interference, not to justify U.S. intervention in their internal affairs. The memo suggested that U.S. intervention in Latin America should be based on the right of self-preservation rather than the Monroe Doctrine itself. This implicitly repudiated the Roosevelt Corollary,

---

187 Thomas Guinsberg, *The Pursuit of Isolationism: In the United States Senate from Versailles to Pearl Harbor*, (New York: Garland Publishing, Inc., 1982).

which had expanded the Monroe Doctrine to justify U.S. intervention in the domestic politics of Latin American countries.

When Franklin Roosevelt, a Democratic president, took office on March 4, 1933, he faced growing anti-American sentiment in Latin America and the declining influence of U.S. economic power in the region. To address this, he implemented the Good Neighbor Policy. On December 28 of that year, Roosevelt publicly declared his opposition to "armed intervention." To counter the growing influence of Germany, Italy, and Japan in Latin America, Roosevelt replaced unilateral intervention with collective intervention, reduced tariffs, and established the Export-Import Bank to provide loans and strengthen economic and trade ties with Latin American countries. At Roosevelt's proposal, the Inter-American Conference for the Maintenance of Peace was held in Buenos Aires in December 1936, where the Convention for the Maintenance, Preservation, and Re-establishment of Peace and the Additional Protocol on Non-Intervention were adopted. The U.S. accepted the principle of "non-intervention" and withdrew its reservations to the 1933 Montevideo Convention on the Rights and Duties of States. At the same time, the U.S. secured provisions urging Latin American countries to engage in collective deliberation when external wars threatened peace in the Americas. In 1938, the 8th Pan-American Conference adopted the Declaration of Solidarity of the American Countries and the Declaration on the Principles of the Americas. Although there was no obligation for collective defense, the declarations stated that all American countries would unite against any foreign intervention or activities that threatened them. The signatories agreed to deliberate in accordance with established procedures if peace, security, or territorial integrity of any American country was threatened.[188]

By restoring U.S. prestige in Latin America, Roosevelt created conditions for the collective neutrality of Latin American countries after the outbreak of World War II. At the Meetings of Consultation of Ministers of Foreign Affairs held in Panama on September 23, 1939, it was agreed that all American countries would remain neutral in the war. In April 1940, the American nations signed the Declaration of Reciprocal Assistance and Cooperation for the Defense of the Nations of the Americas in Havana, announcing that any attempt by a non-American state to impair the territorial integrity, inviolability, sovereignty, or political independence of any American state would be considered an act of aggression against all American countries.[189] The conference also decided

188 Hong Yuyi 洪育沂, ed., *Lamei guojia guanxishigang* 拉美国家关系史纲 [*Outline of Latin American Relations*], (Beijing: Waiyu jiaoxue yu yanjiu chubanshe, 1996), 98–99.

189 Lauterpacht (n. 186), 239.

to temporarily manage European colonies in the Americas to prevent them from falling into German hands. This meant that the Grant Corollary of the Monroe Doctrine, which prohibited territorial transfers to European powers, became a consensus among American nations. The Roosevelt administration promoted defense cooperation with Latin American governments, and after Japan's attack on Pearl Harbor on December 7, 1941, the U.S. entered the war. Most Latin American countries followed the U.S. and sided with the Allies, although Argentina, which had sympathies for Germany and Italy, remained neutral for a significant period but eventually joined the Allies in the final stages of World War II.

Thus, Roosevelt's Good Neighbor Policy was part of a broader strategy to counter the rising threats from Europe and Asia. However, the U.S. path to entering World War II was not straightforward. The traditional spatial mentality shaped by the Monroe Doctrine was so strong that Roosevelt had to restrain his impulse to join the global anti-Fascist alliance until after the Pearl Harbor attack. It had been twenty years since Wilson's internationalist strategy collapsed.

3 Concluding Remarks

Further exploration is needed to understand why the U.S. ultimately broke through the spatial constraints of the Western Hemisphere and transformed the Monroe Doctrine into a principle of global hegemony. In 1917, President Wilson invoked an idealistic reason for intervention: to make the world "safe for democracy." However, this rationale did not convince the isolationists in the U.S., as economic ties between the U.S. and Eurasia were not yet strong enough to necessitate global military and political actions. Wilson's strategy thus failed. The key period for the U.S. to step beyond the Western Hemisphere and build a global empire was World War II.

In 1942, during the Pacific War, Dutch-born American geopolitics scholar Nicholas John Spykman published *American Strategy in World Politics: The United States and the Balance of Power*, which, as Perry Anderson notes, filled "the vacuum of longer-range reflections in Washington."[190] Against the backdrop of rising threats from Germany and Japan, Spykman argued that if the U.S. wanted to ensure the security of the Western Hemisphere, it had to seek a global balance of power. Isolationists in the U.S. believed that the Atlantic and

190 Perry Anderson, *American Foreign Policy and Its Thinkers*, London: Verso, 2015, 20.

Pacific Oceans acted as natural barriers, and that even if Germany and Japan triumphed in the Old World, it would not threaten the Western Hemisphere. Spykman rejected this notion, dividing the Americas into Anglo-Saxon America (the U.S. and Canada) and Latin America. He argued that if Germany and Japan invaded the Americas, Latin American countries would be a hindrance to the U.S. Even without an invasion, Germany and Japan could wage a trade war against the Western Hemisphere, exploiting the vast social and ideological differences between Latin America and Anglo-Saxon America. Spykman speculated that Germany could even establish a puppet regime in Argentina, which would then spread its influence in South America, creating a "Greater South American Co-Prosperity Sphere." Thus, Spykman concluded that to achieve a global balance of power and ensure the security of the Western Hemisphere, the U.S. must proactively join the European and Pacific wars to defeat Germany and Japan.

In 1942, Nicholas John Spykman offered a vision for the post-World War II international system that the U.S. should adopt, learning from the mistakes made after World War I. He argued that the U.S. should not retreat to the Western Hemisphere as it did after the first war but should instead actively engage in the alliance systems of Europe and Asia to maintain the balance of power in the Old World. Spykman notably warned that in post-war Asia, the U.S. needed to be wary not just of Japan, but of China, which had greater long-term economic and military potential than Japan.[191] Spykman famously altered Halford Mackinder's dictum on geopolitical control: "Who rules East Europe commands the Heartland; who rules the Heartland commands the World-Island; who rules the World-Island commands the world." Spykman rephrased it as: "Who controls the Rimland rules Eurasia; who rules Eurasia controls the destinies of the world."[192] China, in Spykman's view, was a key power in this Rimland, representing a significant geopolitical concern.

The balance of power theory, which Spykman supported, is rooted in the political psychology of fear, often justifying preemptive attacks. This idea, with a long intellectual history stretching back to Cicero and later Renaissance

191 Nicholas Speakman, Wang Shan and Guo Xinyu 王珊、郭鑫雨 trans., *Shijie zhengzhizhong de meiguo zhanlue: Meiguo yu quanli pingheng* 世界政治中的美国战略：美国与权力平衡 [*America's Strategy in World Politics: The United States and the Balance of Power*], (Shanghai: Shanghai renmin chubanshe, 2018), 444.

192 Nicholas Spykman, Yu Haijie 俞海杰 trans., Heping dilixue: Bianyuan didai de zhanlue 和平地理学：边缘地带的战略 [*The Geography of the Peace*], (Shanghai: Shanghai renmin chubanshe, 2016), 58.

writers,[193] was invoked by President Monroe in 1823, when he warned that European intervention in the Americas could threaten U.S. independence. Similarly, President Roosevelt in 1904 used the same logic, suggesting that European powers' debt-collecting interventions in Latin America could endanger the autonomy of the region and U.S. security. Spykman expanded this concept further: although Wilhelm II of Germany sent warships to Venezuela, and Nazi Germany never reached Latin America in World War II, Germany still represented a threat in Spykman's thinking. In 1942, while China was fighting Japanese invaders, Spykman was already calculating how to balance China as a rising power.

Spykman's ideas quickly influenced U.S. policy. The U.S. became deeply involved in European and Asia-Pacific affairs. It established NATO in Europe and entered into security treaties with South Korea and Japan to contain both China and the Soviet Union. U.S. officials added a touch of Wilsonian idealism to Spykman's more realist "balance of power" strategy. Today, the U.S. operates more than 800 military bases around the world, many of them encircling China in a C-shaped formation. Despite China's limited naval movements within its own first island chain, U.S. media often escalates these into claims of a "China threat," reflecting a broader U.S. tendency to depict threats from afar while demanding that other nations prove their peaceful intentions.

Thus, the Monroe Doctrine, initially confined to the Western Hemisphere, has expanded globally. U.S. elites now envision the world as they once viewed Latin America—as a region to dominate and control.[194] In May 1903, when Liang Qichao, a Chinese reformist, met President Theodore Roosevelt, he was struck by Roosevelt's vision, summarizing it as "the whole world for the U.S."[195] Spykman's global vision—first conceived in the 1940s—has become a reality, with the U.S. projecting its Monroe Doctrine beyond its original scope.

193 See Richard Tuck, Luo Jiong 罗炯 et al. trans., *Zhanzheng yu heping he quanli* 战争与和平的权利 [*Rights of War and Peace: Political Thought and the International Order from Grotius to Kant*], (Shanghai: Yilin chubanshe, 2009), 20–36.

194 As Graham Allison, who put forward the concept of "the Thucydides' trap," clearly pointed out that the reason why American policymakers did not recognize the "sphere of influence" after the Cold War: "the whole world has essentially become the sphere of influence of the United States." Graham Allison, "The New Spheres of Influence: Sharing the Globe With Other Great Powers," *Foreign Affairs*, March/April 2020.

195 Liang (n. 167), 1155.

CHAPTER 2

"Katechon" in Central Europe? Monroe Doctrine, Großraum and International Law

> Jetzt seh ich Schemen, die vermummt zerstieben,
> Und steh darauf bewußt und fest im Stoffsysteme.
>
> THEODOR DÄUBLERS, Nordlicht[196]

Spatial consciousness similar to the "sphere of influence" exists worldwide. The Monroe Doctrine, established in 1823, provided an American-specific framework for this type of spatial thinking. If the U.S. had remained solely a regional hegemonic power, the Monroe Doctrine would likely have had little influence beyond the Western Hemisphere. However, as the U.S. grew into the world's largest economy by the late 19th century, its political influence began to extend beyond its immediate region. The U.S. became an important reference point for many cultural and political elites in Europe and Asia.

Influenced by the U.S. paradigm, participants in local spatial-political struggles sometimes used the Monroe Doctrine to reformulate their own claims. For instance, when the ruling elites of the British Empire sought to exclude other countries and international organizations from interfering with British colonies and spheres of influence, they appropriated Monroe Doctrine rhetoric, creating what some called a "British Monroe Doctrine."[197] However, in Europe, the most systematic appropriation and theoretical reflection on the Monroe

196 Carl Schmitt, *Theodor Däublers, "Nordlicht," Drei Studien über die Elemente, den Geist und die Aktualität des Werkes*, (Berlin: Duncker & Humbolt, 1991), 23.

197 In 1928, when Britain signed the *Pact of Paris* initiated by France and the United States, it made a reservation: On May 19th, 1928, the British Foreign Office sent a note to the American ambassador to Britain, saying that "there are certain regions of the world the welfare and integrity of which constitute a special and vital interest for our peace and safety. His Majesty's Government have been at pains to make it clear in the past that interference with these regions cannot be suffered." FO 414/262, Sir Austen Chamberlain to Mr. Houghton (19 May 1928), 175.

 | DOI:10.1163/9789004746237_004

Doctrine came not from Britain but from Germany, where the geopolitical environment was more complex and nuanced.

In Central Europe, Germany's main territory largely overlapped with the former Holy Roman Empire. From the Middle Ages until its dissolution in 1806, the Holy Roman Empire remained a loose political confederation, and European powers were accustomed to the absence of a unified, strong state in Central Europe. After the Napoleonic Wars, the Congress of Vienna (1814–1815) reestablished a European balance of power, assuming that Central Europe would remain politically fragmented. Austrian statesman Klemens von Metternich organized the German Confederation, headed by Austria with a parliament in Frankfurt, but he viewed Germany largely as a geographical concept and was not interested in its unification. Under the Vienna system, Britain and Russia were Europe's maritime and land hegemons, respectively, while Prussiaand Austria competed for influence in Central Europe. To the west lay France, which had recently conquered much of Europe under Napoleon. The emergence of a unified Germany would dramatically alter Europe's traditional geopolitical pattern, inevitably pressuring surrounding powers. This rising state was seen as a threat to the status quo, and it faced far greater challenges in asserting a sphere of influence than the U.S. did in Latin America.

From the 19th century onward, the term "Mitteleuropa" was frequently used to describe the sphere of influence envisioned by German elites. For some theorists, "Mitteleuropa" referred to the vast area between France and Russia, particularly regions inhabited by Germans; for others, it could even include France. Concerns about the reproduction and survival of the German population, the supply of raw materials, and the sale of industrialized goods were central to this discourse. The rise of political geography and geopolitics in Germany coincided with this spatial vision. As the U.S. influence on the European continent grew after World War I, the Monroe Doctrine attracted the attention of some German theorists.

While in the U.S., the Monroe Doctrine was championed by politicians, in Germany, it was primarily analyzed by scholars. German politicians, such as Hitler, occasionally invoked the Monroe Doctrine, but they did so opportunistically, without offering a systematic explanation of its underlying principles. Carl Schmitt was one of the few German thinkers who connected Germany's geopolitical ambitions to the Monroe Doctrine discourse in a more thorough and theoretical way. This chapter will examine how Carl Schmitt developed a theory of "multi-polarization" that served Germany's interests, drawing on his analysis and imitation of the U.S. Monroe Doctrine. However, before delving into Schmitt's theoretical framework, it is important to first review the geopolitical environment and ideological context of Germany from the 19th century up to World War I.

1 From the 19th Century to the First World War

Unlike the U.S., systematic thought about spheres of influence existed in Germany even before the founding of the Second German Reich. Before 1871, German elites were already debating the size and influence a unified Germany should have. In the early 19th century, Johann Gottfried Herder envisioned that Prussia and Austria would unite to form a great power in Central Europe, protecting the Germans on the continent.[198] Heinrich Friedrich Karl vom Stein, a Prussian reformer, proposed that the Germans should unite to form a buffer between France and Russia.[199] Friedrich List, the well-known theorist of National Economics, advocated for the German Customs Union, which he hoped would include Austria, Prussia, and other German states. He even envisioned the Danube Valley and the Black Sea coast as potential German colonies.[200] Karl Ludwig Freiherr von Bruck, an Austrian aristocrat and Austrian representative in the Frankfurt Parliament, later served as Trade Minister under Felix zu Schwarzenberg. He proposed a customs union between the German states and Austria and envisioned further economic expansion for the Germans.[201] Through these discussions, the idea that Germany should play a leading role in the vast space between France and Russia began to take shape. However, the concept of Mitteleuropa was still peripheral in their discourse, and their primary concern remained "Deutschland." Their focus was mainly on the economic and political integration of Prussia, Austria, and other German states.[202]

The "Großdeutschland" project of merging Germany and Austria faced significant challenges in practice. The Habsburgroyal family in Austria struggled with the highly diverse national composition of its empire, making it difficult to present themselves solely as representatives of the German nation. Under the leadership of Bismarck, the "Eiserner Kanzler," Prussia pursued a "Kleindeutschland" policy that excluded Austria, leading to the establishment of the Second German Reich in 1871. Bismarck, acutely aware of Germany's precarious geopolitical environment, favored using Europe's balance-of-power mechanisms to maintain the hard-won status quo. He was cautious about

198 Bernhard Suphan, *Herders sdmmtliche Werke*, Vol. 23, (Berlin: Weidmannsche Buchhandlung, 1877–1913), 462.

199 Emil Botzenhart ed., Heinrich Friedrich Karl Freiherr vom Stein, *Briefwechsel, Denkschriften und Aufzeichnungen*, Vol. 4, (Berlin: C. Heymann, 1933), 165.

200 Eduard von Beckenrath et al. eds., Friedrich List, *Schriften, Reden, Briefe*, Vol. 5, (Berlin: R. Hobbing Verlag, 1935), 502.

201 Richard Charmatz, *Minister Freiherr von Bruck*, (Leipzig: S. Hirzel, 1916), 157–281.

202 Otilia Dhand, *The Idea of Central Europe: Geopolitics, Culture and Regional Identity*, (London & New York: I.B. Tauris, 2018), 13–19.

German colonization in Africa and focused primarily on Europe. He advocated maintaining the alliance with Austria-Hungary, avoiding expansionist ambitions that could alarm Austria-Hungary. However, with the rise of German bourgeoisie nationalism, Bismarck's cautious approach as a Junker aristocrat quickly became the target of criticism.

The rise of German bourgeois nationalism was closely tied to Germany's rapid development during the Second Industrial Revolution. As the German economy grew, nationalists began advocating for more expansionist goals, and the concept of Mitteleuropa gained increasing significance. In 1879, Constantin Frantz published Der Föderalismus: Als das leitende Prinzip für die soziale, staatliche und internationale Organisation, criticizing Bismarck's "Kleindeutschland" policy and envisioning a "Mitteleuropäischer Bund" that would include Prussia (including Poland and Baltic states like Lithuania, then occupied by Russia), Austria (including Hungary and the Balkans under its rule), and the remaining German states. Frantz suggested that the Federation could even expand to include the Netherlands, Belgium, and Switzerland. He first considered the threats posed by France and Russia and then addressed how Germany could compete with larger powers like the British Empire, Russia, and the U.S. In his three-volume work Die Weltpolitik, published in 1882, he even contemplated including France in his "Mitteleuropäischer Bund" and emphasized Germany's responsibility to protect Hungarians, West Slavs, and South Slavs from Russia and the Ottoman Empire.

Paul de Lagarde, a biblical scholar and Orientalist, also proposed that Germany should integrate the "Central Europe" zone between France and Russia. In his 1878–1892 anthology, *Deutsche Schriften*, Lagarde identified Russia as Germany's primary threat and Austria as a potential ally. German geographer and historian Berthold Volz expanded the concept of "Central Europe" to include France, Belgium, the Netherlands, Germany, and "the upper Danube Valley." Notably, political geographer Friedrich Ratzel included France in his concept of "Central Europe" in his book *Deutschland: Einführung in Die Heimatkunde*, though it was excluded from the reprint after his death in 1907. Geographer Joseph Partsch published *Central Europe* in 1903 as part of a series hosted by British geographer Halford Mackinder. Partsch's vision of "Central Europe" included Germany, Austria-Hungary, Belgium, the Netherlands, Serbia, Romania, and Bulgaria. He argued that the region needed to unite on the basis of German language and culture to counter threats from both Russia and Britain.[203]

203 Joseph Partsch, *Central Europe*, (London: W. Heinemann, 1903).

The *Geographische Zeitschrift*, founded in 1895, established a dedicated column on "Central Europe." In its first issue, one of the featured articles was Friedrich Ratzel's work on the growth of national organisms. This column published a series of articles, most of which adopted Ratzel's theory of the national organism, viewing "Central Europe" as a sphere of influence that Germany must acquire through its continued growth. However, the authors expressed varying opinions on the geographical boundaries of "Central Europe."[204] In 1902, Albert Sartorius published an article on "Central Europe" in the *Zeitschrift für Sozialwissenschaft*, introducing the perspective of economic geography into the discourse. Sartorius conceived "Central Europe" as an economic region centered on Germany, with its basic organizational form as a customs union, including Germany, Austria, the Netherlands, Switzerland, and Denmark.[205]

After the outbreak of World War I, Germany was forced to strengthen its cooperation with the Austro-Hungarian Empire and Ottoman Turkey due to military pressure and the economic blockade imposed by the Allies. A "Mitteleuropa" extending from the Baltic Sea to the Adriatic and Black Sea soon became a crucial space for military and economic planning. The German Reich quickly devised action plans. In September 1914, with the backing of many German industrial and commercial elites, Chancellor Theobald von Bethmann-Hollweg's cabinet proposed a plan to annex France's Longwy-Briey region, turn France into a market for German goods, make Belgium a dependent state to serve as a military base against Britain, and establish a Central European Economic Zone that included Austria-Hungary, Poland, Denmark, Italy, and the Scandinavian countries. However, with Germany bogged down on the Western Front, the plan quickly faltered. In 1915, Friedrich Naumann, a Christian Socialist statesman, published *Mitteleuropa*, where he predicted that after the war, two major economic blocs, "wirtschaftliche Großräume," would emerge: Anglo-America and Russia-Asia. He argued that Germany should first form a customs union with Austria-Hungary and Romania, eventually creating a political entity based on federalism to offer non-German ethnic groups a more equal status.

Naumann's moderate vision for "Central Europe" had little influence on German authorities. After the military's General Staff took over power, Paul von Hindenburg pursued a more aggressive "Central Europe" plan, aiming to conquer Poland and annex Kurland and Lithuania. On the Eastern Front, the German military capitalized on the instability of the Bolshevik regime following the October Revolution in Russia, extending Germany's borders

---

204 Dhand (n. 202), 19–27.

205 Ibid., 28–30.

eastward through the Treaty of Brest-Litovsk, which furthered the vision of a large "Central European" sphere. However, with the November Revolution in Germany in 1918 and Germany's subsequent surrender to the Allies, these expansionist ambitions collapsed. The focus shifted to how much of its pre-war territory and colonies Germany could retain.

Before World War I, the influence of the United States on the European continent was limited, and German nationalists rarely invoked the language of the Monroe Doctrine to articulate their ambitions for "Central Europe." During the 1848 revolution, the national assembly of the German states in St. Paul's Church in Frankfurt debated German unification and foreign colonization. Friedrich Wilhelm Schulz, a member of the Westendhall, urged Germany to colonize the Danube Valley in the east and southeast as a land-based expansion, in addition to competing with foreign powers for overseas colonies. He famously stated, "Dort an unser Grenze ist unser Texas, unser Mexiko" ("There, at our border, lies our Texas, our Mexico").[206] This analogy reflects a consciousness that saw German expansion into Eastern Europe as akin to the American "Manifest Destiny." However, there was no explicit mention of the "Monroe Doctrine"—in fact, the term "Monroe Doctrine" had not yet entered common English usage at the time. Even Friedrich Naumann, in his influential 1915 work *Mitteleuropa*, referenced America's control over Latin America but did not specifically discuss the Monroe Doctrine, nor did he frame German leadership in Central Europe as a "German Monroe Doctrine." Since the United States maintained an isolationist stance toward European affairs at the time, European powers did not need to invoke the Monroe Doctrine to communicate their ambitions. They could understand each other through other geopolitical frameworks.

In fact, the term "European Monroe Doctrine" might have been coined by Americans rather than Europeans. As early as June 1903, Whitelaw Reid, a diplomat who served as the U.S. negotiator during the Spanish-American War, introduced the concept of a "European Monroe Doctrine" in a speech at Yale Law School. He imagined a scenario in which Britain, along with Belgium, Portugal, Germany, and other countries, would propose to the U.S. that the political system in Africa should be one of constitutional monarchy, and that Africa should be protected from the colonization of republics. Consequently, Reid suggested that the U.S. should cease its support for the

206 Günter Wollstein, *Das "Grossdeutschland" der Paulskirche: Nationale Ziele in der bürgerlichen Revolution, 1848/49*, (Düsseldorf: Droste Verlag, 1977), 302; Matthew P. Fitzpatrick, *Liberal Imperialism in Germany: Expansionism and Nationalism, 1848–1884*, (Oxford & New York: Berghah, 2008), 41.

Republic of Liberia, a state founded by freed black slaves from America.[207] However, this was merely a mirror image Reid had constructed, modeled after the U.S. Monroe Doctrine. It was focused on European colonies in Africa rather than on Europe itself. In reality, European powers at the turn of the 20th century were far more concerned with matters such as the balance of power, territorial control, and spheres of influence than they were with the form of government, as Reid had speculated. For example, France had maintained a republican government since 1870, and although there was tension between royalists and republicans, Bismarck, as the German Chancellor, actually supported French republicanism rather than the Catholic royalists. His reasoning was that a republican France would likely be isolated by Europe's monarchies, which would enhance Germany's geopolitical security.[208] This demonstrates that, for Bismarck, state interests had come to surpass the principle of political homogeneity established by the Congress of Vienna.

Since breaking its "neutrality" and participating in World War I, the U.S. had become a significant player in European affairs, or at least a key audience. This growing presence led to the Monroe Doctrine gaining more attention in Europe than ever before. In 1923, Austrian aristocrat Richard von Coudenhove-Kalergi published *Pan-Europa*, where he argued that "A century after America, Europe ought to proclaim its Monroe Doctrine: 'Europe for the Europeans.'"[209] In Coudenhove-Kalergi's view, the main threat to Europe was the Soviet Union, which, despite sharing a similar historical and cultural heritage with Europe, had adopted principles contrary to those of the West. To prevent the Soviet Union from controlling Eastern Europe and ultimately dominating the entire continent, he proposed that European countries, from Poland to Portugal, unite both politically and economically. The "European Union" he envisioned was to include all non-Soviet countries in Europe, along with their overseas colonies. He did not anticipate Britain's inclusion, given its status as a global empire, but he hoped that the Union could maintain good relations with Britain. Coudenhove-Kalergi suggested that Austria and Czechoslovakia form the initial alliance, which would then extend north to Poland and the Baltic states and south to the Balkans. He envisioned the five Danube countries uniting as the "United States of Eastern Europe" and then expanding into the

207 Whitelaw Reid, "The Monroe Doctrine; The Polk Doctrine; Anarchism," *Yale Law Journal* 13 (1903).

208 Robert A. Kann and Stanley B. Winters, *Dynasty, Politics, and Culture: Selected Essays*, (Boulder: Social Science Monographs, 1991), 96.

209 Richard N. Coudenhove-Kalergi, *Crusade for Pan-Europe: Autobiography of A Man and A Movement*, (New York: G.P. Putnam's Sons, 1943), 10–11.

"United States of Europe." This European federation would coexist alongside the American Federation, the East Asian Federation, the British Federation, and the Soviet Union.

In 1926, Richard von Coudenhove-Kalergi organized the first Pan-European Conference in Vienna, followed by three more conferences in 1930, 1932, and 1935. The Pan-European movement gained support from prominent intellectuals and cultural figures such as Sigmund Freud, Thomas Mann, Stefan Zweig, Albert Einstein, and José Ortega y Gasset. France, as the largest European victor in World War I, showed considerable interest in Kalergi's vision. In 1929, French Prime Minister Aristide Briand delivered a speech at the League of Nations advocating for a European Federation, which garnered support from many German elites. In May 1930, Briand submitted a memorandum to the League of Nations on the establishment of a European Union. That same year, French Prime Minister Édouard Herriot published *The United States of Europe*,[210] which attracted significant attention from Western public opinion.

As a German residing in Austria, Coudenhove-Kalergi envisioned a pro-Entente plan for Pan-European integration, which did not assign Germany a leading role. As a result, this plan was not one that German nationalists found acceptable. In 1919, Germany was severely punished by the Treaty of Versailles, losing vast territories and its overseas colonies, while the Austro-Hungarian Empire disintegrated into Austria, Hungary, Czechoslovakia, and several other new states. After World War I, German cultural and political elites were troubled by the fact that at least 12 million Germans were living outside of Germany. The notion of "Central Europe," which had been revived during the war, did not disappear with Germany's defeat. Given that Austria had lost its empire and now had a more homogeneous population, the idea of Anschluss—unification with Germany—began to seem realistic once again. In the early Weimar period, figures such as Hermann Ullmann, Theodor Heuss, Friedrich Naumann, Ernst Jückh, and Paul Rohrbach advocated for Anschluss.[211] However, under the post-war international system, this was impossible. The Treaty of Saint Germain, signed between the Entente powers and Austria, specifically stipulated that Germany and Austria could not merge without the consent of the Council of the League of Nations.

---

210 The title of the French version of the book is only "Europe," but the title "United States of Europa" is used in the English version. Édouard Herriot, *Europe*, (Paris: Les Éditions Redier, 1930); Édouard Herriot, Reginald J. Dingle trans., *The United States of Europe*, (New York: The Viking Press, 1930).

211 Jorg Brechtefeld, *Miteleuropa and German Politics, 1848 to the Present*, (London: Palgrave Macmillan, 1996), 48.

After World War I, a Pan-European ideology emerged in Germany that opposed the Entente. In 1921, the German historical geographer Walter Vogel wrote *Das Neue Europa und seine historisch-geographischen Grundlage* (The New Europe and its Historical-Geographical Foundations), which explored the geographical basis of the European international system. He argued that Germany could restore its reputation by transcending the nation-state model and leading the creation of an economically federalized Europe.[212] At the same time, he expressed dissatisfaction with how the Paris Peace Conference handled the Rhineland and harbored strong hostility toward Jews and socialists.[213] While the Pan-European plans proposed by Coudenhove-Kalergi and French leaders were aligned with the League of Nations, Vogel's vision was fundamentally hostile to the League. He aimed to bypass it and restore Germany's influence in Europe, relying on Germany's industrial strength. For Vogel, "Pan-Europeanism" was merely a means to an end, with the real goal being the resurgence of German power.

More German geographers and economists, however, turned to the concept of "Mitteleuropa" and tied it to the ideas of *Lebensraum* (living space) and *Volk* (people). Friedrich Ratzel, who had studied zoology in his early years, combined geography with Social Darwinism in his 1897 book *Politische Geographie*. He argued that the state was like an organism, seeking to expand its "living space" in the struggle for survival of the fittest. For Ratzel, "Mitteleuropa" represented Germany's natural living space. He was a prominent figure in the nationalist organization *Alldeutscher Verband* (Pan-German League), founded in 1891, and strongly advocated for Germany's colonial expansion in Africa. Karl Haushofer, who was younger, often accompanied his father, Max Haushofer, on walks with Ratzel as a child and was deeply influenced by his ideas.

In 1924, Karl Haushofer co-founded the journal *Zeitschrift für Geopolitik*, which transformed the concept of "geopolitics," initially coined by Swedish pro-German political scientist Johan Rudolf Kjellén, into a focal point for discussion. The *Zeitschrift für Geopolitik* published numerous articles on topics like the theory of national organisms, geographical determinism, Germany's cultural characteristics and historical mission, Anschluss (unification with Austria), the mistakes of the Versailles Treaty, and autarky. "Central Europe" remained a central spatial concept in these discussions.

Besides *Zeitschrift für Geopolitik*, other publications like *Volk und Reich*, *Deutsches Archiv für Landes- und Volksforschung*, and *Deutsche Rundschau*

212 Walther Vogel, *Das Neue Europa und seine historisch-geographischen Grundlagen*, (Bonn: Schroeder, 1925), 416–422.

213 David Thomas Murphy, *The Heroic Earth: Geopolitical Thought in Weimar Germany, 1918–1933*, (Kent State University Press, 1997), 117–125.

were also keen on debating "Mitteleuropa." Scholars such as Heinrich von Srbik, Hans Rothfels, Wilhelm Schüßler, Martin Spahn, and Paul Rohrbach frequently contributed to these discussions.[214]

In the post-World War I era, the German economy experienced numerous crises. Many German industrialists felt that the international geopolitical landscape greatly restricted Germany's ability to access raw materials and export goods. Numerous industrialists joined the *Mitteleuropäische Wirtschaftstag* (Central European Economic Day). In 1929, the board members of the German branch of the organization received comments from German geographers and economists regarding "autarky" in the 1920s. These discussions culminated in a secret memorandum suggesting that the economic integration of Germany and Austria would create the necessary "Lebens-Großraum" (living space for the nation) and lay the foundation for Germany's future rise as a great power (*Großreich*).[215]

Amidst the global economic crisis, the concept of "autarky" gained heightened significance, as Germany could not achieve a self-sufficient system alone. On March 19, 1931, as European countries grappled with deep economic turmoil, Germany and Austria signed a unified tariff agreement aimed at establishing a customs union. However, this plan was met with strong opposition from the French and Czechoslovak governments. The matter was subsequently referred to the Permanent International Court of Justice in The Hague by the League of Nations. In September, the Court ruled that while the customs union did not directly violate the prohibition of *Anschluss* outlined in the Treaty of Versailles, it endangered Austria's economic independence and therefore contravened Protocol I of the Geneva Agreement of October 4, 1922, which prohibited any direct or indirect threat to Austria's independence. Although the Austrian government supported joining the customs union, Germany and Austria were ultimately forced to abandon the plan. This failure triggered a political crisis in the Weimar Republic, contributing to the Nazi Party's success in the German parliamentary elections in 1932, as well as in the elections in Lower Austria, Salzburg, and Vienna.

It is important to note that during the Weimar period, while many German scholars and political and economic elites were deeply concerned with Germany's survival and development, they rarely connected these concerns to the U.S. Monroe Doctrine discourse. Carl Schmitt, however, delved deeply into the relationship between the Monroe Doctrine, imperialism, and the new international order envisioned by Germany. Schmitt's key argument was that the original U.S Monroe Doctrine, limited to the Western Hemisphere, differed

214 Brechtefeld (n. 211), 50.

215 Ibid., 52.

significantly from the global imperialism of the British Empire. He argued that the U.S., by the late 19th century, had expanded beyond the Western Hemisphere and begun to interfere in European and Asian affairs, while the League of Nations itself was an imperialist-interventionist organization. Schmitt believed Germany should adopt its own version of the Monroe Doctrine in Europe, building a "Großraum" (large space) free from external interference. Unlike other theorists who referred to this space as "Mitteleuropa," Schmitt emphasized that his vision of "Großraum" was rooted in the German national spirit.

Schmitt's German "Monroe Doctrine" was articulated in the fourth edition of his book *Völkerrechtliche Großraumordnung mit Interventionsverbot für raumfremde Mächte: Ein Beitrag zum Reichsbegriff für Völkerrecht*, published in the summer of 1941. This work was based on Schmitt's speech "The Principle of Großraum in International Law," delivered on April 1, 1939, at the 25th anniversary of the Institute of Policy and International Law at Kiel University, and his essay "The Concept of Reich in International Law," published in *Deutsches Recht* on April 29, 1939. In this book, Schmitt fully expounded his principle of "Großraum," refining the concept from the Monroe Doctrine and elaborating on his vision for the future of international law. This chapter will explore a series of Schmitt's works criticizing the Versailles Treaty and the League of Nations, culminating in *Der Nomos der Erde*, published in 1950. Although the latter was written after the war, it served as a further synthesis of his earlier ideas, with no major change in tone, thus warranting discussion in this chapter alongside his pre-war works.

To fully understand Schmitt's vision of international law based on "Großraum," it is crucial to first consider its antithesis: the imperialist-interventionist international law based on universalism that emerged after World War I. In Schmitt's view, the U.S. was the primary force driving this universalist-interventionist law, which was advanced through a reinterpretation of the Monroe Doctrine. Though Schmitt was nostalgic for classical European international law, he recognized that the changes occurring were largely irreversible. His concept of "Großraum" international law was an alternative formulated against this backdrop. To grasp the origins of Schmitt's "Großraum" law, we must first examine his analysis of the collapse of classical European international law.

2 The Decay of European Public Law

After World War I, German nationalists were deeply wounded by the repression imposed by the Versailles system. As one of Europe's foremost powers, Germany was publicly humiliated at the Paris Peace Conference—not only were German representatives excluded from negotiations, but the Versailles

Peace Treaty itself was imposed on Germany by the Entente powers as though declaring war. While disagreements between Britain and France over European power dynamics prevented a more devastating blow to Germany, the treaty was harsh compared to how France had been treated at the Congress of Vienna in 1815. Germany lost 13.1% of its pre-war territory and 10% of its population (based on 1910 statistics) and was subjected to severe military and economic restrictions. The Treaty of Versailles also barred Germany from joining the League of Nations, forbade any political union between Germany and Austria, and required German political and military leaders to be handed over for trial by the International Court of Justice. To ensure compliance with the treaty's military provisions, the Entente occupied the Rhineland for 15 years and established its permanent demilitarization. Additionally, the Saar region was separated from the Rhineland, placed under League of Nations administration for 15 years, and subjected to economic control by France.[216]

Schmitt's fundamental criticism of the Versailles Treaty and the League of Nations system was rooted in his belief that, although Germany had adhered to the classical European international law during World War I, the victorious powers, including the U.S., imposed a new set of rules on Germany. These rules, Schmitt argued, were imperialist-interventionist in nature and lacked a homogeneous political foundation, thus incapable of bringing true peace.

First, Schmitt took issue with Article 231 of the Versailles Treaty, which assigned responsibility for the war to Germany and introduced the concept of "war crimes," listing Kaiser Wilhelm II as a war criminal and calling for his trial. For Schmitt, this violated the spirit of classical European public law, which aimed to regulate wars rather than abolish them. Classical war law recognized that, as long as wars were conducted through established procedures and rules, both sides were considered legitimate combatants, neither party inherently criminal or morally unjust. In the 19th century, legal positivists saw war as a morally neutral phenomenon.[217] Carl von Clausewitz, in his *On War* (1832), famously argued that war was a tool for implementing national policies, and in this context, the concept of "aggression" was not central to discussions of war. The notion of "war crimes" traditionally referred to violations of the laws of war during conflict, such as attacks on civilians or the mistreatment of prisoners, but did not encompass the initiation of war itself.

---

216 Felix Gilbert and David Clay Large, *The End of the European Era: 1890 to the Present* (*The Norton History of Modern Europe*), Sixth Edition, (New York: W.W. Norton & Company, 2008).

217 Kaspar Bluntschli, M.C. Lardy trans., *Le Droit International Codifie*, (Paris: Guillaumin, 1870), 282.

In classical European law, the procedure for declaring war was crucial, as it clearly distinguished between neutral and enemy states, making neutrality a morally innocent stance. Since both sides were legitimate combatants, the neutrality of third-party states was accepted without moral judgment. Post-war treaties often included amnesty provisions, ensuring that each side forgave any harms caused by the other's combatants, thereby preventing lingering grievances from sparking future conflicts.[218] *The Versailles Peace Treaty* requiring the transfer and trial of individuals who waged war was in conflict with the amnesty system in classical international law.[219]

Secondly, Schmitt argue treatment of the Rhineland by the Entente and the League of Nations marked a further departure from classical European law. The occupation of the Rhineland for 15 years aimed to create a demilitarized buffer zone between Germany and France, but the region was governed under the auspices of the League of Nations. In Schmitt's view, this did not follow the classical practice of establishing a "neutral state" (as Belgium had been) or a temporary military occupation. Instead, the Rhineland was managed in a way that created a "state within a state," rendering its legal status distinct from that of the rest of Germany.

The disposal of the Rhineland region did not involve the formal cession of territory. Under classical European public law, when the occupation of enemy land resulted in a change of sovereignty, the "succession of states" principle applied: the obligations of the previous state would be inherited by the successor state, even if the two had been at war. This rule of state succession was designed to maintain social and legal order during transitions of power. A notable example of this can be seen after the destruction of the *Königreich Westphalen* (Kingdom of Westphalia) under Napoleon's control. The former *Landgrafschaft Hessen-Kassel* (Landgraviate of Hesse-Kassel) was restored under the new name *Kurfürstentum Hessen* (Electorate of Hesse), and its ruler, Wilhelm I, had to "succeed the state" from the Kingdom of Westphalia, assuming its legal obligations.[220] Residents of the occupied territories would automatically become citizens of the occupying state, while the occupying power was obliged to assume certain responsibilities of the previous government, including some or all of its debts. Though the process of territorial

218 Stephen C. Neff, *War and the Law of Nations: A General History*, (New York: Cambridge University Press, 2005), 117–118.

219 However, European powers still held the concept of classical international law. Wilhelm II was protected by Belgium, a neutral country. After many unsuccessful efforts, Britain and France finally gave up extradition.

220 Carl Schmitt, *Der Nomos der Erde*, (Berlin: Duncker & Humbolt, 1997), 184.

cession was harsh, it allowed those living in ceded areas to acquire new citizenship, preventing them from becoming stateless and thus reducing the risk of being reduced to mere objects in the international political arena.

However, more importantly, in Schmitt's view, the Versailles Treaty broke the division of political space between Europe and non-Europe in classical international law by applying methods typically reserved for "semi-civilized" and "barbaric" regions to a European "civilized state." Classical European international law was based on the consensus of European great powers: there was a clear internal/external distinction between European and non-European lands, between suzerain states and colonies. This was not only a legal distinction but also a spatial one based on a hierarchy of civilization. Europe, where the colonial suzerains were located, was regarded as the space of civilization, and international law was the product of this space, fully implemented only in civilized nations. Outside Europe, except for states founded by European descendants such as the U.S., there were semi-civilized countries with incomplete sovereignty and savage tribes without any sovereignty.[221] The mission of colonization was to spread the so-called "civilization" globally, and only countries that met the standard of civilization set by European powers could be recognized as members of the "family of nations"—a club of great powers with full sovereignty. This theory of the hierarchy of civilization ensured the *Homogenität* (homogeneity) of the club of great powers. In Schmitt's view, the Versailles Treaty denied Germany the dignity it deserved as a European great power by equating it with many non-European countries. This, he argued, degraded Europe itself.

Specifically, on the issue of the Rhineland, Schmitt pointed out in his 1925 commentary *Die Rheinlande als Objekt internationaler Politik*: "The form and method of turning a part of a country and its people into an international political object have changed, which is different from the 19th century."[222] In the 19th Century European public international law implemented this "objectification" by annexing territory. Historically, there was a tug-of-war over Alsace-Lorraine, exemplifying the classical public international law of the

221 The most typical expression comes from James Larimer, whose three-part expressions are civilized humanity, barbarous humanity, savage humanity, see James Lorimer, *The Institutions of the Law of Nations*, Vol. 1, (Edinburgh & London: William Blackwood and Sons, 1883), 101. Some scholars interpret this as the key to determining what a civilized country is, that is, the willingness and ability of these countries to protect the lives, freedoms and property of European travelers and businessmen, see Georg Schwarzenberger, *The Frontiers of International Law*, (London: Stevens and Sons, 1962), 71.

222 Carl Schmitt, "Die Rheinlande als Objekt internationaler Politik," *Positionen und Begriffe im Kampf mit Weimar-Genf-Versailles 1923–1940*, (Berlin: Duncker & Humbolt, 1994), 19.

time. The old dynastic states sought territory and population, believing that increasing population equated to increased national strength.[223] However, as nationalism began to outweigh dynastic legitimacy, countries emphasizing ethnic homogeneity developed a repulsive attitude toward residents of different nationalities. These nations were less willing to share the benefits of imperial expansion with heterogeneous populations and were reluctant to assume more obligations under the "succession of states" principle. Since foreigners were regarded as burdens rather than assets, international law had to create corresponding rules to retain substantial control over foreign-inhabited lands without granting them citizenship.

Firstly, the European powers established a "protectorate" system for "semi-civilized" countries. Under this system, while these countries retained nominal internal independence, their foreign policy and certain aspects of domestic governance were controlled by the protecting power. By the 20th century, however, even the "protectorate" system appeared outdated. The more modern approach was to grant these weaker nations symbolic sovereignty and the right to make diplomatic decisions while occupying strategically important areas under the guise of "supervision" or ensuring dominance through economic exploitation and exclusive investment rights.[224] For example, what Britain did in Egypt and what the United States did in Cuba, Haiti, the Dominican Republic, Panama, and other Latin American countries exemplified this new mode of domination. Following World War I, Germany's overseas colonies were placed under the League of Nations' mandate system, which avoided outright political annexation. Non-European populations subjected to this form of control were granted a degree of autonomy, but they remained under the intervention of the supervising powers and were not integrated as citizens under the "succession of states" principle in classical European international law. Instead, they were more likely to be treated as mere "objects" of international politics.

Traditionally, these forms of domination were originally directed at non-European "semi-civilized" and "savage" peoples. However, World War I blurred the distinction between "civilization" and "barbarism" when European powers brought colonial armies composed of non-white soldiers to fight on the European continent. Schmitt observed that the Versailles Treaty applied the same traditional European methods used for dealing with non-European "semi-civilized" peoples to Germany, further undermining the privileged status of Europe within classical international law. In his view, this was akin to

223 Ibid., 22.
224 Ibid., 21.

allowing serfs to participate in a duel meant for nobles, which would inevitably destabilize the entire noble system. Schmitt argued that the Treaty of Versailles "contains some dangerous and uncertain concepts which may become the basis for regular intervention," referring to mechanisms such as sanctions, reparations, investigations, and occupations. The power to interpret these measures was monopolized by the victorious powers, leaving Germany in a state of ongoing uncertainty.[225] The victors imposed restrictions on Germany, including the prohibition of fortifications, the banning of permanent or temporary military deployments or gatherings in certain areas, and the outlawing of military exercises or any actions that could be seen as preparations for mobilization.[226] In Schmitt's view, the Entente had effectively legalized politics, punishing Germany under the guise of international law.

Compared with the order pursued by the Holy Alliance in the 19th century, the principle behind Germany's punishment was vague. The Holy Alliance had grounded European order on the principle of dynastic monarchism, establishing a "concert of powers" to ensure mutual support in preventing the rise of popular rebellions like the French Revolution. This system had a clear political basis for distinguishing between enemies and allies. For example, France, despite being the source of the Napoleonic Wars, was not harshly punished at the Congress of Vienna but was reintegrated into the Pentarchy after the restoration of the Bourbon monarchy. In contrast, the Entente's punishment of Germany after World War I lacked such a clear principle of legitimacy, despite being legalized by international law.

Had the classical European public law undergone such significant changes only after World War I? Schmitt argued that the post-war situation was part of a longer process of decline. In the 19th century, the theory of the hierarchy of civilization that underpinned European public law had already faced challenges. In the Western Hemisphere, the United States, with its vast territory and growing population, emerged from the Civil War and the Gilded Age with immense economic success, particularly through the Second Industrial Revolution. With new interpretations of the Monroe Doctrine of 1823, the U.S. expanded its sphere of influence beyond the Americas, vying for global hegemony. Similarly, in Asia, after its victories in the 1894–1895 Sino-Japanese War and the 1904–1905 Russo-Japanese War, Japan was recognized as a member of the "Family of Nations," the exclusive club of great powers. In 1902, Britain and Japan signed a formal alliance treaty as equals. Like the U.S., Japan had developed its own vision of regional order and sought to establish

225 Schmitt (n. 222), 24.

226 Ibid., 26.

hegemony in Asia. The rise of these two non-European powers—the U.S. and Japan—posed a serious challenge to the previously dominant European land, space, and civilization. European international law, long considered a product of European civilization, was now being diluted by the growing influence of these non-European powers.

But the challenge to Europe's dominance didn't only come from external forces. Schmitt argued that Europeans themselves, consciously or unconsciously, blurred the distinction between Europe and its colonies. Schmitt was particularly concerned with how the European powers handled the Congo issue. King Leopold II of Belgium, a neutral state guaranteed by Europe's great powers, spearheaded European colonization in Congo. Since the Belgian government lacked the desire to colonize overseas, Leopold II established the International Association of the Congo (also known as the International Congo Society) in his own name, using the association to carry out colonization, primarily by acquiring land from local African chiefs. Britain, France, and Portugal also engaged in colonization in Congo, and as conflicts between them escalated, German Chancellor Bismarck convened the Berlin Conference (also called the "Congo Conference") in 1884, bringing together 14 nations to resolve these colonial disputes through diplomatic means.

The Berlin Conference is often remembered for its division of Africa, but Schmitt believed the most significant consequence was how the powers handled Congo. Before and during the conference, Leopold II lobbied the elites of various nations, presenting his colonization efforts as promoting "civilization and progress" in Congo. Germany, as host of the conference, recognized the Congo International Association's sovereignty over the "Congo Free State," though Schmitt seemed to downplay Germany's role in this recognition. The U.S. did not participate in the conference but had already acknowledged the Congo International Association's sovereignty over its seized lands before the conference began, setting a precedent for recognizing new states on African soil. Schmitt noted that the U.S. displayed a "mixture of absence in principle and presence in practice" regarding the Berlin Conference, a stance it would later replicate toward the League of Nations.[227] During the conference, representatives from France and Portugal proposed treating overseas territories and colonies as equal to European sovereign states. In Schmitt's view, this set a dangerous precedent by blurring the distinction between European territories and non-European colonies.[228] The powers at the Berlin Conference formally recognized Leopold II's personal occupation and rule over the Congo

227 Schmitt (n. 220), 198.
228 Ibid., 201–202.

River Basin. The Congo Free State (Kongo-Freistaat) under his control was acknowledged as a neutral sovereign state until 1908, when the Belgian government assumed control of Congo from Leopold II.

If the Berlin Conference broke the political distinction between European territories and colonial lands, Schmitt emphasized that the rise of legal positivism made the situation even worse. In 1885, Belgian jurists still acknowledged that the Congo Free State was established based on the collective recognition of European powers, with at least some level of shared European identity playing a role. However, by the early 20th century, when Belgian jurists revisited the legal basis of the Congo Free State, they had forgotten the original premise of political space division. Instead, they cited "effective occupation" as the sole legal foundation for acquiring "open space." In their view, the creation of the Congo Free State was not rooted in the collective recognition of European powers, nor in the numerous agreements between colonizers and local chiefs, but solely in "effective occupation." Schmitt sarcastically noted that these jurists, who relied on the principle of "effective occupation," estimated the population under Belgian rule in Congo to be anywhere between 14 and 30 million people. What an "effective" occupation indeed![229]

The core issue, according to Schmitt, was that "by the end of the 19th century, European powers and the jurists of European international law had not only lost awareness of the spatial foundations of their own international law, but had also lost the political instinct and collective power to maintain their spatial structure and the bracketing of war."[230] Through balance and cooperation, European powers had previously maintained the political space division essential for the effective operation of European public international law. But when every major power pursued "effective occupation" unilaterally, ignoring the established political structure, the order based on the "balance of power" and "concert of powers"—with a degree of shared values and cohesion—was bound to collapse.

3 The Structural Vulnerability of the Versailles System

In Schmitt's view, the Treaty of Versailles itself symbolized the decline of the classical European public law order. The 1919 Paris Peace Conference marked a shift from "Europe deciding the world order" to "the world deciding the order

229 Schmitt (n. 220), 204.

230 Ibid., 205. Also see Carl Schmitt, *The Nomos of the Earth*, translated and annotated by G.L. Ulmen, (New York: Telos Press Publishing), 224.

of Europe."[231] This "world," of course, referred to the major powers outside of Europe, particularly the U.S. and Japan. Although the League of Nations, established after World War I, was still dominated by Britain and France, it was no longer capable of maintaining the balance within Europe, let alone managing global order.

One of the most significant changes to public international law after World War I was the transformation of the law of war. The Covenant of the League of Nations in 1919 did not entirely abandon the classical European international law regarding warfare.[232] Articles 10–17 stipulated that any state initiating war without following specific procedures would be considered a peacebreaker, and other League members could impose sanctions—financial, economic, or military—on the aggressor. However, the League did not criminalize war itself. Schmitt observed: "The idea of the equality of rights for all states, based on equal sovereignty, remained so strong in 1919 that the League Covenant could only implicitly contain a criminal prohibition of war."[233] However, the Geneva Protocol of 1924 (formally known as the Protocol for the Pacific Settlement of International Disputes), discussed at the fifth meeting of the League of Nations, marked a significant step forward. It stipulated that acts of aggression and wars of aggression were to be considered international crimes, with the state itself, rather than individuals, being identified as the subject of these crimes. In cases where an aggressor state refused to submit to arbitration by the League, Article 16 of the League Covenant could be invoked, allowing for the imposition of economic, financial, and military sanctions on the violator.

Schmitt believed that the Geneva Protocol reflected the influence of U.S. views,[234] a judgment supported by historical precedent. In 1890, the U.S. government convened the first Pan-American Conference in Washington, where it discussed a proposal combining compulsory arbitration with the prohibition of territorial conquest. The proposal stipulated that during the validity of an arbitration treaty, any forced territorial cession made under the threat of war or military presence would be considered invalid, and such actions should be submitted to arbitration. Additionally, any waiver of the right to arbitration under the threat of war would be deemed null and void.[235] Since the signing of the Jay Treaty with Britain in 1794, mediation had been a standard tool for

---

231 Schmitt (n. 220), 222.

232 The total abandonment of the classical laws of war did not happen until the end of World War II. Ibid., 286–299.

233 Ibid., 252. Also see Carl Schmitt, *The Nomos of The Earth*, translated and annotated by G.L. Ulmen, (New York: Telos Press Publishing), 270.

234 Schmitt (n. 220), 253.

235 Boyle (n. 119), 104–107.

the U.S. government in resolving international disputes.[236] However, the prohibition of conquest proposed by the first Pan-American Conference never materialized into an effective international treaty. The Geneva Protocol sought to apply on a global scale what the U.S. had attempted in Latin America. Nevertheless, the conservative British government that returned to power in 1925 rejected the protocol, and it was subsequently shelved by the major Western powers.

The U.S. concept of war resurfaced with the signing of the Kellogg-Briand Pact in August 1928. By 1933, 63 countries, including the Soviet Union, Turkey, and others not yet part of the League of Nations, had ratified or acceded to the Convention. Schmitt observed, "The Western Hemisphere now took its place and determined the further development of the transformation of the meaning of war."[237] Article 1 of the Convention declared: "The High Contracting Parties solemnly declare in the names of their respective peoples that they condemn recourse to war for the solution of international controversies and renounce it as an instrument of national policy in their relations with one another."[238] This article directly rejected the classical view of the law of war as articulated by Carl von Clausewitz in *On War* (1832), which framed war as a tool for implementing state policies. According to the Kellogg-Briand Pact, all disputes or conflicts between states, regardless of their nature or causes, were to be resolved solely by peaceful means. However, the Pact did not specify how to judge or prevent violations of these principles. The U.S. also reserved room for its Monroe Doctrine in Latin America through its interpretation of the Pact.[239]

A key issue remained: how to define "war" and "aggression"? Schmitt viewed this as an immensely complex challenge. He noted the rise of a formalist approach to defining these terms, which focused on the territorial status quo without considering its historical origins. This approach, Schmitt argued, was ripe for abuse. For example, if the territorial status quo was the result of prior invasions by a powerful state, any attempts by a weaker state to reclaim lost territory could be labeled as "aggression." Schmitt's concern was closely tied to Germany's own situation. At the Paris Peace Conference, Germany had lost significant territory, and the Rhineland had been designated as a demilitarized

236 Xiaohang Chen, *The Imagination of Alternatives: The History of International Arbitration in the Late Nineteenth Century 1863–1888* (Ph.D. dissertation, European University Institute, 2022).

237 Schmitt (n. 220), 262. Also see Carl Schmitt, *The Nomos of The Earth*, translated and annotated by G.L. Ulmen, (New York: Telos Press Publishing), 280.

238 Kellogg-Briand Pact, 27 Aug.1928, 46 Stat. 2343, 2345–46 (Pt. 2).

239 FO 414/262, Sir Austen Chamberlain to Mr. Houghton, 19 May 1928, 175.

zone. If that moment were taken as the baseline, any effort by Germany to recover lost territory and restore national unity could be construed as "aggression."[240]

In *Völkerrechtliche Formen des modernen Imperialismus* (Forms of International Law in Modern Imperialism), written in 1932, Schmitt further emphasized that the key aspect of the Kellogg-Briand Pact was the dominant role played by the U.S., a non-member of the League of Nations. Although the pact was not integrated into the League's framework, the U.S. could exploit its ambiguity, particularly in its definition of "war," to unilaterally decide what constituted a "war." Schmitt argued that the U.S.'s ability to manipulate broad and undefined concepts to maintain its dominance was a hallmark of "imperialism."[241]

In hindsight, we know that the Kellogg-Briand Pact did not function in the way Schmitt had feared. After the Japanese army occupied Jinzhou, China, on January 3, 1932, U.S. Secretary of State Henry Lewis Stimson sent a note to the Chinese and Japanese governments on January 7, declaring that any violation of the Nine-Power Treaty, signed at the Washington Conference in 1922, and the Kellogg-Briand Pact of 1928—particularly concerning China's sovereignty, territorial integrity, and the Open Door Policy—would undermine U.S. interests and would not be recognized by the U.S. government. Stimson had attempted to rally Britain and France for support prior to issuing the note, but both countries responded with indifference, leaving the U.S. without sufficient international backing to pressure Japan. Shortly after the signing of the Kellogg-Briand Pact, it was already proving ineffective in managing international disputes, such as those triggered by the Mukden Incident. This outcome underscored the fact that, following the peak of Wilsonian internationalism in 1919–1920, the U.S. had retreated to a Western Hemisphere-focused mindset. While it sought greater influence in the Eastern Hemisphere, it remained unwilling to shoulder the corresponding responsibilities.

Amid the global economic crisis of 1929–1933, foreign powers began shifting their domestic conflicts outward, leading to an intensified arms race. Under the auspices of the League of Nations, the World Disarmament Conference was held between 1932 and 1934. However, the conference saw significant disputes between Germany and France. Germany demanded equal rights to rearm, while France insisted that disarmament could only proceed with sufficient

---

240 Carl Schmitt, "Der Status quo und der Friede," in *Positionen und Begriffe im Kampf mit Weimar-Genf-Versailles 1923–1940*, (Berlin: Duncker & Humbolt, 1994), 32.

241 Carl Schmitt, "Völkerrechtliche Formen des modernen Imperialismus," in *Positionen und Begriffe im Kampf mit Weimar-Genf-Versailles 1923–1940*, (Berlin: Duncker & Humbolt, 1994), 176–177.

security guarantees. Britain and the U.S. were unwilling to provide these guarantees, and the Soviet Union, which had long been isolated by the great powers, advocated for universal, comprehensive, and immediate disarmament. At the London Conference in July 1933, the Soviet Union's definition of "aggression" and "aggressor" greatly influenced the debate. Schmitt observed: "The axis of power that had created the concept of war in European international law became unhinged, as power in the East and in the West came to dominate European states no longer certain of themselves."[242] Despite the involvement of the U.S. and the Soviet Union, no substantial progress was made. In October 1933, Germany withdrew from the Disarmament Conference, and although discussions continued for a time, the conference ultimately ended in failure.

While efforts to eliminate war under the Versailles-Washington system were unsuccessful, the pursuit of this goal did not disappear with the collapse of the system. Schmitt argued that the London Agreement of August 8, 1945, signed by the Soviet Union, the U.S., Britain, and France (the Agreement for the Prosecution and Punishment of the Major War Criminals of the European Axis), marked the moment when the East and West finally united, and the process of criminalizing war began. From this perspective, the Nuremberg Trials of 1945 and the Tokyo Trials of 1946 were simply extensions of the "non-war" concept introduced a decade earlier. However, Schmitt questioned the implications of labeling the enemy as a "criminal," as this could create a moral obligation for third parties to join in the punishment. As a result, he argued, true neutrality became impossible, and the scale of war could easily spiral out of control.

Schmitt consistently criticized the League of Nations during the interwar period. As early as 1926, the year Germany was allowed to join the League, Schmitt wrote "*Das Doppelgesicht des Genfer Völkerbundes*" (*The Two Faces of the League of Nations in Geneva*) to caution German public opinion. He argued that the League of Nations was submissive and cautious when dealing with Western powers (referring to the U.S.), but in front of weaker, disarmed countries (such as Germany), it adopted a stern and authoritarian posture, supposedly upholding strict law. Schmitt warned that, without clear principles or established norms, the League was adjudicating the most dangerous conflicts in the name of law, which risked triggering significant international political

242 Schmitt (n. 220), 262. Also see Carl Schmitt, *The Nomos of The Earth*, translated and annotated by G.L. Ulmen, (New York: Telos Press Publishing), 280.

opposition.[243] In 1928, Schmitt further criticized that the League was neither a true European organization nor a genuine universal alliance.[244] By 1936, in "*Die siebente Wandlung des Genfer Völkerbundes*" (*The Seventh Change of the League of Nations*), he commented on the League's inability to prevent one of its members (Italy) from annexing another member (Abyssinia). These critiques underscored Schmitt's view that the League's fundamental problem was that, despite its appearance of universality, its members lacked homogeneity. Particularly, the major powers did not recognize each other's political boundaries. Without a clear plan for dividing political space, even with various rules of international law on paper, the League was incapable of resolving political conflicts involving great powers.

Why, then, could the League of Nations not effectively maintain international order? Schmitt argued that the Vienna Conference of 1814–1815 succeeded in creating an effective European order because it convened all the truly influential European powers and forged a consensus on the arrangement of European space. If the League of Nations aimed to create a peaceful global order, it should have included the world's influential powers and formed a consensus on global arrangements. However, the League excluded two key players: Germany, the defeated nation, and Soviet Russia, which rejected the capitalist order. Moreover, the U.S., one of the key proponents of the League, ultimately chose not to join. This absence of essential powers made it impossible to establish a new and stable political order. As a result, the League could not reach substantive decisions on the truly critical global issues.[245] When examining the relationship between the world's major powers and the League of Nations, an extremely complicated picture emerges:

Firstly, the United States, despite not joining the League of Nations, managed to influence many of its affairs without having to take responsibility for its actions. The League of Nations incorporated the recognition of the Monroe Doctrine into Article 21 of its Covenant, effectively relinquishing any substantive jurisdiction over relations between American countries or between an American country and a non-American country. While the U.S. Senate rejected the Covenant, preventing the U.S. from officially joining the League, many American countries were members of the League, allowing the U.S. to indirectly shape their foreign policies. As a result, the relationship between

243 Carl Schmitt, "Das Doppelgesicht des Genfer Völkerbundes," in *Positionen und Begriffe im Kampf mit Weimar-Genf-Versailles 1923–1940*, (Berlin: Duncker & Humbolt, 1994), 34–36.

244 Carl Schmitt, "Der Völkerbund und Europa," in *Positionen und Begriffe im Kampf mit Weimar-Genf-Versailles 1923–1940*, (Berlin: Duncker & Humbolt, 1994), 84–91.

245 Schmitt (n. 243), 84.

the U.S. and the League of Nations became a peculiar blend of "absence" and "presence." Schmitt noted that during the signing of several treaties in the League of Nations era, American citizens participated, although they did not officially represent the American government.[246] The separation between politics and economics, a common practice in the U.S., also played a significant role.[247] Through their economic power, Americans could influence the League's activities without bearing political responsibility. The U.S. often acted as an arbitrator between the victorious and defeated nations within the League, while the League itself, constrained by the narrow self-interests of certain great powers, failed to fulfill its role as a true arbitrator or a genuinely universal organization.[248]

Secondly, although Japan participated in the creation of the League of Nations and served as a permanent member, it maintained a highly opportunistic stance towards the organization. In the 1870s, Japanese ruling elites learned about the discourse and practice of the U.S. Monroe Doctrine from Charles W. Le Gendre, a French-American advisor hired by Japan's Ministry of Foreign Affairs. Le Gendre suggested that Japan adopt a "Japanese Monroe Doctrine" to dominate Asia, ostensibly to prevent European expansion.[249] After the Russo-Japanese War in 1905, U.S. President Theodore Roosevelt encouraged Kaneko Kentarō, a Japanese diplomatic representative and advisor, to promote an "Asiatic Monroe Doctrine."[250] Japan's expansion into the Korean Peninsula and Northeast China was underpinned by this idea. During World War I, Japan took advantage of the European powers' preoccupation with the war to further expand its influence in China. This was even acknowledged by the United States in the Lansing-Ishii Agreement, signed on November 2, 1917, which recognized Japan's "special interests" in China. In 1919, U.S. President Woodrow Wilson attempted to enshrine the U.S. Monroe Doctrine in the Western Hemisphere into Article 21 of the Covenant of the League of Nations. This led some Japanese elites to believe that such recognition should apply to Japan's sphere of influence in Asia as well. However, the Nine-Power Treaty signed at the Washington

246 Ibid., 103.

247 Schmitt quoted Hegel's comment that the U.S. is only a civil society, not a country, and Marx's similar criticism of the U.S. to strengthen his argument. Schmitt (n. 220), 275–276.

248 Schmitt (n. 243), 89–90.

249 Sophia Su-fei Yen, *Taiwan in China's Foreign Relations, 1836–1874*, (Hamden, CT: Shoe String Press, 1965), 196.

250 Kaneko Kentaro 金子堅太郎, 東洋の平和はアジアモンロー主義にあり [*Peace in the Orient lies in Asian Monroeism*], (Kokikai, 1937), 16–19. See also Carl Schmitt: "Großraum gegen Universalismus," in *Positionen und Begriffe im Kampf mit Weimar-Genf-Versailles 1923–1940*, (Berlin: Duncker & Humbolt, 1994), 338.

Conference in 1922 reinforced the collective control of foreign powers over China and curtailed Japan's claims to "special interests" in the region. After the Mukden Incident in 1931, when Japan sought to establish the puppet state of Manchukuo in Northeast China, the U.S. and the League of Nations opposed these actions. Japanese officials argued that it was unjust for the Covenant of the League of Nations to permit the U.S. to pursue the Monroe Doctrine in the Americas while denying Japan the right to adopt a similar approach in Asia. Eventually, Japan withdrew from the League of Nations and openly embraced the concept of an "Asiatic Monroe Doctrine."

Thirdly, the structural instability of the League of Nations was also reflected in the serious differences between France and Britain, its core members, regarding the arrangement of European order. Schmitt pointed out that Britain had a global vision based on an ocean-centered concept of "maintaining the status quo," which made it more flexible in dealing with European border issues—what was actually implied here is that, after World War I, Britain still tried to contain France and used Germany as leverage, so it had reservations about severely retaliating against Germany. However, as a European country, France's understanding of "maintaining the status quo" differed significantly within the closer confines of European space. At the Paris Peace Conference, it was France that strongly advocated for harsh punishment of Germany. The concepts of land-based order and ocean-based order were uneasily combined in the League of Nations, but the tension between them never fully resolved.[251]

Schmitt wrote the article "Die siebente Wandlung des Genfer Völkerbundes" (The Seventh Transformation of the Geneva League of Nations) in 1936 to discuss Italy's annexation of Abyssinia, a fellow League of Nations member. In response to this annexation, Schmitt sharply pointed out that the League of Nations lacked any true sense of community. So far, there were actually seven League of Nations: the first was the League of Nations advocated by Wilson. The second was the one in which the U.S. failed to join in 1920 and Britain, France, Italy, and Japan were permanent members of the Council. The third was the one after Germany joined in 1926. The fourth was the one after Japan withdrew in 1933. The fifth was the one after Germany withdrew in 1933. The sixth was the one which the Soviet Union joined and became a permanent member in 1934. The seventh was the one which allowed Italy to annex another member, Abyssinia, in 1936. Schmitt commented: "No real world organization can exist with the withdrawal and participation of extremely different members. In and out like this, people think of restaurants, not an alliance.

251 Schmitt (n. 220), 226–227.

Or any lasting political order and organization."[252] The League of Nations remained the same league only in name; it lacked homogeneity and continuity in spirit and essence.

The challenge put forward by Italy in 1936 was that it used the discourse of 19th-century "hierarchy of civilization" to argue that Abyssinia was just a collection of savage tribes, unqualified as a sovereign state, making its inclusion in the League of Nations a mistake. Britain, a member of the League of Nations, let each member state decide whether to recognize Italy's annexation or not, and took the lead in recognizing it. This raised a sharp question—on what basis did the League of Nations decide membership? Schmitt criticized the League of Nations for lacking "homogeneity" and explicitly used the word "Homogenität." This was exactly the word he used when explaining Rousseau's theory of popular sovereignty.[253] In Schmitt's view, the key to people's integration into a political community lied in their "homogeneity." Putting the same principle on the international level, a stable alliance also needed to establish some "homogeneity" among members. The experience of the Vienna system in the 19th century could show that such homogeneity needed the recognition of a common spatial order and a shared discourse on civilization. However, in a highly mobile "restaurant" atmosphere, where every participant brought their own view of order and civilization, it was impossible to produce an effective concrete order.

From the end of World War I to the outbreak of World War II, Europe lacked a clear spatial order and instead was governed by a patchwork of vague and conflicting rules of public international law. There was no genuine consensus among the various visions of order proposed by European powers. This resulted in what Schmitt saw as the illusion of prosperity in positivist jurisprudence. Lawyers, driven by professional self-interest, focused on perpetuating formal rules, appearing diligent in interpreting numerous international treaties but having little practical impact on the realities of international politics. For Schmitt, this legalistic focus obscured the deeper crisis facing the international order. He argued that lawyers often forgot that positive law must rest on more fundamental norms, or *Nomos*. The true importance of these

252 Carl Schmitt, "Die siebente Wandlung des Genfer Völkerbundes," in *Positionen und Begriffe im Kampf mit Weimar-Genf-Versailles 1923–1940*, (Berlin: Duncker & Humbolt, 1994): 214.

253 "On the whole and in every detail of its political existence, democracy presupposes a people whose members are similar to one another and who have the will to political existence. Under this presupposition, it is thoroughly correct when Rousseau states that what the people will is always good. Such a principle is correct not on the basis of a norm. It is correct because a people's existence is based on its homogeneity." Carl Schmitt, *Verfassungslehre*, (Berlin: Duncker & Humbolt, 2010), 235.

norms lies in their ability to establish a stable division of political space. At the international level, the stability of political arrangements depends on both the objective balance of power and a shared subjective consensus on order. Without a stable power structure among the great powers, the positive laws and regulations lack a solid foundation. In such a context, each party's legal interpretation of the rules merely extends their ongoing power struggle. Schmitt, deeply influenced by Hobbes, maintained a profound skepticism toward human language—without a stable allocation of interpretive authority, the act of interpretation alone cannot create a lasting or concrete order.

4 The Großraum Order and the New International Law

How could international law, influenced by "imperialism," be reformed after World War I? In *Völkerrechtliche Probleme im Rheingebiet* (The International Law Issues in the Rhineland), published in 1928, Schmitt anticipated a profound political reorganization in the contemporary world. He argued that the development of modern technology was diminishing the significance of certain political organizations and borders from previous eras: "The earth is getting smaller," he noted, and nations and national systems would inevitably become larger. "Several huge complexes will still exist. According to the common sense of human beings, the era that can be expected may let people enjoy unexpected human happiness based on brand-new technological capabilities. Some smaller entities will gain their own security under the shadow of a wealthy giant."[254] Schmitt urged his German readers to reflect on whether Germany would become a global power capable of enduring into the future or whether it would fall into a state of mental and moral decline.

The thoughts expressed in this 1928 commentary developed further between 1939 and 1941. In the fourth edition of *Völkerrechtliche Großraumordnung und Interventionsverbot für raumfremde Mächte. Ein Beitrag zum Reichsbegriff im Völkerrecht*, published in the summer of 1941, Schmitt examined how to extract core elements from the American Monroe Doctrine and apply them to the construction of a new international order for Germany.

Schmitt clarified that his intention was not to transplant the Monroe Doctrine directly to Germany, but to analyze its core principles and consider how to adapt them to different geopolitical spaces and historical contexts. He recognized that the difficulty lay in the ambiguity of the Monroe Doctrine's

254 Carl Schmitt, "Völkerrechtliche Probleme im Rheingebiet," in *Positionen und Begriffe im Kampf mit Weimar-Genf-Versailles 1923–1940*, (Berlin: Duncker & Humbolt, 1994), 102.

normative implications. From the 19th to the 20th century, the Monroe Doctrine had evolved from a principle of resisting external interference within a defined spatial boundary to a rationale for legitimizing U.S. imperialism. The U.S. government's interpretation of the Monroe Doctrine was highly flexible, giving the impression that the doctrine could be molded to suit any situation as needed. As a result, international law textbooks did not address whether the Monroe Doctrine constituted a principle of international law, leaving positivist jurists uncertain about its meaning.[255]

However, Schmitt argued that this ambiguity could be transformed into a form of decisionistic certainty. He referenced a 1923 discussion by U.S. Secretary of State Charles Evans Hughes about the "true" meaning of the Monroe Doctrine, emphasizing that only the U.S. government could define, interpret, and approve the doctrine's meaning. Schmitt considered this a quintessential example of "Dezisionismus."[256] The term "Dezisionismus" is derived from the Latin words *decidere* and *caedere*, meaning "to cut off" debates and dialogues. In matters involving the Monroe Doctrine, the U.S. government acted like a Roman dictator—its decisions were unpredictable, but its authority to cut off debate was absolute. This, according to Schmitt, was the essence of "decisionistic certainty."

The Monroe Doctrine has been interpreted in various ways throughout history, making any general discussion about it inherently ambiguous. To address this, Schmitt focused his analysis on what he considered the authentic, original version of the Monroe Doctrine, as articulated by President Monroe in 1823. This doctrine contrasted sharply with the principle of monarchical legitimacy promoted by the Holy Alliance. After the Congress of Vienna, European dynastic states elevated the concept of dynastic orthodoxy to a principle of international order, justifying the great powers' intervention in republican revolutions. If this principle were applied to the Americas, it would inevitably lead to European monarchies interfering in the American Revolution. However, the colonial peoples in the Americas had politically awakened and recognized that their continent operated under a political principle distinct from that of European monarchies. This realization became the foundation for their rejection of external interference. Thus, the regional order of republics in the Americas developed a form of "homogeneity" that was fundamentally

255 Carl Schmitt, "Völkerrechtliche Großraumordnung mit Interventionsverbot für raumfremde Mächte: Ein Beitrag zum Reichsbegriff für Völkerrecht," in *Staat, Großraum, Nomos: Arbeiten aus den Jahren 1916–1969*, (Berlin: Duncker & Humblot, 1995), 278–280.

256 Carl Schmitt, *Staat, Grossraum, Nomos: Arbeiten aus den Jahren 1916–1969*, (Berlin: Duncker & Humblot, 1995), 281.

different from that of Europe. Schmitt identified the organic link between a politically awakened nation, its governing principles, and the "Großraum" (large space) governed by these principles, suggesting that this relationship could be applied to other regions, historical contexts, and distinctions between friends and enemies globally.[257]

It is unlikely that Schmitt was aware of Whitelaw Reid's 1903 vision of three different Monroe Doctrines. As previously noted, in a speech at Yale Law School, Reid used the U.S. Monroe Doctrine as a reference point and speculated that European powers in Africa might promote a "European Monroe Doctrine" based on constitutional monarchy. He also imagined that Russia and China could propose an "Asiatic Monroe Doctrine" founded on autocratic monarchy in Asia. Both, according to Reid, could play a role in countering U.S. expansion.[258] Reid's ideas aligned with Schmitt's principles of homogeneity and hostility. The tripartite opposition between America, Europe-Africa, and Asia closely resembled Schmitt's vision of a multipolar world order. However, Reid did not fully grasp that regional "homogeneity" based on a particular form of government was only feasible under specific historical conditions. The Holy Alliance, for example, inspired the American republics to develop their self-awareness regarding political principles. Yet, the "homogeneity" championed by the Holy Alliance—rooted in monarchical and dynastic principles—began to decline with the rise of nationalism in Europe. As European dynasties and aristocracies increasingly sought to emphasize their alignment with their nations' common people, rather than underscoring the differences between the transnational aristocratic elites and the populations they governed, the status of monarchical and dynastic principles as a basis for "homogeneity" was significantly weakened.

To clarify the characteristics of the original Monroe Doctrine, Schmitt contrasted it with the spatial perspective of the British Empire. The fundamental principle guiding British policy was the security of the transport routes that sustained its global empire. This principle was fundamentally different from the original Monroe Doctrine. The Monroe Doctrine focused on a continuous geographic space—the American continent—whereas the British Empire comprised a collection of non-contiguous territories scattered across the globe. The Monroe Doctrine sought to protect a new political idea against interference from conservative European powers by excluding external influence, while the British Empire prioritized the security of its imperial trade

257 Schmitt (n. 255), 281–283.

258 Whitelaw Reid, "The Monroe Doctrine; The Polk Doctrine; Anarchism," *Yale Law Journal* 13 (1903).

routes, seeking to maintain a status quo rather than promoting any specific political ideology.

The British approach was not directed towards the control of a continuous political space but rather emphasized securing the connections between its various possessions. As a result, Britain often framed its geopolitical interests in terms of "humanity" or universal values. For example, Article 8 of the Anglo-Egyptian Treaty signed on August 2, 1936, stated that "In view of the fact that the Suez Canal, whilst being an integral part of Egypt, is a universal means of communication as also an essential means of communication between the different parts of the British Empire," Britain would assume responsibility for the protection of the Suez Canal until Egypt could manage it independently. This argument positioned British interests as aligned with global interests, a typical rhetorical approach for Britain. When Britain was confident in its power, it would directly control such strategic points; when it was less secure, it aimed for internationalization and neutrality. In the Americas, Britain sought control over the Panama Canal but encountered resistance from the Monroe Doctrine, which stressed the regional unity of the Americas. Similarly, after World War I, Britain tried to internationalize and neutralize the Kiel Canal.

Schmitt argued that Britain translated its claims into international law through the concept of "freedom of the seas," which carried connotations of natural law. However, in practical terms, "freedom of the Dardanelles Strait" meant that British warships could pass through the Turkish strait unimpeded to attack the Russian Empire. In Schmitt's analysis, Britain's advocacy for freedom, humanity, and universal values to support its borderless empire should not be dismissed merely as hypocrisy or deception. Instead, it reflected the intrinsic link between a particular mode of political existence and a corresponding way of thinking in international law.[259]

Britain also directly referenced the "Monroe Doctrine" to justify its own geopolitical claims. In 1928, when Britain signed the Pact of Paris, initiated by France and the U.S., it included a reservation. On May 19, 1928, the British Foreign Office sent a note to the American ambassador to Britain, stating that "there are certain regions of the world the welfare and integrity of which constitute a special and vital interest for our peace and safety."[260] The note explicitly treated the American "Monroe Doctrine" as a precedent, suggesting that Britain could make similar claims—often referred to as the "British Monroe Doctrine." However, Schmitt argued that despite the similar language, the underlying spatial logic was fundamentally different from that

259 Schmitt (n. 255), 285–287.

260 FO 414/262, Sir Austen Chamberlain to Mr. Houghton, 19 May 1928, 175.

of the original Monroe Doctrine. The spatial form of the British Empire, with its far-flung colonial territories, was entirely unlike the U.S. as a continental power in 1823.[261]

Thus, from the perspective of their origins, the spatial thinking behind the U.S. Monroe Doctrine was quite distinct from the British vision of a global empire. However, as the U.S. grew in power, its interpretation of the "Monroe Doctrine" increasingly aligned with British imperial thinking. In Schmitt's view, the presidency of Theodore Roosevelt marked a critical shift from a "true Monroe Doctrine" to a form of universal imperialism. Roosevelt, in Schmitt's eyes, misused the Monroe Doctrine to pursue "dollar diplomacy" based on liberal capitalism, which diverged significantly from the original principles of the Monroe Doctrine. Schmitt noted that in 1905, President Theodore Roosevelt encouraged Japanese diplomat Kaneko Kentarō to apply a version of the Monroe Doctrine to Asia. In his 1939 essay "Großraum gegen Universalismus" (Fighting Universalism with Großraum), Schmitt was even more critical of the U.S. than in his 1941 work. He argued that Roosevelt's real objective was to "economically open East Asia to American capital" and that the purpose of this "Monroe Doctrine" in East Asia was to turn China into an Anglo-American colony.[262]

When Japan attempted to adopt a Monroe Doctrine-like policy in Asia, Western theorists often argued that the original Monroe Doctrine was outdated or claimed that Japan lacked the standing to follow the American precedent. Schmitt, however, critiqued the American stance. In 1939, he viewed Japan's "Asiatic Monroe Doctrine" as a counterbalance to Anglo-American imperialism and suggested that it could align with a German-style "Monroe Doctrine."[263]

Building on his critique of Theodore Roosevelt, Schmitt sharply condemned Woodrow Wilson: "When President Wilson solemnly announced on January 22, 1917, that the Monroe Doctrine would become cosmopolitan, the charade reached its peak. His interpretation of cosmopolitanism did not involve extending the regional principle of non-interference inherent in the true Monroe Doctrine to other areas. Instead, it aimed to spread the principles of freedom and democracy to the entire world and all of humanity, disregarding regional differences and boundaries. This shift allowed the U.S. to engage in large-scale interventions in regional matters that did not concern it directly. The true Monroe Doctrine recognized spatial boundaries, but Wilson's doctrine did not. The contrast between them is 'the opposition between a clear

261 Schmitt (n. 255), 288.
262 Schmitt (n. 249), 309.
263 Ibid., 313.

spatial order based on the principle of non-interference by outside powers and a universalist ideology that turns the entire world into a battlefield for intervention, hindering the natural growth of every vibrant nation.'"[264]

Schmitt argued that the principle of liberal democracy and capitalism, which had developed within the "Großraum" of the Americas, had replaced the 19th-century principle of monarchy and dynastic legitimacy, becoming the new justification for interventionism. He suggested that even World War I could be seen as a manifestation of this interventionist drive. In his view, this principle of liberal democracy and capitalism had become the fundamental basis for preserving the existing global order and suppressing the emergence of new political ideas. Schmitt thus positioned Germany as a resister—similar to the role the U.S. once played—and replaced the Monroe Doctrine with his own "Großraum" theory. To Schmitt, the League of Nations was inherently an interventionist institution. In his essay "Großraum gegen Universalismus," Schmitt highlighted how the anticipated German-Austrian Customs Union of 1931 was blocked by a Cuban judge at the Permanent Court of International Justice.[265] He argued that the failure of this Customs Union contributed to the political crisis in the Weimar Republic, ultimately leading to the rise of the Nazi Party. More importantly, Schmitt saw universalism as offering pretexts and opportunities for external powers to interfere in regional matters, once again critiquing the U.S.

For Schmitt, a "Großraum" referred to a contiguous and expansive geographical area, unlike the British model, which connected scattered territories through oceanic trade routes. The true "Monroe Doctrine," in his view, meant protecting the boundaries of a "Großraum" and rejecting any cross-boundary interventions made under the guise of universalism. Schmitt sought to theoretically articulate the U.S.'s role as a leader within the "Großraum" of the Americas.

His book, *Völkerrechtliche Großraumordnung und Interventionsverbot für raumfremde Mächte. Ein Beitrag zum Reichsbegriff im Völkerrecht*, included the 1939 essay "Der Reichsbegriff im Völkerrecht" (The Concept of Reich in International Law), where Schmitt explored the relationship between "Reich" and "Großraum." The existing Chinese translations rendered "Reich" as "Empire," which often led to confusion with the concept of "Imperium"—a distinction Schmitt aimed to clarify. "Imperium" referred to the supreme command authority in Roman public law, associated with universal imperial power during Rome's principality-monarchy era. This idea of universal imperial power was transmitted into the modern era through the Holy Roman Empire

264 Ibid.

265 Schmitt (n. 249), 305–306. Schmitt (n. 255), 294.

of the Middle Ages. Schmitt did not always oppose the concept of "Imperium." In the Middle Ages, the Holy Roman Empire and the imperial power advocated by certain rulers were embedded within the Christian community and operated alongside the authority (*auctoritas*) of the Catholic Pope. In *Der Nomos der Erde*, published in 1950, Schmitt emphasized this idea: "The decisive historical concept of this continuity was that of the restrainer: *Katechon*. 'Empire' in this sense meant the historical power to restrain the rising of the Anti-Christ and the end of the present world."[266]

Der Nomos der Erde clarifies that the concept of the "Katechon" originates from the New Testament, specifically 2 Thessalonians, traditionally attributed to the apostle Paul. In this letter, Paul warns the Thessalonians: "not to become easily unsettled or alarmed by the teaching allegedly from us—whether by a prophecy or by word of mouth or by letter—asserting that the day of the Lord has already come. Don't let anyone deceive you in any way, for that day will not come until the rebellion occurs and the man of lawlessness is revealed, the man doomed to destruction. He will oppose and will exalt himself over everything that is called God or is worshiped, so that he sets himself up in God's temple, proclaiming himself to be God" (2 Thessalonians 2:2–4). This passage introduces the "Antichrist." Paul then explains: "And now you know what is holding him back, so that he may be revealed at the proper time. For the secret power of lawlessness is already at work; but the one who now holds it back will continue to do so till he is taken out of the way. And then the lawless one will be revealed, whom the Lord Jesus will overthrow with the breath of his mouth and destroy by the splendor of his coming" (2 Thessalonians 2:6–8).

Paul outlines a narrative of sacred history: between Christ's resurrection and the Last Judgment, the "Katechon" holds back the rise of the "Antichrist." When the "Antichrist" overcomes the "Katechon," the deceptive spectacle he brings will test believers, separating the truly faithful from the ungodly sinners. This will precede the return of Christ, who will destroy the "Antichrist," ushering in the Last Judgment and the end of worldly history. Humanity thus exists in the era between Christ's resurrection and the Last Judgment, during a period of struggle between the "Katechon" and the "Antichrist." Through the efforts of the "Katechon," the political nature of the world is preserved.[267]

---

266 Schmitt (n. 220), 29.

267 Heinrich Meier, M. Brainard trans., *The Lesson of Carl Schmitt: Four Chapters on the Distinction between Political Theology and Political Philosophy*, (Chicago: The University of Chicago Press, 1998), 161. See also Jens Meierhenrich and Oliver Simons eds., *The Oxford Handbook of Carl Schmitt*, (New York: Oxford University Press, 2016), 46–49. Of course, there are some arguments in the theoretical circle about whether Schmitt can be called a true Catholic, see Aaron B. Roberts, "Carl Schmitt-political theologian?" *The Review of Politics* 77 (2015), 449–474.

In Schmitt's interpretation, the medieval *Imperium* was based on a spatial division between the Christian community and pagans, with a fundamental distinction between friends and enemies. Christian monarchs embodied the spatial role of the "Katechon" through their crusades against non-Christians. However, Schmitt argues that the contemporary visions of *Imperium* held by the United States and the Soviet Union deviate from this concrete spatiality, aiming instead to encompass all humanity as a political unit. In his view, since there are no intelligent creatures other than humans that oppose humans, a global political unit would signify the end of politics as defined by enmity. Referring to the Old Testament, Schmitt notes that it was God who established enmity among humans (Genesis 3:15: "And I will put enmity between you and the woman, and between your offspring and hers; he will crush your head, and you will strike his heel"). A human being, burdened with "original sin," carries this enmity. If humans believe they can eradicate evil and enmity through natural reason alone and create a heaven on earth, Schmitt sees this as an arrogant, anti-Christian delusion.

After World War I, Schmitt's criticism primarily targeted the United States rather than the Soviet Union. He argued that American universalism, compared to that of the Soviet Union, was more deceptive and disorienting. Against this theological backdrop, both the *Reich* and *Großraum* assume the role of "Katechon." The *Großraum* represents a bounded and self-limited space that preserves the world's diversity, thus resisting the realization of the Antichrist's vision. The *Reich* serves as a leader within the *Großraum*, providing political principles that guide and maintain order within this bounded space.[268]

In *Der Reichsbegriff im Völkerrecht*, Schmitt defined *Reich* as "a leading and bearing power, and the political idea of the *Reich* radiates across a certain *Großraum*, for which interference from external powers is fundamentally excluded."[269] The term *Reich* itself implies "domain," and when applied to the political realm, it does not necessarily imply a monarchy. Although Germany experienced a republican revolution at the end of World War I, its official name during the Weimar period remained *Deutsches Reich*, just as it had been during the Second Reich.[270] During World War II, Japanese international jurists translated *Reich* as a "dominating country" in a functional sense, which suited discussions of international order. A *Großraum* might include other nations

268 Schmitt (n. 255), 296–297.

269 Carl Schmitt, "Der Reichsbegriff im Völkerrecht," in *Positionen und Begriffe im Kampf mit Weimar-Genf-Versailles 1923–1940*, (Berlin: Duncker & Humbolt, 1994): 314. Schmitt (n. 255), 295–296.

270 Schmitt (n. 255), 298.

and states that are not part of the *Reich*, just as the U.S. did not claim Argentina or Brazil as part of itself.

For Schmitt, *Reich* was not merely a larger territorial state as conceived after the Peace of Westphalia, nor was it a mechanical governing apparatus tied to a specific territory. Instead, it was fundamentally based on the principle of nationality and aimed to establish a kind of homogeneity within the *Großraum* through national spirit.[271] In the context of 1939, Schmitt's *Reich* certainly pointed to a "Greater Germany" beyond the Third Reich, but he avoided using the term *Mitteleuropa*, which was favored by many contemporary geopoliticians and theorists. While Schmitt did not specify the precise political ideas that the *Reich* should promote within its *Großraum*, he emphasized that it should follow the precedent of the U.S. Monroe Doctrine by excluding foreign interference, thus ensuring the *Großraum's* independence within the global order.

Where classical modern international law treated the state as the basic spatial unit, Schmitt's new international law envisioned *Großraum* as a more critical unit. The expansion of space, he argued, was closely tied to technological advancements. With innovations like aircraft and radio, using the state as the primary unit of analysis had become outdated. Spatial units needed to be larger to facilitate meaningful cooperation. Schmitt's international law concept, centered on *Großraum*, moved beyond the state-centric model of classical international law while rejecting the supranational, universalist international law, which he saw as imperialism. His *Reich*-based international law allowed the national organism to truly embody its state apparatus with its principles and ideals.[272] Given the vastness of the world and the diversity of nations, Schmitt envisioned an ideal global order composed of several distinct *Großräume*, each led by a *Reich* that shaped the worldview and principles of the *Großraum* while preserving global diversity.

Schmitt stressed that the *Großraum* should be led by politically awakened nations, distancing his concept from the notions of "Lebensraum" advanced by Ratzel and Haushofer. He highlighted the initial opposition between the principle of republicanism in the Americas and the monarchic principle of the European Holy Alliance, as seen in the original Monroe Doctrine. This distinction emphasized Schmitt's focus on the fundamental principles that define friend-enemy relationships. The basis of a *Großraum* was not a biological notion of racial hierarchy, nor the expansion of an "organism" driven by population growth, but rather the "political principle" of the leading nation. Schmitt

---

271 Schmitt (n. 268), 315. Schmitt (n. 255), 295–297.

272 Schmitt (n. 252), 304–305.

discussed the contrast between the land-based German national spirit and the sea-based Anglo-Saxon spirit in works like *Land and Sea*. While this distinction might have racial policy implications, such as viewing Jews as a rootless people, it was structurally different from the overt biological racism of Hitler.

In the 1930s, Schmitt's theory clearly served the vision of a German revival. Historically, Germans were dispersed across Germany, Czechoslovakia, Austria, Poland, and other countries. Whether using the concept of *Reich* or *Großraum*, Schmitt aimed to create a framework that integrated different Central European countries under German leadership. Thus, as Germany sought revival and territorial expansion after World War I, Schmitt was not a passive observer or critic—he delivered his *Großraum* lecture at Kiel University shortly after Germany's invasion of Czechoslovakia, clearly echoing contemporary events. Of course, when Germany launched "Operation Barbarossa" after annexing Poland and attacked the Soviet Union, it is reasonable to assume that Hitler's decisions went beyond Schmitt's *Großraum* theory. While Poland and the Baltic regions included many ethnic Germans, leading some theorists of *Mitteleuropa* to include them within Germany's sphere of influence, why did Hitler push all the way to Moscow? If Schmitt's theory applied to the Soviet Union, one might argue that Hitler had entered the *Großraum* of the Slavs.

Karl Haushofer, a German geopolitical scientist who long believed that Germany should align with Russia, a major land power, to counterbalance Anglo-Saxon maritime power, expressed disappointment at Hitler's invasion of the Soviet Union—although he later offered unexpected support.[273] This illustrates the dilemma often faced by theorists: they provide arguments for political actors, but the actions of those actors frequently extend beyond the theories, raising the question of whether it is the actions or the theories that fail.

In the 1930s, Schmitt was just one of many German political and cultural elites who referenced the Monroe Doctrine. It is challenging to assess the extent of his influence on the German ruling elite of the time. On March 4, 1939, German Foreign Minister Joachim von Ribbentrop referenced the "Monroe Doctrine" when discussing the division of Poland with U.S. Under Secretary of State Sumner Welles, insisting that it was a matter to be decided by Germany and the Soviet Union alone, without U.S. interference.[274] In a speech to Congress on April 28, 1939, Hitler criticized President Franklin Roosevelt for

---

273 Patrick O'Sullivan and Jesse W. Miller Jr., *The Geography of Warfare*, (London & New York: Routledge, 1983), 96.

274 Gopal Balakrishnan, *The Enemy: An Intellectual Portrait of Carl Schmitt*, (London: Verso, 2000), 236.

sending him and Mussolini a telegram listing countries in Central Europe that Germany should not invade. Hitler questioned how the U.S. would respond if Germany made similar demands regarding American actions in South America, invoking the Monroe Doctrine to argue that Germany had the right to pursue a similar doctrine for the benefit of Europe, particularly the territories and interests of the Greater German Reich.[275]

In an unpublished manuscript from 1928, Hitler already displayed a mixed attitude of hostility and pragmatism toward the United States. He foresaw that the U.S. would become Europe's primary rival in imperial expansion and hoped for a British-German alliance against France and Russia within Europe and against the U.S. globally. At the same time, he praised the industrial prowess of the U.S. and its selective immigration policies, which he admired for favoring Nordic-Germanic groups.[276]

After Hitler's "Monroe Doctrine" speech, Hans Frank, a minister without portfolio in Hitler's government, called Schmitt to advise him not to publicly discuss the true origins of the European "Monroe Doctrine" concept. Frank noted that "the Führer is proud of his originality."[277] Perhaps in an effort to maintain his relationship with the Nazi leadership, Schmitt refrained from elaborating on the specific worldviews and principles underlying the concept of *Großraum* in his later writings. This silence drew criticism within the Nazi Party itself. In a 1941 article, Werner Daitz, an economic advisor to the party, criticized Schmitt for overlooking the importance of racial homogeneity. Daitz argued that Schmitt's emphasis on the principle of "non-interference" would result in a *Großraum* that could be inhabited by a variety of ethnic groups—Chinese, Malays, Blacks, and Indians.[278] Daitz himself advocated for a biologically defined concept of *Großraum*.[279] Meanwhile, Reinhard Höhn, Schmitt's colleague at Berlin University and someone closer to the Nazi ideology, adopted

275 Adolf Hitler, *Der Führer antwortet Roosevelt*, Reichstagsrede vom 28, April 1939 (Munich: Zentralverlag der NSDAP, FranzEher Nachfolger, 1939), 51.

276 Alton Frye, *Nazi Germany and the American Hemisphere*, (New Haven & London: Yale University Press, 1967), 169–170.

277 Joseph Bendersky, *Carl Schmitt: Theorist for the Reich*, (Princeton: Princeton University Press, 1983), 258–259.

278 Werner Daitz, "Echte und unechteGroßräume," (1941) in *Lebensraum und gerechte Weltordung. Grundlagen einer Anti-Atlantikcharta. Ausgewählte Aufsätze von Werner Daitz*, (Amsterdam: DeAmsterdamsche Keurkamer, 1943), 43.

279 Max Weinreich, *Hitler's Professors: The Part of Scholarship in Germany's Crimes against the Jewish People*, (New York: Yiddish Scientific Institute, 1946), 125.

Schmitt's concept but repeatedly criticized it for being "un-völkisch" (not in line with Nazi racial ideas).[280]

Schmitt joined the Nazi Party in 1933 and initially had a close relationship with the party, earning him the derisive title of "Kronjurist" (Crown Jurist) from exiles. However, before the Nazis came to power, Schmitt had viewed them as a threat to the German state, advocating for a ban on the party based on constitutional theory. Even after joining, Schmitt never fully embraced the party's biological racism. His earlier anti-Nazi stance did not go unnoticed, and some within the Nazi ranks suspected that Schmitt's party membership was a calculated political maneuver. As a result, Schmitt quickly fell out of favor with the Nazi leadership and became politically marginalized. He retreated into academic work, steering clear of sensitive constitutional issues and focusing instead on international law and Hobbes' political philosophy. His development of the *Großraum* theory, despite aligning with Germany's external expansionist goals, did not overcome the party's suspicions, leaving Schmitt in a politically "marginalized" position, though not labeled as an enemy.

This political marginalization turned out to be a double-edged sword for Schmitt. Because he had been sidelined under Nazi rule, he avoided prosecution at the Nuremberg trials after World War II. However, the failure of his *Großraum* theory was evident—his vision of a world divided into several *Großräume* did not come to pass. After the war, the global order was instead dominated by the U.S. and the Soviet Union, each with its sphere of influence but justified through universalist ideologies rather than nationalist-particularism. Germany itself was split into two states, and Schmitt did not live to see the reunification of his homeland, passing away in 1985.

5 Concluding Remarks

Schmitt's theory of international spatial politics and international law proposed a multipolar order deeply rooted in politico-theological concepts. Drawing on Saint Paul's discussion of the "Antichrist" and the "Katechon" in the New Testament's *2 Thessalonians*, Schmitt characterized universalist imperialism, which sought to unify the world, as the "Antichrist." He then explored the spatial political form that could fulfill the role of the "Katechon." From this theological perspective, Schmitt argued that the American "Monroe Doctrine," which originally embodied a spatial principle aligned with the spirit of the

280 Reinhard Hohn, "Grossraumordnung und Volkisches Rechtsought," *Reich, Volksordnung, Lebensraum* 1 (1941), 286.

"Katechon," had degenerated into a discourse of the "Antichrist" that advanced global universalist imperialism. Schmitt hoped that Germany could revive the "Katechon" spirit of the original Monroe Doctrine by creating a *Großraum* in Europe. This *Großraum* would coexist with other *Großräume* worldwide, preserving global pluralism and the essence of "politics."

Based upon existing literature, it is not easy to measure the extent to which Schmitt's analysis of the Monroe Doctrine and his concept of *Großraum* influenced German policymakers of the time. The scope of Germany's Operation Barbarossa likely exceeded the bounds of Schmitt's *Großraum* theory. However, Schmitt's ideas did have some impact on Japan during World War II, notably influencing Japan's development of "large space international law." The next chapter will explore how Schmitt's *Großraum* theory resonated with Japanese geopolitical thought.

At the end of World War II, Schmitt's ideas may have also reached British strategic thinkers. In 1945, Edward Hallett Carr, a scholar who held the Woodrow Wilson Chair at the University of Wales and had experience both at the Versailles Peace Conference and within the League of Nations' Foreign Office in the 1930s, published *Nationalism and After*. In this work, Carr predicted that the post-World War II international order would be built around large political units encompassing multiple nation-states:

> If these predictions are realized, the world will have to accommodate itself to the emergence of a few great multi-national units in which power will be mainly concentrated. Culturally, these units may best be called civilizations: there are distinctively British, American, Russian and Chinese civilizations, none of which stops short at national boundaries in the old sense. Economically, the term *Grossraum* invented by German geo-politicians seems the most appropriate. The Soviet Union is pre-eminently a *Grossraum*, the American continents are the potential *Grossraum* of the United States, though the term is less convenient as applied to the British Commonwealth of Nations or the sterling area which are oceanic rather than continental agglomerations. Militarily, the old and useful term 'zone of influence' has been discredited and may well have become too weak to express the degree of strategic integration required; but the United States has coined the convenient phrase 'hemisphere defence' to cover the zone of influence defined by the Monroe Doctrine.[281]

281 Edward Hallett Carr, *Nationalism and After*, (London: Macmillan, 1945), 52.

While Carr used the term *Großraum* primarily as an economic concept, his analysis contained an unmistakably geopolitical dimension. Although he did not directly reference Schmitt, few European theorists of the time connected the concepts of *Großraum* and the Monroe Doctrine as explicitly as Schmitt did.[282]

Carr, however, did not advocate for establishing a *Großraum* based on the "national spirit." Instead, he argued that: "a political unit based not on exclusiveness of nation or language but on shared ideals and aspirations of universal application may be thought to represent a decided advance over a political unit based simply on the cult of a nation."[283] Carr acknowledged Britain's and Russia's historical roles in Europe. With the rise of Soviet influence in Eastern Europe at the end of World War II, he proposed that Britain should shift its international focus from a global empire to Western Europe: "Western Europe, even if she can renew her vitality and escape from the thrall of traditions once glorious, but now stifling to fresh growth, still lacks the leadership and central focus of power which would be necessary to her among the great multi-national civilizations of the 'hemisphere' or Großraum epoch," and suggested that Britain could assume this role.[284]

However, Britain's power was insufficient to support Carr's strategic vision of making Western Europe its *Großraum*. On March 5, 1946, Churchill delivered the famous "Iron Curtain" speech in the United States, and in 1947, Britain received Marshall Plan assistance from the U.S. By 1948, Britain had allowed the U.S. to establish air force bases on its territory. If there was a transatlantic *Großraum* in the post-war West, the leading power (*Reich*) of this space was clearly the U.S., not Britain. The military might of NATO and the financial strength of the U.S., bolstered by the Marshall Plan, formed the foundation for American influence in Western Europe. Yet, the U.S.'s approach was universalist and imperialist, diverging from Schmitt's *Großraum* concept. In the face of Germany's division after the war, the idea of a European *Großraum* under German leadership became unrealistic.

In *Der Nomos der Erde*, published in 1950, Schmitt reflected on the memory of "European Public Law" from the pre-war era, a time when Europe was still seen as a homogeneous civilization with a regional international law emerging from this shared cultural basis. However, this European order was grounded in

282 See Mika Luoma-aho, "Geopolitics and Grosspolitics from Carl Schmitt to E.H. Carr and James Burnham," in *The International Political Thought of Carl Schmitt: Terror, Liberal War and the Crisis of Global Order*, eds. Louiza Odysseos and Fabio Petito (New York: Routledge, 2007), 42–47.

283 Odysseos and Petito (n. 281), 66.

284 Ibid., 73.

a "balance of power" without a single dominant state (*Reich*)—a vision that did not align with the concept of *Großraum*. In 2017, two authors attempted to apply Schmitt's *Großraum* concept to contemporary Europe, suggesting that the European Union could function as a *Großraum* with the EU as the dominant entity. However, they found challenges in this interpretation: the EU is a complex union of states, and the extent to which it could be considered a "state" remains contentious. Furthermore, the EU's principles are universalist, not substantially different from those of other Western countries, thus contradicting Schmitt's emphasis on regional particularity.[285]

Today, some echoes of Schmitt's *Großraum* principle can be seen among Russian "Eurasianists." Alexander Dugin, a Russian geopolitical theorist, has drawn on Schmitt's *Großraum* theory to envision a multipolar world structure. Like Carr, Dugin links the concept of *Großraum* with "civilization," envisioning distinct *Großräume* such as the North Atlantic (West), Eurasia, the Islamic world, China, Latin America, the South Asian Hindu region, Japan, and Sub-Saharan Africa. For Dugin, Russia is the natural leader of the Eurasian *Großraum*.[286] Dugin's list of civilizations parallels the discussions in Samuel Huntington's *The Clash of Civilizations*. Critics have often compared Huntington's ideas with Schmitt's *Großraum* theory.[287] However, their perspectives differ fundamentally. Huntington warned Americans not to be complacent about Francis Fukuyama's vision of "the end of history" but, as an American patriot, he saw the multipolar world as a reality to be accepted rather than an ideal. For Schmitt and Dugin, however, the coexistence of multiple *Großräume* is a preferable alternative to the interventionist domination of a unipolar hegemony.[288]

For Schmitt and his contemporary followers, a crucial question remains insufficiently explored: does the development of a capitalist economy inherently push the interpretation of the Monroe Doctrine from regionalism to global interventionism? If Germany's industrial economy had been robust enough, could its so-called "national spirit" have prevented a shift towards

285 Walter Rech & Janis Grzybowski, "Between Regional Community and Global Society: Europe in the Shadow of Carl Schmitt and Kojève," *Journal of International Political Theory* 13 (2017), 148–149.

286 Nicolas Laos, *The Metaphysics of World Order: A Synthesis of Philosophy, Theology, and Politics*, (Eugene, Oregon: Pickwick Publications, 2015), 160; Alexander Dugin, *The Fourth Political Theory*, (London: Arktos, 2012), 155–158.

287 Stephen Legg ed., *Spatiality, Sovereignty and Carl Schmitt: Geographies of the Nomos*, (London & New York: Routledge, 2011), 69.

288 See Michael Salter, "Law, Power and International Politics with Special Reference to East Asia: Carl Schmitt's Grossraum Analysis," *Chinese Journal of International Law* 11 (September 2012), 393–427.

universalism and interventionism? Historically, under Emperor Wilhelm II during the Second Reich, Germany had already demonstrated global ambitions. Wilhelm II pursued *Weltpolitik*—a policy aimed at acquiring colonies in Africa and China. He showed interest in colonizing parts of Latin America while simultaneously building a powerful navy to achieve a global "balance of power" with Britain.

If Germany had continued along this path, discussions in Germany around business, naval power, and finance—keywords of maritime empires—would have been inevitable. As a patriot, Schmitt defended Germany's role with the *Großraum* theory. But historical actors often face contexts shaped by fate: Schmitt was only 30 years old when Germany faced defeat in 1918. The loss in World War I stripped Germany of many of its overseas colonies, reducing it to a land-based power in Central Europe under intense pressure from Britain, the U.S., France, and other countries. The leaders of the Weimar Republic could not realistically aspire to challenge British global dominance as Wilhelm II once had. At best, Germany could aim for regional hegemony, a goal to which Schmitt's theory responded.

This is not to suggest that Schmitt should have articulated different theories in the early stages of his career under the reign of Wilhelm II through a "counterfactual" lens. Rather, it highlights that Schmitt's critique of American "imperialism—universal interventionism" does not fully engage with Lenin's theory of imperialism. Schmitt criticized how American elites reinterpreted the Monroe Doctrine, shifting it from the spirit of the "Katechon" to that of the "Antichrist," yet he did not fully explain how this transformation occurred. From Lenin's theoretical perspective, it becomes clear that despite differences in stages of economic development, national strength, and drives for expansion, nations like the U.S. after the Second Industrial Revolution, Germany under Wilhelm II, and the Germany seeking revival after World War I all shared an imperialist nature.

The concept of "Volksgeist" cannot fully account for why Wilhelm II envisioned a world empire while Hitler concentrated on European expansion. Nor can it assure that a future Germany, as a *Reich* within a regional order, would not seek global hegemony. While Schmitt criticized the universalism and interventionism associated with liberal capitalism in Britain and the U.S., revealing the political essence behind economic policies and supporting regional *Großraum* integration, he ultimately placed too much emphasis on political theology and law. He neglected to engage with the development of political economy in Germany, from *Volkswirtschaftslehre* in the 19th century to *Wehrwirtschaftslehre* during World War II.

CHAPTER 3

Ambiguous "Resistance": the Rise of Japan's "Asiatic Monroe Doctrine"

> Pacific Ocean! Pacific Ocean! Before you lies splendid land, and behind you unfolds scenes of bloody slaughter.
>
> LIANG QICHAO, Twentieth Century Pacific Song[289]

∵

From the above study on Germany, we can see that German theorists appropriated the Monroe Doctrine to validate and strengthen Germany's original political spatial demands, and to exclude potential interference by the U.S., especially against the background of U.S. activity in the European political arena after World War I. In Japan, the reason for the popularization of Monroe Doctrine was similar to that in Germany. Japan's expansion to the continent by appealing to the Monroe Doctrine was also similar to that of Germany.

After the Monroe Doctrine was introduced in Japan, it quickly joined with the existing "Asianism" that called on all Asian peoples to unite with Japan to resist the invasion of European powers.[290] The combination of two discourses developed into a "Japanese Monroe Doctrine," which emphasized "the Orient for Oriental people" or "Asia for Asians," and "resisting" interference by some or all Western powers in regional affairs. Regardless of its intention, however, the actual effect of this ostensible emphasis on "regional autonomy" was to provide discourse support for Japan's aggression against Korea, China and other countries. During the Second World War, Japanese international lawyers who were committed to providing legal validation for the Greater East Asia Co-prosperity Sphere drew inspiration from Schmitt's "Großraum" theory to promote Japan's

289 Zhang (n. 3), 5427.

290 Ohara Shiro defined "Asianism" as "an idea that calls on all ethnic groups in Asia to unite with Japan as their ally to resist the aggression of European powers," which was well approved by Takeuchi Yoshimi. See Takeuchi, "The Prospect of Asianism," in *Renjian sixiang* 人间思想 [*Human Thoughts*] (Vol. 4), eds., Gao Shiming and He Zhaotian 高士明、贺照田 (Taipei: Renjian chubanshe, 2016), 256.

 | DOI:10.1163/9789004746237_005

own theoretical construction of "large space international law," attempting to create a legal framework for Japan's domination over "Manchukuo" and Wang Jingwei's puppet regime in Nanjing.

Before Western invasion, countries in East Asia had a concept of tributary order and a conscious differentiation between Xia (the civilized) and Yi (Barbarians), but not a consciousness of "Asia." The gunboats of colonists made the name of "Asia" known to all countries, which then realized their similarly oppressed status. The foreign name "Asia" was increasingly accepted in East Asian countries from the mid-nineteenth century onward. This name not only had geographical meaning, but could also refer to some kind of shared relationship among the oppressed in the imperialist colonial order. In the 1850s and 1860s, Hirano Kuniomi 平野国臣, Satō Nobuhiro 佐藤信淵, Katsu Kaishū 勝海舟 and other Japanese elites advocated "the cooperation of Japan and the Qing Dynasty" 日清提携 in jointly resisting Western invasion. In particular, Katsu Kaishu, known as the "first person" of the modern Japanese navy, actively promoted the idea to Japanese political elites that Japan should build a navy and unite Asian countries to fight against European invasion.[291]

Diplomatic officials of the Qing Dynasty tried to use the new discourse of "Asia" to maintain China's traditional leading role in the tributary system. When Li Hongzhang 李鸿章 talked with Japanese envoy Mori Arinori 森有礼 about the Korean issue on January 24, 1876, he used the concept of "Asia" to question Japan's destruction of tributary relations: "China is the largest country in the East, then Japan. We and all other small countries should act in concert to remedy that situation, so that we can resist European enemies." "Korea and Japan are both in Asia. If there is a war, Korea is China's dependency, and we will handle the issue, since you obviously violated the treaty. If our continent has internal strife, won't it be laughed at by Europe?"[292] When tension between China and Russia came to the fore over the next few years, Zhang Zhidong 张之洞 and Huang Zunxian 黄遵宪 advocated strengthening the relationship between China and Japan. In particular, Huang Zunxian, influenced by Miyajima Seiichirō 宮島誠一郎, advocated cooperation between China and Japan on the Korean issue, and even directly advised the Koreans to regard

291 Chen Haizhong 陈海忠, *Wanqing Zhongguo yu Riben: Boyi bainian* 晚清中国与日本：博弈百年 [*China and Japan in Late Qing Dynasty: A Hundred Years of Game*], (Beijing: Zhongguo fazhan chubanshe, 2018), 39.

292 Zhongguo shixuehui 中国史学会 [Chinese Historical Society] ed., *Zhongguo jindaishi ziliao congkan: Zhongri zhanzheng* 中国近代史资料丛刊:中日战争 [*Series of Modern Chinese History Materials: Sino-Japanese War*] (1), (Shanghai: Shanghai renmin chubanshe, 1957), 298–303.

Russia as the common enemy of Asia.[293] These propositions all reflected the "Asian" consciousness of Qing officials under pressure from the West.

However, in view of the fact that Japan's expansion in Korea, Ryukyu and China's Taiwan constantly endangered the tributary system at the same time, the diplomatic authorities of the Qing Dynasty had to regard Japan as a rival similar to the European powers, so their "Asia" consciousness could not be easily transformed into an "Asianist" foreign policy—as is well known, Li Hongzhang routinely used "playing off one power against another" as his diplomatic strategy. When Japan's influence in Korea was growing, Li Hongzhang's countermeasure was to introduce European powers and the U.S. into Korea to contain Japan, which was fundamentally a "balance of power" strategy.

While Qing officials combined the concept of "Asia" with the tributary system in their discourse, Japan continued to develop its "Theory of Prospering Asia," which differed from the Asia discourse of Qing officials by emphasizing Japan's leadership in Asia. For example, in 1879, Kusama Tokiyoshi 草間時福 stated: "Today, Japan is an advanced country among Asian nations, leading the countries to join the cause of establishing an alliance in East Asia. Nobody can achieve this but Japan."[294] Advocates of the Theory of Prospering Asia founded the Revitalizing Asia Society 振亜社, which was succeeded by the Prospering Asia Association 興亜会 in 1880, and then reorganized as the Asia Association 亜細亜協会 in 1882. In 1891, they founded the Oriental Society 東邦協会.[295] Oi Kentaro 大井憲太郎, the representative of the radical civil rights movement, advocated that Japan, as the forerunner of democracy, should help Asian countries promote democracy at home. In 1885, Oi Kentaro, Kobayashi Kusuo 小林

293 Motegi Toshio, "The Context of Sino-Japanese Relations—the Second Half of the 19th Century," in *Chaoyue guojing de lishi renshi: Laizi Riben xuezhe ji haiwai Zhongguo xuezhe de shijiao* 超越国境的历史认识：来自日本学者及海外中国学者的视角 [*Historical Understanding Beyond National Borders: Perspectives from Japanese Scholars and Overseas Chinese Scholars*], eds., Liu Jie 刘杰 et al. (Beijing: Shehui kexue wenxian chubanshe, 2006), 14–21.

294 Tokifuku Kusama 草間時福 :「東洋連横論」[On Inter-Oriental Union], 『郵便報知新聞』[Yubin Hochi Shimbun], November 19, 1879.

295 Naoki Hazama's *Early Asianism in Japan* attempts to distinguish an early stage with less obvious imperialist characteristics from the development history of "Asianism" in Japan with the East Asian Commonwealth Association in 1898 as the boundary. Naoki Hazama, Zhang Wen 张雯 trans., *Riben zaoqi de yazhou zhuyi* 日本早期的亚洲主义 [*Early Asianism in Japan*], (Beijing: Peking University Press, 2016). However, the problem here is that no matter the "Asia-leaving theorists" or "Asia-rejuvenating theorists," when facing the Japanese policy of invading Korea, Ryukyu and even Taiwan Province, aiming at destroying the Chinese-centered Asian tributary system, there was always a high degree of striking agreement, and few people will criticize the Japanese government's policy.

樽雄 and other leftists of the former Liberal Party tried to buy weapons and made explosives to help members of the Korean Civilization Party who were exiled in Japan to launch a counterattack on Korea, but they were defeated and arrested. This was the so-called "Osaka Incident." In 1993, Tarui Tokichi 樽井藤吉 published *The Great Asian Unification* (大東合邦論) in Chinese characters, calling for "the yellow race" in Korea and Japan to "be united," and then "unite with China" to jointly resist Western aggression. This work could be described as a masterpiece of the Theory of Prospering Asia, which influenced the foreign policy discourse of Kang Youwei and others in China after the Sino-Japanese War of 1894–1895.[296]

At the same time, however, the staged success of the Meiji Restoration and China's repeated failure to resist the aggression of Western powers also gave rise to a strong tendency to despise "stubborn and conservative China" as opposed to "civilized Japan." Japanese politician Sugita Teiichi 杉田定一 criticized China after the Sino-French War in 1884 and opposed cooperating with the Qing Dynasty. Fukuzawa Yukichi 福沢諭吉, a Japanese "enlightenment thinker," put forward the influential "Theory of Leaving Asia," which denigrated China, Korea and other Asian neighbors after the Qing army's suppression of the Gapsin Coup in Korea. When the Sino-Japanese War broke out in 1894, Fukuzawa Yukichi joyfully proclaimed it a war between "civilization" and "barbarism,"[297] and donated generously to the Japanese army. This war dealt a heavy blow to the tributary system. China and Japan signed the Treaty of Shimonoseki 马关条约, and Japan's domination in East Asia became increasingly prominent.

However, in 1895, the governments of Russia, Germany and France decided that Japan had benefited too much from the Treaty of Shimonoseki, which undermined the balance of power in East Asia, so they collectively implemented a Triple Intervention, which constituted a major blow to Japan's continental policy. In 1896, on behalf of the Qing government, Li Hongzhang 李鸿章 signed the Treaty of Mutual Assistance against the Enemy (the Sino-Russian Secret Agreement) with the Tsarist government. Russia's influence in Northeast China was increasing day by day and was regarded as an

296 Mao Haijian 茅海建, *Cong Jiawu dao Wuxu: Kang Youwei Woshi jianzhu* 从甲午到戊戌：康有为《我史》鉴注 [*From the Sino-Japanese War of 1894 to the Reform Movement of 1898: A Review of Kang Youwei's My History*], (Shanghai: Shenghuo, dushu, xinzhi sanlian shudian, 2009), 387.

297 Fukuzawa Yukichi 福沢諭吉,「日清の戦争は文野の戦争なり」[The Sino-Japanese War was a war of civilization (July 29, 1894)], Keio University 慶応義塾 (ed.),『福沢諭吉全集』第14巻 [The Complete Works of Fukuzawa Yukichi, Vol. 14], (Iwanami Shoten, 1961), 491.

eminent threat by Japanese officials. In 1897, Germany sent troops to occupy Jiao'ao, Shandong Province, which apparently triggered a competition between Britain and Germany in China. In 1898, the U.S. won the Spanish-American War and gained dominance over the Philippine Islands.

All of the above events had a great influence on the mentality of Japanese elites in both the ruling and opposition groups: If China was divided up by the great powers, would Japan become the target of the next round of partition? Would the U.S. threaten Japan's survival in Asia after occupying the Philippines? It was against this background that the Japanese government continued to use the European powers as a model to promote domestic reform, in order to meet the "civilized" standards of European powers and to abolish consular jurisdiction. But it also started to publicly express limited support for the discourse of Asianism. The concepts of Asianism and the Monroe Doctrine began coming together against this background.

1 The Confluence of the Concepts of Asianism and Monroe Doctrine

When did the U.S. Monroe Doctrine discourse begin to influence Japanese ruling elites? Of course, those who knew U.S. foreign policy best were American diplomats themselves. In December 1872, while the Iwakura Tomomi 岩倉具視 diplomatic corps that had gone abroad at the end of the previous year was still travelling in European and American countries, the Japanese Ministry of Foreign Affairs hired Charles W. Le Gendre, a French-American who was once the U.S. consul in Amoy, as an advisor in the Japanese invasion of Taiwan. This wily diplomat proposed a Japanese version of the Monroe Doctrine to the Japanese ruling elites, urging Japan to be the protector of Asian nations and prevent Europe from expanding into the sphere. Le Gendre argued that this policy is similar to that adopted by the U.S. when Europe infiltrated and invaded the sphere of influence of the U.S.[298]

In the 1870s, this was a very unusual proposition, because in the eyes of the Western ruling elites, Japan was only a "semi-civilized" country—it did not qualify for equality with the West, not to mention for imitating the U.S. Monroe Doctrine and claiming its own sphere of influence. Le Gendre suggested that Japan's ruling elites must keep this plan in mind, but should publicize internationally as much as possible that Japan was trying to help Asia emerge from

298 Sophia Su-fei Yen, *Taiwan in China's Foreign Relations, 1836–1874*, (Hamden, CT: Shoe String Press, 1965), 196.

barbarism and move towards civilization.[299] The specific approach was to pacify and educate Asian peoples as much as possible; if this is not feasible, destroy them, or treat them in the ways just as the U.S. and Britain have done to the barbarians.[300]

Le Gendre resigned from the Japanese Ministry of Foreign Affairs in 1875 before going to Korea in 1890, and he lived in Japan and worked as a personal adviser to Ōkuma Shigenobu 大隈重信. Against the background of Japan's annexation of Ryukyu, invasion of Taiwan Island and coveting of Korea, Le Gendre passed on the idea of the U.S. sphere of influence to the Japanese ruling elite. They were keen to learn from the West at that time, and it further fueled their ambitions.[301]

Although Le Gendre actively planned for Japan's position in Asia, he was still occidental-centric in his concepts of civilization, which was far from Japan's mainstream Asianism at that time. What we need to ask is, when did Japan's Asianism explicitly seek to merge with Monroe Doctrine discourse? Tōyama Mitsuru 頭山満, one of the representatives of the Theory of Prospering Asia and a founder of the Japanese right-wing group Black Ocean Society 玄洋社, as well as advisor to the Black Dragon Society 黒竜会, once stated: "The person who put forward the slogans of 'the Orient for Oriental people' and 'Asian nations should unite to resist the violence of Western countries and expel their aggressive ambitions' was 霞山公, who initiated the Great Asianism. Taking the Monroe Doctrine of the U.S. as an example, he proposed that the obligation to implement the Asiatic Monroe Doctrine lies in Japan and China. His foresight and grand plan are still admired."[302] Here "霞山公" refers to Konoe Atsumaro 近衛篤麿, the Speaker of Japan's House of Lords and the father of Konoe Fumimaro 近衛文麿, the 34th, 38th and 39th Prime Minister of Japan. Konoe Atsumaro had studied at Bonn University and Leipzig University in Germany.

When the Association for the Unification of Asian Languages was founded in 1898, Konoe Atsumaro served as its first president. The association largely unified Japan's existing Asian Prospering organizations, and many high-ranking officials and nobles joined it. It was called a non-governmental organization

299 Ibid.

300 Robert Eskildsen, ed., *Foreign Adventurers and the Aborigines of Southern Taiwan, 1867–1874*, (Nankang, Taipei: Institute of Taiwan History, Academic Sinica, 2005), 209.

301 On the study of Le Gendre's influence on Japan's foreign policy during Meiji period, See Sandra Carol Taylor Caruthers, "Charles Le Gendre, American Diplomacy, and Expansionism in Meiji Japan" (Ph.D. Thesis, University of Colorado, 1963).

302 Yoshida Tomoaki 吉田鞆明 (ed.),『巨人頭山満翁は語る』[Giant Toyama Mitsuru Speaks], (Kanzanso, 1939), 115.

and actually played the role of non-governmental diplomacy with the support of the Japanese government. At the beginning of 1898, Konoe Atsumaro published a famous article in *The Taiyo*, Volume 4, No. 1, titled "Alliance of the Same Race—With the Necessity of Studying Chinese Issues." Like Tarui Tōkichi 樽井藤吉, he highlighted the conflict between the yellow and white races: "In my opinion, the future of East Asia will inevitably reach the stage of racial competition. Even if a temporary situation can be resolved through foreign policy, that is just an expedient measure. The ultimate fate is still the rivalry between the yellow and white races. In this competition, Chinese and Japanese are in the position of regarding the whites as their enemies."[303] Konoe Atsumaro advocated that "the survival of China is closely related to other countries and the fate of Japan. Therefore, from today onward, we should treat China with friendship, persuade it, enlighten it, bring progress to it, motivate it, get rid of its suspicion and jealousy, and make it feel close to and dependent on Japan, so as to create a tacit understanding between the two peoples to protect the yellow race."[304] This was the famous "Theory of Preserving China." Konoe Atsumaro held that "although the strength of the Qing Dynasty has declined, its disadvantage lies in the politics, not the nation. Is it difficult to inspire and guide Chinese, and join hands to preserve East Asia?"[305]

When receiving exiled Chinese reformist Kang Youwei in November 1998, Konoe Atsumaro explained: "Today, the problem of East Asia is no longer just a problem of East Asia, but a world problem. European powers are competing in East Asia for their own benefit. East Asia is East Asia for East Asians. We must have the right to solve the oriental issue independently. This is also the meaning of the Monroe Doctrine in the Americas. In fact, the obligation to realize the Asiatic Monroe Doctrine in East Asia falls on the shoulders of our two nations."[306] However, when Kang Youwei raised the idea of borrowing Japanese troops to attack Empress Dowager Cixi 慈禧 and rescue the Emperor Guangxu 光绪, Konoe Atsumaro's attitude became very cautious, emphasizing

303 Konoe Atsumaro 近衛篤麿,「同人種同盟附支那問題研究の必要」[The Necessity of Studying the Racial Alliance and the Chinese Problem],『太陽』[Taiyō], Vol. 4, No. 1, 1898, p. 1.

304 Ibid.

305 Konoe Atsumaro Diary Publishing Committee 近衛篤麿日記刊行会 (ed.),『近衛篤麿日記 別巻 近衛篤麿日記付属文書』[Konoe Atsumaro Diary, Supplementary Volume: Documents Added to the Konoe Atsumaro Diary], (Kajima Institute Publishing, 1969), 401.

306 Konoe Atsumaro Diary Publishing Committee 近衛篤麿日記刊行会 (ed.),『近衛篤麿日記』第2巻 [Konoe Atsumaro Diary, Volume 2], (Kajima Institute Publishing, 1968), 195.

that the response of other powers must be taken into account. Konoe's circumspection reflected the complicated mentality of the Japanese ruling elites at that time. On the one hand, Japan urgently needed the European powers to fully recognize its status as a "civilized nation," so theories such as "the rivalry between the yellow race and the white race" could never became official statements. On the other hand, Japan was worried that the foreign powers' partition of China would lead to a situation in which "if the lips are gone, the teeth will be cold." Although Japan also sent troops to participate in the invasion of China by the Eight-Nation Alliance in 1900, foreign powers' talk of dividing up China also made many Japanese elites worry about Japan's future.

Imperialism and Education 帝国主義と教育, published in 1901 by Ukita Kazutami 浮田和民, a professor at Waseda University and leading writer for *Taiyo* Magazine, expressed this sense of powerlessness: "Although I want to advocate the Japanese Monroe doctrine of 'Asia for Asians,' I feel helpless for its backwardness. The only imperialism that Japan can advocate today is one that upholds the rights of our own people according to international law. At the same time, we should encourage and promote the reform of Asian countries to foster their independence."[307] Ukita believed that in China at this time, "Japan's economic status falls behind Britain's, and its political status falls behind Russia's." Given that China was less able than Korea to meet Japan's urgent needs, Japan's responsibility for China was to a large extent a burden.[308]

On February 3, 1901, people who called for Japan to adopt a tough policy towards Russia, such as Uchida Ryōhei 内田良平 and Hirayama Shū 平山周, established the Black Dragon Society (黒竜会, Kokuryū-kai). The name of the association was taken from the Heilongjiang River, indicating their ambition to compete with Tsarist Russia for regional hegemony in the Heilongjiang River basin. The first item of the constitution of the Kokuryū-kai stated, "We aim to promote the profound culture of our country, to explain the essence of Eastern culture, to pursue peaceful coexistence between East and West, and to establish Japan as a leader in the revitalization of the Asian nation," reflecting a distinct "Asianism."[309] Tōyama Mitsuru 頭山満 served as a consultant to the Kokuryū-kai. It is worth mentioning that at that time, such political figures as Konoe Atsumaro 近衛篤麿, Itō Hirobumi 伊藤博文, Inoue Kaoru 井上馨 and

---

307 Ukita Kazutami 浮田和民,『帝国主義と教育』[Imperialism and Education], (Minyusha, 1901), 35–36.

308 Ibid., 74.

309 Hori Yukio, Xiong Dayun 熊达云 trans., *Zhanqian riben guojia zhuyi yundongshi* 战前日本国家主义运动史 [*History of Japanese Nationalist Movement before the World War II*], (Beijing: Shehui kexue wenxian chubanshe, 2010), 26.

Ōkuma Shigenobu 大隈重信 all advocated adopting a tough policy toward Russia at that time. In order to contain Tsarist Russia, Britain in 1902 signed an equal alliance treaty with Japan, which greatly improved Japan's international status. When the Russo-Japanese War broke out in Northeast China in 1904, Japan was supported by British and U.S. capital. In cooperation with the Japanese military headquarters, the Kokuryū-kai organized a guerrilla group called the Manchuria Volunteer Army to fight against the Russian army. After the war, the Kokuryū-kai was committed to consolidating Japan's rule in Korea and its expansion in Northeast China, playing a vanguard role in the expansion of Japan on the continent.

On October 23, 1904, Ōkuma Shigenobu 大隈重信, who was Prime Minister in 1898 and vigorously promoted the alliance between Britain and Japan in 1902, delivered a speech titled "On Peace in East Asia" at the Korea and Chinese Association of Waseda University. Responding to the ongoing war between Japan and Russia, he describe it as a war between "civilization" and "barbarism." Japan represented constitutionalism and Tsarist Russia represented despotism. But if Japan wanted to stand rock-firm in the "family of nations," it needed to consider its role in East Asia as the only power qualified to guide and treat China as the sick man of Asia out of a sense of friendship toward people of the same culture and race. The peace terms in the war between Japan and Russia should also ensure that Japan was "the pillar of peace in East Asia."[310] The speech conceptualized the Russo-Japanese war from the perspective of race and civilization, and clearly expressed Japan's position in the sphere of influence, which major Tokyo newspapers referred to as the "Okuma Doctrine." In 1905, Japan defeated Russia and was accepted by the Western powers as a member of the "family of nations," joining the club of the world's top powers. Japan obtained from Russia the lease rights to Lushun, Dalian Bay, its adjacent territories and other privileges. It also acquired the South Manchurian Railway and its subsidiary rights. The victory was widely interpreted as an event in which the yellow race defeated the white race in both China and Japan. The Japanese effort to establish a "sphere of influence" in Southern Manchuria was also interpreted as an action to "preserve" China by theorists of the Japanese Monroe Doctrine such as Kodera Kenkichi 小寺謙吉, who held that the move helped China as a member of the "yellow race" and saved China from falling into the hands of European powers such as Britain and Russia.

310 Ōkuma Shigenobu 大隈重信:「東亜の平和を論ず」[Discussing Peace in East Asia], Waseda University Editorial Department 早稲田大学編輯部 (eds.),『大隈伯演説集』[Collected Speeches by Count Okuma], (Waseda University Press, 1907), 101–123.

However, in Kodera Kenkichi's works, the "China" to be "preserved" actually meant what Japan often called "China proper," which didn't include Northeast China, Inner and Outer Mongolia, Xinjiang and Tibet.[311] Kodera Kenkichi's view of China's territory was not unique in Japan at that time.[312] In 1858, Yoshida Shōin, the spiritual leader and theoretical founder of the Meiji Restoration, proposed that Japan needed to carve out Northeast China from China. After the Russo-Japanese war, a "Manchu learning" or "Manchu-Mongolian learning" that was parallel to "China studies" emerged in Japanese academic circles. Aggressors toward the mainland such as Uchida Ryōhei had long imagined pushing Japan's border from the Korean Peninsula to Siberia, and his "theory of preserving China" always served the needs of Japan's expansion in competition with Russia for Northeast Asia. In the words of Japanese scholar Fujimura Michio 藤村道生: "The so-called 'theory of preserving China' aimed at expelling Russia from Northeast China, but it did not imply de-legitimizing Japan's invasion of China."[313]

Even so, China's anti-Manchu revolutionaries and Japan's "Asianists" began allying with each other. The establishment of the Revolutionary Alliance 同盟会 in 1905 was strongly supported by the Black Dragon Society 黒竜会. Members of the Kokuryū-kai such as Uchida Ryōhei 内田良平, Hirayama Shū 平山周 and Kita Ikki 北一輝 joined the Revolutionary Alliance one after another. There were various reasons for the two organizations to approach each other: Both were worried that the Western powers would first carve up China and

311 In his *Theory of Greater Asianism*, Kodera Kenkichi argued that the Japanese-Russian War was the "preservation" of China. So what is "territorial preservation"? Kodera Kenkichi defined the so-called territorial preservation as a country that cannot preserve its territory by itself, relying on external forces to stop the declining trend, rather than preserving something that has been lost, or lifting the accepted sovereignty restrictions. According to this standard of Kodera Kenkichi, what China can "preserve" is the 18 provinces in the mainland, the vassal departments are not in here. See Wang Xiangyuan 王向远, *Riben dui Zhongguo de wenhua qinlue* 日本对中国的文化侵略 [*Japanese Cultural Aggression against China*], (Beijing: Kunlun chubanshe, 2015), 98–103. Gu Jiegang wrote an article in 1939, pointing out that the word "China's headquarters" itself contained evil intentions, Gu Jiegang 顾颉刚, "'Zhongguo benbu' yiming jidai feiqi '中国本部' 一名亟待废弃" [The name of "China's headquarters" needs to be abandoned urgently]," *Yishibao xingqi pinglun* (1 January 1939).

312 Yoshida Shoin 吉田松陰,「丙辰幽室文稿·久坂玄瑞に復する書」[The Manuscripts of Hei-chin Yushitsu: A Letter Returning to Kusaka Genzui], Yamaguchi Prefectural Education Association 山口県教育会 (ed.),『吉田松陰全集』第4巻 [Complete Works of Yoshida Shoin, Vol. 4], (Iwanami Shoten, 1938), 152.

313 Fujimura Michio 藤村道生:「日本の対アジア観の変遷」[Changes in Japan's View of Asia], Sophia University Historical Society 上智大学史学会 (ed.):『上智史学』第22号 (Sophia Historical Studies, No. 22, 1977), 30.

then seize control of Japan. They all thought that China and Japan needed to unite to resist Western invaders (especially Russia). At the same time, they also thought that China's Qing government was not competent for achieving this goal. China needed to carry out internal transformation to mobilize its strength for self-preservation. But for Asianists such as Miyazaki Tōten 宮崎寅藏 and Kita Ikki 北一輝,[314] who were influenced by certain socialist ideas and were trying to promote social transformation in Japan, the Chinese revolution and Japan's social transformation were intrinsically interconnected. In particular, Kita Ikki's *Kokutairon and Pure Socialism*, published in 1906, had been banned, and he was deeply conscious of the difficulties in reforming Japanese society. Kita Ikki decided to first devote himself to the Chinese Revolution, and then use the Chinese revolution to drive the social transformation of Japan.

For Asianists such as Uchida Ryōhei 内田良平 who were more interested in Japan's mainland expansion, cooperation with China's anti-Manchu revolutionaries was also in line with their goals. Uchida pointed out: "The reason why we spared no effort to help Sun [Yat-sen]'s revolution is that it is consistent with the interests of Japan. The purpose of the revolution is to expel Manchus and to establish a Han China, so we will help the Han people force the Manchus to turn toward Russia. Later, Japan and China can cooperate to defeat Russia, and then we can take Manchuria and Siberia as our own territory, so as to lay a solid foundation for mainland operations."[315] At that time, the Revolutionary Alliance adopted the slogan of Ming Dynasty's founder Zhu Yuanzhang 朱元璋 "to expel the northern barbarians and to revive China." The traditional differentiation between the civilized and barbarians converged with modern nationalism to form a kind of anti-Manchu Han nationalism. Many members of the alliance did not strongly disagree with the notion that "preserving China" was actually the preservation of "eighteen provinces" (or "China proper"), and regarded Japan's presence in Northeast China as a barrier to Russian invasion. In this way, Japan's continental expansionists could consolidate their colonial rule over Korea by emphasizing Russia as a common enemy, and further extended their influence to Northeast China.[316]

314 Kita Ikki published *The Outline of Japan's Reform Act* in 1923, which marked his trend towards militarism, while China was the inevitable target of aggression in the implementation of Japan's reform plan. However, in the early years, Kita Ikki really had high hopes for the Chinese revolution and deeply participated in it.

315 Ryohei Uchida 内田良平,『硬石五拾年譜』 [Fifty-Year Chronicle of Ryohei Uchida], (Yoshi Shobō, 1978), 77.

316 Wang Ke 王柯, "Minquan, zhengquan, guoquan—Zhongguo geming yu heilonghui 民权、政权、国权——中国革命与黑龙会 [Civil Rights, Political Power and State Power—Chinese Revolution and Kokuryū-kai]," *21 shiji* 127 (2011).

However, we should also see the differences within the Revolutionary Alliance. Some members were aware of the oppression and hypocrisy of Japan's discourse of Asianism. For example, Song Jiaoren 宋教仁 was obviously in great conflict with the Black Dragon Society's mainstream concept of Chinese territory. In 1907, when Uchida Ryōhei tried to create an issue over Kanto 間島 on the border of China, Korea and Russia with the intention of taking China's territory, Song Jiaoren wrote *The Issue of Jiandao* under a pseudonym based on an on-the-spot investigation and sent it to key Qing officials.[317] In this way, he contributed significantly to the diplomatic negotiations between the Qing government and Japan.

There were also thinkers such as Zhang Taiyan 章太炎 who had insights into the fundamental tension between the Anglo-Japanese Alliance and the alliance of Asia. In 1907, Zhang Taiyan joined Japanese socialist Kōtoku Shūsui 幸徳秋水 and the Indians Mohamed Barkatullah and Surendramohan Bose in launching the Asian Solidarity Association. The Charter of the Association, which was drafted by him, advocated that China and India should be taken as the main axis to carry out "peace and friendship in Asia," calling on the oppressed peoples of Asia to unite in resistance against the great powers and to seek liberation by themselves.[318] It was no accident that the Charter did not mention the role of Japan. In some political commentaries during that same period, Zhang criticized Japan's suppression of the national liberation movements in India and Korea.[319] This repression resulted from the signing and implementation of the Anglo-Japanese Alliance.[320]

---

317 Chen Xulu 陈旭麓 ed., *Song Jiaoren ji* 宋教仁集 [*The Collection of Song Jiaoren*] (1), (Beijing: Zhonghua shuju, 1981), 57–135.

318 *Zhang Taiyan quanji: Taiyan wenlu bubian* 章太炎全集·太炎文录补编 [*Complete Works of Zhang Taiyan, Supplement to the Records of Taiyan Literature*] (1), (Shanghai: Shanghai renmin chubanshe, 2017), 341, 279–281.

319 In the 1908 political treatise "The Benefits and Diseases of the Qing-U.S. Alliance," Zhang Taiyan said: "Japan is proud of itself, not our good friend." Ibid., 341. After the Korean patriot An Jung-geun assassinated Japanese Prime Minister Itō Hirobumi in 1909, Zhang Taiyan wrote "Ode to An Sir" to commemorate him. On October 10th, 1911, in a letter to Manchuria students studying in Japan, Zhang Taiyan even criticized Japan for clamping down on Korea, and warned royalist students not to expect Japan to support the Qing government. *Zhang Taiyan quanji: Shuxinji* 章太炎全集·书信集 [*Complete Works of Zhang Taiyan (Letters)*] (1), (Shanghai: Shanghai renmin chubanshe, 2017), 395–396.

320 For the influence of Anglo-Japanese Alliance on Zhang Taiyan's thought, see Lin Shaoyang 林少阳, *Dingge yiwen—Qingji geming yu Zhang Taiyan 'fugu' de xinwenhua yundong* 鼎革以文——清季革命与章太炎"复古"的新文化运动 [*The Revolution in late Qing and Zhang Taiyan's "Retro" New Culture Movement*], (Shanghai: Shanghai renmin chubanshe, 2018), 177–224.

Faced with Russia's expansion in Northeast China, not only did Britain use Japan to contain Russia through the Anglo-Japanese Alliance, but U.S. President Theodore Roosevelt also viewed Japan as an important force for containing Russia. On June 6, 1904, while the Russo-Japanese war was still ongoing, Roosevelt proposed to his Harvard classmate, Japanese diplomatic representative Kaneko Kentarō 金子堅太郎, and the Japanese ambassador to the U.S., Takahira Kogoro 高平小五郎, that Japan should have paramount interest in the surrounding areas of the Yellow Sea, just as the U.S. had paramount interest in the Caribbean Sea.[321] When Japan won the Russo-Japanese war in 1905, President Roosevelt presided over the Portsmouth Conference in an attempt to mediate between Japan and Russia. As Japan's then diplomatic representative Kaneko Kentarō recalled, while discussing the upcoming Portsmouth Conference with him on July 8, 1905, Roosevelt proposed that Japan, as the only nation in Asia to understand the principles and methods of Western civilization, was qualified to lead Asia by carrying out the Asiatic Monroe Doctrine, playing a leading role in the vast area from Suez Canal to Russia Kamchatka (excluding Russian territory and British, French and Portuguese colonies), and resisting the interference and aggression of European powers, just as the U.S. had done in the Americas.[322]

In the context of the aftermath of the Russo-Japanese War, Roosevelt's main purpose in promoting the Asiatic Monroe Doctrine was to recognize Japan's privileges in Korea and Northeast China in exchange for Japan's recognition of the U.S. occupation of the Philippines, its agreement to implement the U.S. Open Door Policy in its new sphere of influence, and its playing an active role in blocking Russia's eastward advance. Although Roosevelt never publicized this internal dialogue, it fueled the Japanese government's aggression against Korea and China, and also provided an excuse for Japan to curb U.S. intervention in regional affairs. After the Mukden Incident, Japanese expansionists maximized the surplus-value of Roosevelt's remarks to justify an aggressive policy toward China.

After the Russo-Japanese War, Ōkuma Shigenobu 大隈重信 expressed a series of new opinions on the East Asian order. Against the background of the New Policy Era in the late Qing Dynasty, Okuma advocated that Japan should "preserve" and "develop" China through "supervision and guidance" of China's

321 TR to Cecil Arthur Spring-Rice, June 13, 1904, Elting Morison and John Blum, eds., *The Letters of Theodore Roosevelt*, 8 vols. (Cambridge, MA: Harvard University Press, 1951–1954), 833.

322 Kaneko Kentarō 金子堅太郎,『東洋の平和は亜細亜モンロー主義にあり』[Peace in the East Lies in the Asian Monroe Doctrine], (Kokikai, 1937), 16–19.

modernization, and should establish an awe-inspiring image in China that would prevent the Qing government from containing Japan along with the Western powers.[323] Okuma also introduced the popular theory of "civilizational hierarchy" in Europe and the U.S., saying that there were differences between the world's civilized and uncivilized countries. Japan, which had already kept pace with Western powers, needed to play the role of coordinator between higher and lower civilizations.[324] In particular, as a pioneer and representative of East Asia, Japan needed to guide the civilizational progress of Asian countries with inferior levels of civilization.[325] Japan's defeat of Russia, backed by the Anglo-Japanese Alliance concluded in 1902, had instilled Okuma with a measure of confidence: As an absorber and conveyor of Western civilization, Japan could play a role in coordinating Western powers and Asian countries in this region. Okuma clearly recognized Britain as the most civilized country, while also believing that Japan had achieved a status comparable to that of Britain, as evidenced by the Anglo-Japanese Alliance.

Okuma's Theory of Civilization was probably influenced by the Monroe Doctrine of his personal adviser, French American William Le Gendre. It had a different theoretical background from discourses of Asianism based on the independence and superiority of East Asian Culture (such as the Asia discourse of Okakura Tenshin 岡倉天心). Okuma's vision was fundamentally based on Westernization. It also duplicated the discourse of "the Mission to Civilize" of Western colonialism and imperialism.[326] In 1915, Japan assisted the British army in suppressing an anti-British uprising by Indian soldiers in Singapore, and Okuma was quite proud of this.[327] However, Okuma's close attention to and public promotion of Japan's sphere of influence in Asia made him one of the key representatives of the Asiatic Monroe Doctrine after Konoe Atsumaro 近衛篤麿. In other words, the discourse of Asiatic Monroe Doctrine was not necessarily based on opposing the West and the so-called "white race," but might also be based on a kind of coordination with the West, in exchange

---

323 Ōkuma Shigenobu 大隈重信,「再び東亜の平和を論ず」[Peace in East Asia Revisited], Waseda University Editorial Department 早稲田大学編輯部 (ed.),『大隈伯演説集』[Collected Speeches of Count Okuma], (Waseda University Press, 1907), 133.

324 Ōkuma Shigenobu 大隈重信,『経世論』[Economic and Social Theory], (Tomiyama Publishing, 1912), 29–30.

325 Ibid., 38.

326 Nomura Koichi, Zhang Xuefeng 张学锋 trans., *Jindai riben de Zhongguo renshi: Zouxiang yazhou de hangzong* 近代日本的中国认识：走向亚洲的航踪 [*Understanding of China in Modern Japan: A Journey to Asia*], (Beijing: Zhongyang bianji chubanshe, 1999), 6–11.

327 Nagasaki Nobuko 長崎暢子,「日本のアジア主義とインドの民族運動」[Japanese Asianism and the Indian National Movement], in Ogata, Kohei 大形孝平 (ed.),『日本とインド』[Japan and India], (Sanseido, 1978), 71.

for the latter's recognition of Japan's sphere of influence in Asia. Once Okuma's "Civilization" theory modeled on Europe was replaced by a new theory centered on Kokutai/state form 國體 and kōdō/imperial way 皇道 (alternatively, "kingly way"), Japan's concept of regional hegemony after the Mukden Incident was easily derived.

In the Russo-Japanese War, President Theodore Roosevelt supported Japan in order to expand U.S. interests in China. It then became necessary to curb Japan's ambition to monopolize China's interests. Emperor Wilhelm II of Germany sought to establish an alliance between China, the U.S. and Germany from 1907 to 1908. However, the Qing government was afraid that getting too close to one power might cause suspicion among other powers; the U.S. had similar considerations.[328] Ultimately, the idea of such an alliance was not put into practice. The U.S. believed that the greatest threat to China's independence and territorial integrity came from Japan. In 1909, the U.S. signed the Root-Takahira Agreement with Japan, and reached a series of agreements with Japan on the Pacific order. At the same time, the third paragraph of the agreement required that China's independence and territorial integrity should be respected, and that equal business opportunities for the major powers within the country should be maintained.

The U.S. diplomatic authorities supported a proposal by railway tycoon E.H. Harriman to buy the Japanese-controlled Southern Manchu Railway in 1906, but Japan declined. In 1909, Philander C. Knox, Secretary of State under President William Howard Taft, further proposed the Knox Plan to seek "the neutralization of the Manchuria Railway" based upon international co-management, forcing Japan to abandon the Southern Manchu railway and Russia to give up the Chinese Eastern Railway. If Japan refused to comply, the Knox Plan's alternative was to build a railway from Jinzhou 锦州 to Aigun 瑷珲 to compete with Japan and Russia. Under U.S. pressure, Japan and Russia signed the Second Russo-Japanese Secret Treaty in 1910, which confirmed the sphere of influence defined in the first secret agreement between the two countries in 1907. It also stipulated that when the special interests of the two countries were threatened, they should not only focus more on self-protection, but also strengthen mutual cooperation, such as taking joint action or providing other forms of assistance. The treaty therefore established a military alliance between Russia and Japan. Theodore Roosevelt's plan to use Japan to contain Russia and expand U.S. interests in China can be said to have suffered a major setback.

---

328 Li Yongsheng 李永胜, "1907–1908 nian zhongdemei lianmeng wenti yanjiu 1907–1908 年中德美联盟问题研究 [Research on Sino-German-American Alliance from 1907 to 1908]," *Shijie lishi* 4 (2011).

After the Russo-Japanese War, the focus of Japan's defense increasingly shifted from Russia to the U.S. Japan renewed the Anglo-Japanese Alliance in 1905 and 1911, but Japan remained the relatively weaker party in this alliance, and had difficulty taking action without consulting Britain. After supporting Japan's victory in the Russo-Japanese War, the U.S. government was dissatisfied with not enjoying the expected returns. After the Russo-Japanese War, the Japanese government and the public were worried by Anti-Japanese sentiment among the U.S. public. It is worth mentioning that as early as 1909, Homer Lea, a U.S. citizen who served as a military adviser to Kang Youwei and Sun Yat-sen, published *The Valor of Ignorance*, which held that Japan and the U.S. were destined to go to war. The book's immediate translation into Japanese and publication in 1911 indicates the attention it received in Japan.[329]

In October 1907, the vice-president of Bank of Japan, Takahashi Korekiyo 高橋是清, visited the U.S. during the Japanese exclusion period. According to a report in the *San Francisco Call*, Takahashi publicly announced that Japan's new national policy was "Asia for the Asians," and the commentators of the *San Francisco Call* were quick to summarize it as a Japanese Monroe Doctrine similar to "America for the Americans."[330] But Takahashi was to a large extent expressing his personal emotions rather than the key thinking of Japan's top policymakers. In September 1907, there was a talk between the president of the Manchurian Railway, Gotō Shinpei 後藤新平, and Ito Hirobumi 伊藤博文, who at that time was the commissioner of Korean Tōkanfu. Gotō described to Ito the prospect of "Asia for the Asians," but Ito warned him that "greater Asianism" might cause misunderstanding among Western powers as evidence of the "Yellow Peril."[331]

Ito's views could be said to represent the cautious attitude of Meiji reformers toward the international situation. It was because of this caution that the Japanese government was extremely wary of links between Japanese Asianism and national liberation activists in other Asian countries. For example, the Japanese government in 1907 gave Sun Yat-sen a grant while politely urging him to leave the country. During World War I, when Japan's advocator of Asianism, Ōkawa Shūmei 大川周明, became too close to activists in the Indian national liberation movement, Britain put pressure on Japan to curb this activity, and the Japanese government complied.

---

329 Homer lea, *The Valor of Ignorance*, (New York: Harper & Brothers, 1909).

330 "Japan Promulgates 'Monroe Doctrine' Affecting Korea and Encroachment by Russia Means Declaration of War," *San Francisco Call* 94 (13 October 1903).

331 Tsurumi Yusuke 鶴見祐輔,『後藤新平』第2巻 [Gotō Shinpei, Volume 2], (Keiso Shobō, 1965), 960–961.

The European powers also restricted the Japanese government’s China policy after the outbreak of the 1911 Revolution. After the Wuchang Uprising broke out in 1911, many members of the Black Ocean Society 玄洋社 and the Black Dragon Society 黒竜会 supported the revolutionaries. Uchida Ryōhei 内田良平 even served as diplomatic adviser to the Nanjing Provisional Government. However, elders in the Japanese government such as Yamagata Aritomo 山縣有朋 and Terauchi Masatake 寺内正毅 rejected the revolutionaries, and advocated coordinating with the Western powers led by Britain in foreign policy. Many in Japan doubted whether China could take the republican road. In 1911, Nakajima Tan 中島端 published his book *China’s Destiny of Partition*. He held that the Chinese people were unqualified to establish a republic, that they had no belief in a republic, no history of a republic, no concept of a republic, no qualities for a republic, and only had a conception of provinces and not of a state; the Chinese people were corrupt, divided and dependent; the Han people had bent their knees to other nations throughout history. Therefore, by taking the road of republicanism, China was bound to split into provinces and become divided among the great powers, inevitably leading to the subjugation of the country. Facing this prospect, Nakajima called on Japan to implement an East Asian Monroe Doctrine towards China in order to take on the “bounden duty of the great nation” with “great determination, great strength and great spiritual aspirations.”[332]

The co-existence of various internal opinions caused the Japanese government to vacillate in its China policy: In the early period of the revolution, the Japanese government provided loans to the Qing government and tried to force the revolutionaries to accept the idea of constitutional monarchy; in the later period, the Japanese government placed its bet on the revolutionaries and tried to provide loans to the Nanjing Provisional Government. Britain was worried about the possible partition of China, which might damage British commercial interests and benefit Japan and Russia, which were directly adjacent to China. Britain therefore maintained “financial neutrality” by refusing to provide loans to either side, urged both sides to find a political way out through negotiation, and supported Yuan Shikai’s rise to power.

Based on the Anglo-Japanese Alliance, Britain had repeatedly thwarted unusual changes in Japan’s China policy. After Yuan Shikai became Provisional

---

332 Nakajima Tan 中島端,『支那分割の運命』[The Fate of the Division of China], (Seikyosha, 1912), 234–235. For similar arguments in similar periods, see Sakamaki Teiichirō 酒巻貞一郎,『支那分割論』[On the Division of China], (Keiseisha, 1913), 275–276. Uchito Konan 内藤湖南,『支那論·附支那新論』(On China and New Theory on China), (Sogensha, 1938).

President of the Nanjing government, the Japanese government's foreign policy kept pace with that of Britain. In May 1912, the Japanese ronin Kawashima Naniwa 川島浪速 instigated "Manchu and Mongolian independence" in Northeast China. The Japanese army first expressed support but later withdrew aid.[333] In 1913, Uchida Ryōhei 内田良平 and others established the China Research Association, and continued to encourage the Japanese government to take the opportunity to solve the so-called "Manchu and Mongolian issue." Inconsistency between the radical Chinese policy of non-governmental personages and the prudent foreign policy of the Japanese government also led to the assassination of Abe Moritarō 阿部守太郎, head of the Political Affairs Bureau of the Ministry of Foreign Affairs.[334]

Generally speaking, there was a rather complicated relationship between the discourse of the Asiatic Monroe Doctrine and Japan's state establishment during the Meiji and Taisho periods. All the proponents of the Asiatic Monroe Doctrine were deeply concerned with the expansion of Western powers (especially Russia) in Asia. Many of them were also dissatisfied with the Japanese government's compromising attitude towards the West and its collaborationist diplomatic line; however, in terms of Japan's expansion in Korea, Ryukyu, Taiwan and Northeast China, the proponents of Asiatic Monroe Doctrine discourse seldom expressed their criticism. Some of them were even the vanguard of Japan's expansion policy in mainland China; their "theory of preserving China" was not completely hypocritical. After all, if China were completely divided up by the great powers, Japan would inevitably be in a very vulnerable position. However, as mentioned above, in the minds of many proponents of the Asiatic Monroe Doctrine, the territory of this "China" to be "preserved" had shrunk considerably compared with that of the Qing Dynasty. From the perspective of the territorial integrity of China, so-called preservation and partition differed only in degree.[335]

333 For the role of "the concert of the great powers" in the Revolution of 1911, see Zhang Yongle 章永乐, "Daguo xietiao yu datuoxie: Tiaoyue wantluo, yinhangtuan yu Xinhai geming de lujing 大国协调与大妥协：条约网络、银行团与辛亥革命的路径 [Great Power Concert and Great Compromise: Treaty Network, Banking Group and the Path of the Revolution of 1911]," *Xueshu yuekan* 10 (2018).

334 Hori Yukio 堀幸雄, Xiong Dayun 熊达云 trans., Zhanqian Riben Guojiazhuyi yundong shi (*History of Japanese Nationalist Movement before the World War II*), (Beijing: Shehui kexue wenxian chubanshe, 2010), 35–36.

335 A similar situation also exists in Britain's attitude towards China. In the Revolution of 1911, Britain opposed the partition of China by the great powers, but Tibet had already been excluded from its envisaged territory of China. Britain's policy towards Tibet was an extension of its "great game" with Russia in Central Asia. Britain was worried that Russia would march southward to occupy Tibet, which would threaten British India. Therefore,

2 The First World War and the Vicissitudes of the Japanese Monroe Doctrine

On July 28, 1914, the Austro-Hungarian Empire declared war on Serbia. As the major European powers declared war one after another, the First World War broke out. The rivalry among European powers led to a power vacuum in East Asia that created an opportunity for Japan's Asiatic Monroe Doctrine to be transformed from ideological trend to national policy. Ōkuma Shigenobu 大隈重信 seized the opportunity on August 23, 1914, after forming the cabinet for the second time. He declared war on Germany under the banner of "maintaining peace in East Asia," and then took advantage of the weakening presence of European powers to issue "Twenty-one Demands" to Yuan Shikai's government.[336] The Japanese government told Yuan Shikai's government not to cede or grant concessions on coastal bays, ports or islands to any major powers, and prohibited China from accepting foreign investment in Fujian Province.

---

it tried to separate Tibet from China and form a buffer zone. In 1903, Curzon, governor of British India, put forward that China only enjoyed "suzerainty" rather than "sovereignty" over Tibet. In 1904, Britain forced Tibetan nobles and monks to sign the Lhasa Treaty, and at the same time tried to force the Qing court to admit that China only enjoyed "suzerainty" in Tibet, which was rejected by the Qing government. In 1907, Britain signed a treaty with Russia, which confirmed this view. See G.P. Gooch and Harold Temperley eds., *British Documents on the Origin of the War, 1898–1914*, Vol. 4, (London: H.M.S.O., 1929), 352. Britain opposed the Bureaucratization of Native Officers by the Qing government in the part of Sichuan province where Tibetans reside. In February 1910, the Qing army stationed in Sichuan entered Lhasa, the Dalai Lama fled to British India, and the Qing court deprived the Dalai Lama of his title. Bound by the 1907 Anglo-Russian Treaty, Britain did not send troops to intervene. However, the outbreak of the Revolution of 1911 gave Britain another opportunity to intervene in Tibet affairs. Britain reiterated the claim that China had only "suzerainty" on Tibet and supported separatist forces. But legally speaking, Britain's proposition is a continuation of its consistent position. In 1912, Britain and Russia reached a new compromise because the 1907 Anglo-Russian Treaty was too restrictive on British intervention in Tibet. It was recognized that Britain and Russia enjoy the freedom of movement outside Mongolia, while Russia recognizes Tibet as the British sphere of influence. Britain then sent a large number of troops to Tibet.

336 In 1933, Wang Zaoshi discussed the change of situation and order brought about by World War I in this way: "In 1915, Japan took the opportunity of the European War to put forward Twenty-one Demands to China, which was the period when Asiatic Monroe Doctrine defeated Open Door Policy; It was not until after the Washington Conference in 1922 that the balance of power in the Far East was restored." Wang Zaoshi 王造时, "Jiashi yuandong dazhan 假使远东大战 [If the Far East War break out]," in *Zhongguo wenti de fenxi: Huangmiuni* 中国问题的分析·荒谬集 [*Analysis of Chinese Problems* (*Absurd Problems Collection*)], (Shanghai: Fudan daxue chubanshe, 2015): 243. The original title is "*What If the Far East War Break Out—What to do*" which was published in *Free Speech* 19 (1 November 1933).

Foreigners other than Japanese were not allowed to engage in mining, railway construction or seaport construction. In essence, the Japanese government did not allow any third country to maintain Army or Navy forces in Fujian, so as to maintain Japan's occupation of Taiwan. These demands were highly similar to those imposed by the U.S. on Latin American countries.[337]

Shuntian Shibao 顺天时报, a Chinese-language newspaper published by the Japanese Ministry of Foreign Affairs in Beijing, was very active during this period. Yuan Shikai's government leaked the contents of the Twenty-one Demands to the great powers in an attempt to leverage the Western powers, especially the U.S., against Japan. According to a *Shuntian Shibao* commentary, Yuan Shikai's expectation of U.S. intervention in the Far East would violate the U.S. Monroe Doctrine. "How can the United States interfere in distant East Asian affairs if it abides by the Monroe Doctrine?" It then quoted newspapers from Britain, France, the U.S. and Russia to demonstrate that all powers had actually agreed to Japan's policy, and admonished Yuan Shikai to give up the struggle.[338] At that time, U.S. political elites were quite displeased with Japan. On April 7, 1915, *News Press* 新闻报, one of the four major newspapers in Shanghai, quoted Japanese reports as saying that the U.S. Senate Committee on the Philippines had invited William Morgan Shuster, a U.S. financial expert who had served as financial secretary to the Persian imperial government, to give a speech on the independence of the Philippines. In a subsequent interview with the *Times*, Shuster talked about how Japan had developed its own Monroe Doctrine since its victory in the Russo-Japanese War, and would certainly support the Philippines independence movement and exclude American influence from Asia.[339]

After receiving the Yuan Shikai government's request for help, the Wilson government put pressure on Japan, reiterated the principle of the Open Door Policy and stressed that Japan should not harm U.S. interests and Chinese territorial integrity. However, its efforts to negotiate with Japan were very limited, and ultimately it failed to stop Japan from imposing the "Twenty-one Demands" on China. In a note to Japan on March 13, Secretary of State William Jennings Bryan acknowledged that Japan had "special relations" with China

---

337 In a commentary, Bao Mingqian clearly regards Twenty-one Demands as the policy of the Asiatic Monroe Doctrine. Bao Mingqian 鲍明钤, *Bao Mingling wenji* 鲍明钤文集 [*Selected Works of Bao Mingqian*], (Beijing: Zhongguo fazhi chubanshe, 2011), 763.

338 "Qiyu kelian 其愚可怜 Its stupidity is pitiful (11)," *Shuntian shibao* (10 March 1915), second edition.

339 Yu Gong 瑜公, "Riben zhi menluo zhuyi 日本之门罗主义 [Monroe Doctrine in Japan]," *Xinwenbao* (7 April 1915).

because of its territorial contiguity.[340] This actually provided a stimulus for the further development of the Asiatic Monroe Doctrine in Japan.

After Yuan Shikai proclaimed his Hongxian monarchy, the cabinet of Okuma decided to eliminate Yuan in December 1915. A series of anti-Yuan movements had been launched in China, such as the second Manchu-Mongolian Independence Movement promoted by Kawashima Naniwa 川島浪速 in cooperation with the Royalist Party in Northeast China, the Third Revolution of Sun Yat-sen, and the National Protection War launched by Cai E 蔡锷 and Liang Qichao 梁启超. These movements enjoyed varying degrees of support from the Japanese government and the public. The second Manchu-Mongolian Independence Movement promoted by Japanese forces did not succeed, due to the vigilance of the European powers and the U.S. against Japan's domination of Northeast China, as well as the Japanese cabinet's fear of Western powers on this issue. However, the anti-Yuan movement supported by Japan achieved remarkable results. Under domestic and external pressure, Yuan Shikai issued the Order of Revocation of the Imperial System to restore the Republic of China on March 22, 1916, and died of illness on June 6. After Yuan, China's political situation became more fragmented, and local powers gained greater autonomy. This fragmented situation was even more conducive to the growth of Japanese power in China than Yuan Shikai's personal dictatorship.

In 1917, President Li Yuanhong 黎元洪 and Prime Minister Duan Qirui 段祺瑞 of the Beiyang government engaged in fierce debate over whether or not to participate in World War I and how to participate. Local powers became involved, triggering the Zhang Xun Restoration on July 1. The restoration was suppressed in less than two weeks. Because Duan Qirui advocated the formulation of a new Constitution and refused to restore the Provisional Constitution, Sun Yat-sen went south to launch the Constitution Protection Movement and set up a military government. The constitutional order of the Republic of China was thus divided. The Japanese government adopted the policy of supporting the Beiyang government, and provided the Nishihara Loan 西原借款 to the Duan Qirui government through Nishihara Kamezo, to ensure that China joined the entente to fight under Japanese domination. After the downfall of the Anhui Clique of Duan Qirui, Japanese officials successively supported the Zhili Clique and Fengtian Clique that controlled the Beijing government. The military government of South China, led by Sun Yat-sen, constantly sought Japan's official recognition and support, but did not get any positive response.

---

340 Noriko Kawamura, *Turbulence in the Pacific: Japanese-U.S. Relations During World War I*, (Westport & London: Praeger, 2000), 45.

Japan's China policy during World War I triggered severe criticism from Kita Ikki 北一輝. In his *An Informal History of the Chinese Revolution*, which was published in 1915–1916 and revised in 1921, Kita Ikki argued that an authentic policy to preserve China was incompatible with the Anglo-Japanese Alliance, and the Japan actually played the role of British diplomatic lackey under the Anglo-Japanese Alliance in the name of preserving China. Japan participated in the banking consortium, committed economic aggression against China with Western powers, and provided loans to warlords in the north, but did not support the revolutionary forces that actually sought China's self-preservation. Kita Ikki exposed the hypocrisy of Ōkuma Shigenobu 大隈重信's Asiatic Monroe Doctrine, and demanded that Japan truly put it into practice by breaking away from British foreign policy, playing the role of "the protector of China and other parts of the yellow race" and "leader of Asia," supporting the revolutionaries opposed to the warlords in the north, and then launching an Anglo-Japanese War and Russo-Chinese War to truly liberate Asia from the oppression of European imperialism.[341] After the disillusionment of the Chinese revolution, Kita Ikki 北一輝 published *The Outline of Japan's Reform Act* in 1923, which changed its policy toward China. However, the core proposition that Japan should act as leader of Asian allies against the West remained intact.[342]

With the growing strength of Japan in China, the contradiction between the U.S. and Japan had become increasingly prominent. In 1917, the U.S. and Japan started negotiations. Japanese Extraordinary and Plenipotentiary Ambassador Ishii Kikujirō 石井菊次郎 made public speeches in New York on September 29 and October 1 while engaged in talks with U.S. Secretary of State Robert Lansing, saying that ideas similar to the Monroe Doctrine existed not only in the Western Hemisphere but also in East Asia.[343] Ishii further pointed out: "There is a basic difference between the Monroe Doctrine of the U.S. towards Central America and South America and the statement of Japan's attitude towards China. First of all, in the U.S., there was no agreement or promise, while Japan voluntarily declared its promise not to undermine the political or territorial integrity of our neighbors and to abide by the principles of Open Door and

341 Kita Ikki 北一輝,『支那革命外史』[Unofficial History of the Chinese Revolution], (Seiki Shobō, 1921), 184–187, 242.

342 Nomura (n. 325), 31–41.

343 Ikeda Jugo 池田十吾, 「石井·ランシング協定をめぐる日米関係(一)——中国に関する日米両国交換公文の成立過程から廃棄に至るまで」[U.S.-Japan Relations Regarding the Ishii-Lansing Agreement (1)—From the Establishment of the Japan-U.S. Exchange of Notes on China to its Termination], in『國士舘大學政經論叢』[Kokushikan University Political Science Review, Vol. 63, No. 4, 1988], 116.

equal opportunities, and asked other countries to respect these principles."[344] When Lansing testified to the Foreign Relations Committee of the U.S. Senate in 1919, he briefed the Senate on his communications and negotiations with Ishii. He held that the central principle of the U.S. Monroe Doctrine was the principle of "non-interference," and Ishii's speech spirit was consistent with this.[345] Ishii believed that according to the U.S. Monroe Doctrine, the U.S. had the "paramount interest" in Mexico, and Japan could have the same interests in China. Lansing denied that the U.S. Monroe Doctrine included such an element, but he was prepared to admit the special interests arising from territorial proximity.[346] In the process of negotiation between Lansing and Ishii, the U.S. Monroe Doctrine was always the frame of reference for Japan to put forward its own ideas. Japan even actively interpreted the U.S. Monroe Doctrine, forcing the U.S. to define the Monroe Doctrine more in line with the current Japanese interests.

In the Lansing-Ishii Agreement signed On November 2, 1917, by the U.S. and Japan, Ishii made concessions to Lansing, and the text did not include the "paramount interest" initially advocated by Ishii, but stated that "the governments of the United States and Japan recognize that territorial propinquity creates special relations between countries, and, consequently, the government of the United States recognizes that Japan has special interests in China, particularly in the part to which her possessions are contiguous ..."[347] Accordingly, Japan recognized the Open Door principle and the right of "equal opportunities" enjoyed by the U.S. in China. The secret agreement also included a clause that Germany's privileges in China's Shandong Province would be transferred to Japan. It can be seen that from the Roosevelt administration to the Wilson

344 Quoted from Bao (n. 336), 764–765. Bao Mingxian published the book *The Foreign Relations of China: A History and A Survey* in the U.S. in 1921, in which there was a special chapter to discuss Japan's "Asiatic Monroe Doctrine," and the translation of this book was included in Bao Mingxian's Collection. Bao Mingqian compared the similarities and differences between the Monroe Doctrine of Japan and the Monroe Doctrine of the U.S., but this comparison did not fully consider the massive interference of the U.S. in other countries' internal affairs in Latin America.

345 Hearings on the Treaty of Peace with Germany signed at Versailles on June 28, 1919, before the Senate Committee on Foreign Relations. Sixty-sixth Congress, First Session, Senate Document No. 106: 226.

346 Ibid., 147, 223–224.

347 Wang, He and Wu (n. 147), 447; Ross. Kennedy ed., *A Companion to Woodrow Wilson*, (Malden, Oxford & Chichester: John Wiley & Sons, Ltd., 2015), 234. For the discussion of the Lansing-Ishii Agreement and Monroe Doctrine in Chinese newspapers, see Tu Ruyang 屠汝涑, "'Teshu liyi' yu Riben menluo zhuyi ‘特殊利益’ 与日本之门罗主义 [Special interests" and "Monroe Doctrine]," *Liumei xuesheng jibao* 2 (1918), 155–160.

administration, the United States always acquiesced to and even condoned Japan's use of its Monroe Doctrine precedent in Asia.

The First World War provided a good opportunity for Japanese expansion, and also greatly stimulated the geopolitical imagination in Japanese public opinion and theoretical circles, bringing the discourse of the Japanese Monroe Doctrine to a climax. In 1916, Kodera Kenkichi 小寺謙吉, an active figure in Japanese politics, published *The Theory of Great Asianism* 大亞細亞主義論, which vividly played up the Western Yellow Peril Theory, and held that "Great Asianism means that Asia is Asia for Asians." In view of the great ambition of Western powers towards China, Japan "in terms of the China issue, has the lofty mission of being the core of maintaining peace in East Asia, rescuing China from the oppression of the white race, and assuming the leader of the yellow race."[348] Kodera Kenkichi pointed out that Japan's military strength could keep pace with Western powers, but it lacked natural resources; while China was rich in natural resources, but weak in military strength. China and Japan could therefore "support and help each other, and fight against whites for Asia and even all colored peoples."[349] His Asiatic Monroe Doctrine thus contained the notion of division of labor within the region. China's significance for Greater Asianism lay in providing economic resources, while Japan could provide protection for the whole region with its powerful military force.

In 1916, Tokutomi Sohō 徳富蘇峰, a critic who proposed the "Great Japan Expansion Theory" in 1894 and was ecstatic about Japan's victory in the Sino-Japanese War of 1894–1894, wrote a book titled *Taisho Youth and the Future of Empire* that trumpeted the Asiatic Monroe Doctrine. Tokutomi Sohō declared bluntly: "I firmly believe that the mission of the Japanese Empire is to fully realize the Asiatic Monroe Doctrine. The so-called Asiatic Monroe Doctrine is that Asian affairs are to be handled by Asians." Tokutomi Sohō held that Europeans should handle European affairs, Americans should handle American affairs and Asians should handle Asian affairs, without interfering with each other. But in "Asian affairs," Japan was the inevitable leader: "No one but Japanese can take on this task. Therefore, the Asiatic Monroe Doctrine means that the Japanese deal with Asian affairs." The article accused Chinese of "kowtowing to white people to get a moment's peace," but said that Japan should still "try its best to be friendly to China as members of the same race." As for the relationship with the "white race," Tokutomi Sohō emphasized that "Oriental autonomy" did not necessarily mean excluding white people, but rather "striving to be qualified to

348 Kenkichi Kodera 小寺謙吉,『大亜細亜主義論』[On Greater Asianism], (Tokyo Hobunkan, 1916), 12–13.

349 Ibid., 466.

surpass white people. Let the white people be convinced by the fact. Then, we will guide oriental people to interact with white people on an equal footing."[350]

Tokutomi Sohō 徳富蘇峰's exposition aroused the doubts of Ukita Kazutami 浮田和民. In 1918, Ukita Kazutami published "Neo-Asianism—A New Interpretation of East Asian Monroe Doctrine" in the journal *Taiyō* 太陽, referring to the "lock-up doctrine" of China, Japan and Korea before the Western invasion as "Old Asianism," and the Asiatic Monroe Doctrine of Tokutomi Sohō as "New Asianism." He himself advocated "Neo-Neo-Asianism," criticized Tokutomi Sohō for "making race a foothold," and contended that all nationalities living in Asia, regardless of their race, should belong to the category of Asians. This position could bring European colonists into the category of "Asians." Ukita Kazutami believed that if Tokutomi Sohō put too much emphasis on Japan as the center in foreign policy, "it will lead to opposition from the powers that maintain interests in East Asia, and at the same time, it will lead to resistance from other countries in East Asia." The goal of his Neo-Neo-Asianism was "not to expel European and American forces from Asia. The reason why Japanese should deal with Asian affairs is that we don't want Asia, like Africa, to be divided up by European and American powers." In terms of China policy, Ukita Kazutami insisted that Japan was "the protector of Oriental countries" and should not take a tough attitude towards the protected peoples. "We should first abandon the policy of placing China or several provinces of it into Japan's sphere of influence. We should not only pay special attention to China proper, but also preserve the territories outside of the 18 provinces. Then we can announce the great justice of the Asiatic Monroe Doctrine and implement it throughout East Asia."[351]

Kita Ikki 北一輝's brother, Kita Reikichi 北昤吉, also wrote an article in 1917 comparing the U.S. Monroe Doctrine with Japanese Greater Asianism. Kita Reikichi pointed out that the U.S. Monroe Doctrine was meant neither to defeat European forces and unify America, nor to publicize a unique American culture against European culture. Fundamentally, it was a disguised doctrine that focused on the interests of the U.S. Accordingly, the significance of Greater

---

350 Tokutomi Sohō 徳富蘇峰,「大正の青年と帝國の前途」[The Youth of the Taisho Era and the Future of the Empire], in Kamishima Jiro 神島二郎 (ed.),『徳富蘇峰集』[Tokutomi Soho Collection], (Chikuma Shobō, 1978), 229–231.

351 参见 Kazutami Ukita 浮田和民,「新亜細亜主義——東洋モンロー主義の新解釋」[New Asianism: A New Interpretation of the Oriental Monroe Doctrine],『太陽』Taiyō, Vol. 24, No. 9, 1918, pp. 2–17. For a Chinese translation of the essay on Dongfang Zazhi, see Kazutami Ukita 浮田和民,「新亜細亜主義——東洋モンロー主義の新解釋」[New Asianism: A New Interpretation of the Oriental Monroe Doctrine], Dongfang Zazhi, vol. 15, No. 11, November, 1918.

Asianism was not to mobilize the yellow race to defeat the white race, to stop the aggression of the white race by cooperating with Asia's weaker countries, or to wage a cultural war against the white race with the concept of Oriental civilization. Its goal was similar to the Monroe Doctrine, in that it aimed at eliminating Western oppression from Asia and establishing Japan's dominant position in Asia in order to seek Japan's political survival and the development of Japanese culture. "Greater Asianism" therefore essentially meant "Japanism." Kita Reikichi stressed that Japan's national interests should be taken into consideration, and Japan could form an alliance with some Asian countries in order to eliminate white oppression, but Japan didn't need to take on some imagined obligation to help weak countries in Asia. When necessary, Japan could also ally with Western powers, so it was not necessary to stir up strife between the yellow race and the white race.[352] We can see that Kita Reikichi's Japanese centralism was more obvious than that of Tokutomi Sohō 徳富蘇峰. However, in terms of the means of realizing Japan's interests, Kita Reikichi 北昤吉, like Ukita Kazutami 浮田和民, was concerned that the discourse of racial conflict might lead to conflict between Japan and Western powers. He advocated a more flexible posture.

It is difficult for us to understand the May Fourth Movement that broke out in China in 1919 without understanding the development of the Asiatic Monroe Doctrine as Japan's official policy during World War I, and the significant growth of Japan's influence in China. At the 1919 Paris Peace Conference, the Japanese representative asked for the inclusion of "racial equality" in the Covenant of the League of Nations, successfully forcing Wilson to make concessions. Wilson agreed to transfer German privileges in Shandong to Japan. Article 21 of the Covenant of the League of Nations, which made concessions to the Monroe Doctrine, was also regarded by the Japanese delegation as recognition of Japan's special regional interests.[353] The Paris Peace Conference's handling of the Shandong issue aroused anger in China. We can say that the May Fourth Movement was a response to Japan's Asiatic Monroe Doctrine after the outbreak of World War I, and also expressed dissatisfaction with the complicity of the U.S. Wilson government in Japan's Asiatic Monroe Doctrine. Under strong domestic pressure, the representatives of the Beiyang government did not sign the Treaty of Versailles.

352 Kita Tokichi 北昤吉,「誤解されたる亜細亜主義」[Misunderstood Asianism],『東方時論』[Oriental Journal, Vol. 2, No. 7, 1917], 8–10.

353 Thomas W. Burkman, *Japan and the League of Nations: Empire and World Order, 1914–1938*, (Honolulu: University of Hawai'i Press, 2008), 79.

At the beginning of 1920, Japan successfully won a permanent seat in the Council of the League of Nations. There was no second seat for Asia. At that time, Liang Qichao complained that Asia was not fully represented in the Council of the League of Nations, but "if we say that Asia is represented by Japan, how can it be different from recognizing Japan's Asiatic Monroe Doctrine? This is sufficient to create the hotbed of World War."[354] At the same time, the Treaty of Versailles met with great obstacles in U.S. Congress. In November 1919, when the U.S. Senate raised an objection to the handling of the Shandong issue, *Yomiuri Shimbun* 読売新聞 published a heated commentary accusing the U.S. of disrespecting the freedom of other countries: It promoted its own Monroe Doctrine, but did not respect Japan's Monroe Doctrine on the Shandong issue.[355] For Japanese public opinion, the response of the U.S. was a reversal of the consistent practice from Roosevelt to Wilson to allow Japan to cite the precedent of the U.S. Monroe Doctrine in East Asia.

Japan's Asiatic Monroe Doctrine was soon attacked by Western powers. The Washington Conference of 1921–1922 ended the Anglo-Japanese Alliance, replacing it with the Four-Power Treaty and the Nine-Power Treaty. Japan was forced to give up a number of military and political interests. The great powers strengthened their joint control over China and restrained Japan's pursuit of "special interests" in China. In 1924, the U.S. passed a new immigration act known in public as the Japanese Exclusion Act, which caused anger in Japan. Japan's Ministry of Foreign Affairs had a strong tradition of diplomatic coordination with Western powers. However, under the pressure of Western powers, the Japanese Army Headquarters' inclination toward the Asiatic Monroe Doctrine had strengthened, and line struggle within Japanese diplomacy became increasingly fierce in the 1920s.

Japanese military and political elites continued to seek new breakthroughs in China. In June 1927, Japanese Prime Minister Tanaka Giichi 田中義一 presided over the Oriental Conference on the governance of Manchuria and Mongolia, formulated *The Outline of China Policy*, and advocated Japan's "special status" in Manchuria and Mongolia, and especially in the three Northeastern provinces, in order to exclude other powers from the region. Tanaka's Cabinet planned to lay five main railways in Northeast China to control Manchuria and Mongolia by economic means. Tanaka had a close relationship with Zhang Zuolin 张作霖, the so-called "king of Northeast China." At the same time, Tanaka also planned to establish contact with Chiang Kai-Shek. In September 1929, Chiang Kai-Shek was defeated within the Kuomintang and announced that he would

354 Zhang (n. 167), 3037.
355 Burkman (n. 352), 101.

step down, after which he went to Japan for support. Matsui Iwane 松井石根, then chief of the Second Department (Intelligence Department) of the General Staff of the Japanese Army, helped Chiang Kai-Shek's lobbying efforts and introduced him to Tanaka Giichi 田中義一. After securing a promise of support from Tanaka Giichi, Chiang Kai-Shek returned to Nanjing to take charge of the Nationalist Government. Tanaka made a political investment in North China and South China in an attempt to expand Japan's interests in China.

However, as Samuel Huntington pointed out, due to the nature of Japan's national ideology and its deep-rooted feudal tradition, the military professionalism of Japanese military officers at that time was weak. They were rather highly politicized.[356] Japan's young officers wanted to see immediate results, and had no patience with Tanaka's long-term fishing expedition. On May 3, 1928, the Japanese army suddenly attacked Jinan 济南, killing and injuring thousands of Chinese soldiers and civilians; on June 4, Zhang Zuolin 张作霖 was killed at the Huanggutun 皇姑屯 railway station in Shenyang 沈阳 under the planning of Kōmoto Daisaku 河本大作, a senior staff officer of the Kwantung Army. As a result, Zhang Xueliang announced a "change of flag in the Northeast" and declared allegiance to the Nanjing Nationalist Government. Tanaka's "boiling frogs in warm water" tactic for Manchuria and Mongolia was defeated.

Tanaka petitioned the Japanese Emperor to impeach Kōmoto Daisaku 河本大作, but was criticized by the Japanese Army Headquarters. On July 2, 1929, Tanaka resigned. As Tanaka's moderate line lost ground, the radical invasion of China by young military officers came to the fore. Especially after the moderate prime minister Inukai Tsuyoshi 犬養毅 was assassinated by soldiers on May 15, 1932, Japan's pre-war party cabinet came to an end. The situation of Japanese military intervention in politics spun even more out of control. The Asiatic Monroe Doctrine of the Japanese Army Headquarters was increasingly transformed into the official policy of the Japanese government.

In August 1928, the U.S. and France initiated the Kellogg-Briand Pact (also known as the Pact of Paris), which required the contracting parties to abandon war as a tool for implementing national policies.[357] When Britain signed the treaty, it made a reservation: In a note to the U.S. ambassador on May 19, 1928, the British Foreign Ministry said, "There are certain regions of the world the

356 Samuel Huntington, Li Sheng 李晟 trans., *Junren yu guojia: Junzheng guanxi de lilun yu zhengzhi* 军人与国家：军政关系的理论与政治 [*The Soldier and the State: The Theory and Politics of Civil-Military Relations*], (Beijing: Zhongguo zhengfa daxue chubanshe, 2017), 114.

357 Wang, He and Wu (n. 147), 630.

welfare and integrity of which constitute a special and vital interest for our peace and safety." In these areas, Britain could exercise the right of self-defense.[358] In December 1928, Tachi Sakutarō 立作太郎, Emperor Hirohito's instructor in international law and a senior researcher on the Monroe Doctrine, commented that the British government's reservation represented a new Monroe Doctrine: "Britain does not recognize the application of the Pact of Paris in the sphere of influence in which it has close interests. The U.S. is also likely to claim that the pact is not applicable to some places based on the Monroe Doctrine. Therefore, due to the Monroe Doctrine of the U.S. and the new Monroe Doctrine of the sphere of influence claimed by the United Kingdom, there will be wars that cannot be prohibited by the Pact of Paris."[359]

Tachi Sakutarō 立作太郎's intention was to prove that Japan had the right to carry out a similar Monroe Doctrine in Northeast China. The Japanese government did not state a reservation on this point, however. Instead, it proposed that the expression "in the names of their respective peoples" in the treaty was contrary to Japan's state form 國體.[360] However, with the development of the situation, the idea of Tachi Sakutarō 立作太郎's idea quickly became the standard proposition of Japanese officials over the next few years.

3 The Full Flowering of the Japanese Monroe Doctrine

If the 1921–1922 Washington Conference suppressed the Japanese Monroe Doctrine, the world economic crisis of 1929–1933 brought new opportunities to Japan. In 1930, Ishii Kikujirō 石井菊次郎, who was then a privy counsellor, published his *Diplomatic Memoir* 外交余録 and vigorously promoting the Asiatic Monroe Doctrine, claiming that Japan's special interests in China were a permanent reality and did not need to be recognized by other countries. If there was a major upheaval in China, Europeans and Americans could pack up and leave at any time. However, Japan was adjacent to China and would inevitably be affected. Japan therefore needed to take measures to calm internal

358 Lauterpacht revised, *Oppenheim's International Law* (Part II Volume 1), (Beijing: Shangwu chubanshe, 1989), 137, Note 1.

359 Tatsusaku Taro 立作太郎, 「英国の新モンロー主義の宣言及不戦条約の実効」 [Britain's Declaration of the New Monroe Doctrine and the Effectiveness of the Kellogg-Briand Pact], 『外交時報』[Diplomatic Times, Vol. 48, No. 12, Issue No. 577, December 15, 1928], 3.

360 See Herbert Bix, Wang Liping and Sun Shengping 王丽萍、孙盛萍 trans., *Zhenxiang: Yuren tianhuang yu qinhua zhanzheng* 真相：裕仁天皇与侵华战争 [*Hirohito and the Making of Modern Japan*], (Beijing: Xinhua chubanshe, 2004), 129–131.

turmoil in China.[361] On the way to his "Staff Tour" in Northeast China from July 1929 to July 1931, Kwantung Army staff officer Ishiwara Kanji 石原莞爾 spoke in favor of Japan, representing the East Asian nations, carrying out a "final war" with the U.S., representing Western civilization. To that end, Japan urgently needed to incorporate "Manchuria—Mongolia" into Japan's territory in order to strengthen its war preparation. He made specific plans for this goal.[362] Japan's Kwantung Army launched the Mukden Incident in Northeast China in 1931. However, Ishiwara's idea that China's Northeastern provinces should be directly incorporated into Japanese territory was not accepted by the Japanese Army Ministry. The puppet state of Manchuria was founded on March 1, 1932, and Puyi was appointed puppet ruler.

If Kita Ikki tried to change China by supporting Chinese revolutionaries, and in turn promoting change in Japan, some proponents of Japan's Asiatic Monroe Doctrine in the 1930s also tried to promote the transformation of Japan's domestic order by experimenting with the puppet state of Manchukuo. Tachibana Shiraki 橘樸, the editor-in-chief of *Manchuria Review*, agreed with Okakura Tenshin 岡倉天心's idea of "Asian integration." Based on the Self-Government Guidance Department jointly established by the Kwantung Army and the South Manchuria Railway Company, he tried to influence the construction of the Manchurian puppet state order. He advocated "the imperial way of self-government" and expected to foster a non-capitalist "decentralized autonomous state" in Northeast China, based on the autonomy of families, tribes, gangs, peasant associations and various mutual aid groups. The autonomous system would be constructed on multiple levels, such as villages, towns, counties, provinces and the nation.

---

361 Ishii Kikujirō 石井菊次郎,『外交余録』[Diplomatic Commentaries], (Iwanami Shoten, 1930), 132–163.

362 Zhang Bofeng and Zhuang Jianping 章伯峰、庄建平 eds., *Kangri zhanzheng diyijuan: Cong jiuyiba zhi qiqi* (*Zhongguo jindaishi zilliao congkan*) 《抗日战争·第1卷：从九一八至七七（中国近代史资料丛刊）[*War of Resistance against Japan* (*Volume 1: From Mukden Incident to Marco Polo Bridge Incident*) (*Series of Modern Chinese History Data*)], (Chengdu: Sichuan daxue chubanshe, 1997), 94–95; Literature and History Committee of Jilin Provincial Political Consultative Conference eds., *"Jiuyiba" shibian ziliao huibian* "九·一八"事变资料汇编 [*Compilation of Mukden Incident Data*], (Changchun: Jilin wenshi chubanshe, 1991), 109–110; Mizuno Akira, "Ishihara's Strategy before the Manchurian Incident" in, *Shenyang wenshi ziliao dishibaji: Jinian "jiuyiba" liushi zhounian shiliao zhuanji* 沈阳文史资料第18辑：纪念"九·一八"六十周年史料专辑 [*The Album of Historical Materials Commemorating the 60th Anniversary of Mukden Incident* (*No. 18 Series of Shenyang Literature and History Materials*)], eds., Literature and History Research Committee of the Shenyang Municipal Committee of the Chinese People's Political Consultative Conference (1991): 165–173.

Tachibana Shiraki 橘樸 regarded the Mukden Incident as imbued with the significance of "Asian liberation." It led to so-called "nation-building" in the territory of the four Northeast provinces. This would lend a certain impetus to the transformation of Japan's domestic order: "The indirect intention is to expect the transformation of the motherland, so that the industrious masses will be liberated from the dictatorship and oppression of capitalist parties. Only in this way can we truly obtain the driving force for the liberation of Asia and engender the power to build an ideal country."[363] However, as is well known, the essence of regime-building in the Manchukuo puppet state was Japan's colonialism in China, and the Kwantung Army always occupied a dominant position. All discussion of "autonomy" was a political veil over the actual historical process.

After the Japanese occupied Jinzhou 锦州 on January 3, 1932, U.S. Secretary of State Henry Lewis Stimson held a meeting with the Chinese and Japanese governments on January 7, stating that the U.S. Government would not recognize any treaty or agreement that violated the Treaty of Nine Powers signed in 1922 or the Kellogg-Briand Pact signed in 1928, as well as any situation that effectively violated U.S. treaty rights, including China's sovereign independence or territorial and administrative integrity or the Open Door Policy. This was Stimson's so-called "non-recognition doctrine." Stanley Hornbeck, chief of the State Department's Division of Far Eastern Affairs, wrote to Stimson on January 14, further accusing Japan of pursuing the Japanese Monroe Doctrine: "For nearly twenty years, Japanese statesmen and writers have been speaking of 'Japan's Monroe Doctrine for Asia.' Some years ago they were given to comparing the position of Japan vis-à-vis China with that of the United States vis-à-vis Mexico. More recently they have insisted that Japan's relationship to Manchuria is essentially that of the United States toward weak countries of the Caribbean. They not infrequently say: 'The South Manchuria Railway is our Panama Canal.' During the past few weeks they have compared their activities in Manchuria with those of the United States in Nicaragua."[364]

In September 1932, *Time* Magazine reported a speech by Mori Kaku 森恪, a member of the Japanese House of Representatives, on Japan's national policy of pursuing a "Far Eastern Monroe Doctrine." It also noted that the Japanese Army Minister said that East Asian countries were oppressed by the white

363 Nomura (n. 325), 262–263.

364 Stanley Hornbeck Memorandum, 14 January 1932, "Manchuria? ... for Asia," in *The Diplomacy of Frustration: The Manchurian Crisis of 1931–1933 as Revealed in the Papers of Stanley K. Hornbeck*, ed. Justus D. Doenecke (Palo Alto, CA: Hoover Institution Press, 1981), 127.

race, and that while the U.S. openly advocated justice and humanity, its policy towards Cuba, Panama, Nicaragua and other Latin American countries contradicted its rhetoric. When Japanese officials advocated that Japan should protect Asia, they often traced the idea back to President Theodore Roosevelt.[365]

At the request of China, the Council of the League of Nations established an investigation team headed by Rufus Daniel Isaacs, first Marquess of Reading, on January 21, 1932. The team completed the investigation report on September 4 and published it on October 2. The report held that China had sovereignty over Northeast China, that the Mukden Incident was an act of Japanese aggression against China, and that "Manchukuo" had no legitimacy, but at the same time acknowledged that Japan had "special interests" in Northeast China. Japan responded to the Lytton Commission sent by the League of Nations and Stimson's "non-recognition doctrine" by emphasizing its right to exclude the domination of other powers in the name of "maintaining peace in Asia."[366]

To deal with the report, Japanese international jurist Matsubara Kazuo 松原一雄 tried to find a legal basis for Japanese aggression. What he found was Theodore Roosevelt's approval of Japan's Asiatic Monroe Doctrine. Matsubara said that the Japanese Monroe Doctrine was the guiding principle tailored by Roosevelt for Japan, and the core of the doctrine was that, "as the leader and protector of Asian peoples, Japan has the obligation to eliminate the encroachment of European powers on Asia." The territory of so-called Asian peoples ranged from the Suez Canal to the Kamchatka Peninsula, excluding India, Annan, the Philippines, Hong Kong and other European colonies. Since Japan also had its own Monroe Doctrine, U.S. interference in Japan's actions in East Asia violated the principles established by President Roosevelt.[367]

Takagi Yasaka 高木八尺, a prominent Japanese expert on American Studies and the student of Frederic J. Turner, the academic leader of "American frontierism" in the U.S., tried to establish an analogy between the U.S. Monroe Doctrine and the Japanese policy of expansion. He compared Japan's expansion in Northeast China to the expansion of the U.S. into Florida, Texas, California, Cuba and Hawaii. His rationale for Japan's use of military force in Northeast China was similar to that of the U.S. in the Caribbean. Takagi Yasaka said that among all the nations on earth, the U.S. might be the first to understand Japan's position and even appreciate the Japanese people's mentality

365 "Japan: Fissiparous Tendencies," *Time* (5 September 1932).

366 Xu Gongsu 徐公肃, "Suowei yazhou menluo zhuyi 所谓亚洲门罗主义 [The so-called Asiatic Monroe Doctrine]," *Wajjiao pinglun* 2 (1932).

367 Matsubara Kazuo 松原一雄,「リットン報告と日本モンロー主義」[The Lytton Report and the Japanese Monroe Doctrine],『東亜』(East Asia, Vol. 5, No. 11, 1932), 7.

towards Manchuria. He questioned the internal consistency of the U.S. application of the Monroe Doctrine in the Americas and the Open Door Policy in Asia, and suggested holding an international conference to discuss how to define "Monroe Doctrine."[368] Similarly, in a 1932 commentary, the foreign policy critic Inahara Katsuji 稲原勝治 complained that the U.S. adopted double standards by pursuing a closed-door policy in the Americas but implementing the Open Door Policy in the Far East. Fairness demanded that Japan be allowed to implement the Asiatic Monroe Doctrine in East Asia as a closed-door policy, and at the same time implement the Open Door Policy in Central and South America.[369]

On January 21, 1933, Japanese Foreign Minister Uchida Kōsai 内田康哉 delivered a speech in Congress, holding that article 21 of the Covenant of the League of Nations applied to the conflict between Japan and the League of Nations.[370] On February 21, the General Assembly of the League of Nations started discussing the draft report of the Committee of Nineteen. Japanese representative Matsuoka Yōsuke 松岡洋右 strongly opposed the intervention of the League of Nations, repeatedly emphasizing the regional specificity of the current situation and questioning the League of Nations' "co-management" plan for Northeast China: "Will the people of the U.S. agree to this kind of control over the Panama Canal? Will the British people allow this to happen in Egypt?"[371] However, the General Assembly of the League of Nations passed the draft report of the Committee of Nineteen on February 24, with only Japan opposing it. Japan withdrew from the League of Nations on March 27, 1933, and then withdrew from the Washington Naval Treaty and the London Naval Treaty on December 29, 1934. The withdrawal lifted the Versailles-Washington System's restrictions on the expansion of the Japanese Navy. On October 6, 1937, the General Assembly of the League of Nations adopted the report of the Far East Advisory Committee, ruling that Japan's actions violated the Pact of Paris; moreover, Japan could not claim that its Japanese Monroe Doctrine in

368 Yasaka Takagi, "World Peace Machinery and the Asia Monroe Doctrine," *Pacific Affairs* 5 (1932). See also George Blaustein, *Nightmare Envy and Other Stories: American Culture and European Reconstruction*, (Oxford: Oxford University Press, 2018), 63–64.

369 This article was published separately in 1938. Katsuji Inahara, *Japan's Continental Policy*, (Tokyo: Foreign Affairs Association of Japan, 1938), 32.

370 Uchida Kōsai 内田康哉,「第六十四回帝国議会ニ於ケル内田外務大臣演説」[Speech by Foreign Minister Uchida at the 64th Imperial Diet], 外務省 [Ministry of Foreign Affairs, 1933], 9.

371 Japanese Delegation to the League of Nations, Japan's Case in the Sino-Japanese Dispute as Presented Before the Special Session of the Assembly of the League of Nations, Geneva (1933): 60.

Northeast China was justified by "self-defense."[372] But with Japan having withdrawn from the League of Nations, this resolution no longer had binding force.

The atmosphere of the Asiatic Monroe Doctrine in Japan was already very strong by 1933. Yokota Kisaburō 横田喜三郎, a law professor at Tokyo University and successor to the chair held by Tachi Sakutarō 立作太郎, summarized the Japanese Monroe Doctrine prevailing in Japan from three aspects: First, "Japan can claim special rights and interests in Asia, especially in China"; second, "with regard to Asian issues, especially those concerning disputes, European and American interference must be excluded"; third, "the territory of Asia under the control of Europe and the U.S. should be liberated and their nations should be independent. Then, all the Asian nations should be united, and Japan should take the leader's position to compete with Europe and the U.S.." This summary attracted notice in China and was translated into Chinese.[373] After bidding farewell to the Versailles Washington system after World War I, Japan accelerated its efforts to create a regional order under its own domination.

George Hubbard Blakeslee, a part-time consultant to the State Department's Far East Division and a professor at Clark University, refuted the Japanese Monroe Doctrine in *Foreign Affairs* in 1933. Blakeslee pointed out that Japan was very small compared with Asia, while the U.S. was a giant compared with its neighbors in the south. It was therefore natural for the U.S. to adopt a proactive policy towards the Americas, while it was unnatural for Japan to adopt a similar policy towards Asia. This proposition was largely based on the argument of "the rights of the strong." Blakeslee further believed that the principle of the right to survival, lifeline and political expansion used to legitimize Japanese expansion in Manchuria was entirely fabricated by the Japanese themselves. There was no need for the U.S. to coerce the Caribbean republics into opening their doors to American capital. These countries opened their doors to the U.S. voluntarily. U.S. public opinion did not want to change the status quo in the Caribbean, while discussion of Manchuria in Japanese public media was completely focused on the interests of Japan. The last difference Blakeslee pointed out was that many other powers also had privileges in China and other parts of the Far East, but none of them had a similar claim to the Caribbean.[374]

---

372 Lauterpach (n. 357), 137, Note 2.

373 Yokota Kisaburō 横田喜三郎,「アジア・モンロー主義批判(亚细亚门罗主义批判)」[Criticism of the Asian Monroe Doctrine]『中央公論』[Chūōkōron, July 1933], 92–104. The Chinese version of the article was translated by Wang Mingzhang and published on Waijao Yuebao (Diplomatic Monthly), Vol. 3, No. 2, 1933.

374 George H. Blackslee, "The Japanese Monroe Doctrine," *Foreign Affairs* 11 (July 1933).

Blakeslee naturally presented a greatly embellished image of the U.S. Monroe Doctrine, reflecting U.S. double standards on the issue of sphere of influence. However, we can see how much pressure had been brought to bear on U.S. diplomats by Japan resorting to the precedent of the U.S. Monroe Doctrine. In 1936, Stanley Henpeck, director of the U.S. State Department's Far East Divison, delayed official publication of the *Lansing-Ishii Agreement* signed by the U.S. and Japan in 1917, in order to prevent adding fuel to the flames of Japan's Asiatic Monroe Doctrine; but in fact, the formal content of the agreement had long been no secret in the U.S. press.[375]

Facing increasing pressure from Japan, the Nanjing Nationalist Government strengthened its economic and technological ties with European powers and the U.S.. The London Monetary and Economic Conference was held in June 1933 with 66 countries as participants. The Nanjing Nationalist Government sent T.V. Soong (Song Ziwen 宋子文) as its representative. Soong said at the conference, "We do not want to adopt the Asiatic Monroe Doctrine, we welcome Western technology and capital, and we are willing to maintain a financial policy that does not prevent the import of foreign goods."[376] At the end of May 1933, China and the U.S. reached a "cotton and wheat loan contract," in which the U.S. promised to grant $50 million in cotton and wheat material loans to the Nanjing Nationalist Government; on July 3, the Council of the League of Nations decided to establish the Committee of the Council for Cooperation between the League of Nations and China;[377] the Nationalist Government also strengthened its relations with Germany and Italy, upgrading bilateral relations from the minister level to the ambassador level in 1933 and 1934, respectively. During his visit to Italy on July 12, 1933, T.V. Soong directly criticized Japan's policy of invading China and its ambition to dominate the world.

---

375 John R. Murnane, "Japan's Monroe Doctrine?: Re-Framing the Story of Pearl Harbor," *The History Teacher* 40 (August 2007), 514.

376 *Shen Bao*, 16 June 1933; see Qin Bangxian 秦邦宪, "Wei fensui diren de wuci 'weijiao' yu zhengqu duli ziyou de suweiai Zhongguo er douzhegn 为粉碎敌人的五次'围剿'与争取独立自由的苏维埃中国而斗争 [Struggle to Smash the Enemy's Five Encirclement and Suppression Campaigns and Fight for the Independence and Freedom of Soviet China]," in *Jiandang yilai zhongyao wenxian xuanbian (1091–1949)* 建党以来重要文献选编（1921 – 1949）[*Selected Works of Important Documents since the Founding of the Party (1921–1949)*] (Volume 10), (Beijing: Zhongyang wenxian chubanshe, 2011), 369.

377 Zhang Li 张力, "Gu Weijun yu 20 shiji 30 niandai Zhongguo yu guolian de jishu hezuo 顾维钧与20世纪30年代中国和国联的技术合作 [Gu Weijun and the Technical Cooperation with China and the League of Nations in the 1930s]," in *Gu Weijun yu Zhongguo waijiao* 顾维钧与中国外交 [*Gu Weijun and China's Diplomacy*], ed. Jin Guangyao 金光耀 (Shanghai: Shanghai guji chubanshe, 2001), 220–236.

Targeting the economic and technical cooperation between China and the League of Nations and European and American countries, Japanese Foreign Minister Hirota Kōki 広田弘毅 delivered a speech on foreign policy in the imperial Diet on January 23, 1934, opposing the expansion of British and U.S. power in China and advocating the implementation of the Asiatic Monroe Doctrine. On April 17, the Chief of Intelligence of Japan's Foreign Ministry, Amō Eiji 天羽英二, issued a statement which embodied Hirota Kōki's policy of Asiatic Monroe Doctrine: "if China uses other countries to reject Japan, or uses the means of violating the peace in East Asia, or adopts the policy of playing one foreign state against another, Japan can do nothing but fight back." As the statement contended, many countries that were concerned about the situation caused by the Manchuria Incident and Shanghai Incident and took joint action with China, "even if it is referred to as financial or technical assistance, it must have political implications in China," and this might result in the division of spheres of influence, co-management and even partition of China, which would affect peace in East Asia.[378]

This rhetoric imitated the expression of the U.S. Monroe Doctrine in many respects, and treated China as the exclusive sphere of influence of Japan.[379] There were urgent interests behind it. After the world economic crisis of 1929–1933, the U.S. and European powers established exclusive trade groups, established trade barriers to foreign countries, and reduced the competitiveness of imported products. In the face of these trade barriers, Japan's export of light industrial products had dropped dramatically, and economic pressure had quickly turned into the pressure of social stability. However, racist immigration laws in Western countries had prevented the poor people of Japan

378 Gong Gujin and Yun Xiu 龚古今、恽修 eds., *Diyici shijie dazhan yilai diguo zhuyi qinhua wenjian xuanji* 第一次世界大战以来帝国主义侵华文件选辑 [*Selected Documents of Imperialist Aggression against China since World War I*], (Beijing: Shenghuo, Dushu, Xinzhi sanlian shudian, 1958), 171.

379 After the publication of the Amau Doctrine, Ta Kung Pao wrote the *Statement of Japan's Ministry of Foreign Affairs* to analyze Japan's intention: "On the positive side, it is best for China to be under the control of Japan's so-called East Asiatic Monroe Doctrine politically and economically. On the negative side, at least, it is necessary that let other counrties not to help China increase its military strength on a large scale. The foregoing statement is an expression of its negative determination. On the positive side, Japan also knows that it is not easy to achieve, and now it shows its clue, and it wants to make a preliminary attempt." At the same time, the editorial pointed out that "this time, Japan only relies on a high-pressure statement to face China and to scare the world, and China will not be responsible for the possible major damage to peace in East Asia in the future." "Statement of Japanese Ministry of Foreign Affairs," *Ta Kung Pao Social Review* (20 April 1934), second edition.

from making a living through immigration. This greatly increased China's importance for Japan in solving its own economic and social crisis: China could provide Japan with markets for raw materials and commodities, and with space to settle Japanese immigrants. In this context, the growing influence of Western powers in China was undoubtedly very unfavorable to Japan's planning.

At a time when China and Japan had repeatedly negotiated on issues such as Northeast China and the League of Nations, there was considerable discussion and refutation of the Japanese Monroe Doctrine or Asiatic Monroe Doctrine in Chinese public opinion circles. In November 1932, *Ta Kung Pao* published an editorial that said: "Since the Mukden Incident, the so-called East Asian Monroe doctrine has predominated among Japanese thinkers, and is one of the movements against European and American interference in the Far East. According to the current situation, Japan's so-called Monroe Doctrine is a doctrine for the conquest of China. Its significance is to oppose any interference by European and American forces during its conquest of China."[380] On December 15, 1934, Du Chongyuan 杜重远, a well-known journalist, published an article titled "Greater Asianism" in Volume 1, issue 45 of *New Life*. He pointed out that Japan's "Greater Asianism" was Asia's version of the Monroe Doctrine, which centered on Japan and conquered and swallowed up other countries. It was no different from the "Greater Germanism" advocated by German imperialism in the past. Du Chongyuan also pointed out that the doctrine was copied from the U.S., an advanced imperialist country, and was similar to the U.S. clamoring for "America for the Americans." Its purpose was to invade Asia on its own.[381] Fang Jisheng 方济生's *Study of Greater Asianism*, published in 1937, criticized Greater Asianism as "a kind of Asiatic Monroe Doctrine, an exaggeration of Japanese imperialism, and an Asian crown for the Japanese Emperor."[382] Even Shanghai's *Pupils* magazine published fables titled "The Monroe Doctrine of Little Fox" and "The Monroe Doctrine of Goat" to discuss the international situation in East Asia in 1935.[383] The appearance of the Monroe Doctrine in

380 "Riben suowei dongyang menluo zhuyi 日本所谓东洋门罗主义 [Japan's so-called Oriental Monroe Doctrine]," *Ta Kung Pao Social Review* (30 November 1932), second edition.

381 Du Chongyuan 杜重远, "Dayaxiya zhuyi 大亚细亚主义 [Great Asianism]," *Xinsheng zhoukam* 1 (1934).

382 Fang Jisheng 方济生, *Dayaxiya zhuyi zhi yanjiu* 大亚细亚主义之研究 [*A Study of Greater Asianism*], (Beijing: The First Branch of Oriental Studies Association of New Asia Publishing House, 1937), 4.

383 In these two fables, the image of Japan is a fox, who, under the banner of uniting with the goat family to resist leopard and tiger, deceives the fatuous old goat, drives away the

primary school magazines shows how wary the Chinese public had become of Japan's Asiatic Monroe Doctrine.

The 1937 Marco Polo Bridge Incident marked the resolute resistance of the Chinese army and people against Japanese aggression, and frustrated the Japanese fantasy of conquering China in a short period of time (the most extreme version of which was the clamoring of Army Minister Sugiyama Hajime 杉山元 to "solve the China Incident in one month"). In this context, Japan launched the so-called "East Asian New Order" theory in an attempt to divide China's Anti-Japanese forces. The Konoe Cabinet issued a series of statements on China on January 16, November 3 and December 22, 1938, with the statement on November 3 saying, "The construction of such a new order should be based on the cooperation of Japan, Manchuria and China, and the establishment of a series of mutual aid relations in politics, economy and culture. We hope to establish international justice in East Asia, to realize common defense against Communism, to create a new culture and to realize economic integration." The Japanese government hoped that the Nationalist government would abandon its policy of "opposing Japan and tolerating Communists" and cooperate with Japan. Meanwhile, it hoped that Britain, the U.S. and other powers would "adapt to the new situation in East Asia."[384]

Here, Konoe Fumimaro 近衞文麿 translated his father's Asiatic Monroe Doctrine into very concrete policies. In the statement on December 22, Konoe Fumimaro explicitly proposed the three principles of "good-neighborly friendship, active defense against Communism and economic cooperation," and particularly stressed that "in the world of East Asia, there should be no Comintern power," which more clearly excluded the Communist Party from the space of its Asiatic Monroe Doctrine.[385] Wang Jingwei sent a telegram in response to the statement of the Konoe Cabinet on December 29. In March 1940, Japanese militarist forces supported the establishment of Wang Jingwei's puppet regime in Nanjing. As early as December 16, 1938, the Japanese

alert little goat, and finally occupies the house of the goat family and eats the uncle and aunt of the goat. This is the Monroe Doctrine of the fox. "Xiaohuli de menluozhuyi 小狐狸的门罗主义 [The Monroe Doctrine of Little Fox]," *Xiaoxuesheng* (Shanghai) 5 (1935). The escaped kid joined forces with chickens, ducks, geese, pigs and other animals in the valley, defeated the fox, established the Monroe Doctrine of the weak, and prohibited the fox from setting foot in the valley. This is the Monroe Doctrine of the kid. "Shanyang de menluo zhuyi 山羊的门罗主义 [Monroe Doctrine of Goats]," *Xiaoxuesheng* (Shanghai) 6 (1935).

384 Gong and Yun (n. 377), 183–184.

385 Ibid., 184.

government had set up the East Asia Development Board 興亜院, which took charge of puppet regimes in Japanese-occupied areas and coordinated the Japanese government's policy towards China.

Around 1938, the concept of the "East Asian Co-Prosperity Sphere" was proposed in the National Defense Policy jointly drafted by Iwakuro Hideo 岩畔豪雄 and Horiba Kazuo 堀场一雄. On July 26, 1940, the Konoe cabinet issued "Outline of the Basic National Policy," which proposed building "a new order of Greater East Asia with Japan as the core and the firm integration of Japan, Manchuria and China as the backbone" and "establishing an economic cooperation circle covering the whole of Greater East Asia." On August 1, Japan's Foreign Minister, Matsuoka Yōsuke 松冈洋右, issued a statement on the Greater East Asian Co-Prosperity Sphere and again raised the question of why the U.S. could rely on the Monroe Doctrine to maintain its dominant position in the Western Hemisphere so as to maintain the stability and prosperity of the American economy, but Japan could not use the Asiatic Monroe Doctrine to do the same thing in Asia.[386] The Japanese militarists advocated carrying forward the spirit of the so-called "imperial way," liberating Asia from the oppression of Western colonists, and establishing a regional order led by Japan. The scope of the so-called Greater East Asian Co-Prosperity Sphere designated by the Konoe cabinet extended from east of Siberia to the South Pacific Ocean, and from Japan to British India.

In April 1940, Nazi Germany launched its Blitzkrieg in Europe and rapidly conquered Denmark and Norway, then invaded the Netherlands, Belgium, Luxemburg and France in May. Japan began to worry that the ownership of Southeast Asian colonies ruled by the European powers newly conquered by Germany might give rise to disputes among the great powers. Japan therefore issued notes to several Western powers from April to May of 1940, hoping to maintain the original state of the Dutch East Indies and the French Indochina Peninsula, in the same way that the U.S. interpretated the Monroe Doctrine in the nineteenth century to prevent the "transfer" of territories in the Americas to European powers. Japan was worried that Dutch and French colonies in Southeast Asia would fall into the hands of Britain and the U.S.

On July 6, 1940, President Roosevelt's press secretary, Stephen Early, issued an announcement on behalf of the president, stating that the U.S. was not prepared to send troops to war: "The government of the United States wants

386 Kimitada Miwa, "Japanese Images of War with the U.S.," in *Mutual Images: Essays in American-Japanese Relations*, ed. Akira Iriye (Cambridge, MA: Harvard University Press, 1975): 133.

to see, and thinks that there should be, an application of the Monroe Doctrine in Europe and Asia similar to its interpretation and application of the Monroe Doctrine for this hemisphere"; the colonies in Americas and Asia formerly ruled by defeated European powers could be handled by countries in the region through consultation.[387] Japanese ruling elites were excited by this announcement. Secretary of State Cordell Hull rushed to put out the fire and issued a statement on July 8, saying that the Monroe Doctrine was misinterpreted in some parts of the world, and was only a policy of collective defense as opposed to U.S. hegemony, and was different from the military occupation and complete economic and political control implemented in these places.[388] Early further stated that there was no sign or evidence of true Monroe Doctrine in other hemispheres.[389] The Japanese government's attempt to reach an understanding with the U.S. government on the scope of mutual respect for each other's Monroe Doctrine failed.

The French Vichy government surrendered to the Nazi German government on June 22, 1940. On September 22, the Japanese army entered the northern part of Indochina with the consent of the local authorities under the French Vichy puppet government. The Vichy government recognized Japan as a "co-protector" of French Indochina. On September 27, 1940, Germany, Italy and Japan signed a military agreement stipulating that Japan recognized and respected Germany's leading position in the establishment of a new European order, while Germany and Italy recognized and respected Japan's leading position in the establishment of the "new Greater East Asian order."[390] To a certain extent, Japan had extricated itself from its isolated situation in the world since the Mukden Incident. On November 30, 1940, *The Joint Declaration of Japan, Manchuria and China* was signed by Wang Jingwei 汪精卫, President of the Executive Yuan of the Wang puppet government, Abe Nobuyuki 阿部信行, the "ambassador" of Japan to the puppet government, and Zang Shiyi 臧式毅, Speaker of the Senate of the Manchukuo puppet state.[391] The "Greater East Asia Co-Prosperity Sphere" envisaged by the Japanese government seemed to have taken shape.

---

387 Gerald K. Haines, "American Myopia and the Japanese Monroe Doctrine, 1931–41," *Prologue* 13 (Summer 1981), 113.

388 Francis O. Wilcox, "The Monroe Doctrine and World War II," *The American Political Science Review* 36 (Jun., 1942), 452.

389 Division of American Republics, Memorandum, 8 July 1940, DS 710.11/2527, RG59, NA.

390 Gong and Yun (n. 377), 229.

391 Ibid., 239.

The Konoe Cabinet strengthened its alliance with Germany and Italy, while concurrently maintaining a coordination relationship with Britain and the U.S.. It pursued intermittent negotiations with the U.S. during the following year, aimed at gaining U.S. recognition for the sphere of influence outlined by the Japanese Monroe Doctrine and a mutual agreement not to interfere in each other's affairs. However, the U.S. government insisted that the U.S. Monroe Doctrine had nothing in common with the Japanese Monroe Doctrine; the U.S. version had become a kind of multilateralism with the promotion of the Roosevelt administration's "good neighbor policy," which had been approved by the American Republics, while the Japanese version had coercively imposed its will on other countries and nations in the region. This statement of course ignored the continuous reaffirmation by the U.S. State Department that U.S. had the right to unilateral action.[392]

During the period of "neutrality," the U.S. made money from both sides: It helped Chiang Kai-Shek resist Japanese aggression, while continuously selling oil, steel and other materials that were helpful to Japan's war of aggression according to the Treaty on Trade and Navigation signed by the U.S. and Japan in 1911. However, Japan's ambition for Southeast Asia and the Pacific region posed a serious threat to U.S. interests in Asia. On 26 July 1941, President Roosevelt issued an executive order to freeze Japanese assets in the U.S., and then imposed an oil embargo on Japan. Since most of Japan's oil was supplied by the U.S., the U.S. government's move dealt a heavy blow to Japan's war capability. On December 7, 1941, the Japanese army raided Pearl Harbor, and the Pacific War broke out. The Japanese army quickly marched into Southeast Asia, transforming the Greater East Asia Co-Prosperity Sphere from a plan on paper to active colonial conquest. On November 1, 1942, the imperial government of Japan set up a Ministry of Greater East Asia 大東亜省, and the former colonial governing institution the East Asia Development Board 興亜院 was incorporated into this new institution.

According to the new arrangements under Japan's policy toward China formed by the Imperial Council of Japan on December 21, 1942, the provisional meeting of the Central Political Committee of Wang Jingwei's puppet regime in Nanjing passed a resolution to declare war on Britain and the U.S. on January 9, 1943, saying that "Britain, the U.S. and other countries are still following their old policy of splitting East Asia, and they have intensified their efforts to lure the Chongqing government to join the so-called Anglo-American

392 Haines (n. 386), 103.

group and send troops to Myanmar and India." Wang's puppet regime declared, "We should exert our full strength to cooperate with Japan, a friendly country, in sweeping away the brutality of Britain and the U.S., so as to seek the rejuvenation of China, the liberation of East Asia, and friendship between Manchukuo and China. We should make a concerted effort to promote the future common prosperity of East Asia, so as to jointly build a new East Asian order based on moral principles." The declaration of war on Britain and the U.S. was associated with "realizing the Great Asianism of the Father of the Nation."[393] This was a comprehensive reiteration of the Japanese government's Greater Asianism discourse. The Japanese government also formally returned the Japanese concession to the Wang puppet government, abolished extraterritorial jurisdiction, and forced the French Vichy regime to return the French concession to the Wang puppet regime and abolish extraterritoriality.

How do we explain the history of Japanese expansion since the nineteenth century when Japanese militarism turned to confront Britain and the U.S.? *The Construction of East Asian Order*, published by Ōkawa Shūmei 大川周明 in 1943, serves as an example of the discourse in Japan's historical narrative of the Asiatic Monroe Doctrine towards full-scale aggression. Ōkawa Shūmei said that Japan awakened earlier than other Asian countries and made great sacrifices for Asia, and it therefore should wield the guiding power of the Greater East Asia Co-Prosperity Sphere. He reviewed several Japanese wars against China throughout history, and interpreted the Sino-Japanese War of 1894–95 as Japan's first counterattack against the European invasion of East Asia. The reasoning was that the Qing government had at that time become the puppet of Europe, not only selling its own rights and interests to European powers, but also introducing European powers into Korea. Okawa likewise explained the Russo-Japanese war as Japan's second counterattack against the European invasion of East Asia, and held that it brought courage and hope to Asian countries oppressed by the white race.

For Ōkawa Shūmei, the process from the launch of the Mukden Incident to the establishment of the Manchukuo puppet state was remarkable for Japan abandoning its accord with the Anglo-American powers that oppressed Asia, and turning to the great cause of "rejuvenating Asia." Ōkawa Shūmei argued

---

393 "Wangwei zhegnfu dui yingmei xuanzhanwen 汪伪政府对英美宣战文 [Wang Puppet Government's Declaration of War against Britain and America]," in *Wang Jingwei jituan maiguo toudi pipan ziliao xuanbian* 汪精卫集团卖国投敌批叛资料选编 [*Selected Works of Wang Jingwei Group's Traitors, Enemies and Rebellions*], eds. Selected Works of Wang Jingwei's Research Group of Marxism-Leninism Teaching and Research Section of Nanjing University (Nanjing: Nanjing daxue xuebao bianjibu 1981), 282.

that China's War of Resistance against Japan was based upon a profound misunderstanding of Japan's painstaking efforts to revive Asia, and that Britain and the U.S. were responsible for instigating discord between Japan and China. Ōkawa Shūmei demonstrated that Japan's war against China was fundamentally for the "rejuvenation of China" and that Japan would ultimately join hands with the rejuvenated China to realize the "rejuvenation of Asia."[394] It is worth mentioning that Ōkawa Shūmei was the only civilian figure among the war criminals tried in the International Military Tribunal for the Far East after World War II. He was ultimately exempted from prosecution because of mental illness.

So, what kind of political and ethical principles underpinned the internal homogeneity of the so-called Greater East Asia Co-Prosperity Sphere? Various discussions of "Tao" (*dao*, "way") emerged at this time. In his book *Oriental Culture and the Future of China*, published in 1939, Inoue Tetsujirō 井上哲次郎 advocated replacing the KMT government's Three Principles of the People with the "Tao" of Japan. He said that the "Tao" of Japan was a continuation of Chinese culture, but was tempered by Japanese spirit to finally surpass Chinese culture. He did not directly refer to the term "imperial way," but his discussion actually pointed to the "imperial way" with the "state form" as its core.

In 1942, Kuwahara Tamaichi 桑原玉市 directly advocated the slogan of "imperial way" in his *The Idea of the Empirization of Great East Asia*, calling the ongoing Greater East Asia War an "imperial movement" that liberated Asian nations from the "Shina spirit" or "European and American spirit." According to Shinto beliefs, the emperor of Japan was not only a political and legal sovereign, but also a descendant of God, and people should not only obey him, but also believed in him whole-heartedly. This discourse was not just for propaganda purposes.[395] When Pu Yi was in power in the Manchukuo puppet state, the Japanese asked him to build a Founding Temple to worship the Shinto goddess Amaterasu Ōmikami 天照大神. The Japanese army also built a shrine in Nanjing, and coerced the Wang puppet regime to send military and political officials and people's "representatives" to participate in so-called "Rituals for the Souls" 慰灵祭. All of this was the concrete practice of the imperial way within the sphere of influence of the Asiatic Monroe Doctrine.

---

394 See Ōkawa Shūmei 大川周明,『大東亜秩序建設』[The Construction of East Asian Order], (Daiichi Shobō, 1943).

395 See Wang Xiangyuan 王向远, *Riben dui Zhongguo de wenhua qinlue* 日本对中国的文化侵略 [*Japanese Cultural Aggression against China*], (Beijing: Kunlun chubanshe, 2005), 117–124.

After the Japanese government began supporting the puppet Manchukuo and Wang Jingwei regimes, it still faced the problem of how to explain their relations with Japan in terms of international law. From the Asiatic Monroe Doctrine to the Greater East Asia Co-Prosperity Sphere, Japanese political elites constantly refined their political discourse based on the U.S. Monroe Doctrine. At the same time, they also tried to reform the existing rules of international law to create a Greater East Asia International Law that provided legitimacy for the Greater East Asia Co-Prosperity Sphere. Carl Schmitt's theory (in a Japanese translation of the "Theory of Large Space Order") provided the inspiration for Japanese international jurists to construct their discourse. Considering Schmitt's use of Japan's Asiatic Monroe Doctrine as backup in his exposition of international law in 1939, the attraction of his theory to Japanese international jurists can be imagined. Japanese scholars such as Yasui Kaoru 安井郁 (a professor at Tokyo University), Matsushita Masatoshi 松下正寿 (a professor at Rikkyo University) and Tabata Shigejirō 田畑茂二郎 (an associate professor at Kyoto University) had carefully examined the Monroe Doctrine and Schmitt's "Großraum Theory,"[396] and then combined them with Japan's own Asianism. Schmitt's sharp criticism of universalism in international law and his exploration of the regional concept of "Großraum" between the global order and nation-state were well-suited to the practical needs of Japan's construction of the Greater East Asia Co-Prosperity Sphere.[397]

Schmitt emphasized the exclusion of external interference from Großraum and the role of the leading nation in Großraum, but his minimal discussion of the internal structure of Großraum provided Japanese international law

396 During the Second World War, the Japanese international law academia had a plan to publish twelve volumes of the Great East Asian International Law Series, and finally four volumes were published, two of which are: Matsushita Masatoshi 松下正寿,『米洲広域国際法の基礎理念』 [Fundamental principles of American Large-Space International Law] (有斐閣 Yuhikaku, 1942). Yasui Kaoru 安井郁,『歐洲広域国際法の基礎理念』[Fundamental principles of European Large-Space International Law] (有斐閣 Yuhikaku, 1942). 参见 Akashi Kinji 明石欽司:「『大東亜国際法』理論-日本における近代国際法受容の帰結」[Theory of "Greater East Asian International Law"—The Consequences of Japan's Acceptance of Modern International Law], (『法学研究』Legal Studies, Vol. 82, No. 1, 2009), 261–292. For the translation and introduction of Japan's "Large Space International Law" by Chinese scholars, see Wei Leijie 魏磊杰 (ed.), *Guojifa zhixu: Yazhou shiye* 国际法秩序：亚洲视野 [*International Law Order: Asian Perspective*], (Beijing: Dangdaishijie chubanshe, 2020), 67–159.

397 Tabata Shigejirō 田畑茂二郎,「ナチス国際法学の轉開とその問題史的考察」[The Development of Nazi International Law and a Historical Consideration of Its Problems], 『外交時報』[Diplomatic Times, Vol. 107, No. 1, Issue No. 926, July 1, 1943], 5–17.

scholars with room for theoretical development. Tabata Shigejirō 田畑茂二郎 believed that East Asian International Law needed to go beyond the "principle of absolute equality of states" in modern international law: "The fundamental legal concept of modern international law is not applicable to the states in the Greater East Asia Co-Prosperity Sphere, and we should not follow this concept in understanding and building the legal relationship among the states in the Co-Prosperity Sphere in the future. The legal relations among states in the sphere have gone beyond the preset scope of modern international law. Its formation does not simply depend on the agreement of the free will of the states concerned, which has nothing to do with objective values. The legal relations among the states in the Co-Prosperity Sphere should be based on the full understanding of their own destiny, and on their common moral consciousness, that is, to realize the great ideal of common prosperity for all nations declared at the beginning of the Greater East Asia Joint Declaration."[398] The so-called Co-Prosperity Sphere was not a treaty-based combination of equal states according to free will, but a union of destiny beyond free will. "As members of the Co-Prosperity Sphere, it is impossible for states to leave it at will."[399]

Matsushita Masatoshi 松下正寿 pointed out more specifically: "The principle of internal composition of the Coprosperity Sphere is not the formal collection of equal states in previous international law, but the organic combination of unequal states, so there should be different classes in law. Among them, the state that is positioned at the top and is responsible for maintaining the Coprosperity Sphere is the leading power. I therefore define the leading power as: the state that should not only fully exercise rights and fulfill obligations in international law independently, but also make legal acts for states in the Coprosperity Sphere when they cannot fully exercise their rights and fulfill their obligations in international law."[400] The "leading power" here was the Japanese counterpart of Schmitt's concept of "Reich." Matsushita Masatoshi 松下正寿's exposition shows that the internal order of the Co-Prosperity Sphere was unequal, that Japan was dominant as the leading state, and that the Manchukuo and Wang puppet regimes would be dominated by Japan according to the so-called "organism" principle. At the same time, following Schmitt's

398 Tabata Shigejirō 田畑茂二郎,「東亜共栄圏国際法への道」[The Path to International Law for the East Asia Co-Prosperity Sphere],『外交評論』[Diplomatic Review, Vol. 23, No. 1, 1943], 14.

399 Matsushita Masatoshi 松下正寿:『大東亜国際法の諸問題』[Problems of International Law in Greater East Asia], 日本法理研究会 [Japan Legal Principles Research Association, 1942], 25–26.

400 Ibid., 43–44.

analytical framework, Matsushita Masatoshi clearly divided international law into "intra-sphere law" and "inter-sphere law." The former was applicable to the relationships within the Co-Prosperity Sphere or Greater Space, while the latter regulated the relationships between Co-Prosperity Spheres or Large Spaces.[401]

Of course, with Japan's defeat, the efforts of Japanese international jurists to reform modern international law came to an abrupt end. The development from Schmitt's *Großraum* theory to Japan's large space international law is a segment that cannot be ignored in the history of the Monroe Doctrine's global circulation. Like Germany, Japan also limited the U.S. Monroe Doctrine to its pre-Wilsonian form, excluded interference from Britain and the U.S. in the name of regional autonomy, and then strengthened its control over other countries and nations in the region. In its heyday, Japanese militarists did not seek a global balance of power with maritime hegemony like Wilhelm II, the emperor of the Second German Reich, but were satisfied with conquering and dominating Greater East Asia. However, even such apparently limited imperial expansion caused great disaster to the region.

4 Concluding Remarks

The rising of the Monroe Doctrine discourse in Japan can be read as the story of a latecomer seeking the recognition of the privileged in the imperialist order. In the 1870s, the U.S. diplomat Le Gendre taught the Monroe Doctrine to Japanese ruling elites. By the end of the nineteenth century, Monroe Doctrine discourse merged with the discourse of Asianism. From the Russo-Japanese War to the Lansing-Ishii Agreement of 1917, the U.S. government attempted to compete with European powers in East Asia by condoning and even encouraging Japan to use the Monroe Doctrine as a reference in dealing with its relations with its Asian neighbors, with the result that the U.S. was ultimately hit by its own boomerang. It was impossible to limit the targets of exclusion in Japan's Asiatic Monroe Doctrine to the European powers alone. Starting from the end of the nineteenth century, the integrated version of Asianism and the Monroe Doctrine in Japan reiterated the "rivalry between the yellow race and the white race," and held that Japan should be the leader of Asia in liberating Asia from Western colonial rule. The growing pressure of Western powers in Asia, as well as the exclusion of Asian immigrants by racist forces in the West, lent appeal to

401 Ibid., 45–50.

the Asianist rhetoric of "resisting European powers and the U.S.," and allowed Japanese Monroe Doctrine discourse to gain a degree of endorsement among Chinese cultural/political elites.

However, this rhetoric of resistance was ambiguous, and it had long been distant from Japan's foreign policy. In 1902, Japan and Britain entered into an alliance that lasted until December 13, 1921, when the Washington Conference signed the Four-Power Treaty. During the alliance, Japan helped Britain suppress the uprising of Indian soldiers stationed in Singapore, while Britain also supported Japan in strengthening its colonial rule over Korea. The Russo-Japanese War, which Japanese Asianists boastingly described as "the yellow race defeating the white race," actually reflected internal contradictions among the Western powers, in which Britain and the U.S. supported Japan's confrontation with Russia. During World War I, the discourse of Asiatic Monroe Doctrine was rampant in Japan, but Japan's actual policy was to sign secret treaties with Western powers and seek their recognition of Japanese rights and interests in Shandong through an exchange of interests. There is a stark and obvious contrast between the rhetoric about "the competition between the yellow race and white race" and "Asia for the Asians," and these various cases of conspiracy and coordination between Japan and Western powers.

However, this ambiguity was not without political grounds. Japan's diplomatic authorities had long adopted a diplomatic line in harmony with European and American powers because of their strength, and fierce critics of the West among the advocates of Asiatic Monroe Doctrine were often regarded as excessively radical troublemakers and excluded from the decision-making core. Elites such as Okuma gave priority to the Anglo-Japanese Alliance, but selectively borrowed some phrases of Asianism to legitimate the outcome of the Russo-Japanese War and the establishment of spheres of influence in China. However, the conflict between Japan's expansion and European and American powers became increasingly prominent after World War I, and the diplomatic line coordinated with Europe and America gradually degenerated with the rising power of the Japanese military and the decline of the party cabinet. In the 1930s, Japan broke with the League of Nations led by Britain and France, and later declared war on Britain and the U.S. directly.

In Southeast Asia, the Japanese army did wage wars against British and Dutch colonial troops and won some local support, which made its rhetoric of "resistance" look less awkward. However, the unchangeable fact was that at this time, Japan was seeking domination over China more blatantly than ever, and it had inflicted great disasters on many of the nationalities and peoples included in the Greater East Asia Co-Prosperity Sphere. This kind of Asianism was along the lines of what Tokutomi Sohō said in 1916 about the Asiatic Monroe Doctrine being Japan's doctrine for dealing with Asia, or what Kita Reikichi proposed in 1917 that equated Asianism with Japanese Doctrine—there was no real respect for the subjectivity of other countries and nations in the region.

Against this background, we can better understand the profound reflection expressed by Japanese thinker Takeuchi Yoshimi 竹内好 in *Asia as Method* in 1961. Takeuchi pointed out that while exporting the positive values of freedom and equality to areas beyond Europe, Western Europe had established a new hierarchy in the world, thus limiting the effective domain of these values to the metropolis, and denying that colonial and semi-colonial peoples could cite these values in their interaction with the West. Colonial and semi-colonial peoples could therefore establish their own subjectivity and truly turn these values into genuine universal human values only by launching profound internal movements and resisting Western colonialism-imperialism.[402] Takeuchi Yoshimi's "Asia" here was not a cultural-geographical concept, but a political subject generated through resistance. Israel is geographically located in "Asia," but it does not belong to "Asia" as defined by Takeuchi. Cuba is geographically located in America, but it can belong to what Takeuchi likes to call "Asia." Asianism in modern Japan once had a certain connotation of resisting imperialism and colonialism, but eventually it became imperialism and colonialism.

Takeuchi keenly felt the absence of resistance in Japanese Asianism, but this absence might have been the inevitable result of the so-called "success" brought by the Meiji Restoration. During the Meiji Restoration, Japanese elites imitated the "civilization" of European powers, and quickly built a powerful nation. Japan won the Sino-Japanese War of 1894–1895 and the Russo-Japanese War of 1904–1905. The international environment of the Great Game between Britain and Russia also brought favorable conditions for the rise of Japan. Japan became an ally of Britain and was soon recognized as a member of the family of nations, the club of colonial empire. The contradiction between Japan and other great powers was essentially the contradiction between colonial empires, and the "resistance" rhetoric of Asianism served to compete with other powers in the imperialist club for control of East Asia.

Compared with modern Japan, modern China's resistance to the unfair international order was more resolute and profound. However, this was not out of some "inborn" quality, but rather the result of China's failure to follow the Japanese Road. During that period, numerous political and cultural elites admired the prestige of colonial empire, and envied Japan's path through the Meiji Restoration from a "semi-civilized country" toward a "first-class power"

402 Takeuchi Yoshimi 竹内好,「方法としてのアジア」[Asia as Method],『日本とアジア 竹内好評論集』[Japan and Asia: Takeuchi's Collected Essays, Vol. 3], 419–420.

recognized by other great powers. However, from the perspective of geopolitics, the "success" of the Meiji Restoration in Japan itself also blocked the possibility of China's joining the club of great powers and attaining regional hegemony through a similar approach, not to mention the direct damage to China caused by the Sino-Japanese War and the Russo-Japanese war. During the First World War, when Yuan Shikai's government, which remained more or less outside of Japan's control, tried to improve China's international status by joining the Entente, the Okuma cabinet's response was to try to stop it and to impose its Twenty-one Demands on China.

Oppressed by both regional and global hegemony, China was too poor and weak to genuinely conceive of the possibility of building regional hegemony through reforms similar to the Meiji Restoration. On the brink of partition, China rose to seek independence, launching a magnificent political and social revolution. The new subjectivity China gained in the revolution was based on more resources against the hegemonic mentality. China's new political agenda was not to replace the old hegemonic powers in a hierarchical order, but to deeply reflect on the hegemonic mentality itself, so as to shape a new and more just international system.

CHAPTER 4

The Genealogy of Provincial Monroe Doctrine Discourses in Modern China

> The land is torn in pieces, and the setting sun is dark red.
> I hold up the sky with my hands and sing of the strong gale.
> Who on earth will command the vast Central Plains?
> In the wilds and marshes, heroes are rising everywhere.
>
> YANG YULIN, No. 2 of Miscellaneous Poems on the Way North[403]

When the U.S. Monroe Doctrine spread to China at the end of the Qing Dynasty and the beginning of the Republic of China, what kind of chemical reaction did it trigger? Judging from historical materials, the most influential Monroe Doctrine discourse that emerged in China at that time did not focus on the configuration of regional and global order at the supranational level, but rather on provincial autonomy at the subnational level. Among the typology of Monroe Doctrine discourse analyzed in this book, the "Provincial Monroe Doctrine" in modern China is the most unique.

Accurately positioning the encounter between the Monroe Doctrine and modern China requires starting with the U.S. Before the U.S. became an independent country, the British East India Company played an intermediary role in commercial exchanges between China and the North American colonies. What the Boston Tea Party dumped in 1773 was tea shipped by the East India Company from Guangzhou, China, and most of it was red tea from the Wuyi Mountains of Fujian Province. Direct business contacts with China began shortly after the U.S. achieved independence. Following the arrival of the U.S. merchant vessel Empress of China in Guangzhou in 1784, a total of 118 merchant vessels went to China in the remaining years of the eighteenth century.[404] At the beginning of the nineteenth century, American

403 Rao Huaimin 饶怀民 ed., Yang Yulin Ji 杨毓麟集 [Collected Works of Yang Yulin], (Changsha: Yuelu Shushe, 2008), 365.

404 Wang Xi and Zou Mingde 汪熙、邹明德, "Yapian zhanzheng qian de zhongmei maoyi 鸦片战争前的中美贸易 [The Sino-U.S. Trade before the Opium War]," in *Zhongmei*

 | DOI:10.1163/9789004746237_006

merchants became involved in opium smuggling to China. For example, Warren Delano, the grandfather of President Franklin Delano Roosevelt, was a senior partner of Russell & Co., and played a significant role in expanding the company's opium business. American merchants mainly imported opium from Turkey, which at one point accounted for 10% of all of the opium that the great powers exported to China, even impacting the opium profits of the British East India Company.[405] Many wealthy families benefited from the opium trade with China, and used the profits to invest in industry and infrastructure in the U.S. For example, much of the construction in Boston benefited from the opium trade profits of several families known as the Boston Brahmans.[406]

On July 3, 1844 (the 24th year of Daoguang Emperor), the Qing imperial government and American diplomatic representatives signed the Treaty of Peace, Amity, and Commerce between the U.S. and China in Wanghia Village, Macao. Its exquisite legalese made this treaty a model for similar unequal treaties that China signed with many other great powers. However, the term "Monroe Doctrine" did not yet exist in 1844. Soon after that, the U.S. experienced fierce conflict between the North and the South, which developed into a brutal civil war in the 1860s. After the Civil War, the U.S. rebuilt its domestic order, and with the help of the Second Industrial Revolution emerged as a major industrialized power. Consequently, even though the U.S. had approached China as a colonial power very early on, it did not acquire ceded territory or establish its sphere of influence in China like other European powers or Meiji Japan, and the psychological pressure it imposed on Chinese elites was much lighter than that of other major powers. It was only after the Spanish-American War in 1898 that the U.S. became more aggressive toward East Asia, seizing the Philippines from Spain as a base for its imperial expansion in Asia. It seems no coincidence that the Monroe Doctrine did not become popular in China until the end of the nineteenth century, especially after the Spanish-American War.

Professor Guo Shuanglin pointed out in a groundbreaking article[407] that it took a long time for Chinese to know the specific content of the Monroe

guanxishi luncong 中美关系史论丛 [*Historical Essays on Sino-US Relations*], ed. Wang Xi 汪熙 (Shanghai: Fudan daxue chubanshe, 1985), 95–96.

405 Hunt Janin, *The India-China Opium Trade in the Nineteenth Century*, (Jefferson, North Carolina & London: McFarland & Company, Inc.), 62–63.

406 Peter Dobkin Hall, Family Structure and Class Consolidation Among the Boston Brahmins, (New York: State University of New York at Stony Brook, 1975).

407 Guo Shuanglin 郭双林, "Menluo zhyi yu qingmo guojia minzu rentong 门罗主义与清末国家民族认同 [Monroe Doctrine and National Identity in the Late Qing Dynasty]," in *Zhongguo jindaishi shang de minzu zhuyi: di'er jie zhongguo jindai sixiangshi guoji xueshu yantaohui wenji* 中国近代史上的民族主义——第二届中国近代思想史国际

Doctrine before they knew of the existence of president James Monroe in the nineteenth century. In 1838, the American missionary Elijah Coleman Bridgman published in Singapore a Chinese book titled *Concise Records of the United States* 美理哥合省国志略, which first mentioned the name of President Monroe, transliterated into Chinese as "Man Luo" 瞞罗. Some parts of the book were absorbed into Wei Yuan 魏源's *The Illustrated Annals of Overseas Countries* 海国图志 and Liang Tingnan 梁廷枏's *Four Treaties on Overseas Countries* 海国四说. As a result, the name "Man Luo" became widespread, but the substantial ideas of "Man Luo" were still unknown.[408] In 1880, the *Shen Bao* Newspaper Office in Shanghai published *History of History of the World* 万国史记, written by Japanese scholar Okamoto Kansuke 岡本監輔, which introduced President Monroe's idea: "In 1817, James Monroe was made president. Monroe often said that the U.S. was a world unto itself and had nothing to do with European disputes. Most commentators agreed with him."[409] However, Okamoto Kansuke did not refer to President Monroe's thinking as the "Monroe Doctrine."

It can be added here that English newspapers founded by the British in China, such as *North-China Herald* and its successor *North China Daily News*, had reported the development of the Monroe Doctrine in the U.S. since 1838.[410] However, because these newspapers were run mainly for the foreign readership in China, their discussion of the Monroe Doctrine did not have substantial repercussions among Chinese political and cultural elites. According to existing historical materials, the keen interest in the Monroe Doctrine developed among Chinese elites travelling in Japan. After the failure of the Hundred Days Reform in 1898, Kang Youwei and Liang Qichao fled to Japan, attempting to

学术研讨会论文集 [*Nationalism in Modern Chinese History: Proceedings of the Second International Symposium on the History of Modern Chinese Thought*], (Beijing: Shehui kexue wenxian chubanshe, 2006), 331. This paper by Professor Guo Shuanglin is an important starting point of this chapter.

408 Eligah Coleman 高理文, "Meilige hesheng zhilue 美理哥合省国志略 [Concise records of the United States]," in *Jindaishi ziliao* 近代史资料 [*Modern History Materials*], No. 92, eds. Editorial Department of Institute of Modern History, Chinese Academy of Social Sciences (Beijing: Zhongguo shehuikexue chubanshe, 2006), 199.

409 This book has several editions, such as Shanghai Liuxian Press edition in 1897, Shanghai Yizhitang edition in 1898 and Shanghai Publishing House edition in 1901. What I read during my research is the following edition, Okamoto Kansuke 岡本監輔, *Wanguo shiji* 万国史记 [*Historical Records of Nations*], Vol. 19, (Shanghai: Liuxian chubanshe, 1897), 10.

410 For examples, "Extension of the Monroe Doctrine," *Zilin xibao* (27 December 1893), third edition; "The Monroe Doctrine," *Zilin xibao* (13 December 1895), fourth edition; "Proposed Enlargement of the Monroe Doctrine," *Zilin xibao* (23 January 1896), third edition; "The German Press and the Monroe Doctrine," *Zilin xibao* (17 November 1896), third edition; "The Monroe Doctrine," *Zilin xibao* (19 June 1900), fourth edition.

borrow Japanese troops to defeat the political faction of Empress Dowager Cixi, release the imprisoned Emperor Guangxi, and continue their unfinished reforms. The constitutional monarchist forces they led played an extremely important role in the spread of the Monroe Doctrine. Unintentionally, however, their translation and introduction of the Monroe Doctrine provided anti-Manchu revolutionaries with a new discursive weapon in the shape of an anti-Manchu provincial Monroe Doctrine.

Kang Youwei appealed for aid from Konoe Atsumaro 近衛篤麿, speaker of the House of Peers, in November 1898. In his letter to Konoe Atsumaro on November 2, Kang Youwei compared his appeal to Shen Baoxu 申包胥's "cry at the Qing court" in the Spring and Autumn period, and emphasized that "our two brother countries are like lips and teeth. We belong to the same race and the same continent, and share joys and sorrows."[411] The metaphor of "lips and teeth" was more fully expressed in Kang Youwei's article "The Worry of Lips and Teeth" (*Chun chi you* 唇齿忧), written in Japan at the end of October, which emphasized that Chinese and Japanese belonged to the same race, and shared the same writing system, customs, and political and moral cultivation systems; China and Japan could be characterized as brother countries of Huaxia 华夏 (the civilized).[412] The term *Zhu Xia zhi guo* 诸夏之国 (the countries of Huaxia) can be said to combine Japanese Asianism with the Chinese traditional differentiation between the civilized and barbarians.

It was not surprising that these explicitly "Asianist" terms appeared in Kang Youwei's writings. After the Sino-Japanese War of 1894–1895, Kang Youwei was influenced by *Da Dong Hebang Lun* 大东合邦论 (*On the Great East Union*) by the Japanese author Tarui Tōkichi 樽井藤吉; Japan also sent envoys to lobby Kang Youwei and other reformers.[413] During the Reform Movement of 1898, the reformers put forward the idea of "allying with Japan" and even "the union of China, Britain, the U.S. and Japan." The reformers even recommended Itō Hirobumi 伊藤博文, the former Japanese prime minister, to the Emperor Guangxu, hoping that Itō would be appointed an advisor on reform

411 Jiang Yihua and Zhang Ronghua 姜义华、张荣华 eds., *Kang Youwei quanji* 康有为全集 [*Complete Works of Kang Youwei*] (Volume 5), (Beijing: Renmin daxue chubanshe, 2007), 40.

412 Kang Youwei 康有为, "Chunchiyou 唇齿忧 [Worry about your lips and teeth]," in *Kang Youwei quanji* 康有为全集 [*Complete Works of Kang Youwei*] (Volume 5), (Beijing: Renmin daxue chubanshe, 2007), 141.

413 See Qiu Tao and Zheng Kuangmin 邱涛、郑匡民, "Wuxu zhengbian qian de Rizhong jiemeng huodong 戊戌政变前的日中结盟活动 [Japan-China Alliance before the coup of 1898]," *Jindaishi yanjiu* 1 (2010).

so as to weaken the political faction of the Empress Dowager Cixi.[414] After the failure of the Hundred Days Reform of 1898, Kang Youwei fled to Hong Kong and turned to Britain for help. When the British government showed indifference, Kang Youwei turned to the Japanese government, following the example of Shen Baoxu's "cry at the Qin Court." In eagerly seeking help, Kang Youwei adopted Asianism, which was rising in Japan at that time, as one of his major discourse resources.

The Japanese political elites who came into contact with the exiled reformers also responded to them with the discourse of Asianism. When Kang Youwei finally met with Konoe Atsumaro on November 12,[415] the latter went straight to the point with the following observations: "Today's East Asian issue is not just about East Asia; it has become a problem for the whole world. European powers are competing in the Orient for their own benefit. East Asia is East Asia for East Asians. East Asians must have the right to solve the East Asian problem independently. This is also what the Monroe Doctrine in the U.S. implies. Indeed, the obligation to realize the Asiatic Monroe Doctrine (亜細亜のモンロー主義) in East Asia falls on the shoulders of our two countries."[416]

414 On the evening of September 19th, 1898, Kang Youwei discussed with Yang Shenxiu and Song Bolu to sponsor Ito Bowen and Timothy Richard. Yang Shenxiu immediately played to Emperor Guangxu: "Today's crisis, without joining Britain, the United States and Japan, there is no way to save the picture. The situation is that Ito Bowen of Japan traveled in the capital, and he once won the fame of the East, and he will be deeply willing to join China and seek self-protection together. Not for the sake of borrowing talents, First, raise money through it. I especially wish my emperor to make plans early and consolidate Britain, the United States and Japan. Don't be too beautiful in the name of the alliance, and be sincere in the blessing of the whole world." Ming and Qing Archives of National Archives Bureau, *Wuxu bianfa dangan shiliao* 戊戌变法档案史料 [*Historical Materials of Archives of the Reform Movement of 1898*], (Beijing: Zhonghua shuju, 1958), 15.

415 At the beginning of 1898, Konoe Atsumaro published the famous article "The Necessity of Studying the Racial Alliance and the Chinese Problem" in Volume 4, No. 1 of Taiyō, which placed the conflict between the Yellow and White races in a prominent position: "In my opinion, the future of Orient will inevitably become a stage for racial competition. Even if a temporary situation can be solved through foreign policy, it is only a provisional measure. The final fate is still the competition between the yellow and white races. In this competition, the Chinese and the Japanese are in the position of taking the white people as enemies." Konoe Atsumaro advocated that "the survival of the Chinese people is closely related to other countries and the fate of Japan. Therefore, from today, we should treat China with friendship, persuade it and enlighten it. Make progress for it, stimulate it, get rid of its suspicion and jealousy, and make it feel close to Japan, cooperating with each other to protect the same race." Konoe Atsumaro 近衛篤麿,「同人種同盟附支那問題研究の必要」[The Necessity of Studying the Racial Alliance and the Chinese Problem], 『太陽』[Taiyo], Vol. 4, No. 1, 1898, 1.

416 Konoe Atsumaro Diary Publishing Committee 近衛篤麿日記刊行会 (ed.),『近衛篤麿日記』第2巻 [Konoe Atsumaro Diary, Volume 2], (Kajima Institute Publishing, 1968), 195.

Konoe Atsumaro's distillation of the Asiatic Monroe Doctrine into the slogan "East Asia is East Asia for East Asians" resonated deeply with a sentence pattern in ancient Chinese: "X is X for Xans." Indeed, it expressed the classical spatial-political question in ancient China—who is the master of Tianxia 天下 (all-under-heaven). We can see discussion of this question in many writings in the Confucian tradition.

After Qin defeated six other states in 221 BC, a unified dynasty based on the Central Plains and surrounded by a series of vassal states gradually became the historical norm accepted by official Chinese historiography. In theory, "Under heaven, all is the king's land. Within the sea-boundaries of the land, all are the king's subjects" (溥天之下，莫非王土；率土之滨，莫非王臣). There was no strict Westphalian internal/external distinction based on the physical boundaries between the Central Plains Dynasty and vassal states, or even between vassal states.[417] The question of who was the master of Tianxia did not lead to the discussion on the legitimacy of monarchy as a form of government, but rather on who was qualified to be an emperor.[418] In the ancient

417 The Sino-Russian Treaty of Nerchinsk of 1689 demarcated the eastern border between China and Russia. In 1711, Kangxi issued a decree to map the northeast region, specifically ordering to draw a clear line between the "Chinese places" and the "Korean places." As Huang Xingtao pointed out, Kangxi's "China" began to bear the meaning of modern national concept closely related to "national boundaries." See Huang Xingtao 黄兴涛, Chongsu zhonghua 重塑中华 [*Reshaping China*], (Beijing: Beijing shifan daxue chubanshe, 2017), 14–15. Kangxi was keen to draw a clear line, which was related to the influence of Catholic Jesuits with European knowledge of international law. See Ceng Tao 曾涛 "Jindai Zhongguo yu guojifa de zaofeng 近代中国与国际法的遭逢 [Modern China and International Law Encounter]," *Zhongguo zhengfa daxue xuebao* 5 (2008).

418 Here are a few examples: Book of Han: Biographies of Gu Yong and Du Ye: 'The world belongs to all people in the world, not to one person alone.' Records of the Three Kingdoms: Book of Wei, Biography of Gaotang Long: 'The world belongs to all under heaven, not solely to Your Majesty.' Book of Jin: Biography of Duan Zhuo: 'The world belongs to all under heaven, not to one person.' Book of Jin: Biography of Pan Yue (with nephew Pan Ni): '... therefore saying "the world is not one person's possession but belongs to all under heaven." How can it be seized or relinquished at will!' Book of Sui: Biography of Yang Su: 'The world is the domain of the late emperor.' Such discussions were not confined to the literati elites. The Ming dynasty novel Investiture of the Gods, centering on King Wu's campaign against King Zhou, declares through Jiang Ziya's voice that 'the world belongs to its people.' It affects the middle and lower classes of society except the scholar-bureaucrat. In the transcript of "Xilu Myth" of the Tiandihui (Heaven and Earth Society), a secret society in Qing Dynasty, there is a statement that "The world ... is not the world of one person, but the world of everyone under heaven." See Wang Xuetai 王学泰, *Youmin wenhua yu Zhongguo shehui* 游民文化与中国社会 [*Wandering Culture and Chinese Society*] (part two), (Beijing: Tongxin chubanshe, 2007), 590.

Chinese context, an emperor's failure to abide by the normal political and moral standards of rule would not lead to the change of the form of government, but might result in a change of the throne. As stated in the Confucian classic *Shang Shu* 尚书: "The mandate of heaven is not constant and will help only the virtuous ones" (天命靡常，惟德是辅).[419]

In the Qing Dynasty, the phrase "Tianxia for the people of Tianxia" was also cited to address the legitimacy of Manchu rule. In the traditional Chinese world order, the most important spatial distinction was not the physical boundary, but the distinction between Yi 夷 and Xia 夏, that is, between the uncivilized peoples and the civilized ones. It was regarded as normal for Yi and Xia to coexist in peace, or for Yi to evolve in the direction of Xia. The suppression of Xia by Yi was regarded as an anomaly in Tianxia. Fearing that the Manchus might be classified as Yi, Emperor Qianlong attempted to downplay the distinction between Yi and Xia, arguing that "Tianxia is for the people of Tianxia and should not be monopolized by any specific people. Shun came from Dong Yi (Eastern barbarians), and King Wen of the Zhou Dynasty came from Xi Yi (Western barbarians). But is it possible to make a distinction between them by referring to the East or the West? Legitimate kingship must have its own standard."[420] Here, "Tianxia is for the people of Tianxia" was not a criticism of absolute monarchy, but a criticism of the monopoly of legitimate rulership by specific ethnic groups.

However, due to the uneven geographical distribution of agricultural civilization and the Yi/Xia differentiation, the competition for Tianxia did not necessarily mean competition for all the known inhabited geographical space, but only for the mature agricultural civilization zone centered on the Central Plains. Whoever unified the core agricultural civilization zone was likely to gain hegemony over the "barbarians" in all four directions. Therefore, in

---

419 It is worth mentioning that, in 1779 (the eighth year of the An'ei era), Japanese Hiraga Kennai 平賀源内's Fūryū Shidōken den (The Modern Life of Shidōken) criticized China's consciousness that "the world is not a world for one person, but a world for all the people," and thought that it encouraged rebellions aimed at usurping monarchical power. The stable lineage of Japanese monarchs is the basis of Hiraga Kennai's exposition. See Watanabe Hiroshi 渡辺浩, Ou Jianying trans., Dongya de Wangquan yu sixiang 东亚的王权与思想 [Monarchy and Ideas in East Asia], (Shanghai: Shanghai guji chubanshe, 2016), 129.

420 *Qinggaozong shilu* 清高宗实录 [Veritable Records of the Qianlong Reign] (Vol. 784), (Beijing: Zhonghua shuju (photocopy), 1986), 424. Qianlong's posture was supported by scholars in the middle Qing Dynasty. See Wang Hui 汪晖, *Xiandai Zhongguo sixiang de xingqi* 现代中国思想的兴起 [*The Rise of Modern Chinese Thought*] (Volume I, Part II: Empire and State), (Beijing: Shenghuo, Dushu, Xinzhi sanlian shudian, 2004), 519–578.

ancient Chinese, "Tianxia" might also be characterized as a deer to be hunted, a bounded space to be dominated.[421] The question "who is the master of Tianxia" could be applied to all kinds of bounded space. When the tributary system was increasingly threatened by the European international law system, Chinese scholar-officials realized that the geographical reach of Tianxia might cover a very limited number of countries.[422] The revival of the Gongyang school of Confucianism in the late Qing Dynasty was closely related to the drastic change of spatial consciousness in China from the centering of Tianxia to one among the nations, and Kang Youwei was a key figure in this revival movement. If the theories *Zhang san shi* 张三世 (unfolding the three ages) and *Tong san tong* 通三统 (channeling the three traditions) in the Gongyang school were directly related to time and history, *Yi nei wai* 异内外 (distinguishing the internal and the external) was directly related to space, involving a series of categories such as "Tianxia," "the country," "Yi" and "Xia," etc.

"天下人の天下" was not a common phrase in Japanese. In fact, the connotation of "天下人" in Meiji Japan was quite different from the meaning of "天下人" in ancient Chinese. It signified not the multitude, but those powerful men capable of ending political turmoil and dominating the state, for example, Minamoto no Yoritomo 源頼朝, Ashikaga Takauji 足利尊氏, Oda Nobunaga 織田信長, or Toyotomi Hideyoshi 豐臣秀吉. As a member of the Japanese political and cultural elite who was capable of writing poetry directly in Chinese, Konoe Atsumaro may have learned the sentence pattern "X is X for Xans" directly from Chinese, rather than adapting the original Japanese sentence pattern. This sentence pattern could stimulate the spatial political consciousness of Chinese Confucian scholar-officials better than any similar English expression. Although newspapers run by the British in China had introduced the Monroe Doctrine in English, those reports never sparked any focused discussion among Chinese scholar-officials.

After Kang Youwei raised his appeal for help, Konoe Atsumaro expressed a conservative and cautious attitude and did not make any substantive commitment. Eager to ask the Japanese government for help, Kang Youwei further

421 For example, the last sentence of Luo Binwang's "A Manifesto to Proclaim the Punitive Expedition Against Wu Zhao for Xu Jingye" shows a strong sense of spatial politics: "Look now upon the realm: to which house, after all, does this Tianxia belong?" Wang Fuzhi, a great scholar in the late Ming Dynasty and early Qing Dynasty, said in "Reflections on the Comprehensive Mirror" that "The Tianxia of China was, in the era before Xuan-yuan, likely composed of barbarians as well."

422 Jiang and Zhang (n. 409), 107.

strengthened his rhetoric of Asianism. On February 13, 1899, Kang Youwei visited Konoe Atsumaro for the second time. In their correspondence, Kang Youwei emphasized that "in the overall situation of East Asia, our two countries are comparable to twin brothers."[423] Kang Youwei also turned to other Japanese political dignitaries for help. In late November 1898, Kang Youwei sent a letter to Okada Masaki 岡田正樹, specifically emphasizing that China and Japan "share the same writing system, the same race and the same continent." He said that Emperor Guangxu had personally revised his letter of credentials before sending ambassador Huang Zunxian to Japan, adding "a country with the closest affinity on the same continent," and proposed that the Qing court should enlist Japanese talent to advise its reforms. In this way, China and Japan could be "equivalent to the same country, not just two countries on the same continent."[424] In another letter, Kang Youwei mentioned that Guangxu changed his letter of credentials and talked about "East Asia" and the "yellow race."[425] Kang also reported Guangxu's revision of the letter of credentials in his article "In Praise of Emperor Guangxu's Virtue as a Sage" 光绪圣德记, published in *Qing Yi Bao* 清议报, which was edited by Liang Qichao.[426]

In the process of Kang Youwei's seeking help from Japanese political circles, Liang Qichao often accompanied him and helped draft letters and documents. On December 23, 1898, the exiled reformists founded *Qing Yi Bao* in Yokohama, Japan, with Liang Qichao presiding over the editorial board. Since 1899, Konoe Atsumaro's expression "X is X for Xans" had suddenly become popular among Chinese elites traveling in Japan. Did this sentence pattern used by Konoe Atsumaro to explain the Monroe Doctrine inspire Kang Youwei, and then stimulate his student Liang Qichao, a giant in public media? I can't verify this chain of transmission from current historical data, but the evidence shows that *Qing Yi Bao*, run by Liang Qichao from December 1898 to December 1901, played a pioneering role in promoting the concept of the Monroe Doctrine and the sentence pattern "X is X for Xans."

1 Supranational, National, and Provincial: Three Spatial Aspects of the Monroe Doctrine

While the discourse of the Monroe Doctrine was mainly concerned with the supranational spatial plane, it touched upon three aspects of space in

423 Ibid., 43.
424 Ibid., 44–45.
425 Ibid., 115.
426 Zhang (n. 167), 168.

modern China: supranational, national, and subnational, especially provincial. Chinese elites appropriated this discourse not only to address the problem of state-building and nation-building, but also to respond to claims of autonomy on the provincial level. Both of these aspects could be seen in the anti-Manchu political mobilization in the late Qing era.

In December 1898, Liang Qichao stated four main purposes in the inaugural editorial of *Qing Yi Bao*: "First, to maintain discussion by the righteous literati of China and to stimulate the uprightness of the people; second, to increase the knowledge of the Chinese; third, to communicate the voices of China and Japan and improve their friendship; fourth, to develop East Asian learning in order to preserve Asian quintessence." He made appeal for "we four hundred million compatriots to jointly learn from it; we yellow people who hope to pursue the cause of Asian autonomy in the twentieth century to jointly support it."[427] "East Asia," "Asian quintessence" and "yellow race" were the prevalent concepts of Japanese Pan-Asianism at that time. Japan's public opinion atmosphere of Asianism strengthened Liang Qichao's awareness of the ties among Asian countries, which soon led to new progress in his writing.

Qing Yi Bao was founded during the American colonial conquest in the Philippines after the 1898 Spanish-American War. Liang Qichao, as editor-in-chief, paid close attention to the increasingly tense relationship between the U.S. and the Philippines. This conflict sparked his interest in the Monroe Doctrine. The second volume of *Qing Yi Bao*, published on January 2, 1899, included a translation of "New Monroe Doctrine in the Far East" 极东之新木爱罗主义 under the translator's name, Kataoka Tsuruo 片岡鶴雄. The translation introduced a U.S. senator's interpretation of the New Monroe Doctrine in the Far East and proposed that the American occupation of the Philippines could be understood according to this interpretation. The essence of this doctrine was that "the U.S. and Britain presided over a shared new imperialism in the world," replacing the imperialism of ancient Rome. It comprised five aspects: First, Britain, the U.S. and the Netherlands jointly negotiated to create an international arbitration institution supported by various states; second, member states should limit the use of lethal weapons in war; third, U.S.-annexed territories were open to free trade by all countries; fourth, Britain, the U.S. and Japan jointly implemented the New Monroe Doctrine to protect China, confronting "European powers, stopping their land grabbing"; fifth, before the U.S., Britain and the Netherlands formally established international arbitration institutions, "this doctrine should be maintained and applied to the Indian

427 Zhang (n. 167), 168.

Islands."[428] Here the "Indian Islands" referred to the "East Indies," including the Philippines occupied by the U.S., Indonesia occupied by the Netherlands, and Malaysia occupied by Britain. This doctrine therefore meant a concerted effort by the great powers in the Far East—Britain, the U.S., Japan and the Netherlands—to maintain regional order and especially to prevent other great powers from carving up China.

On January 23, 1899, the Republic of the Philippines was proclaimed, with Emilio Aguinaldo as its president. On February 4, the American-Philippine War broke out. The *Qing Yi Bao* editorial board paid close attention to the war and regarded the invasion by American troops as an invasion against Asia. In August 1899, Ou Jujia, a member of the editorial team of *Qing Yi Bao* and one of the disciples of Kang Youwei, published "On the Philippine Islands' Independence" in Volume 25 of *Qing Yi Bao*, arguing that the Philippine leaders advocated freedom and independence and inspired Filipinos with a consciousness of "the Philippines is the Philippines for Filipinos." Here, Ou Jujia used the sentence pattern "X is X for Xans" on the nation-state level. Ou Jujia was enthusiastic about the Filipino war of resistance and predicted that it could be effective. He further saw the prospect of "Asian autonomy": "There has never been anyone in Asia who advocated autonomy; if there is, they must begin with the Philippines."[429] This sentence indicated Ou's consciousness of "Asian solidarity," which was obviously related to the atmosphere of Asianism in Japanese public opinion circles.

A similar sentence pattern soon appeared in the article "A Theory of Independence" authored by "Feng Ziqiang" in Volume 58 (September 1900) of *Qing Yi Bao*: "China is China for Chinese; China could not be preserved by foreigners; the responsibility to preserve China belongs to the Chinese people, not any other people."[430] According to Guo Shuanglin's statistics, starting with Feng Ziqiang's discussion, "China is China for Chinese" appeared at least

428 "Jidong zhi xinmuailuo zhuyi 极东之新木爱罗主义 [The New Monroe Doctrine in the Far East]," *Qingyibao* 2 (2 January 1899).

429 Ou Jujia 欧榘甲, "Lun feilübin qundao zili 论菲律宾群岛自立 [On the Independence of the Philippine Islands]," *Qingyibao* 25 (26 August 1899). It is worth mentioning that, in December 1903, the Philippine Governor sent by the United States, later President Taft, gave a speech to discuss the slogan "The Philippines for the Filipinos" and dressed himself as a supporter of this slogan. "The Duty of Americans in the Philippines," speech delivered by Taft before the Union Reading College in Manila, 17 December 1903; Reproduced in official gazette (supplement), 23 December 1903 (Vol. 1, No. 68): 3. His explanation of this slogan is to distinguish it from national independence, but only to emphasize that the United States governs the Philippines for the benefit of Filipinos themselves.

430 Feng Ziqiang 冯自强, "Dulishuo 独立说 [Independence Theory]," *Qingyibao* 58 (24 September 1900).

twenty times in newspapers and periodicals in the late Qing Dynasty, and the sources included Ou Jujia's *New Guangdong*, Zou Rong's *Revolutionary Army*, Lu Xun's *A Brief Discussion on China's Geology*, Tao Chengzhang's *History of the Growth and Decline of the Power of the Chinese Nation*, Sun Yat-sen and others' *Revolutionary Strategies of the Revolutionary Alliance*,[431] Yang Du's "The Doctrine of Gold and Iron" and other famous essays.[432] Among them were both revolutionaries and royalists, which showed the wide influence of the sentence pattern "X is X for Xans."

In 1900, Liang Qichao invited his student Cai E, who fled to Japan after the failure of the Independence Army uprising led by Tang Caichang, to join the editorial board of *Qing Yi Bao*. The 67th volume of *Qing Yi Bao* published Cai E's article "Monroe Doctrine," which directly introduced and commented on the U.S. Monroe Doctrine: "What is the Monroe Doctrine? It prevailed in the first half of the nineteenth century in the U.S. It means 'America is America for Americans.'"[433] Here, the sentence pattern of "X is X for Xans" appeared again. Cai E reviewed the territorial expansion of the U.S. in the nineteenth century, and commented that the U.S. Democratic Party "always adheres to the Monroe Doctrine" and that the Republican Party "adheres to imperialism." Following the thinking on the relationship between "Monroe Doctrine" and "Imperialism" published in the second volume of *Qing Yi Bao*, Cai E regarded them as polar opposites. Against the background of Republican Theodore Roosevelt's presidency, Cai E believed that the U.S. was turning to imperialist expansion. However, "In the past, the U.S. was founded with the Monroe Doctrine. Now it has abandoned the doctrine and turned to imperialism due to changes in the general trend and the necessity of time." When Filipinos showed signs of losing their resistance against the U.S., Cai E worried about

431 In 1906, Sun Yat-sen and his colleagues clearly announced that "China is China for Chinese and China's politics should be run by Chinese" under the entry "Restoring China" in "The Revolutionary Strategy of the Revolutionary Alliance." *Sun Yat-sen quanji* 孙中山全集 [*Complete Works of Sun Yat-sen*] (Vol. 1), (Beijing: Zhonghua shuju, 1981), 297.

Guo Shuanglin 郭双林, "Menluo zhuyi yu qingmo guojia minzu rentong 门罗主义与清末国家民族认同 [The Monroe Doctrine and National Identity in the Late Qing Dynasty]," *Nationalism in Modern Chinese History: Proceedings of the Second International Symposium on the History of Modern Chinese Thought*, (Beijing: Shehui kexue wenxian chubanshe, 2006): 328.

432 Guo Shuanglin 郭双林, "Menluo zhuyi yu qingmo guojia minzu rentong 门罗主义与清末国家民族认同 [The Monroe Doctrine and National Identity in the Late Qing Dynasty]," *Nationalism in Modern Chinese History: Proceedings of the Second International Symposium on the History of Modern Chinese Thought*, (Beijing: Shehui kexue wenxian chubanshe, 2006): 328.

433 "Menglu zhuyi 孟鲁主义 [The Monroe Doctrine]," *Qingyibao* 67 (22 December 1900).

the destiny of the whole East Asia, and even the whole "yellow race."[434] This was the theme of "the war between yellow and white races" embedded in the popular Pan-Asianism in Japan at that time.

It is very likely that Cai E discussed with Liang Qichao before publishing "Monroe Doctrine." In his 1902 article "On the Implications of the U.S.-Philippines War and the Boer War for China," Liang praised the Philippines for fighting against Spain and the U.S. He believed that the Philippines "is the pioneer of independence in Asia, and the beginning of the yellow race's striving for civil rights!" If the Philippines won, "it can bring a feeling of exaltation to the yellow race, and of fear to the white race." Liang Qichao particularly emphasized that the grandmother of Emilio Aguinaldo was Chinese by origin, and that many Chinese were participating in his movement. If the Philippines could gain independence in the western Pacific Ocean, there would be Japan, the Philippines and China supporting each other to "join forces to resist the eastward movement of European power."

In 1902, Cai E published "A Treaty on Military, State, and People" in *Xin Min Cong Bao*, edited by Liang Qichao. Cai came up with this observation: "The U.S. is regarded as a country of peace and republicanism, adhering to the Monroe Doctrine. However, even the lyrics of children's songs in the elementary schools are actually majestic and fierce military songs."[435] When discussing the "national soul" of the great powers, he commented on the U.S. again: "The Monroe Doctrine in the U.S. means 'America is America for Americans,' and other countries are not allowed to interfere in the affairs of the Americas. These words have been imprinted on the American minds. Now, they are turning to the doctrine that 'the world is the world for the whole world' and should not be monopolized by any power. Therefore, Americans have changed from a defensive strategy to an offensive one."[436] Cai E reiterated here the judgment in his

434 Cai E's exposition may be the result of discussion with Liang Qichao. In 1902, in the article "On the Relationship between the United States, the Philippines, Britain and DUZH War and China," Liang Qichao praised the Philippines for fighting against Spain and the United States, and believed that the Philippines "is the pioneer of advocating independence in Asia, and I am the ancestor of Huang Zhongxing's civil rights!" If the Philippines wins, "it can breathe out for the yellow race and make the white race lose their guts." Liang Qichao particularly emphasized that the grandmother of the leader of the Philippine independence movement is Chinese, and his subordinates are mostly Chinese. If the Philippines is independent and on the east coast of the Pacific Ocean, Japan, the Philippines and China will support each other and "join forces to resist the eastward spread of European power." Zhang (n. 167), 949.

435 Zeng Yeying 曾业英 ed., *Cai Songpo ji* 蔡松坡集 [*Cai Songpo Collection*], (Shanghai: Shanghai renmin chubanshe, 1984), 18.

436 Ibid., 34.

previous article in 1900 that the U.S. was moving from the Monroe Doctrine to imperialism, and further refined the American *zeitgeist* as "the world is the world for the whole world," which indicated the continuity of political rhetoric in the American transition from the Monroe Doctrine to imperialism. Liang Qichao visited North America in 1903 and met President Theodore Roosevelt. In his *Travel Notes to the New World*, he analyzed changes in the essence of the Monroe Doctrine from "America is America for Americans" to "America is America for the U.S." and then to "the world is the world for the U.S." He was amazed at the flexibility of American politicians in adjusting their interpretation of the Monroe Doctrine.[437] Both Cai E's "the world is the world for the whole world" and Liang Qichao's "the world is the world for the U.S." point to President Theodore Roosevelt's global imperialist gestures beyond the Western Hemisphere after winning the Spanish-American War.

If Cai E's exposition regarded Monroe Doctrine and Imperialism as two concepts with opposite meanings, other comments in the same period reached different conclusions.[438] The column "Explanation of New Terms" in *Zhejiang Chao*, a revolutionary journal published in Tokyo, held that "Monroe Doctrine" was just another name for "imperialism." In 1903, the fifth issue of *Hubei Student Circle*, founded in Tokyo, published the article "A Brief Account of the Destruction of the Philippines" in the *Historical Biography* column, which was reprinted in the first issue of *Cuixin Bao* published in Jinhua, Zhejiang Province, in 1904. This article not only discussed the history of the U.S. conquest of the Philippines, but also revealed the imperialist nature of American Monroe Doctrine.[439] Yang Du's "The Doctrine of Gold and Iron," written in Japan in 1907, stated that the U.S. "changed its Monroe Doctrine into imperialism." While the former was civilized, the latter was slightly barbaric, but one could hardly survive in a dangerous world without the latter. Yang Du was deeply worried about the survival of China in the world of imperialism and

437 Zhang (n. 167), 1155.

438 On December 28, 1912, when Cai E called Yuan Shikai, Li Yuanhong, the State Council and the provincial governors on the principles formulated by the Constitution, he also mentioned that "North America is an advanced Republic, and it is always a Monroe Doctrine, and it also vigorously advocates nationalism in order to plot development." Zeng (n. 433), 630. The core of "nationalism" emphasized by Cai E is to build a strong central government, concentrate domestic forces and compete internationally. Therefore, it belongs to different dimensions of the same proposition as "imperialism" in the interpretation article of "Menglu Doctrine" in 1900.

"Feilubin wangguo canzhuang jilue 菲立宾亡国惨状记略 [A brief account of Philippine Libin's tragic subjugation]," No. 5 of *Hubei xueshengjie* 5 (1903) and *Cuixinbao* 1 (1904).

439 Ou (n. 427).

suggested that China should imitate the methods of the great powers. Despite their different views about the past of the U.S., all these commentators shared the conclusion that the U.S. was now an imperialist power. This was not necessarily derogatory, because most Chinese commentators regarded imperialism as the norm in the social Darwinist world, and hoped that China could learn imperialism for her own survival.

Accepted and transformed by Chinese cultural and political elites in Japan, the Monroe Doctrine spread quickly in the Chinese world and merged with anti-Manchu sentiments and localism, especially with the concept of provincial autonomy, or even independence. As mentioned earlier, inspired by the Philippine War against the U.S., Ou Jujia in 1899 praised the Philippines for its spirit of independence and expressed admiration for the spirit of "the Philippines for Filipinos."[440] In 1902, Ou Jujia published *New Guangdong* in Yokohama, Japan, and proposed Guangdong's separation from the Manchu court. In response to the "traitorous" behavior of the Qing court, Ou Jujia called for "China is China for the Chinese." Unlike the similar slogan in the article "On Independence" published by *Qing Yi Bao* in 1900, Ou Jujia's slogan was full of anti-Manchu sentiment. Ou's argument was that since the Qing government was so ineffectual, the forces of Britain, France and many other great powers had already entered Guangdong, and Guangdong was on the verge of destruction. Ou Jujia therefore proposed that "Guangdong is Guangdong for the Cantonese, not any other people; Cantonese are the masters of the land of Guangdong," and "Cantonese should dominate the affairs of Guangdong."[441] Ou Jujia called for Guangdong to claim independence from the Manchu court, and for all provinces to respond in concert with Guangdong and separate themselves from the Qing court. They would unite again on the basis of new political principles. Various issues of concern to the editorial team of *Qing Yi Bao*, such as the Philippines' resistance to the U.S., the Boers' resistance to Britain, the partitioning of Poland and the annexation of India, were all mentioned and analyzed in *New Guangdong*. *New Guangdong* cited the example of the founding of the U.S. on the basis of federalism. It did not directly

440 Ou Jujia 欧榘甲, "Xinguangdong 新广东 [New Guangdong]," in *Xinhai geming qianshinianjian shilun xuanji* 辛亥革命前十年间时论选集 [*Selected Works on Time in the Ten Years Before the Revolution of 1911*] (Volume 1, Volume 1), eds. Zhang Fang and Wang Renzhi 张枬、王忍之 (Beijing: Shenghuo, Dushu, Xinzhi sanlian shudian, 1960): 287.

441 欧榘甲： "新广东，" 张枬、王忍之编：《辛亥革命前十年间时论选集》（第一卷上册），北京：生活·读书·新知三联书店1960年版，第287页。 Ou Jujia, "New Guangdong," edited by Zhang Fang and Wang Renzhi, "Selected Works on Time in the Ten Years Before the Revolution of 1911" (Volume 1, Volume 1), Beijing: Life, Reading and New Knowledge Joint Publishing Company, 1960, p. 287.

mention the Monroe Doctrine, but as analyzed above, Ou Jujia was already tacitly aware of the Monroe Doctrine. All in all, provincial autonomy, federalism and the Monroe Doctrine encountered each other and formed a common "meaning field" in this text.

Ou Jujia's creative exposition of a "Guangdong Monroe Doctrine" soon had a significant impact. In 1903, Yang Yulin, a Hunanese anti-Manchu revolutionary in Japan, followed up with *New Hunan*. At the beginning of the book, he acknowledged taking Ou Jujia's *New Guangdong* as his inspiration. Yang Yulin imitated Ou Jujia's *New Guangdong* from the overall structure to specific examples. He also began with the geography and history of his province, then listed the imperialist aggression of the great powers in East Asia, and proposed the independence of Hunan from the Manchu court in order to avoid falling into the hands of "white men." Like Ou Jujia, he proposed the slogan "Hunan is Hunan for the Hunanese," and called on Hunanese to set up a revolutionary army against the Manchu court and seek support from other provinces. He also argued that "if Hunan were the Philippines, there must be people like Aguinaldo."[442]

Professor Guo Shuanglin[443] cites the article "On the Future of China and the Responsibility of the People" published in the third issue of *Hubei Student Circle* in Tokyo in April 1903, to prove that the nationalist slogan "China is China for the Chinese" is intrinsically related to the U.S. Monroe Doctrine. His article in *Hubei Student Circle* remarked: "I heard that Americans have a saying: America is America for Americans, and should not accept interference by non-Americans. The Japanese have a saying: Asia is Asia for Asians, and should not accept interference by white men. I hope that my people will also say: China is China for Chinese, and should not be interfered with by foreigners."[444] This article combined the discourse of the U.S. Monroe Doctrine and the Japanese Monroe Doctrine with the anti-Manchu slogan "China is China for the Chinese."[445] The sentence also provides clues for reconstructing the

442 Here's "Ajun Yadu," that is, "Aguinado" written by Ou Jujia, that is, Emilio Aguinaldo, the leader of the anti-American war in the Philippines. Rao Huaimin 饶怀民 ed., *Yang Yulin ji* 杨毓麟集 [*Yang Yulin Collection*], (Changsha: Yuelu shushe, 2008), 45.

443 Guo (n. 430), 334.

444 Zhang (n. 167), 473.

445 Of course, in the newspapers and periodicals of the late Qing Dynasty, the slogan "China is China for Chinese" may not have a clear anti-Manchu conotation. For example, Feng Ziqiang's slogan "China is China for Chinese" in his "Independence Theory" published in Qingyibao was against the invasion of eight powers in 1900. Feng (n. 428). Liang Qichao further commented on the Yihetuan movement in 1901, "On the New Method to Destroy a Country": Chinese people have been sleeping for thousands of years, and now they

chain of communication: the Monroe Doctrine of the U.S. inspired Japan's Pan-Asianism, and then prompted the anti-Manchu slogan "China is China for the Chinese." This piece of evidence that Professor Guo Shuanglin discovered is very important, but it appeared as late as 1903. How about the period before 1903? By investigating on the agendas set by the editorial team of *Qing Yi Bao* in earlier times, I have determined the relationship between the anti-Manchu slogan "China is China for the Chinese," the anti-Manchu Provincial Monroe Doctrine and the U.S. Monroe Doctrine transmitted by the Japanese. This can further reinforce Professor Guo Shuanglin's textual research.

2 The Development of the Provincial Monroe Doctrine after the 1911 Revolution

The increasingly anti-Manchu sentiment of the Provincial Monroe Doctrine in the late Qing Dynasty was strongly expressed in the struggle of the gentry around railway rights, which led to the Revolution of 1911. A mass rally of 10,000 people concerning railway rights took place in Changsha on May 14, 1911, followed by a demonstration by more than 10,000 railway workers from Changsha to Zhuzhou, which spread to Hubei, Guangdong, Sichuan and other places. In a report to the Japanese Minister to China, Ijūin Hikokichi, on May 30, 1911, Japan's Acting Consul in Changsha, Yamazaki Takesige, pointed out that some radical gentry in Hunan "believed that the Beijing government was bound to die, shouted that Hunan was Hunan for the Hunanese, and wanted to finance the construction of the railway by themselves." Among the radical local gentry, "businessmen are in the majority, with support from some members of the Provincial Consultation Bureau."[446] The Road Protection Movement in Sichuan was even more strident, and armed conflict broke out between local gentry and the government. The Qing court ordered the transfer of the Hubei New Army to Sichuan to suppress the popular uprising, but this weakened the Qing court's military strength in Wuchang. The Central China branch of the Revolutionary Alliance took this opportunity to launch the Wuchang

have a big dream, and they gradually have "idea of 'China for the Chinese.'" Therefore, the Yihetuan movement was actually caused by their patriotism, with the aim of strengthening China against foreign invaders." Therefore, the Yihetuan movement is regarded as a movement with the spirit of "China for Chinese," which was not taken as an anti-Manchu slogan. Yang Du's "Theory of Gold and Iron Doctrine" criticized the great powers for coveting China and treating China as a country belonging to great powers, not the Chinese people; it emphasizes "anti-imperialism" rather than "anti-Manchu." Liu (n. 432), 217.

446 Mi Rucheng 宓汝成, *Zhongguo tielushi ziliao* 中国铁路史资料 [*Materials of Chinese Railway History*] (Volume 2), (Beijing: Zhonghua shuju, 1963), 1259–1260.

Uprising. Following the example of Hubei Province, other provinces declared independence from the Qing court.

After Guangdong declared independence on November 9, 1911, Liu Yongfu 刘永福, a general of the Qing army who had participated in the Sino-French War in 1883–1885 and had led the Taiwan people's anti-Japanese struggle after the signing of Treaty of Shimonoseki in 1895, was appointed head of the Guangdong Civil Corps at the request of Hu Hanmin, the governor of the Guangdong Revolutionary Government. The documents of the Revolution of 1911 include a publicly issued "Notice of Liu Yongfu, Chief of Guangdong Civil Corps," which carries a strong tone of Guangdong regionalism: "Our Guangdong has Fujian to the east, Guangxi to the west, the five mountains to the north and the ocean to the south. Our customs, language and habits are different from those of the Central Plains. We are an independent country by nature." His notice ended with the slogan "Guangdong is Guangdong for the Cantonese."[447]

As the North-South peace talks progressed, the Qing Emperor issued his last imperial edict announcing his abdication on February 12, 1912. On February 15, the Nanjing Provisional Senate elected Yuan Shikai as provisional president of the new republic, thus unifying the legal and political order of the North and South. With the withdrawal of the Aisin Gioro family from the political stage, anti-Manch sentiment gradually ebbed. Revolutionaries abandoned their anti-Manchu stand in the compromise between the North and South, and accepted "the republic of five nationalities." In other words, the central government of the republic held that the Chinese nation included Han, Manchu, Mongol, Tibetan and Muhammadan peoples within Chinese territory, not just Han. Consequently, the phrase "China is China for the Chinese" ceased to be an anti-Manchu slogan.

In the political system of the Qing dynasty, the provincial government was not institutionally regarded as "local" government. Provincial governors were called "external officials" as opposed to the "internal officials" in Beijing. Both were appointed by the imperial court and followed the system of avoiding the appointment of officials to their places of origin (for example, as a Fujianese, Lin Zexu was not allowed to be governor of Fujian and Zhejiang, and as a Hunanese, Zeng Guofan was not allowed to be governor of Hunan and Hubei). During the Revolution of 1911, many provinces announced their separation from the Qing court. From then on, provincial governors could control the army and taxes, and appoint provincial officials by themselves. This not only weakened the power of the Qing government, but also undermined the leadership of the revolutionary Nanjing Provisional Government. After unifying the

447 Li Shiyu 李世瑜, *Shehui lishixue wenji* 社会历史学文集 [*Anthology of Social History*], (Tianjin: Tianjin guji chubanshe, 2007), 589.

North and South into one constitutional order, Yuan Shikai devoted himself to centralizing provincial power. However, his attempt was resisted by powerful factions in many provinces. In 1915, Yuan Shikai's claim to the imperial throne triggered a new local separation movement, and nullified his recent achievements in centralizing military power, financial power and personnel power. After Yuan Shikai's death in 1916, the Beijing government remained the nominal central government, but its control over local governments was even weaker than in the Yuan Shikai era. After Zhang Xun's monarchical restoration in 1917, Premier Duan Qirui 段祺瑞 refused to restore the 1912 Provisional Constitution. Sun Yat-sen went South to "protect the 1912 constitution," and the constitutional order of the Republic of China was torn apart, resulting in the emergence of two power centers that each claimed to be the "central government." China's political fragmentation reached a new height.

However, since the Qin's unification of the six ancient states, the agricultural areas centered on the Central Plains had become increasingly accustomed to unification. Confucian scholar-officials had originally advocated the rituals of the Zhou Dynasty based on the enfeoffment system, but after the Qin unification, they gradually adapted to the county-prefecture system and the emperor system. Scholars such as Dong Zhongshu 董仲舒 actively cooperated with Emperor Wu of the Han Dynasty 汉武帝 to weaken enfeoffment and strengthen imperial power; in the Tang Dynasty, Liu Zongyuan 柳宗元's "On Feudalism" affirmed the county-prefecture system and opposed the restoration of "feudalism"; Huang Zongxi 黄宗羲 and Gu Yanwu 顾炎武 in the late Ming and early Qing period criticized the over-concentration of political power on the emperor, but they did not abandon the concept of unification. Gu Yanwu once commented: "The shortcomings of feudalism lie in the arbitrariness of the lower strata; the shortcomings of the county and prefecture system lie in the arbitrariness of the upper strata." He proposed an appropriate mixture of the two systems, "incorporating feudalism into the county and prefecture system."[448] In the Qing Dynasty, Western nationalist thinking resonated with the traditional Chinese resources of identity politics, and finally led to self-consciousness of "the Chinese nation."[449] Against this background, even local warlords wouldn't publicly oppose national unification after the Revolution of 1911. Political debate did not focus on whether unification was desirable, but on how to reach a better state of unification. It was in this

448 Gu Yanwu 顾炎武, *Gu Tinglin shiwenji* 顾亭林诗文集 [*Collection of Poems and Essays by Gu Tinglin*], (Beijing: Zhonghua shuju, 1983), 12.

449 See Huang (n. 415).

context that the Monroe Doctrine became an extremely important symbol in the debate surrounding the vertical separation of powers.

During the era of the Republic of China, U.S. ruling elites reinterpreted the Monroe Doctrine based on regional hegemony for global hegemony, and this had a great influence on China. President Woodrow Wilson's January 22, 1917, speech to the U.S. Senate, "Peace without Victory," was interpreted as calling for each country and nation decided its own development path. It was applicable not only to the U.S.-dominated Americas, but also to the rest the world:

> I am proposing, as it were, that the nations should with one accord adopt the doctrine of President Monroe as the doctrine of the world: that no nation should seek to extend its polity over any other nation or people, but that every people should be left free to determine its own polity, its own way of development, unhindered, unthreatened, unafraid, the little along with the great and powerful.[450]

An English-language newspaper published in China, *North China Daily News*, reported Wilson's speech the next day, and used a small paragraph to sum up Wilson's new interpretation of the Monroe Doctrine: "... that no nation should seek to extend itself or its policy over any other nation or people but that each, little and great, should be free to develop unhindered and unafraid."[451] *Ta Tung Monthly*, edited by the Englishman Evan Morgan, described this speech in its third issue of 1917: "Wilson also said that all countries in the world should take Monroe Doctrine as the exemplar, and must not impose their own policies upon other countries; all the countries, no matter they are strong or weak, can govern their countries according to their free will and should not be hindered by other countries."[452] On March 8–9, 1918, *The News*, sponsored by American John C. Ferguson, published the article titled "The Post-War Monroe Doctrine (the U.S. public law Professor Wilson's speech)," which introduced Wilson's speech of January 22, 1917 in this way: "The declaration of the President on the 22nd indicates how the government treats this doctrine. The government attempts to implement this doctrine to respond to the peace negotiation. Therefore, the Monroe Doctrine should broaden its scope, which is not as narrow as before, but attempts to lay a broad foundation for all-under-heaven. The

450 President Woodrow Wilson, "Peace Without Victory," Speech (22 January 1917) 64th Cong., 23 Sess., Senate Document No. 685: "A League for Peace."

451 "Pres. Wilson on Peace Terms," *Zilin xibao* (23 January 1917).

452 Yi Wei 一苇, "Meizongtong weierxun zhi yanshuo heping 美总统威尔逊之演说和平 [American President Wilson's Speech on Peace]," *Datong yuebao* 3 (1917).

interpretation of the Doctrine is that each country should develop freely without interference from other countries."[453] The author even proposed: "From a broader perspective, the purpose of this war can be described as the Monroe Doctrine for all-under-heaven."[454]

Wilson set up a wartime propaganda agency, the Committee on Public Information, on April 13, 1917. In September 1918, the agency set up a branch in Shanghai, China, called the Oriental News Agency (later renamed the China-U.S. News Agency), to increase Chinese awareness of the Sino-U.S. friendship, America's national development path and Wilson's thinking. Oriental News Agency provided international news and reviews for more than 300 Chinese newspapers. International information from the U.S. quickly overwhelmed that from the United Kingdom; Oriental News Agency published posters and pictorial magazines in China's major cities. Its leader, Carl Crow, carefully selected Wilson's speeches for translation and publication by the Commercial Press. These volumes included *American President Wilson's Speech at Peace Conference*, translated by Qian Zhixiu 钱智修 (the first edition in March 1919), and *American President Wilson's Speech at War* (the first edition in November 1918), translated by Jiang Menglin, which circulated widely in Chinese public opinion circles. Karl Crowe collected the names and addresses of 25,000 local elites in China through missionaries and international companies. Wilson's lectures were sent to them, and more than 5,000 replies were received, indicating significant influence on Chinese public opinion.[455] In China's intellectual and public opinion circles, Peking University led by Cai Yuanpei 蔡元培, the Jiangsu Education Association led by Huang Yanpei 黄炎培, Commercial Press led by Zhang Yuanji 张元济 and even the Yan Jiu Xi 研究系 (the research faction) led by Liang Qichao, all actively spread Wilson's ideas through their social status and communication channels.[456]

---

453 "Zhanhou zhi menluo zhuyi (meiguo gongfaxue jiaoxi weierxunshi yanshuo wen) 战后之门罗主义（美国公法学教习威尔逊氏演说文） [Monroe Doctrine after World War II (American public law Professor Wilson's speech)]," *Xinwenbao* (8 March 1918).

454 Ibid.

455 Ren Yi 任一, "Huanshi dumei: Wusi qianxi meiguo zaihua xuanchuan yu Zhongguo dui xinguoja shenfen de zhuiqiu 寰世独美:五四前夕美国在华宣传与中国对新国家身份的追求 [No One but the U.S.: the U.S. propaganda in China and China's pursuit of a New National Identity on the Eve of the May Fourth Movement]," *Shixue jikan*, 1 (2016.).

456 Ma Jianbiao 马建标, "Suzao jiushizhu: 'yizhan' houqi 'weierxun zhuyi' zai zhongguo de chuanbo 塑造救世主: '一战' 后期 '威尔逊主义' 在中国的传播" [Shaping the Savior: The Spread of the Wilson Doctrine in China in the Late World War I], *Xueshu Yuekan* 6 (2017).

In Article 5 of the Fourteen Principles of Peace published on January 8, 1918, Wilson proposed only that "a free, open-minded, and absolutely impartial adjustment of all colonial claims, based upon a strict observance of the principle that in determining all such questions of sovereignty the interests of the populations concerned must have equal weight with the equitable claims of the government whose title is to be determined."[457] Wilson did not use the Bolshevik-style concept of "national self-determination," and the portion of the Fourteen Principles concerning national independence focused on the treatment of nations in the former Russian, German, Austro-Hungarian and Ottoman empires, and was not intended to promote the independence of nations in the colonies and semi-colonies in general. However, the China Branch of the Committee on Public Information enlarged Wilson's proposition to create the image of Wilson as a passionate supporter of "national self-determination," emphasizing the support of the U.S. for China's participation in the peace conference after the war and its recovery of interests and rights from the great powers.[458] Mediated by the image of Wilson in China, the Monroe Doctrine as traditional American foreign policy was closely affiliated with the concepts of "democratic autonomy" and "national self-determination," and even American federalism was brought into the same "meaning field" as the Monroe Doctrine. All these concepts were believed to embody the spirit of "democratic autonomy." The following paragraphs will focus on the existence of this "meaning field," taking the participation of the young Mao Zedong in the Hunan constitutional movement as an example.

The publicity generated by the China Branch of the Committee on Public Information made Wilson's prestige flourish rapidly in China. However, the image of Wilson as a "lucky star of world peace" created by this publicity triggered the excessive expectations of Chinese elites, which was highly risky for Wilson. At the Paris Peace Conference in 1919, Wilson agreed to transfer Germany's privileges in Shandong to Japan, which contrasted sharply with the publicity of the China Branch of the Committee on Public Information. This was a blow to Wilson's reputation in China, but could hardly be called a total reversal. Chen Duxiu (eventually party secretary of the Chinese Communist Party), who criticized Wilson publicly at that time, only called Wilson "Wei Da

457 Woodrow Wilson, Jiang Menglin 蒋梦麟 trans., *Meiguo zongtong weierxun canzhan yanshuo* 美国总统威尔逊参战演说 [*American President Wilson's Speech at the War*], (Shanghai: The Commercial Press, 1918), 41.

458 Hans Schmidt, "Democracy for China: American Propaganda and the May Fourth Movement," *Diplomatic History* 22 (Winter 1998), 1–28.

Pao" 威大炮, or "Big Gun Wilson,"[459] essentially criticizing Wilson for spouting off without taking real action. In 1919, Mao Zedong still tended to view Wilson as a good guy surrounded by a group of cunning bad guys and often making compromises against his own will. The words of Chen Duxiu and Mao Zedong

459 One question that arises from this is why Wilson's interpretation of Monroe Doctrine can still be popular in China for several years after he suffered the prestigious Waterloo in 1919. This has a lot to do with the way Chinese public opinion reported and commented on Wilson and Wilson Doctrine in 1919. Chen Duxiu, who attacked Wilson fiercely at that time, only called Wilson a "mighty cannon," but he didn't pay attention to digging more black materials of Wilson. Chen Duxiu 陈独秀, "Weidapao 威大炮 [Wilson the Braggart]," *Meizhou pinglun* 8 (9 February 1919). Mao Zedong still tended to understand Wilson as a good man in Xiangjiang Review in 1919, But surrounded by a group of cunning bad guys, I had to make compromises and do things against my will. Mao Zedong 毛泽东, "Kelian de weierxun 可怜的威尔逊 [Poor Wilson]," *Xiangjiang pinglun* (14 July 1919). Many people in China's public opinion circles know that when the representative of Japan put forward a motion on racial equality, President Wilson sided with the representatives of Australia and Britain who supported racism. The Journal of Geosciences also published a series of articles, discussing the practical application of "national self-determination" after World War I, pointing out that the vast majority of border changes were the result of the continued expansion of the great powers, especially Britain instigated separatism in Tibet, China under the banner of "national self-determination." Han Ziqi 韩子奇, "'Dixue zazhi' yu yici dazhan qianhou zhongguoren de shijieguan 《地学杂志》与一次大战前后中国人的世界观 [Journal of Geosciences and Chinese World Outlook before and after World War I]," in Minguo shijia yu shixue 1912–1949: *Minguo shijia yu shixue guoji xueshu yantaohui lunwenji* 民国史家与史学1912 - 1949：民国史家与史学国际学术研讨会论文集 [*Historians and Historiography of the Republic of China 1912–1949: Proceedings of the International Symposium on Historians and Historiography of the Republic of China*], ed. Chen Yong 陈勇 (Shanghai: Shanghai daxue chubanshe, 2014): 103–104. But even so, no one has systematically explored the history of President Wilson's racist speech. As a matter of fact, President Wilson, who grew up in the American South immersed in racist culture and showed a strong racial prejudice. After World War I, his support of national self-determination did not go beyond his own racism. First of all, national self-determination served the punishment of the defeated powers, and what he admitted was basically the independence of those white nations; When faced with America's own colony, Philippines, President Wilson said that Filipinos have not yet reached the ability of self-government and still need American guardianship. See Woodrow Wilson, "The Ideals of America," *Atlantic Monthly* 90 (December 1902), 721–734. If these facts were known to Chinese public opinion circles at that time, Wilson's image would be different. However, the failure of historical actors to dig up these materials at that time was not only due to lack of knowledge, but also due to the fact that the political and cultural elites in China at that time did not have particularly strong ill feelings towards the United States. Therefore, there is not much motivation to defame Wilson. The general perception of the U.S. is that compared with other powers, the United States does not have colonies or definite spheres of influence in China, and its Open Door Policy, to a certain extent, also constrains other powers' attempts to carve up China, although it is ultimately calculated for the benefit of the United States itself.

can give us clues as to the general image of Wilson in China after the Paris Peace Conference: inefficient and unreliable, but not evil or malicious.

Many people in China's public opinion circles knew that when the representative of Japan proposed a motion on writing racial equality into the Convention of the League of Nations, President Wilson sided with the representatives of Australia and Britain against this motion. But even so, no one in China did a systematic study of the history of President Wilson's racist speeches. As a matter of fact, President Wilson, who grew up immersed in the racist culture of the post-civil war South, had deep racial prejudices and enacted a series of racially discriminatory policies. His support for national determination after World War I was also very limited. Most of those nations allowed to establish independent states were in the defeated countries and the former Russian empire. Wilson did not expect independence for colonized or semi-colonized countries ruled by the victors of the war. As for the Philippines, President Wilson said explicitly that Filipinos had not yet achieved the capacity for self-government and still needed American guardianship. But for Lenin, national self-determination was a universal principle, applied not only to Europe, but also to the colonies and semi-colonies dominated by Western powers.

Few Chinese elites took notice of Wilson's dark side apart from his concession to Japan in Paris. This was not simply due to lack of information. Essentially, China's mainstream political and cultural elites did not have strong negative feelings toward the U.S. at that time. Compared with other great powers, the U.S. did not own colonies or definite spheres of influence in China, and its Open Door Policy also constrained the ability of other powers to carve up China to a certain extent. During the First World War, many Chinese elites expected the U.S. to play a role in balancing the rising Japanese power. Although the U.S. acted according to its own calculation of national interests, its self-interest was perceived to be less harmful than that of most other great powers. Ultimately, the deterioration of Wilson's reputation in China did not harm the popular image of the U.S. to the same extent—just as Mao's 1936 interview with Edgar Snow indicated, his disenchantment with Wilson in 1919 did not reverse his attitude toward the Monroe Doctrine and the Open Door Policy. The associative mechanism among the Monroe Doctrine, federalism, autonomy and national self-determination shaped by the American wartime propaganda machine continued to exert influence in Chinese public opinion.

Against the background of the confrontation between the North and the South in 1920–1921, many local elites actively promoted the autonomy of provinces, seeking to formulate provincial constitutions and expecting to rebuild a new central government in a way similar to American federalism. The United Provincial Autonomy Movement arose. A series of publications advocating provincial autonomy were founded one by one: *New Hubei* in September 1920, *New Anhui* in December 1920, *New Zhejiang* in December 1921, *New Sichuan* in April 1921, *New Jiangxi* in May 1921, and *New Shandong* in July 1921, ushering in a climax of Provincial Monroe Doctrine in China. However, this climax passed quickly, and the reputation of the Monroe Doctrine soon underwent a dramatic reversal.

The following is an overview of Provincial Monroe Doctrine discourse in the Republic of China. I set a threshold for the selection: To prove the existence of a strict Provincial Monroe Doctrine, we need to find that local elites explicitly used the term Monroe Doctrine to refer to the autonomy of their province, or that newspapers or other elites used the Monroe Doctrine to comment on the exercising of provincial autonomy. In some provinces, we cannot find explicit use of the term "Monroe Doctrine," but local elites might use the phrase "Xans govern X" instead. This is a lesser form of Provincial Monroe Doctrine. I will start with the most explicit types of Provincial Monroe Doctrine, and then descend to less explicit types. This spectrum can demonstrate the gradual change in the reception of the Monroe Doctrine in China.

1. Hunan Monroe Doctrine 湖南门罗主义. Hunan's local identity had been on the rise since the Taiping Rebellion. Yang Du 杨度, the leading constitutional monarchist in the late Qing era, wrote in "Hunan Youth Song" that "if China were Greece, Hunan should be Sparta; if China were Germany, Hunan would be Prussia." The anti-Manchu revolutionary Yang Yulin 杨毓麟 wrote *New Hunan*, advocating Hunan's independence from the Qing court. Modern events such as the suppression of the Taiping Rebellion by the Hunan Army led by Zeng Guofan 曾国藩, Zuo Zongtang 左宗棠's pacification of Xinjiang, and Tan Sitong 谭嗣同 sacrificing his life for reform, all became important symbolic resources of Hunan's local identity in the late Qing Dynasty. In the mass protests of the Railway Protection Movement in Hunan on May 30, 1911, some radical gentry had already shouted the slogan "Hunan is Hunan for the Hunanese."[460] After the Wuchang Uprising broke out, Hunan responded quickly and declared its separation from the Qing court, with its local elites grasping military and political power. After the split of the constitutional order and the formation of the confrontation between the North and South in 1917, Hunan Province became a battlefield contested by the military forces of the South and the North. This became increasingly unbearable for the gentry and people in the province. A new movement therefore came into being, calling for Hunan's autonomy and neutrality in the confrontation between North and South.

460 Mi (n. 444), 1259–1260.

Mao Zedong was very active in Hunan's autonomy movement. From 1919 to 1920, Mao was the young leader of the "Zhang-expelling movement," in which Hunan students expelled Zhang Jingyao 张敬尧, a warlord of the Anhui faction. After Tan Yankai 谭延闿 and Zhao Hengti 赵恒惕 led the Hunan Army in successfully driving Zhang Jingyao out of Hunan in 1920, Mao Zedong and other members of the Xinmin Society proposed the idea of autonomy for Hunan. As he recalled to American journalist Edgar Snow in 1936: "Our group [the Xinmin Society] is disgusted with the Beiyang government. It was believed that Hunan could achieve modernization more quickly if it was separated from Beijing, so separation from Beijing was encouraged. At that time, I was a strong supporter of the American Monroe Doctrine and Open Door Policy."[461] Tan Yankai 谭延闿 and Zhao Hengti 赵恒惕 also endorsed the United Provincial Autonomy Movement and planned to formulate a constitution for Hunan Province. The term "Hunan Monroe Doctrine" emerged in the process of formulating the provincial constitution. Shanghai's English-language newspaper, *Continental Daily*, published a report with the following title on November 25, 1920: "Hunan Government to Redeem Bank Currency: Province to Have 'Monroe Government' and Will Regulate Its Own Affairs."[462]

Long Jiangong 龙兼公, the chief writer for *Ta Kung Pao* in Changsha, was one the key proponents of the Hunan Monroe Doctrine. During the Constitutional Movement in Hunan Province, he wrote articles titled "Hunan Monroe Doctrine," "Cantonese Governing Guangdong," "The Autonomy of Hunan People," "People-oriented Constitution," and "A Brief History of Hunan

---

461 Liu Peng 刘朋 et al. eds., *Zhonggong dangshi koushu shilu* 中共党史口述实录 [*Oral Record of the History of the Communist Party of China*] (Volume 1), (Beijing: Zhongguo guji chubanshe, 2010), 3. However, it is worth mentioning that when Mao Zedong was studying in Changsha in 1916, he once questioned "Hunan people governing Hunan." On July 18, 1916, Mao Zedong analyzed the political situation in Hunan in "Letter to Xiao Zisheng" and thought that the expulsion of Hunan Governor Tang Yuming (Hubei Lishui people) was Hunan's misfortune: "Tang can be acquitted in the world, and can be acquitted in Hunan people. It is also unfortunate to go to Hunan." Mao Zedong's Early Manuscripts, Changsha: Renmin chubanshe, 1995, p. 49. On July 25, Mao Zedong sent a letter to Xiao Zisheng again, summarizing the content of the former letter as "saying that Hunan people take the Romanticism for their own sake," and made it clear that Hunan constantly boycotted foreign officials. Cause "the wind of tilting, forming, gaining," "this kind of self-pushing, chief executive's ethos, can't be opened. People in this province are officials of this province, which is very harmful." *Mao Zedong zaoqi wengao* 毛泽东早期文稿 [*Mao Zedong's Early Manuscripts*], (Changsha: Renmin chubanshe, 1995), 49.

462 "Hunan Government To Redeem Bank Currency," *Dalubao* (25 November 1920). It is precisely because Zhao Hengti won the name of "Monroe Doctrine" that when he launched the Hunan-Hubei War in the name of "aiding Hubei" in 1921, it caused some discussion among the people. See Xiang E wenti yu baoding huiyi 湘鄂问题与保定会议 [Hunan and Hubei Issues and Baoding Conference], *Shenbao* (2 August 1921).

Autonomy" etc., among which "Hunan Monroe Doctrine" was published on September 5, 1920. Before Long Jiangong published "Hunan Monroe Doctrine," Mao typically used the term "Hunan people's self-determination." In a letter to Zeng Yi on June 23, Mao Zedong said that the enemies of "Hunan people's self-determination" were "those who oppose the creation of Hunan civilization, the warlords, the inspector of Hunan, Guangdong and Guangxi, the inspector of Hunan and Hubei, the national defense army, the Jingguo army and the Zhengnan army." "Hunan people's self-determination" called for all of these forces to withdraw from Hunan, and for "Hunan people to calmly develop their nature and create their civilization."[463] On the day after Long Jiangong published "Hunan Monroe Doctrine," Mao Zedong wrote "Absolutely in Favor of Hunan Monroe Doctrine," arguing that Long Jiangong put forward three explanations of the Monroe Doctrine: "We should do what we should do with our heart," "We will never interfere in other people's affairs" and "Never allow others to interfere in our affairs." Mao argued that these conditions were in tune with the mentality of most Hunan people.[464] At the same time, Mao Zedong published "Hunan is Burdened by China: Proofs from History and the Present Situation," which further contended that "in the next twenty years, people in all provinces should pay full attention to their own provincial policies, and all provinces should close their doors to other provinces and pay no attention to affairs outside their doors."[465]

At the same time, Mao Zedong emphasized that what he advocated was "Hunan people's autonomy," not the general slogan "Hunanese governing

463 Mao Zedong 毛泽东, "Hunan gaizao cuchenghui fu Zeng Yi shu 湖南改造促成会复曾毅书 [Zeng Yishu (23 June 1920)]," in *Zhongguo yida daibiao zaoqi wengao xuanbian: 1917.11–1923.7* 中共一大代表早期文稿选编：1917.11 - 1923.7 [*Selected Early Manuscripts of the First Congress of the Communist Party of China: 1917.11–1923.7*] (1), eds. Memorial Hall of the First Congress of the Communist Party of China (Shanghai: Shanghai renmin chubanshe, 2011): 885.

464 Mao Zedong 毛泽东, "Juedui zanchegng hunan menluo zhuyi 绝对赞成湖南们罗主义 [Absolutely in favor of Hunan Menluo Doctrine (6 September 1920)]," in *Zhongguo yida daibiao zaoqi wengao xuanbian: 1917.11–1923.7* 中共一大代表早期文稿选编：1917.11 - 1923.7 [*Selected Early Manuscripts of the First Congress of the Communist Party of China: 1917.11–1923.7*] (1), eds. Memorial Hall of the First Congress of the Communist Party of China (Shanghai: Shanghai renmin chubanshe, 2011): 900.

465 Mao Zedong 毛泽东, "Hunan shou Zhongguo zhilei yilishi ji xianzhuang zhengmingzhi 湖南受中国之累以历史及现状证明之 [Hunan is burdened by China and proved by history and present situation (September 6, 7, 1920)]," in *Zhongguo yida daibiao zaoqi wengao xuanbian: 1917.11–1923.7* 中共一大代表早期文稿选编：1917.11–1923.7 [*Selected Early Manuscripts of the First Congress of the Communist Party of China: 1917.11–1923.7*] (1), eds. Memorial Hall of the First Congress of the Communist Party of China (Shanghai: Shanghai renmin chubanshe, 2011): 903.

Hunan." The difference between the two slogans was that the former referred to the true democratic autonomy of the vast majority of Hunan people, while the latter might be reduced to the monopoly of a few local bureaucrats and warlords in the name of Hunanese.[466] On October 5–6, *Ta Kung Pao* published a joint statement by 377 representatives from all walks of life in Hunan, including Mao Zedong, Peng Huang 彭璜 and Long Jiangong, titled "Proposal for Hunan People's Constitutional Assembly to be Convened by Hunan Revolutionary Government to Formulate Hunan Constitution in Order to Build a New Hunan," arguing for the banner of "Hunan Revolutionary Government" under which every 50,000 people in Hunan should choose one representative to participate in the constitutional assembly to formulate the Hunan Constitution.[467] The article said: "We think that the autonomy law that Hunan wants now is equivalent to the constitutions of the U.S. and Germany. China is now in a divided situation, and I don't know when the national constitution will come into being. In fact, I am afraid that there must be a sub-constitution of each province before there is a general constitution of the whole nation, just like the path that the U.S. and Germany have taken."[468] This shows how Mao Zedong, Long Jiangong and others equated the Monroe Doctrine with Federalism. On October 8, a broadly representative group of people held a mass rally demanding the "convening of the People's Constitutional Convention," and Mao Zedong was elected chairman of the meeting.

However, Tan Yankai 谭延闿 and Zhao Hengti 赵恒惕 did not accept the proposal by Mao Zedong et al. of opening up the constitutional drafting process to ordinary citizens. Tan Yankai 谭延闿 tried to formulate a draft of the constitution by the provincial council. Tan was soon driven out of Hunan by

466 Mao Zedong 毛泽东, "'Xiangren zhixiang' yu 'xiangren zizhi' '湘人治湘' 与 '湘人自治' ['Hunan people govern Hunan' and 'Hunan people's autonomy' (September 30, 1920)]," in *Zhongguo yida daibiao zaoqi wengao xuanbian: 1917.11–1923.7* 中共一大代表早期文稿选编：1917.11 – 1923.7 [*Selected Early Manuscripts of the First Congress of the Communist Party of China: 1917.11–1923.7*] (1), eds. Memorial Hall of the First Congress of the Communist Party of China (Shanghai: Shanghai renmin chubanshe, 2011): 908.

467 Mao Zedong 毛泽东, "You 'hunan geming zhengfu' zhaoji 'hunan renmin xianfa huiyi' zhiding 'hunan xianfa' yijianshe 'xinhunan' zhi jianyi 由 '湖南革命政府' 召集 '湖南人民宪法会议' 制定 '湖南宪法' 以建设 '新湖南' 之建议 [The Hunan Revolutionary Government convened the Hunan People's Constitution Conference to formulate the Hunan Constitution to build a new Hunan (October 5, 6, 1920)]," in *Zhongguo yida daibiao zaoqi wengao xuanbian: 1917.11–1923.7* 中共一大代表早期文稿选编：1917.11 – 1923.7 [*Selected Early Manuscripts of the First Congress of the Communist Party of China: 1917.11–1923.7*] (1), eds. Memorial Hall of the First Congress of the Communist Party of China (Shanghai: Shanghai renmin chubanshe, 2011): 911–913.

468 Ibid.

Zhao Hengti 赵恒惕 due to internal military strife. Zhao Hengti 赵恒惕 completely denied citizen participation in the drafting process. He instead invited experts and scholars to draft the constitution, which would then be submitted to the provincial referendum for ratification. Mao Zedong's stand of "rule by the people" was consequently frustrated in the process of constitution-making. As Mao described the situation to Edgar Snow, he turned to a new approach to save China at the end of 1920: "In the winter of 1920, I organized the workers politically for the first time. In this work, the influence of Marxist theory and Russian revolutionary history began to play a guiding role."[469]

On January 1, 1922, Zhao Hengti 赵恒惕 officially promulgated the Constitution of Hunan Province in his capacity as provincial governor. The Constitution stipulated that "Hunan is an autonomous province of the Republic of China," and that autonomy "belongs to all the people of the province," "the people of the province should jointly protect the law and order of the province; troops from outside the province may never be stationed or pass through the province without the approval of the provincial council and the permission of the provincial government."[470] The regulations on troops from outside the province embodied the core concerns of Zhao Hengti 赵恒惕 in formulating the provincial constitution. Against the background of confrontation between the two governments in 1921, Sun Yat-sen took Guangxi with the help of Chen Jiongming 陈炯明's Guangdong Army, and then set up a base camp in Guilin to prepare for the Northern Expedition. However, in the name of "Hunan Autonomy," Zhao Hengti 赵恒惕 remained neutral and refused permission for the Northern Expeditionary Army sent by Sun Yat-sen to pass through Hunan. Finally, Sun's army was forced to go north from Jiangxi Province, and the Northern Expedition failed. On May 23, 1921, *Shen Bao* published "Hunan Province's Attitude towards the Guangdong-Guangxi War—Hunan Province Responded to the Guangdong-Guangxi War with the Old Signboard of Autonomy and the Old Way of Monroe Doctrine," commenting on Zhao Hengti's actions: "At present, Hunan Province can only handle the Guangdong-Guangxi War with the old signboard of autonomy and the old way of Monroe Doctrine. Hunan therefore politely refused Sun's demand."[471] On October 12, 1922, *Shi Bao* reported:

---

469 Liu (n. 459), 4.

470 "Hunansheng xianfa 湖南省宪法 [Constitution of Hunan Province]," *Dongfang zazhi* 19 (25 November 1922).

471 "Xiangsheng duiyu yuegui zhanshi zhi taidu—Xiangshegn yi zizhi laozhaopai yu menglu zhuyi laobanfa yingfu yuegui zhanzheng 湘省对于粤桂战事之态度——湘省以自治老招牌与孟禄主义老办法应付粤桂战争 [Hunan province's attitude towards the Guangdong-Guangxi war—Hunan province responded to the Guangdong-Guangxi war with the old signboard of autonomy and the old way of Monroe Doctrine]," *Shenbao* (23 May 1921).

"Zhao Hengti recently declared to county representatives: Hunan Province is still following the Monroe Doctrine and has no bias toward either the South or the North, with the hope of letting the people rest and recuperate within three years."[472]

After being driven out of Hunan by Zhao Hengti 赵恒惕, Tan Yankai 谭延闿 returned to Hengyang, Hunan Province, in August 1923 with the help of Sun Yat-sen to confront Zhao Hengti 赵恒惕 under the banner of the "Provincial Constitution Amendment Office." In response, Zhao Hengti 赵恒惕 struck the banner of "protecting the Constitution." In order to defeat Tan Yankai 谭延闿, he introduced the army of the Zhili faction into Hunan. This move actually violated the provisions of the Constitution of Hunan Province that restricted the presence of troops from other provinces. In the conflict between Tan and Zhao, "Hunan Autonomy" became a melodrama. In the inaugural July 1, 1923, issue of *Qian Feng* 前锋, a monthly magazine published by the Central Committee of the Communist Party of China, Mao Zedong published the article "Hunan under the Provincial Constitution" under the pseudonym of Shi Shan 石山, pointing out that Hunan's economic situation was better than that of Sichuan, Yunnan and some other provinces and could maintain an army of moderate size. This was the economic base of its "provincial Monroe Doctrine."[473] But ultimately, "there is no reason that the life of the provincial constitution could last long. Provincial autonomy is something that can never be realized."[474]

The Constitution of Hunan Province was nominally effective until the Northern Expedition. On July 14, 1926, Tang Shengzhi 唐生智, the commander of the middle route branch of the Northern Expeditionary Army send by the Guangdong Nationalist Government, arrived in Changsha and abolished the provincial constitution. At this point, the Hunan Monroe Doctrine came to an end. A few months later, Mao Zedong made an in-depth investigation of the peasant movement in Hunan, and wrote *Investigation Report of the Hunan Peasant Movement*. As a former pioneer of the Hunan Autonomy Movement, Mao Zedong once again stood at the forefront of the times in a new movement to reunify the country through military struggle and social revolution.[475]

---

472 "Zhao Hengti zuijin zhi taidu 赵恒惕最近之态度 [Zhao Hengti's recent attitude]," *Shibao* (12 October 1922).

473 Memorial Hall of the First Congress of the Communist Party of China and Preparatory Office of Shanghai Revolutionary History Museum eds., *Shanghai gemingshi ziliao yu yanjiu* 上海革命史资料与研究 [*Materials and Research of Shanghai Revolutionary History* (Series III)], (Shanghai: Shanghai guji chubanshe, 2003), 556.

474 Ibid., 554.

475 From studying in Changsha, Mao Zedong paid attention to Monroe Doctrine throughout his life. After the moment of "Hunan Monroe Doctrine" in 1920, Mao Zedong also mentioned "Monroe Doctrine" in some reports, declarations and talks, for example, in

2. Zhejiang Monroe Doctrine 浙江门罗主义: Zhejiang had been headed by local elites since the Revolution of 1911. In 1916, various factions in the province competed for the post of governor, which caused political turmoil. On January 3, 1917, the Beijing government appointed Yang Shande 杨善德 (Anhui native) and Qi Yaoshan 齐耀珊 (Shandong native) as military governor and governor of Zhejiang Province. Zhejiang gentry boycotted the appointments. Starting on January 5, a "citizens' congress" was held in Hangzhou for several days, with more than 4,800 people attending. Provincial Councilor Xu Zuqian pointed out in his speech that the "Zhejiang Monroe Doctrine has been broken ever since."[476] Members Shen Dingyi 沈定一, Ren Fenggang, 任凤冈, Jin Xie 金燮, Zhang Yuqiao 张雨樵 and Congress member Chu Fucheng 褚辅成 delivered speeches calling on people from all walks of life to refuse entry to troops from other provinces. Shen Dingyi cried out: "Zhejiang is Zhejiang for the Zhejiang people. If Zhejiang people cannot protect our province, we cannot protect the state, either … if Zhejiang cannot have autonomy, and other

---

the report "Current Situation and Party Policy" on July 13, 1940, Mao Zedong analyzed the struggle between Germany, Italy, Japan and Britain and the United States, and pointed out that its main battlefield has shifted from land to sea. Here Mao Zedong commented on the United States: "The United States is Monroe Doctrine plus cosmopolitanism, 'mine is mine, yours is still mine.' It is unwilling to give up its interests in the Atlantic and Pacific." So China can take advantage of the contradictions between imperialist countries. Literature Research Office of the Central Committee of the Communist Party of China ed., *Mao Zedong wenji* 毛泽东文集 [*Selected Works of Mao Zedong* (Volume 2)], (Beijing: Renmin chubanshe, 1999), 287. On October 6, 1958, Mao Zedong drafted and issued the Letter of the Ministry of National Defense of the People's Republic of China to Taiwan Province Compatriots in the name of Peng Dehuai, criticizing the military presence of the United States in the Western Pacific; "An eastern Pacific country, why did it come to the western Pacific? The western Pacific is the western Pacific of the western Pacific people, just as the eastern Pacific is the eastern Pacific of the eastern Pacific people." Literature Research Office of the Central Committee of the Communist Party of China eds., *Mao Zedong wenji* 毛泽东文集 [*Selected Works of Mao Zedong* (Volume 7)], (Beijing: Renmin chubanshe, 1999), 421. On March 18th, 1959, when Mao Zedong met with Asanuma Inejirō, secretary of the Japanese Socialist Party, he clearly pointed out that "the western Pacific should be managed by its own country." This is to advocate the joint efforts of China and Japan to jointly reject American occupation and interference in regional affairs. Ministry of Foreign Affairs of the People's Republic of China and the Literature Research Office of the Central Committee of the Communist Party of China eds., *Mao Zedong waijiao wenxuan* 毛泽东外交文选 [*Selected Diplomatic Works of Mao Zedong*], (Beijing: Zhongyang wenxian chubanshe, 1994), 371.

476 Xu Xingbin 许行彬, "Shinian liuwang zhi shengriyin 十年流亡之生日吟 [Singing the Birthday of Ten Years in Exile]," quoted from Shen Xiaomin 沈晓敏, *Chuchang yu qiubian: Qingmo minchu de zhejiang ziyiju he shengyihui* 处常与求变：清末民初的浙江咨议局和省议会 [*Managing and Seeking Change: Zhejiang Consultative Bureau and Provincial Council in the Late Qing Dynasty and the Early Republic of China*], (Beijing: Beijing: Shenghuo, Dushu, Xinzhi sanlian shudian, 2005), 193.

provinces cannot have autonomy like Zhejiang, how can the foundation of the central government be consolidated?"[477]

Lu Yongxiang 卢永祥 (native of Jiyang, Shandong Province), a local warlord of the Anhui faction, was appointed governor of Zhejiang Province in 1919. In 1921, under the control of the Beijing government by the Zhili faction, Lu Yongxiang refused entry to Zhejiang by Zhili forces in the name of "local autonomy," and sent a telegram on June 4, calling for the provinces to first formulate the provincial constitution, after which provincial military and political chiefs should send representatives to negotiate, and finally put the plan of unification to a referendum.[478] This gesture was well received by local elites such as Chen Jiongming in Guangdong, and was also welcomed by the gentry in Zhejiang. In December 1921, the newly founded *New Zhejiang* magazine published an editorial saying: "… Who owns Zhejiang? Everyone knows that Zhejiang is Zhejiang for the Zhejiang people, and I would emphasize that Zhejiang belongs to all the Zhejiang people … Therefore, those who love Zhejiang should set the governing of Zhejiang by the Zhejiang people as the primary aim."[479] Amidst this atmosphere of "Zhejiang people governing Zhejiang," Lu Yongxiang even changed the registration of his native place from Shandong to Ningbo, Zhejiang.

The Constitution of Zhejiang Province of the Republic of China was officially promulgated on September 9, 1921. However, Article 54 of the Constitution stipulated that "voters in this province who are at least thirty-five years old may be elected as governors, and if they are serving soldiers, they must be relieved of their military duties before they can take office."[480] This meant that Lu Yongxiang, as a military commander, could not become governor. In addition, some people questioned Lu Yongxiang's registration of native place. Lu Yongxiang suspended this constitution. Later, the gentry in Zhejiang drafted the Three-Color Constitution and the Zhejiang Autonomy Law. They even organized the Zhejiang Autonomous Government, which collapsed after only three days.

In 1924, Lu Yongxiang found himself surrounded by the military forces of the Zhili faction, so he joined forces with the Fengtian faction and Sun Yat-sen

477 "Zhejiang zhi shanhou wenti 浙江之善后问题 [The aftermath of Zhejiang]," *Shenbao* (7 January 1917).

478 Lu Yongxiang guanyu shengxian zizhi zhi tongdian 卢永祥关于省宪自治之通电 [Lu Yongxiang's Telegram of Provincial Constitutional Autonomy], *Shenbao* (5 June 1921).

479 Zhang Jinglu 张静庐, "Fakanci 发刊辞 [Speech on Publishing]," *Xinzhejiang* 1 (1921).

480 Xia Xinhua 夏新华 et al., *Jindai Zhongguo xianzheng licheng: Shiliao huicui* 近代中国宪政历程：史料荟萃 [*The History of Constitutional Government in Modern China: A Collection of Historical Materials*], (Beijing: Zhongguo zhengfa daxue chubanshe, 2004), 600.

to form an "Anti-Zhili Triangle Alliance." Lu Yongxiang also incorporated Zang Zhiping 臧致平 and Yang Huazhao 杨化昭 of the Fujian Army into his own military force. This caused great dissatisfaction among the Zhili faction, who accused him of violating the Jiangsu-Zhejiang Peace Convention's stipulation against incorporating the armies of other provinces. On September 3, 1924, the Jiangsu-Zhejiang War broke out. Qi Xieyuan 齐燮元, the military governor of Jiangsu Province who belonged to the Zhili faction, joined forces with Sun Chuanfang 孙传芳, who had been stationed in Fujian to defeat Lu Yongxiang. However, Feng Yuxiang 冯玉祥 launched a military coup in Beijing on October 23, 1924, and then Duan Qirui 段祺瑞 of the Anhui faction came to power again with the support of Zhang Zuolin of the Fengtian faction to form a new provisional government. Qi Xieyuan was removed from office by Duan Qirui. Sun Chuanfang took power over Zhejiang, and announced in early 1926 that the "Monroe Doctrine of Five Provinces" should be implemented in Jiangsu, Zhejiang, Fujian, Anhui and Jiangxi. However, war was imminent as the Northern Expeditionary Army of the Guangzhou Nationalist Government approached Zhejiang. On November 25, 1926, *Ta Kung Pao* reported: "The Zhejiang military wants to pursue a kind of Zhejiang Monroe Doctrine and intends to stand outside the whirlpool." However, "since the gentry are full of empty talk, and the Zhejiang army lacks strength, few achievements can be expected from the current situation."[481] In February 1927, the Northern Expeditionary Army controlled the whole of Zhejiang Province, and the Zhejiang Monroe Doctrine vanished.

3. Monroe Doctrine of Five Provinces 五省门罗主义: In October–November 1925, Sun Chuanfang 孙传芳 (native of Tai 'an, Shandong Province) and Zhang Zuolin 张作霖 fought for the domain of Jiangsu and Anhui. With the military forces of five provinces, Sun Chuanfang finally forced Zhang Zuolin's Fengtian army to retreat to Shandong. On November 25, 1925, Sun Chuanfang officially announced the establishment of the coalition forces in Jiangsu, Zhejiang, Fujian, Anhui and Jiangxi provinces. At the meeting of major generals in Nanjing in February 1926, Sun Chuanfang announced that he would adhere to "The Monroe Doctrine of Five Provinces" and emphasized the aim of "recognizing the five provinces to protect the domain and the people."[482] The five southeast provinces remained neutral in the ongoing wars in Henan and

481 "Huzhe qingxing 沪浙情形 [The situation in Shanghai and Zhejiang]," *Ta Kung Pao* (25 November 1926).

482 Shen Yunlong 沈云龙 et al., "Guowen zhoubao: Guoneiwai yizhoujian dashiji 国闻周报·国内外一周间大事记 [National News Weekly, Memorabilia in a Week at Home and Abroad] (Vol. 3, No. 1 to Vol. 3, No. 50)," (Taiwan: Wenhai chubanshe, 1985, photocopy), 503.

Hubei. On June 9, 1926, the *Shuntian Shibao*, a Chinese newspaper published by the Japanese Ministry of Foreign Affairs in Beijing, reported the development of the situation with "Sun Chuanfang's Adherence to the Monroe Doctrine of Five Provinces."[483] In May, 1926, due to rumors that there would be a meeting of Zhang Zuolin, Wu Peifu, Sun Chuanfang and Yan Xishan, Sun Chuanfang responded to the reporter that "I have no intention of being so active," and he hoped that Wu Peifu and Zhang Zuolin would join hands. As for himself, he "intends to extend the Monroe Doctrine in the Southeast provinces to the whole country, giving assistance to the good government and taking an indifferent attitude towards the bad government. And we must abide by democracy as our policy."[484]

We don't know whether Sun Chuanfang's speech intentionally referred to the speech of "Peace without Victory" by U.S. President Wilson in 1917, which interpreted the Monroe Doctrine as a doctrine of self-determination in the development paths and political systems of all nations and peoples. As Sun Chuanfang advocated that "the Monroe Doctrine in the southeast provinces should be extended to the whole country," his discourse contained a similar rhetorical structure: It downplayed the problem of interference and anti-interference, and focused on the spirit embodied in the governance of this region. Sun Chuanfang interpreted this spirit as "democracy," so "pushing the Monroe Doctrine of Southeast Provinces to the whole country" meant that when the Beijing government and other provincial governments pursued this doctrine, he would support it; if they did not pursue this doctrine, Sun would keep his distance from them. Of course, Sun Chuanfang himself firmly controlled the power to interpret what "democracy" meant.

Soon, the Guangdong Nationalist Government launched the Northern Expedition. The Northern Expeditionary Army approached the sphere of influence of Sun Chuanfang, and Feng Yuxiang 冯玉祥's National Army in the North also attacked the forces of Wu Peifu. Wu Peifu hoped to concentrate on dealing with Feng Yuxiang's army, expecting his ally Sun Chuanfang to resist the Guangdong Northern Expeditionary Army. Sun Chuanfang once again showed

---

483 "Sun Chuanfang queshou wusheng menluo zhuyi 孙传芳确守五省门罗主义 [Sun Chuanfang really abides by the Monroe Doctrine of Five Provinces]," *Shuntian shibao* (9 June 1926) and *Zhonghua minguoshi shiliao waibian* 中华民国史史料外编 [*The Historical Materials of the Republic of China* (Volume 16)], 35.

484 "Sun Chuanfang qianri zhi tanhua 孙传芳前日之谈话 [Sun Chuanfang's conversation the day before yesterday]," *Shijie ribao* (29 May 1926), 2nd edition; "Wu Peifu nengxie Sun Chuanfang beilaiye 吴佩孚果能偕孙传芳北来耶 [Wu Peifu can bring Sun Chuanfang to the north]," *Shijie ribao* (23 May 1926), 3rd edition; "Sun Chuanfang yu rijizhe tanhua 孙传芳与日记者谈话 [Sun Chuanfang talks with Japanese reporters]," *Shenbao* (29 May 1926).

the true nature of the local warlord's Monroe Doctrine. While cooperating with Wu Peifu perfunctorily, he negotiated with Chiang Kai-shek and declared that if the Northern Expeditionary Army did not attack Zhejiang and Jiangxi, he would stay out of the war.

How did Sun Chuanfang respond to Zhang Zuolin, who held the Beijing government? The observation of *Shuntian Shibao* was: "Sun Chuanfang's attitude towards the political situation of the central government is essentially a kind of neutrality based upon the Monroe Doctrine of the Southeast, and he does not want Wu (Peifu) and Zhang (Zuolin) to be strong in any aspect."[485] However, the Northern Expeditionary Army made smooth progress in the Hunan and Hubei region. The Northern Expeditionary Army attacked Jiangxi on September 5, and Fujian on October 5th. In October 1926, Xia Chao 夏超, the governor of Zhejiang Province, announced that he had withdrawn from the alliance of five provinces. He joined the Guangdong Nationalist Government and was appointed commander of the 18th Army of the National Revolutionary Army. This highlighted the anti-interference side of the Monroe Doctrine. Sun Chuanfang dispatched troops to suppress Xia Chao, killing Xia as well as He Weisheng 贺威圣, secretary of the CPC Hangzhou District Committee. Sun Chuanfang was soon defeated by the Northern Expedition, and the Monroe Doctrine of Five Provinces became obsolete.

4. Yunnan Monroe Doctrine 云南门罗主义: Tang Jiyao 唐继尧, whose native place was Huize County, Yunnan Province, was the protagonist of the Yunnan Monroe Doctrine, which arose not from Tang's self-promotion, but from comments published in newspapers. In 1920, Tang Jiyao's Jingguo Army attacked Sichuan. According to *Ta Kung Pao*, the Sichuan provincial council lambasted Tang Jiyao's expansion measures as "imperialism": "Since the founding of the Republic, the military figures controlled and abused power. Ignorant of the overall situation, they picked up imperialism and advocated actions that harm our compatriots."[486] Tang Jiyao lost the war in Sichuan and retreated to Yunnan. On December 15, 1920, *Ta Kung Pao* commented: "Tang Jiyao of Yunnan declared self-defense and purely adopted the Monroe Doctrine. But he also declared that he would resolutely protect the 1912 constitution. His intention is simply to avoid the attention of Guizhou and Sichuan. This has been known to everyone." The report also mentioned that Tang Jiyao privately convened secret meetings with prominent people from all walks of life. "It is said

485 Sun Chuanfang qianzhi fengpai yi zhuwu 孙传芳牵制奉派以助吴 [Sun Chuanfang restrained Fengpai to help Wu], *Shuntian shibao* (1 July 1926).

486 "Chuanshenghui tongma Tang Jiyao 川省会痛骂唐继尧 [Sichuan provincial capital lambasted Tang Jiyao]," *Ta Kung Pao* (19 June 1920), sixth edition.

that the topic of discussion was to attack Sichuan, and next to take Guizhou."[487] *Ta Kung Pao* implied that Tang Jiyao's Monroe Doctrine was only superficial, and that what Tang pursued was essentially expansionism.

In 1921, Gu Pinzhen 顾品珍, a subordinate of Tang Jiyao, expelled Tang and became commander-in-chief of the Yunnan Army. In February 1922, Tang led the army to counterattack. Gu Pinzhen committed suicide, and Tang Jiyao regained power in Yunnan. On May 18, 1922, *Shuntian Shibao* published a report titled "Monroe Doctrine in Yunnan," which commented on the current situation in Yunnan: "After Tang Jiyao returned to Yunnan, all his declarations were worthy of attention. He seems to realize that it has been unfeasible to attack neighboring provinces as a means of expanding Yunnan. It is likely that he is focusing on the internal governance of the province and completing the organization of the provincial government. His policy is neither to invade other provinces nor to allow other provinces to invade; in other words, it seems that he has abandoned the greater Yunnan Doctrine, and sought to build a small Yunnan autonomous state for the purpose." However, like *Ta Kung Pao*, *Shuntian Shibao* also had doubts about Tang Jiyao's real intentions: "We whole-heartedly support the Yunnan Monroe Doctrine. It is in the interests of all of China and Yunnan Province to strive with all our strength for the establishment of the provincial government and provincial autonomy. Tang himself can also gain prestige from it. However, does Tang sincerely believe in this doctrine?"[488]

Naturally, Tang Jiyao would not be satisfied with ruling only Yunnan. After regaining military and political power in Yunnan, Tang Jiyao expanded the Yunnan Army into the "Jianguo Army" and became commander-in-chief of the coalition forces of Sichuan, Yunnan, Guizhou, Hubei, Henan and Shaanxi provinces. He first controlled Guizhou, and then launched the first Yunnan-Guangxi War, which suffered setbacks. After the Guangdong Nationalist Government launched its Northern Expedition, Tang Jiyao stood on the opposite side. On February 6, 1927, his subordinates Hu Ruoyu 胡若愚, Zhang Ruji 张汝骥, Shi Longyun 史龙云 and Li Xuanting 李选廷 jointly launched a "military remonstration," forcing Tang Jiyao to give up his power. Tang Jiyao died of illness two months later.

487 "Tan baozhong Tang Jiyao zhi cunxin 探报中唐继尧之存心 [Exploring Tang Jiyao's Intention in Newspaper]," *Ta Kung Pao* (15 December 1920).

488 "Yunan zhi menluo zhuyi 云南之门罗主义 [Monroe Doctrine in Yunnan]," *Shuntian shibao* (18 May 1922), quoted from *Zhonghua minguo shishi jiyao (chugao): Zhonghua minguo shiyinian* (1922) (*sizhiliu yuefen*) 中华民国史事纪要（初稿）·中华民国十一年（1922）（四至六月份）[*Editorial Committee of Historical Records of the Republic of China (First Draft), Eleventh Year of the Republic of China* (1922) (*April to June*)], (Taipei: Research Center for Historical Materials of the Republic of China, 1982 edition), 1239.

After a transitional period, Long Yun 龙云 became the new ruler in Yunnan and held great power independent of the Nanjing Nationalist Government. However, Long Yun became closer to Chiang Kai-shek before the War of Resistance against Japanese Invasion. During the Xi'an Incident, he declared that he would attack Zhang Xueliang and Yang Hucheng and save Chiang Kai-shek. During the War of Resistance against Japanese Invasion, the Chongqing Nationalist Government carried out a systematic policy to undermine Long Yun's power in Yunnan, and the conflict between them gradually intensified. On October 3, 1945, Chiang Kai-shek ordered Du Yuming 杜聿明 to launch a coup in Kunming, stripping Long Yun of his power. However, this process was implemented in a way similar to "boiling frogs with warm water," and mainstream public opinion did not label Long Yun as a Monroe Doctrine figure like Yan Xishan. When general Lu Han 卢汉 later took over as chairman of Yunnan Province, the main force of the Yunnan Army was transferred to Northeast China by Chiang Kai-shek to engage in the civil war, and there was no space for the Yunnan Monroe Doctrine.

5. Guizhou Monroe Doctrine 贵州门罗主义: In Guizhou, due to internal strife within the military government initiated by Sun Yat-sen in 1917, a confrontation between the old and new factions arose. The old faction was headed by Liu Xianshi 刘显世, the chief administrative officer of the military government and the military governor of Guizhou. He formed an alliance with Tang Jiyao 唐继尧, and allowed the Yunnan Army into Guizhou. The new faction, headed by his nephew Wang Wenhua 王文华, commander-in-chief of the Guizhou Army, supported Sun Yat-sen. In November 1920, when Wang Wenhua was still in Shanghai, the new faction threatened by the old faction took preemptive military action, forcing Liu Xianshi to step down. During Wang Wenhua's stay in Shanghai, Lu Tao 卢焘 (from Si'en, Guangxi) acted as commander-in-chief of the Guizhou Army. After Wang Wenhua's assassination by Yuan Zuming 袁祖铭, a general of the Guizhou Army who surrendered to Beiyang Government in March 1921, Lu Tao officially served as commander-in-chief of the Guizhou Army. After the 1920 Incident, there were reports in the media that "Lu Tao is committed to the Monroe Doctrine in governing Guizhou, although neighboring provinces did not respond to him actively."[489] This meant that Lu Tao would neither interfere with neighboring provinces such as Sichuan and Yunnan, nor accept interference from neighboring provinces. The real reason

489 "Yesterday (23rd), I met a politician from Guizhou and talked about the present situation in Guizhou. According to the cloud, Lu Tao ruled Guizhou, taking Monroe Doctrine, although neighboring provinces did not approach ...." "Zuijin zhi tongyi xiaoxi 最近之统一消息 [Recent Unified News]," *Shenbao* (26 December 1920), sixth edition.

for non-interference was that the Guizhou army had been divided into five parts after a period of turmoil, and had no capacity to attack other provinces. Meanwhile, the neighboring provinces were in the hands of the pro-Tang forces, which were hostile to Sun Yat-sen. In 1922, the forces of Yuan Zuming and Liu Xianshi returned and recognized the Beiyang government in the North. Lu Tao resigned as commander-in-chief of the Guizhou Army, and the brief period of Guizhou Monroe Doctrine under his rule ended.

6. Fujian Monroe Doctrine 福建门罗主义: Li Houji 李厚基 (native of Fengxian, Jiangsu Province), who came from the Beiyang Army, joined the Anhui faction in 1916 and was appointed military governor and governor of Fujian. In July 1920, the Anhui faction lost the Anhui-Zhili war, and the Zhili faction and Fengtian faction controlled the Beijing government jointly. Li Houji alienated the Anhui faction and approached the Zhili faction. On September 17, 1921, *The News* published a comment under the title "Li Houji's Recent Attitude: Fujian Province Adopted Monroe Doctrine" to analyze Li Houji's ruling strategy in Fujian. Li Houji approached the Zhili faction instead of the Fengtian faction, which displeased Zhang Zuolin, so Zhang persuaded Wang Yongquan, Li Houji's subordinate, to drive Li out of Fujian. However, Li Houji regained his firm foothold in the face of internal and external challenges. The report in *The News* mentioned that on September 3, Li Houji held a military meeting to discuss strategies for the current situation: "It was finally decided that Fujian Province aims to ensure neutrality and protect the people. No matter how the current situation changes, Fujian Province will never take sides. We need to take proper measures toward those who do not understand the difficulties of Fujian Province and violate our interest."[490] *The News* referred to Li Houji's neutral posture in complex times as "Monroe Doctrine." It is worth mentioning that, in the public opinion at that time, if a warlord took "protecting the domain and the people" as his guideline, this political posture was usually regarded as the embodiment of Monroe Doctrine. This applied to Sun Chunfang 孙传芳 and Li Houji 李厚基. It also applies to Yan Xishan 阎西山, analyzed below.

7. Guangdong Monroe Doctrine 广东门罗主义: Guangdong had been a politically active province in China since the nineteenth century. This province had a large number of immigrants living overseas, and neighbored Hong Kong, which was controlled by Great Britain. Scholars and intellectuals of Guangdong origin came into contact with Western learning very early, which

490 "Li Houji zuijin taidu: Minsheng caiyong menluo zhuyi 李厚基最近态度：闽省采用们罗主义 [Li Houji's Recent Attitude: Fujian Province adopts Menlo Doctrine]," *Xinwenbao* (17 September 1921).

led to ideas of reform and revolution. The most famous constitutional monarchist, Kang Youwei 康有为, and the most famous revolutionary, Sun Yat-sen 孙中山, both came from Guangdong. However, Guangdong is located south of the five mountains, far from Beijing, which easily engendered a local-oriented mindset. The anti-Manchu revolutionaries of the late Qing period strategically proposed the separation of eighteen provinces from the Manchu court. Ou Jujia 欧榘甲, under the influence of anti-Manchu revolutionaries, wrote *New Guangdong*, which started expressing concern about imperialism and then proceeded in an anti-Manchu direction, proposing "Guangdong is Guangdong for the Cantonese, not others. Cantonese are the masters of Guangdong," and "using Cantonese to work for Guangdong."[491] This was a very important product of the discourse of Guangdong Monroe Doctrine, which greatly influenced anti-Manchu elites in other provinces.

After the Revolution of 1911, the discourse of Guangdong Monroe Doctrine broke out in the context of the Constitution-Protection Movement and the United Provincial Autonomy Movement. In 1917, Sun Yat-sen and Hu Hanmin 胡汉民 went South to protect the 1912 provisional constitution. Zhu Qinglan 朱庆澜, the governor of Guangdong appointed by the Duan Qirui government, expressed his support. Duan Qirui was displeased and announced that he would swap the governors of Guangdong and Guangxi. Zhu Qinglan had no roots in Guangxi and had to resign. The Guangdong Provincial Council elected Hu Hanmin as the new governor, but the Guangxi faction was worried that Sun Yat-sen's faction might occupy a major position in Guangdong, so Deng Jiayan, a congressman from Guangxi, sent a telegram attacking Hu Hanmin as inconsistent with Sun Yat-sen's idea of protecting the law: "Mr. Sun Yat-sen felt distressed about the illegal dissolution of Congress and sought a pure land in the Southwest, so he called members of congress to hold an extraordinary meeting in Guangdong Province. Congressmen's interests are in one country, not in one province; in the constitution, not in the governor. If Cantonese learn from the Monroe Doctrine and implement this idea, saying that Guangdong is for Cantonese, then we are likely to see another Yunnan military supply dispute. Brave men have been held back, and lofty-minded people have been frustrated—this is not what Mr. Sun intended."[492] Sun Yat-sen asked Hu Hanmin to resign from the post of governor to the provincial council. Hu Hanmin obeyed sullenly. At that time, Zhang Taiyan 章太炎, secretary-general of the military government, observed: "The Cantonese under Sun were seeking

491 Ou (n. 439), 287.

492 "Deng Jiayan zhi Hu Hanmin dian 邓家彦致胡汉民电 [Deng Jiayan's telegram to Hu Hanmin]," *Tianjin Yishibao* (6 September 1917), 3rd edition.

to take the military government to practice their Guangdongism. I know Sun's effort will be in vain, so I decided to go west."[493]

In April, 1918, internal strife broke out within the Guangzhou military government. The Grand Marshal system was changed into the collegial system of seven committee members, and Sun Yat-sen was demoted from Grand Marshal to one of the seven committee members. Sun left Guangdong, and the leadership of the military government fell into the hands of Cen Chunxuan 岑春煊 and Lu Rongting 陆荣廷. In 1920, Sun Yat-sen, Tang Shaoyi 唐绍仪, Wu Tingfang 伍廷芳 and Tang Jiyao 唐继尧 jointly opposed the dominating power, the Guangxi faction. Chen Jiongming 陈炯明 led the Guangdong army to defeat the Guangxi Army entrenched in Guangdong, and then became governor of Guangdong Province and commander-in-chief of the Guangdong Army. On November 4, Chen Jiongming issued his "Announcement to the People of Guangdong," declaring that he had expelled the army of other provinces and restored the right of Guangdong people to self-government: "From now on, Guangdong will be Guangdong of the Cantonese, by the Cantonese and for the Cantonese."[494] Chen Jiongming was obviously imitating Abraham Lincoln's articulation of the principles of democratic government. On January 13, 1921, Chen Jiongming declared at the provisional meeting of the Guangdong Provincial Council: "The purpose of governing Guangdong by Cantonese has been achieved."[495]

In 1920, *Ta Kung Pao* in Changsha, which was vigorously advocating Hunan Autonomy, published "A Talk on the Factions in Guangdong" on December 14, commenting on political forces in Guangdong: "One is the Chen Jiongming faction, which advocates the Guangdong Monroe Doctrine against invading other provinces or being invaded by other provinces, just as Hunan has done. The way to carry it out is to establish a federal government and change Guangdong Province into Guangdong State. People in business, education and other sectors who do not have much to do with politics belong to this faction. The other is the military government faction headed by Sun Yat-sen. They sought to re-establish the military government and convene an extraordinary congress to elect an extraordinary president. Advisers and politicians

493 Tang Zhijun 汤志钧 ed., *Zhang Taiyan nianpu changbian* 章太炎年谱长编 [*Zhang Taiyan Chronicle*] (Vol. 1), (Beijing: Zhonghua shuju, 1979), 549.

494 "Yuejun chenzongsiling zhi xuanyan 粤军陈总司令之宣言 [Declaration of Commander-in-Chief Chen of Guangdong Army]," *Shanghai Minguo ribao* (12 November 1920), 6th edition.

495 "Shengyihui kai linshi huiji 省议会开临时会纪 [Provisional Meeting of Provincial Council]," *Guangdong qunbao* (14 January 1921), 3.

from other provinces, and vagrants or politicians of Guangdong origin should agree with them."[496]

The difference in political lines between Sun and Chen was quite obvious by 1921. Chen Jiongming made this explicit in a conversation with a reporter from *North China Daily News* in mid-February 1921: "Dr. Sun Yat-sen once tried to unify China by force, but he failed. Today, it seems quite clear that if there are still individuals or groups who embrace militarism, they should never be entrusted with great power." Chen also said that Guangdong would implement an experiment in bottom-up autonomy, hoping that other provinces would follow suit, "finally creating a great united provincial government for China."[497] When Lu Yongxiang, the military governor of Zhejiang Province, sent telegrams on June 4, 1921, advocating the formulation of provincial constitutions in each province and called an assembly of provincial representatives, Chen Jiongming responded quickly. When Zhao Hengti 赵恒惕 promoted the formulation of a provincial constitution in Hunan, Chen Jiongming also responded to him positively.

During the United Provincial Autonomy Movement from 1920 to 1921, Chen Jiongming stood at the forefront. He advocated consolidating the Guangdong base area and "recuperating the people's strength," opposing Sun Yat-sen's agenda to attack and take Guangxi.[498] He even sent telegrams to eight provinces to advise Guangxi to join the United Provincial Autonomy Movement.[499] After Lu Rongting sent troops to attack Guangdong, Chen Jiongming fought back passively. In June 1921, Chen Jiongming served as Commander-in-Chief of the army against Guangxi and captured the whole domain of Guangxi. However, his rhetoric still emphasized that this was a necessary response to Guangxi's repeated provocations, which seriously influenced the autonomy of Guangdong. His aim was to help Guangxi's autonomy get on the right track, and to turn it into an ally of Guangdong in the United Provincial Autonomy

496 "Yuezhong zhi paibietan 粤中之派别谈 [Talk about factions in Guangdong and China]," *Ta Kung Pao* (14 December 1920).

497 "Zilin xibao tongxinyuan pilu guangdong zhenxiang 字林西报通信员披露广东真相 [The correspondent of Linxi Newspaper disclosed the truth of Guangdong]," *Shanghai Minguo ribao* (18 February 1921), 3rd edition.

498 Chen Jiongming 陈炯明, "Yu mouyiyuan de tanhua 与某议员的谈话 [Conversation with a Member of Parliament]" and "Guanyu gonggui de tanhua 关于攻桂的谈话 [Conversation on Attacking Guangxi]," in *Cheng Jiongming ji* 陈炯明集 [*Chen Jiongming Collection*] (2), eds. Duan Yunzhang and Ni Junming 段云章、倪俊明 (Guangzhou: Guangzhou daxue chubanshe, 2007): 587–588.

499 Chen Jiongming 陈炯明, "Dianqing basheng quan guisheng zizhi 电请八省劝桂省自治 [Call Eight Provinces to Advise Guangxi Province to Autonomy]," *Hong Kong huazi ribao* (19 May 1921).

Movement.[500] However, Sun Yat-sen's goal after taking Guangxi was still to push forward with the Northern Expedition. When Chen Jiongming and Sun Yat-sen discussed the Northern Expedition in Nanning, Chen thought that the revolutionary camp was not strong enough to launch a Northern Expedition. Chen soon issued a statement stating, "I am not able to sponsor the Northern Expedition, so let Sun develop it on his own. If anyone in my army decides to follow Sun, please go ahead."[501]

As early as June 6, 1921, while talking with Wu Zongci 吴宗慈, Chen Jiongming said: "I don't agree with today's Sun Yat-sen government, but it has already happened. I just avoid paying money to it, so as not to waste money. In short, Guangdong's money can only be invested on Guangdong affairs."[502] After Sun Yat-sen decided on the Northern Expedition, Chen Jiongming took a passive-aggressive attitude toward the issue of raising logistic funds, and in February 1922, he refused an appointment as commander-in-chief of the left wing of the Northern Expedition. The line struggle between Chen and Sun concerning the Northern Expedition to unify China versus the autonomy of the provinces deepened continuously, finally leading to the "June 16 mutiny" in 1922, when they broke completely.

Chen Jiongming was defeated by the Eastern Expedition Army of the Nationalist Government in 1925, and then withdrew from the political arena. Chen never said explicitly called his policy the Guangdong Monroe Doctrine, but the label of Guangdong Monroe Doctrine accompanied him from then on. Because Chen Jiongming was born in Huizhou and advocated "Huizhou people governing Huizhou," Japanese scholar Takeuchi Minoru 竹内実 even named Chen Jiongming's idea the "Huizhou Monroe Doctrine" 惠州门罗主义 in an article in 1977.[503] The dispute between Sun and Chen was not a simple dispute

500 Chen Jiongming 陈炯明, "Zai guangxisheng yihui de yanshuo 在广西省议会的演说 [Speech in Guangxi Provincial Council]" and "Yu moujunguan de tanhua 与某军官的谈话 [Conversation with an Officer]," in Duan Yunzhang and Ni Junming 段云章、倪俊明 eds., *Cheng Jiongming ji* 陈炯明集 [*Chen Jiongming Collection*] (2), (Guangzhou: Guangzhou daxue chubanshe, 2007): 671–672.

501 Chen Jiongming 陈炯明, "Guanyu Sun Yat-sen beifa de tanhua 关于孙中山北伐的谈话 [Talking about Sun Yat-sen's Northern Expedition]," in *Cheng Jiongming ji* 陈炯明集 [*Chen Jiongming Collection*] (2), eds. Duan Yunzhang and Ni Junming 段云章、倪俊明 (Guangzhou: Guangzhou daxue chubanshe, 2007): 703.

502 Chen Jiongming 陈炯明, "Yu Wu Zongci tanhua 与吴宗慈谈话 [Talking with Wu Zongci]," in *Cheng Jiongming ji* 陈炯明集 [*Chen Jiongming Collection*] (2), eds. Duan Yunzhang and Ni Junming 段云章、倪俊明 (Guangzhou: Guangzhou daxue chubanshe, 2007): 625.

503 Takeuchi Minoru, Cheng Ma trans., *Zhongguo lishi yu shehui pinglun* 中国历史与社会评论 [*Review of Chinese History and Society*], (Beijing: Zhongguo wenlian chubanshe, 2006), 66.

over personal grievances or personal qualities, but over the political line on how to unify China. Chen Jiongming was one of the most enthusiastic representatives of the United Provincial Autonomy Movement at that time. Chen's failure also marked the complete failure of the United Provincial Autonomy line within the revolutionary camp.

8. Monroe Doctrine of Guangdong and Guangxi 两广门罗主义: The phrase Monroe Doctrine of Guangdong and Guangxi arose during the period of the "Nanjing-Wuhan Opposition" in 1927. Li Jishen 李济深, who was born in Wuzhou, Guangxi, had been chairman of the Guangdong provincial government since November 1926. In August and September 1927, the director of the Guangdong Finance Department, Gu Yingfen 古应芬, and his cronies colluded with profiteers to manipulate financial trends in Guangzhou and made a fortune, which caused resentment among businessmen. Li Jishen passed a political branch resolution and ordered Deng Shizeng 邓世增, the police commander, to take action on September 6. Hearing the news, Gu Yingfen 古应芬 fled, but dozens of his henchmen were arrested and brought to justice.[504] *Ta Kung Pao* published an article on the matter on September 10, saying that "Li's action is nothing more than to realize the Monroe Doctrine of Guangdong and Guangxi, so that Guangdong and Guangxi are in fact independent of the Nationalist Government, and on the surface maintain a neutral or coordinated attitude towards the two governments. Li pretends to be the Feng Yuxiang 冯玉祥 of the South."[505] Here, of course, "Monroe Doctrine" was used as a derogatory term meaning that Li wanted to break away from the Nanjing and Wuhan Nationalist Governments and stand on his own two feet, and fundamentally wanted to "expand the doctrine of Greater Guangdong and Guangxi."

But the "Nanjing-Wuhan confluence" was soon completed, and the Guangxi faction gained hegemony within the KMT. Li Jishen, reputed as a "half-member of the Guangxi faction," was involved in the conflict between Chiang Kai-shek and the Guangxi faction within the Kuomintang from 1928 to 1929. He was detained by Chiang Kai-shek in Nanjing in March 1929, and lost control of the

---

504 Literature and History Data Committee of Wuzhou CPPCC and Cangwu CPPCC, Guangxi eds., *Wuzhou wenshi ziliao di15ji: Li Jishen minzhu sixiang yanjiu* 梧州文史资料第15辑：李济深民主思想研究 [*Wuzhou Literature and History Data No. 15: Research on Li Jishen's Democratic Thought*], (Literature and History Data Group of Wuzhou Committee of Chinese People's Political Consultative Conference 1991) 324.

505 "Biaomian tiaohe, yin caizhegn fengchao jinzhu hujiang liangxi 表面调和，因财政风潮尽逐胡蒋两系 [On the surface of harmony, the two departments of Hu and Jiang should be pursued because of the financial agitation]," *Ta Kung Pao* (10 September 1927), 3rd edition.

Guangdong army after he was freed. The label "Monroe Doctrine of Guangdong and Guangxi" was therefore a flash in the pan.

9. Sichuan Monroe Doctrine 四川门罗主义: During the United Provincial Autonomy Movement, on October 4, 1920, Liu Xiang 刘湘, head of a powerful Sichuan faction, sent telegraphs nationwide advocating Sichuan autonomy. On December 13 of the same year, Liu Xiang 刘湘, Dan Maoxin 但懋辛 and Yang Sen 杨森 jointly sent telegraphs to Xiong Kewu 熊克武 and Liu Cunhou 刘存厚 to advocate "rallying the general will of the citizens of Sichuan and implementing autonomy."[506] Xiong Kewu and Liu Cunhou gave positive responses. On January 8, 1921, Liu Xiang and others jointly sent telegraphs to the entire country, saying that "Sichuan Province was completely autonomous before the establishment of the legally unified government of the Republic of China."[507] *New Sichuan*, sponsored by the Chengdu Association of the Sichuan Autonomous Period, which was established in Shanghai, advocated civilian politics. However, recognizing the strong power of Sichuan martial arts, its minimum aim was nothing more than "to hope that the generals in Sichuan will implement independent autonomy after expelling the Yunnan-Guizhou army."[508] The Provincial Constitution Drafting Committee was established in Chengdu in January 1923, and soon drafted four draft laws, including the Draft Charter of Sichuan Province. But there was soon a scuffle among the warlords in Sichuan, and the provincial constitutional movement dissipated.

In the course of the United Provincial Autonomy Movement, quite a few newspaper reports mentioned Sichuan's Monroe Doctrine. In 1921, Sun Yat-sen contacted the local powers in Hunan and Sichuan to oppose Wang Zhanyuan 王占元, the military governor of Hubei. On July 29, 1921, Liu Xiang, commander-in-chief of Sichuan Army and governor of Sichuan, led the Sichuan Army in an attack on Hubei, and the Sichuan-Hubei War broke out. The Beijing government replaced Wang Zhanyuan with Wu Peifu and Xiao Yaonan 萧耀南, who were appointed military overseer of Hunan and Hubei and military governor of Hubei, respectively. Wu Peifu defeated the army of Hunan, but he made peace with Sichuan because he feared the Fengtian Army in the North and Sun

506 Sichuan Literature and History Research Institute, *Sichuan junfa shiliao* 四川军阀史料 [*Historical Materials of Sichuan Warlords*] (Volume III), (Chengdu: Sichuan renmin chubanshe, 1985), 183–185.

507 Zhou Kaiqing 周开庆, *Minguo Li Fucheng xiansheng xiangnianpu* 民国刘甫澄先生湘年谱 [*Chronicle of Mr. Liu Fucheng in Hunan*], (Taipei: Shangwu yinshuguan, 1981), 23–24.

508 Research Office of Ma, En, Lie and Si Works Compilation Bureau of the Central Committee of the Communist Party of China, *Wusi shiqi qikan jieshao* 五四时期期刊介绍 [*Introduction to Periodicals during the May Fourth Movement*] (Volume III, Volume I), (Beijing: Shenghuo, Dushu, Xinzhi sanlian shudian, 1959), 428.

Yat-sen's army in the South. On December 22, Sun Chuanfang 孙传芳 and Liu Xiang sent representatives to sign a draft peace treaty, and the Sichuan Army gradually withdrew to Sichuan. On February 21, 1922, *Ta Kung Pao* published an article to refute a rumor that the Sichuan-Hubei peace talks would fail: "Although there are a few ambitious schemers and Hubei immigrants in Sichuan trying to mobilize the Sichuan Army to act in concert with Sun Yat-sen in Guangdong against Hubei, Liu Xiang still adheres to the Monroe Doctrine to consolidate the foundation of Sichuan's autonomy in view of the overall situation of Sichuan, and has not yielded an inch to exaggerated remarks."[509] The Sichuan-Hubei Peace Treaty was formally signed on March 7, and the war between the two provinces ended. In this report in *Ta Kung Pao*, "Monroe Doctrine" was still used in a positive sense. A special commemorative issue No. 4,000 of *Xin Shu Bao* 新蜀报 in 1934 published an article analyzing the situation in Sichuan, saying that after the National Protection Movement, the Yunnan-Guizhou army held political power in Sichuan. Dan Maoxin 但懋辛 and Liu Xiang 刘湘 drove Gu Pinzhen 顾品珍 and Zhao Youxin 赵又新 of the Yunnan Army out of Sichuan. Part of the Sichuan Army was commanded by Liu Xiang and Yang Sen, while the other part was under the control of Xiong Kewu and Dan Maoxin, who were "singing the hymn of the Monroe Doctrine and declaring that Sichuan people should govern Sichuan."[510] Here, the phrase "Monroe Doctrine" was still descriptive and carried no explicitly derogatory meaning.

The derogatory use of "Monroe Doctrine" appeared in the expressions of pro-Sun Yat-sen revolutionaries in Sichuan. According to *Records of Sichuan Province*, Lu Yifeng, a native of Jincheng Township, Yibin County, participated in the May Fourth Movement. At the end of July 1920, he contacted the progressive students of Peking University to form the Sichuan, Yunnan and Guizhou Cultural Association and put forward three propositions: 1) to support Sun Yat-sen's revolutionism; 2) to oppose the Monroe Doctrine that "Sichuan should be governed by Sichuan people"; 3) to oppose the aggression of the Yunnan and Guizhou armies. Lu Yifeng soon went to Shanghai to visit Sun Yat-sen, and reiterated the above three points, which Sun appreciated. Lu Yifeng then returned to Sichuan at Sun Yat-sen's order, and lobbied

509 "Chuan'e heyi jiangcheng 川鄂和议将成 [Hubei, Hunan and Sichuan-shaped distribution in the sound of potential drums]," *Ta Kung Pao* (Tianjin Edition) (21 February 1922).

510 He Zhijun 贺植军, "Siqianhao de zhuiyi 四千号的追忆 [Remembrance of No. 4,000]," in *Wusi yundong zaichongqing* 五四运动在重庆 [*The May Fourth Movement in Chongqing*], eds. Party History Working Committee of Chongqing Municipal Committee of the Communist Party of China (published internally in 1984), 206–207.

warlords from Sichuan, Yunnan and Guizhou to unite to defeat the Xong Kewu.[511] In these statements, the "Sichuan Monroe Doctrine" was regarded as the reactionary doctrine of Sichuan warlords as opposed to Sun Yat-sen's idea of unifying the whole country through revolution. During the Northern Expedition, *Ta Kung Pao* published a comment on November 23, 1926, saying that some Sichuan local warlords such as Liu Cunhou 刘存厚, Deng Xihou 邓锡侯, Tian Songyao 田颂尧 and Li Jiayu 李家钰, "always cling to the Monroe Doctrine and stay in the defense zone, so that Sichuan plays no significant part in the national affairs."[512] This comment clearly set the "Monroe Doctrine" and "national affairs" against each other.

10. "Henan Monroe Doctrine" 河南门罗主义: In 1922, Zhao Ti 赵倜 lost power. When Feng Yuxiang 冯玉祥, who was attached to the Zhili faction, became the military governor of Henan, Wu Peifu, a warlord of the Zhili faction, tried to recommend his confidant Li Jichen (from Xian County, Zhili) to become the governor of Henan. "Henan people in Beijing saw this dramatic turn of affairs, so they advocated the Monroe Doctrine, and calls for 'Henan to be governed by Henan People' spread all over Beijing and Kaifeng."[513] Its core appeal lay in abolishing the military governor and electing the provincial governor by themselves. Feng Yuxiang once appointed Bao Shibin 暴式彬 and other Kuomintang members to promote local autonomy in Henan, but the autonomy movement came to a standstill in September 1923. Another moment for the slogan "Henanese govern Henan" was during the Northern Expedition in 1926. When Fan Zhongxiu 樊钟秀 (from Baofeng, Henan Province), who belonged to the Second Army of Feng Yuxiang's National Revolutionary Army, entered Henan to exchange fire with the Zhili army of Wu Peifu, he struck the banner of "Henanese governing Henan."[514] This may have been only a slogan of war propaganda. Compared with the slogan "Xans govern X" in the United

511 "Hundun zhi sichuan yu daju wugan yi duobing weilei 混沌之四川 与大局无干 以多兵为累 [Chaos in Sichuan and the General Situation: Too Many Soldiers Are Tired]," *Ta Kung Pao* (Tianjin Edition), (23 November 1926).

512 "Hundun zhi sichuan yu daju wugan yi duobing weilei 混沌之四川 与大局无干 以多兵为累 [Chaos in Sichuan and the General Situation: Too Many Soldiers Are Tired]," *Ta Kung Pao* (Tianjin Edition), (23 November 1926).

513 "Lvjing yuren zhi feidu yizhang yundong 旅京豫人之废督易长运动 [The Movement of Abolishing the Governor and Changing the Growth of People in Beijing and Henan]," *Shenbao* (26 October 1922), 6th Edition.

514 "Fan Zhongxiu 樊钟秀声势甚盛 [Fan Zhongxiu has a strong momentum]," *Minguo ribao* (20 August 1926); "Fanjun zhanling xuchang 樊军占领许昌 [Fan Jun occupied Xuchang]," *Minguo ribao* (22 August 1926).

Provincial Autonomy Movement, it did not have the connotation of distancing the province from the central government.

11. "Hubei Monroe Doctrine" 湖北门罗主义: In autumn 1920, Wang Zhanyuan 王占元 (Shandong native), the military governor of Hubei Province, tried to sponsor his relative in marriage, Sun Zhenjia 孙振家, as governor of Hubei Province. Hubei elites in Beijing quickly mobilized against Sun Zhenjia, and won the support of Li Yuanhong 黎元洪, Zhou Shumo 周树模 and other high officials of the Hubei origin in Beijing. Under pressure, President Xu Shichang 徐世昌 re-appointed Xia Shoukang 夏寿康, president of the Administrative Court, as provincial governor. Before Xia Shoukang took up his post, the Hubei Hometown Association in Beijing raised four slogans: "Hubei should be governed by Hubei people," "distinguish between the military and the civilian," "Hubei autonomy" and "abolish the military governor and reduce armament" as prerequisites for supporting Xia Shoukang.[515] After Xia Shoukang took office, he promoted the autonomy of Hubei people. Wang Zhanyuan was strongly opposed to Xia, and once even sent troops to surround the provincial government. The Hubei Hometown Association in Beijing and local gentry launched a new movement to expel Wang Zhanyuan 王占元 from Hubei. On September 30, 1920, Mao Zedong's articles "Hunan People Governing Hunan" and "Hunan People's Autonomy" contained the expression "Wang Zhanyuan against governance of Hubei by Hubei people," which showed that the movement had significant trans-provincial influence.[516] Wang Zhanyuan recommended Liu Cheng'en 刘承恩, a native of Xiangyang, Hubei Province, as provincial governor in order to enhance the appeal of Hubei autonomy. On March 8, 1921, Liu Cheng'en was officially appointed the chief of Hubei Province, but he was also boycotted by anti-Wang local elites, who further sought help from neighboring provinces and tried to introduce external forces to expel Wang Zhanyuan. In this situation, Zhao Hengti 赵恒惕 in Hunan and Liu Xiang 刘湘 in Sichuan all struck the banner of "aiding Hubei autonomy." Eventually, Wang Zhanyuan stepped down, but the Zhili army took advantage of the situation to seize control of Hubei. Wu Peifu became

515 Lu Weigan 卢蔚乾, "Beiyang shiqi hubei de shengzhang gengdie ji 'erenzhi'e" 北洋时期湖北的省长更迭及"鄂人治鄂" [Governor Change and' Hubei People Governing Hubei' during the Northern Warlords Period] in *Hubei wenshi ziliao: Beiyang junfa tongzhi hubei* 湖北文史资料：北洋军阀统治湖北 [*Hubei Literature and History Materials (Volume 2, Volume 27, 1989): Northern Warlords Ruling Hubei*], (Wuhan: Literature and History Materials Committee of Hubei Provincial Committee of Chinese People's Political Consultative Conference, 1989), 19.

516 Literature Research Office of CPC Central Committee and Hunan Provincial Committee of CPC (n. 459), 651.

the miliary overseer of Hubei and Hunan, and Xiao Yaonan (from Huanggang, Hubei), a Zhili figure who had less intersection with local elites in Hubei, became the miliary governor of Hubei. Liu Cheng'en, who was widely regarded as Wang's partisan, was not replaced. In 1922, Tang Xiangming became the governor of Hubei Province, supported by the faction against Wang Zhanyuan and Liu Cheng'en. However, Tang was boycotted by the military governor Xiao Yaonan and was unable to take office. Soon after that, Xiao Yaonan became provincial governor until he died of illness in February 1926.

On April 24, 1922, *Ta Kung Pao* remarked that since Wu Peifu had become the military overseer of Hubei and Hunan, he "regarded Hubei as a conquered domain," and his army obtained supplies from Hubei, thus imposed heavy burdens on the local people. With the outbreak of the first Zhili-Fengtian War, most of the Zhili troops previously stationed in Hubei were withdrawn from Hubei Province. In Hubei, "local gentry planned to launch a mass petition in order to reduce the burden on the province's people. They sent the following requests to the military and civilian departments and the provincial council: The Zhili troops withdrawn from Hubei Province should not return to Hubei, and none of their expenses should be covered by Hubei; if the war is fierce, Wusheng Pass should be blocked, and the Monroe Doctrine of Hubei should be declared so that armies of other provinces will not enter."[517] In fact, this was the proposition that Hubei should remain neutral in the wars between the Zhili and Fengtian faction, and take the opportunity to expel the Zhili troops from Hubei. This was not feasible under the circumstances at that time. The first Zhili-Fengtian war lasted from April 28 to May 5, when the troops of the Fengtian faction were driven out of Shanhaiguan Pass, and Wu Peifu 吴佩孚 consolidated his control over Hubei.

12. "Fengtian Monroe Doctrine": "Fengtian Monroe Doctrine" referred not to the Monroe Doctrine of Fengtian Province, but rather to the Monroe Doctrine pursued by Zhang Zuolin 张作霖 and his son Zhang Xueliang 张学良, whose rule covered the three provinces in the Northeast, with expansion or contraction in different periods. An early leader of the Chinese Communist Party, Li Dazhao 李大钊, once commented on Zhang Zuolin's decision-making and actions in the article "Recent Situation of the Northern Political Situation" (under the byline "Lie Wu" 列武) in April 1927: "The military and politics of Fengtian have strictly adhered to the Monroe Doctrine and no outsiders are

517 "Yantiaotingzhe keyi xiuyi 言调停者可以休矣 [Say the mediator can retire]," *Ta Kung Pao* (Tianjin Edition) (24 April 1922).

allowed to participate."[518] During the 1916 National Protection War, Zhang Zuolin struck the banner of "Fengtian governed by Fengtian people," and instructed the chief of Fengtian Security Council, Yuan Jinkai, and others to draft The Constitution of the Security Council of Fengtian in order to drive out Duan Zhigui 段芝贵, the general of Fengtian. Later, Zhang Zuolin forced Yuan Shih-Kai to appoint him general of Shengjing with jurisdiction over the military affairs of the whole Fengtian province. After Yuan Shikai's death, Zhang Zuolin formed an alliance with Premier Duan Qirui. In 1917, he supported Duan Qirui in the dispute between the premier and the president, and once declared "independence" from the Beijing government. In 1922, Zhang Zuolin was defeated in the first Zhili-Fengtian war, and the Beijing government controlled by the Zhili faction relieved him of all his posts. While in Luanzhou on May 12, Zhang Zuolin declared "independence" on behalf of the whole of Northeast China. He then took advantage of the United Provincial Autonomy Movement initiated by the local Northeast power faction based on the Fengtian provincial council, and announced the implementation of "united provincial autonomy" in the three eastern provinces, appointing himself military overseer of the three Eastern provinces, as well as governor and military governor of Fengtian and commander-in-chief of the security force of the three eastern provinces. Zhang Zuolin also used the declaration of "independence" to intercept taxes that should have been transferred to the central government, and used the taxes to strengthen his own power. *Ta Kung Pao* reported on July 7, 1922, that Zhang Zuolin held a military and political conference on July 3 to decide that he would not accept a command or request for negotiation from the central government or any other party. The report explained that "this decision is to adopt the measures of Zhejiang Province. Adhering to the Monroe Doctrine, he even rejected negotiation with other parties."[519] In other words, Zhang Zuolin took advantage of the slogan of the military governor of Zhejiang Province, Lu Yongxiang, calling for the United Provincial Autonomy Movement, and ignored the Beijing government's orders and attempts to negotiate.

---

518 Li Jihua, Feng Tiejin and Zhou Fang 李继华、冯铁金、周芳 eds., *Li Dazhao yiwen jizhu yu yanjiu* 李大钊轶文辑注与研究 [*Annotation and Research on Li Dazhao's Yi Wen*], (Beijing: Xianzhuang shuju, 2013), 71.

519 "Fengsheng zhi junzhenghui biaojue shijian wuxiang zhangjiang xunshi jihei 奉省之军政会 表决事件五项 张将巡视吉黑 [Voting Events of the Military and Political Council of the Province]," *Ta Kung Pao* (7 July 1922). See also "Zhang Zuolin zhaoji junzheng huiyi 张作霖召集军政会议 [Zhang Zuolin Convening Military and Political Conference]," *Shenbao* (8 July 1922); "Zhang Zuolin gaishou menluo zhuyi shuo 张作霖改守门罗主义说 [Zhang Zuolin changed to Monroe Doctrine]," *Shenbao* (19 July 1922). All the above reports mentioned Zhang Zuolin's "Monroe Doctrine."

In 1924, Zhang Zuolin won the second Zhili-Fengtian war. This victory not only greatly expanded his domain, but also won him a major say over the Beijing government. However, with the deterioration of his relations with Feng Yuxiang and Duan Qirui, Zhang Zuolin once again declared "independence" at the beginning of 1926, and the Joint Association of Corporations of the Three Eastern Provinces sent telegrams stating support for Zhang Zuolin and the implementation of "united provincial autonomy" in the three Eastern provinces. However, Zhang Zuolin's concern was not to implement genuine local autonomy, but to use the name of "united provincial autonomy" to intercept taxes that should be transferred to the central government, and then deploy his troops inside the Shanhaiguan Pass. Zhang Zuolin never announced the formal cancellation of his third "independence," but under pressure from the Northern Expeditionary Army, the Fengtian faction organized the An Guo military government in Beijing in June 1927, with Zhang Zuolin as the Grand Marshal. On September 15, 1926, the *Shuntian Shibao*, edited by the Japanese Ministry of Foreign Affairs in Beijing, published an editorial on the so-called "responsibility of the Fengtian faction," calling on Zhang Zuolin to actively reform the Beijing government and give some assistance to Wu Peifu and Sun Chuanfang 孙传芳, but also to "always respect the Monroe Doctrine of six provinces and three special zones." It meant that the Fengtian faction should be careful of overextending its power.[520] On October 12, 1926, the Declaration of the 12th Congress of the Hunan Region of the Communist Party of China responded to this comment, pointing out that "Japanese imperialism is planning for the government of the Fengtian faction at this time, asking the latter to adhere to the Monroe Doctrine, control the Beijing government and avoid direct conflict with the Northern Expeditionary Army."[521]

Under pressure from the Northern Expeditionary Army, Zhang Zuolin retreated to the Northeast from Beijing in June 1928 and was killed in Huanggutun, Shenyang, by a bomb buried by the Japanese Kwantung Army. On December 29, his son Zhang Xueliang pledged allegiance to the Nanjing

520 "Shiju yu fengpai zhi zeren 时局与奉派之责任 [The Current Situation and the Responsibility of the School]," (editorial), *Shuntian shibao* (15 September 1926). So-called "six provinces and three special zones," the "six provinces" are the three eastern provinces originally controlled by Fengsi plus Shanxi controlled by Zhili and Shandong and its ally Yan Xishan, and the "three special zones" are Jehol, Chahar and Suiyuan.

521 Yi Liangru 易亮如 et al. eds., *Hunan geming lishi wenjian huiji (shengwei wenjian): 1923–1926* 湖南革命历史文件汇集（省委文件）: 1923–1926年 [*Compilation of Hunan Revolutionary Historical Documents (Documents of the Provincial Party Committee): 1923–1926*], (Central Archives and Hunan Archives, 1983), 85.

Nationalist Government, bringing an end to the Beiyang clique.[522] However, during the Central Plains War in 1930, both Chiang Kai-shek and the anti-Chiang alliance sent representatives to ask the Northeast Army to send relief troops. On August 22, Zhang Zuoxiang 张作相 (sworn brother of Zhang Zuolin), an elder of the Fengtian faction, telegraphed Zhang Xueliang to suggest embracing the "Northeast Monroe Doctrine." Wang Shuhan 王树翰 responded on behalf of Zhang Xueliang, saying that Zhang would maintain strict neutrality and would never send troops.[523] Zhang Xueliang was actually waiting for a better deal. He finally rendered aid to Chiang Kai-Shek, dealing a heavy blow to the anti-Chiang alliance.

13. "Shanxi Monroe Doctrine" 山西门罗主义: The protagonist of the "Shanxi Monroe Doctrine" was Yan Xishan 阎锡山, who was born in Wutai, Shanxi. After the Revolution of 1911, Yan Xishan occupied Shanxi, which was difficult to attack and easy to defend. Facing the confrontation between the North and the South in 1918, Yan Xishan struck the banner of "protecting the domain and the people" and announced the principle of "Three Noes and Two Necessities": not to join a party faction, inquire into the business of other provinces, or use soldiers for the expansion of personal power; and the necessity to obey the central government's orders and to safeguard local public order. "Protecting the domain and the people" meant that the Shanxi army should not leave Shanxi, but that the armies of other provinces were also not allowed to enter Shanxi. Shanxi would remain neutral in the conflict between neighboring provinces, but it would also resolutely repel any invading enemy.[524] At the same time, Yan Xishan expanded his army, developed military industry and accumulated strength day by day. After Cao Kun 曹锟 of the Zhili faction became president in 1923, there were rumors that Beijing would remove Yan Xishan from Shanxi. On December 3, 1923, *Ta Kung Pao* reported that Yan Xishan called the Beijing government to recommend a military governor for Shanxi, and said that he could serve as governor, but that he would not allow the army of any other province to enter Shanxi. *Ta Kung Pao* commented: "Yes,

---

522 Li, Feng, and Zhou (n. 516), 71.

523 "Dongbei yuanlaopai bao menluo zhuyi 东北元老派抱门罗主义 [Northeast Yuan Old School Embrace Monroe Doctrine]," *Shengjing shibao* (26 August 1930).

524 Luo Chunpu 雒春普, *Yan Xishan zhuan* 阎锡山传 [*Biography of Yan Xishan*], (Taiyuan: Shanxi Renmin chubanshe, 2004), 120–121. "Shen Bao" commented in October 1922 that Yan Xishan "holds the Monroe Doctrine, and the four sides and eight sides, such as the central place, use the wrist that is not sticky and does not take off, and has no determination to fight with people. Even if he is forced to fight, he may not be able to take the lead." Ou Cang 欧沧, "Shanxi tongxin 山西通信 [Shanxi Communication]," *Shenbao* (2 October 1922).

Yan still insists upon one end of the Monroe Doctrine."[525] After the second Zhili-Fengtian war broke out in 1924, Yan Xishan broke the defensive policy and sent troops to fight against the Zhili faction, but soon joined forces with the Zhili faction against the Fengtian faction. In 1926, Yan Xishan joined forces with both the Zhili faction and the Fengtian faction in an "anti-red" war against Feng Yuxiang's National Army. The Shanxi Army fought fiercely against the Northwest Army of Feng Yuxiang in Northern Shanxi, and emerged victorious. On July 21, 1926, *Shanghai Times* reported the war situation with the title "Monroe Doctrine of Yan Xishan," commenting that Yan advocated "protecting the domain and the people" and did not pursue the enemy outside of his province. However, this description was soon outdated.[526] In August, the Shanxi Army marched into Suiyuan and soon changed its name to the Jin-Sui (Shanxi-Suiyuan) Army.

After the Guangzhou Nationalist Government launched the Northern Expedition, Shanxi became one of the fortresses to be taken. A June 21, 1927, letter from Shanxi students in the Wuhan archives of the Kuomintang mentions "Yan Xishan's Shanxi Monroe Doctrine": "After the revolutionary army recovered Nanjing, Yan Xishan saw that the wave of revolution had soared and surged, progressing to the Yellow River Basin, especially the geographically critical Shanxi. Yan Xishan felt that his position was shaken. He gave up his Monroe Doctrine, which claimed to protect the domain and the people, in order to cope with the climax of the revolution and maintain his home turf in Shanxi and Suiyuan."[527] This letter referred to Yan Xishan's banner of "protecting the domain and the people" as "Monroe Doctrine," which shows that the Provincial Monroe Doctrine had become synonymous with parochialism against national unity. However, Yan Xishan once again showed his ability to "protect the domain and the people" by announcing "replacement of the flag" on June 3, 1927. In the "dispute between Nanjing and Wuhan," Yan bet on Nanjing as the victor and cooperated with Chiang Kai-shek. Soon after that, in response to Chiang Kai-shek's purge within the KMT against members

525 "Yan Xishan zhi menluo zhuyi duli youyan baojian buyuan kejun rujing 阎锡山之门罗主义督理由阎保荐不愿客军入境 [Yan Xishan's Monroe Doctrine Supervisors Reason Yan Sponsors Unwilling to Enter the Foreign Army]," *Ta Kung Pao* (3 December 1923).

526 Xue Jun 雪筠, "Yan Xishan zhi menluo zhuyi 阎锡山之门罗主义 [Yan Xishan's Monroe Doctrine]," *Shibao* (21 July 1926).

527 "Dong Yongwei zhizhongzhenghui fu shanxi xuesheng zhaowang liangjun zhi dengtongzhi han yijian 董用威致中政会附山西学生赵、王两君致邓同志函一件 [Dong Yongwei sent a letter to Comrade Deng from Shanxi students Zhao and Wang Jun] (June 21, 1927)," in *Kuomintang dangshiguan dang'an* 国民党党史馆档案 [*Archives of Kuomintang Party History Museum*], Han No. 2617.

of the Communist Party and the left-wing of the KMT, Yan Xishan also suppressed the forces of the Central Club Clique within the KTM in Shanxi to prevent losing control over Shanxi's KMT party organization.

Next, Yan Xishan cooperated with Chiang Kai-shek to push forward the Second Northern Expedition and managed to enlarge his sphere of influence in North China. Before long, Chiang Kai-shek began to weaken the power of local warlords, which caused a major rebound. Yan Xishan once became one of the leaders of the anti-Chiang allied forces. The military failure of the Central Plains War in 1930 severely frustrated his ambition to grasp national hegemony, and his spheres of influence shrank. Yan Xishan regained control of Shanxi after one year. Amidst the treacherous political environment, Yan Xishan once again carried out the strategy of keeping a low profile and hiding his real strength. He tried to build an independent financial and industrial system in Shanxi. Under his rule, even the Tong-Pu Railway 同蒲铁路 was built using a narrower gauge than the national standard.[528]

Yan Xishan's Shanxi Monroe Doctrine was widely known, and even the Japanese used this label to refer to his policy of rule in Shanxi. Xu Yongchang 徐永昌, who once assisted Yan Xishan, recorded in his diary on April 12, 1936, that the Counsellor of the Japanese Embassy, Itagaki Osamu 板垣修, and other visitors asked him many complicated questions, "the strangest one being whether Yan Xishan would still maintain the 'Monroe attitude' in the future."[529] In 1938, Volume 3 of *The Record of Chinese Incidents* edited by the Editorial Bureau of Japan's Yomiuri Shimbun News Agency talked about the Japanese offensive in Shanxi, describing it as the Japanese expedition against the "Shanxi Monroe Doctrine."[530] Furumi Tadayuki 古海忠之, a Japanese prisoner of war, commented in his later writings: "Shanxi Province has formed a closed economy like an independent kingdom, which constitutes Yan Xishan's Shanxi Monroe Doctrine. However, the Japanese army cut off the traffic between Shanxi and Henan by force, and completely controlled the transportation lines

528 The narrow gauge of Tongpu Railway is widely regarded as the symbol of Yan Xishan's "Shanxi Monroe Doctrine." However, some commentators believe that the narrow gauge of Tongpu Railway is mainly for the sake of saving money and should not be counted as the proper example of Yan Xishan's "Shanxi Monroe Doctrine." Guo Xuewang 郭学旺, "Shanxi zhaigui tielu chengyin kaobian 山西窄轨铁路成因考辨 [Study on the Causes of Shanxi Narrow Gauge Railway]," *Jindaishi yanjiu* 4, (1988).

529 Institute of Modern History, Academia Sinica, *Xu Yongchang riji* 徐永昌日记 [*Xu Yongchang Diary*] (Volume III), (Taipei: Institute of Modern History, Academia Sinica, 1991), 404.

530 Editorial Bureau of Yomiuri Shimbun 読売新聞社編輯局 ed., 『支那事變實記』 [*China* Incident], Vol. 3, (Hibonkaku, 1938), 246–248.

from Taiyuan to other cities—railways and highways. ... The first army [i.e., the first army of Japanese invaders] inherits this 'tradition,' emphasizing 'the particularity of Shanxi' and implementing the Monroe Doctrine of Shanxi, which is a sort of complete market monopoly."[531]

Uchida Tomoyuki 内田知行's *The Conditions of Taiyuan Iron Works under Japanese Occupation* also discussed the Japanese army's continuation of Yan Xishan's "Shanxi Monroe Doctrine." After the Japanese occupation of Taiyuan, in June 1938, Ōta Fumio 太田文雄, representative of Japan's Okura Kogyo, proposed an operation policy for Taiyuan Iron Works, especially regarding how to fully meet local needs as the first stage task, arguing that it was necessary to "enlarge the Shanxi Monroe Doctrine of the old Northwest Industrial Company and take part of Henan and Shaanxi as its supply areas."[532] The so-called "Old Northwest Industrial Company," an example of Yan Xishan's economic Monroe Doctrine, was one of the largest bureaucratic capital enterprises in Shanxi.

After the War of Resistance against Japanese Invasion, the Shanxi Monroe Doctrine remained a problem in the eyes of the Nanjing Nationalist Government. The Japanese journalist Matsumoto Shigeharu 松本重治 described in his *Shanghai Times* how Chiang Kai-shek took the opportunity of pursuing the Communist army to let the KMT Central Army enter Shanxi, thus breaking Yan Xishan's Shanxi Monroe Doctrine.[533] After the liberation of Shanxi in 1949, the PLA Financial Takeover Group of the Taiyuan Military Management Committee criticized the Yan Xishan government for "adopting Monroe Doctrine for a long time and forming a semi-independent financial system." The effort of the takeover group was to break this Monroe Doctrine and connect Shanxi's financial system with the entire liberated area.[534]

---

531 Central Archives, Second Historical Archives of China and Jilin Academy of Social Sciences, eds., *Huabei jingji lueduo* 华北经济掠夺 [*Economic Plundering of North China*], (Beijing: Zhonghua shuju, 2004), 739.

532 Uchida Zhixing, Ye Xiaotong 叶晓彤 trans., "Rijun zhanlingxia de taiyuan tiechang de jingying zhuangkuang 日军占领下的太原铁厂的经营状况 [Operation Status of Taiyuan Iron Works under Japanese Occupation]," in *Minguo shanxishi* 民国山西史 [*History of Shanxi in the Republic of China*], eds. Li Maosheng 李茂盛 et al., (Taiyuan: Shanxi Renmin chubanshe, 2011), 387–388.

533 Matsumoto Shigeharu, Cao Zhenxian, and Shen Zhongqi 曹振咸、沈中琦 trans., *Shanghai shidai* 上海时代 [*Shanghai Times*], (Shanghai: Shanghai shudian chubanshe, 2010), 424–425.

534 Shanxi Provincial Archives, *Zhongguo renmin jiefangjun taiyuanshi junguanhui jinrong jieguanzu dang'an* 中国人民解放军太原市军管会金融接管组档案 [*Archives of Financial Takeover Group of Taiyuan Military Management Committee of Chinese People's Liberation Army*], 1949.

In addition to the thirteen Provincial Monroe Doctrines above, there were other provinces that did not directly use the label of "XX Monroe Doctrine" in the United Provincial Autonomy Movement, but appropriated the phrase "Xans govern X," which is just one step away from the phrase "XX Monroe Doctrine."

1. Jiangsu 甘肃: In 1920, the Jiangsu Provincial Council decided to unseat Governor Qi Yaolin 齐耀琳 (from Yitong, Jilin), thus mobilizing local elites in the name of "Jiangshu people governing Jiangsu." Zhang Jian 张謇 and other local elites initiated the Jiangsu Society 苏社, advocating "Jiangsu people governing Jiangsu" and promoting local autonomy. After their success in expelling Qi Yaolin, the gentry in Jiangsu went on to discuss new candidates for governor with the Beijing government and Li Chun 李纯 (a Zhili native), the military governor of Jiangsu Province. However, the slogan of "Jiangsu people governing Jiangsu" promoted by local gentry was largely a part of their negotiation strategy; they finally accepted Wang Hu 王瑚 (a Zhili native) as governor. After Li Chun's sudden death in October 1920, the local gentry sought to abolish the military governor and implement provincial autonomy. They tried to formulate a provincial constitution or a provincial autonomy law for Jiangsu Province, but their achievements were rather limited. Local gentry managed to induce the succeeding military governors, Qi Xieyuan 齐燮元 (Zhili native) and Sun Chuanfang 孙传芳 (Shandong native), to pursue the policy of "protecting the domain and securing the people" and to remain neutral in the Hunan-Hubei War and the first Zhili-Fengtian war.[535] However, with the intensification of tangled warfare among warlords, Jiangsu became caught up in the Jiangsu-Zhejiang War in September 1924 and the Fengtian-Zhejiang War in October 1925. After the war, Jiangsu fell under the control of Sun Chuanfang until the Guangzhou Nationalist Government took over Jiangsu.

2. Jiangxi 江西: As early as March 1912, Li Liejun 李烈钧 seized the position of Governor of Jiangxi from Ma Yubao 马毓宝 (a native of Kunming, Yunnan Province) with the slogan "Jiangxi people governing Jiangxi."[536] In November 1920, the Jiangxi Hometown Association in Beijing submitted a petition to the Beijing government, proposing the removal of Jiangxi Governor Qi Yang 戚扬 (from Shanyin, Zhejiang Province) and opposing Ding Naiyang

535 See Chen Mingsheng 陈明胜, "Minchu difang shishen yu junfa zhengfu de maodun gongsheng—Yi jiangsu 'shengzizhi' yundong weizhongxin 民初地方士绅与军阀政府的矛盾共生——以江苏"省自治"运动为中心 [Contradictions and symbiosis between local gentry and warlord government in the early Republic of China-centered on Jiangsu's 'provincial autonomy' movement]," *Minguo dangan* 4, (2018).

536 Editorial Committee, *Liehuowanjun renpingsheng: Li Liejun wenji* 烈火千钧任平生：李烈钧文集 [*Collected Writings of Li Liejun*], (Beijing: Tuanjie chubanshe, 2013), 67.

丁乃扬 (from Wuxing, Zhejiang Province) as his possible successor. Other groups and individuals of Jiangxi origin living in other provinces also sent telegrams or organized meetings to support the proposal, accelerating the autonomy movement in Jiangxi. At the beginning of December 1920, Qiu Yulin 邱玉麟, a member of the provincial Council, drafted a Jiangxi Autonomy Law and submitted it to a provisional meeting of the provincial council for discussion and adoption. Subsequently, the provincial council held several meetings to discuss the draft Autonomy Law. The provincial council also passed two bills: one to impeach Qi Yang, and the other to have the Jiangxi governor be elected by Jiangxi people. On February 21, 1921, the Beijing government removed Qi Yang from his post as governor, and Ding Naiyang retired under pressure. The successor governor, Zhao Congfan 赵从藩 (a native of Nanfeng, Jiangxi Province), was welcomed by the province's local elites. However, Chen Guangyuan 陈光远 (from Wuqing, Zhili), the military governor of Jiangxi Province, prevented Zhao Congfan from taking office, and convinced the Beijing government to appoint his confidant Yang Qingjian 杨庆鉴 as acting governor of Jiangxi Province. Jiangxi's local elites launched a campaign to expel Yang and urge Zhao Congfan to take office. The movement failed. Against the background of the Guangzhou government's commitment to the Northern Expedition, Jiangxi's local elites pointed the spearhead of struggle directly at military governor Chen Guangyuan. In 1922, the Guangzhou government's Northern Expeditionary Army expelled Chen Guangyuan from Jiangxi. The Jiangxi Autonomous Movement continued to advance, and the third Jiangxi provincial council passed the "Bill Concerning County Autonomy of Jiangxi Province." The Association for the Promotion of Jiangxi People's Autonomy in Shanghai discussed and adopted "An Outline Concerning the Organizational of Jiangxi Autonomous Government." However, the Beijing government appointed Cai Chengxun 蔡成勋 (a native of Tianjin County, Zhili Province) as commander-in-chief of the relief military force for Jiangxi. Cai Chengxun reoccupied Jiangxi and became the province's acting military governor. He later supported his close confidant Li Tingyu 李廷玉 to become governor. Jiangxi elites launched a movement to expel Cai. Finally, Li Tingyu resigned and left Jiangxi in September 1922, after just one month in office. In autumn 1924, Cai Chengxun was ousted by Fang Benren 方本仁 (from Huanggang, Hubei Province), the military leader in South Jiangxi. Jiangxi local elites mobilized again and petitioned Duan Qirui to respect the spirit of "Jiangxi people governing Jiangxi" and to appoint Li Liejun as the military governor and governor of Jiangxi. This effort failed, and Fang Benren took military power over Jiangxi Province. In 1925, Fang served as commander-in-chief of the Jiangxi Army in a joint defense army of five southeastern provinces led by Sun Chuanfang

孙传芳. In April 1926, Wu Peifu 吴佩孚 instigated the defection of Fang's subordinate, Deng Ruzhuo 邓如琢 (a native of Fuyang, Anhui Province). Fang fell from power and went over to the Guangzhou Nationalist Government. Deng Ruzhuo took Fang Benren's position in Jiangxi until he was defeated by the Northern Expeditionary Army sent by the Guangzhou Nationalist Government.

3. Anhui 安徽: When the revolutionary leader Bai Wenwei became governor of Anhui in 1912, he promoted the idea of "Anhui people governing Anhui affairs."[537] However, after the failure of the Second Revolution in 1913, Anhui fell into the hands of Ni Sichong 倪嗣冲 (from Fuyang, Anhui Province). Although there was an episode in which Li Yuanhong 黎元洪 appointed Zhang Xun 张勋 as Anhui's military governor, Ni Sichong regained the position of military governor by soliciting the help of Duan Qirui, and even annexed Zhang Xun's Dingwu Army. After the war between the Zhili faction and Anhui faction in 1920, the Anhui faction collapsed, and Ni Sichong resigned on the grounds of ill health. After taking control of Anhui after the Second Revolution, Ni Sichong had dominated and manipulated the provincial council elections. Ni Sichong's nephew Ni Daolang 倪道烺 also tried to manipulate the third provincial council election in 1921, and many politicians and speculators cheated in the election. Although Ni Sichong and Ni Daolang were both from Anhui Province, the warlords of Anhui Province had become so unpopular that local elites rose up to expose the shady election. Ni Daolang and his former subordinate Ma Lianjia 马连甲 tried to cooperate to acquire the post of provincial governor. Their attempt was resisted by Anhui local elites. Two candidates for the position of provincial governor, Li Guoyun 李国筠 and Lyu Tiaoyuan 吕调元, were also boycotted on suspicion of having political dealings with Ni Daolang and Ma Lianjia. On August 21, 1921, President Xu Shichang appointed Li Zhaozhen 李兆珍, an aide to Ni Sichong and a native of Fujian, as the chief of Anhui Province. Before Li took office, Finance Minister Tao Rong (from Shucheng, Anhui Province) acted as governor. On August 21, people from Anhui who had traveled to Beijing and Shanghai created a public uproar by accusing the Beijing government of appointing Li Zhaozhen, who was "nearly eighty years old and long in poor health," and Tao Rong, who was "greedy and trivial," to be in charge of Anhui. Accusing the government of "deliberately trapping our Anhui in fire and water," they demanding that "Anhui people should govern Anhui."[538] On September 10, gentry, businessmen and scholars held a meeting in Anqing, the

537 Sun Caixia 孙彩霞 et al. eds., *Bai Wenwei wenji* 柏文蔚文集 [*Collected Works of Bai Wenwei*], (Hefei: Huangshan shushe, 2011), 83.

538 "Lvjing wanren fandui Li Zhaozhen 旅京皖人反对李兆珍 [Wan people in Beijing oppose Li Zhaozhen]," *Ta Kung Pao* (24 August 1921).

capital city of Anhui, to boycott Li Zhaozhen's appointment, and in a subsequent street protest displayed the slogan "Anhui people should govern Anhui."[539] Li Zhaozhen gave up his post under pressure. On September 29, 1921, Xu Shiying 许世英 (from Zhide, Anhui), who enjoyed much more favor among Anhui's local elites, became provincial governor. After Xu took office, he actively dealt with the fraud in the election of the third provincial council, which brought him into conflict with remnant allies of Ni Sichong. Meanwhile, he promoted "abolishing the military governor and reducing armaments," which caused a major conflict with military governor Ma Lianjia. In February 1923, Xu Shiying resigned. The Beijing government appointed Lyu Tiaoyuan 吕调元 (from Taihu Lake, Anhui Province), who served as the chief of Anhui Province from 1919 to 1920. A protest against Lyu's appointment by eleven local elite groups failed.[540] Lyu Tiaoyuan 吕调元 was soon removed from his post, and Ma Lianjia was temporarily appointed governor of Anhui Province. We can therefore see that Anhui's discourse of "Anhui people governing Anhui" in the early 1920s did not directly oppose forces from other provinces, but first targeted Anhui province's own unpopular warlords.

According to existing historical materials, the more direct expression of Monroe Doctrine related to Anhui's local power structure probably didn't appear until the Northern Expedition of the National Revolutionary Army in 1926. The Northern Expeditionary Army captured Nanchang on November 8 of that year. On November 18, *Ta Kung Pao* reported a rumor: Chen Tiaoyuan, deputy military affairs officer of Anhui Province and commander-in-chief of the Fifth Army (Anhui Army) of Sun Chuanfang's Five Provinces Allied Forces, and Wang Pu, governor of Anhui Province, sent a telegram to announce their policy of neutrality in the conflict between the Beiyang Clique and the Revolutionary army, in other words, "maintaining the Monroe Doctrine."[541] This was probably just a rumor. Soon after that, Chen Tiaoyuan crossed swords with the National Revolutionary Army, but in March 1927, he turned his troops over to the Northern Expeditionary Army. After the founding of the Nanjing Nationalist Government, Anhui Province's close proximity to the Nanjing Nationalist

539 "Anhui gejie juli dayouxing 安徽各界拒李大游行 [All walks of life in Anhui refused to March on Li]," *Minguo ribao* (15 September 1921).

540 "Lvhu wanren youyi ju Lyu zhi tongdian 旅沪皖人又一拒吕之通电 [Another telegram of Anhui people traveling in Shanghai against Lyu]," *Shenbao* (23 February 1923).

541 "Wanchenwang tongdian baojinghou suowen zuori fengchuan anqing weiji 皖陈王通电保境后所闻昨日风传安庆危急 [Anhui Chen Wang heard the news of Anqing's crisis yesterday after he was telegraphed to protect the domain]," *Ta Kung Pao* (18 November 1926).

Government prevented it from practicing the Anhui Monroe Doctrine any longer.

4. Shaanxi 陕西: Chen Shufan 陈树藩 (from Ankang, Shaanxi), the provincial governor of Shaanxi Province and warlord of the Anhui faction, lost Duan Qirui as a backer after the war against Anhui in 1920. Within his province, the Jingguo Army supported by Sun Yat-sen resisted Chen's rule. In June 1920, the Shaanxi Anti-Chen Shufan Federation of All Walks of Life was established in Xi'an. In order to maintain his hold on power, Chen Shufan struck the banner of "Shaanxi people governing Shaanxi" to counter the external threat from the Zhili faction. At the same time, he released Hu Jingyi 胡景翼, who had been detained for two years, to ease the relationship with the Jingguo Army. In December 1920, Chen Shufan raised the banner of "Abolishing the military governor and formulating a Constitution," and asked the provincial council to prepare a draft provincial constitution as soon as possible. In many other provinces, local elites expelled a provincial miliary governor or provincial governor from another province, but in Shaanxi, local elites expelled a native miliary governor who had lost the support of the Beijing government, and who furthermore struck the banner of Provincial Monroe Doctrine in Shaanxi. But even this banner couldn't save Chen Shufan. In May 1921, the Beijing government removed Chen from the post of military governor. Yan Xiangwen (a native of Shandong) and Feng Yuxiang 冯玉祥 (a native of Zhili) successively served as governors of Shaanxi Province, but the local elites who had expelled Chen Shufan did not form a strong Provincial Monroe Doctrine against them.

5. Gansu 甘肃: In 1921–1922, local warlords surnamed Ma took advantage of the failure of the Anhui faction in the Zhili-Anhui war to drive out military governor Zhang Guangjian 张广建 (from Hefei, Anhui Province). They later opposed the Zhili faction's arrangement for Cai Chengxun (from Tianjin County, Zhili Province) to become military governor of Gansu. At that time, a newspaper reported that "Gansu people opposed Cai Chengxun 蔡成勋's taking the post of governor concurrently. They announced the principle 'Gansu people govern Gansu' and sent telegrams to people inside and outside of Beijing to organize a petition to the government. Cai Chengxun heard about this and decided to resign from his concurrent post."[542] Cai Chengxun was boycotted and did not take up his post in Gansu. In June 1922, he became military governor of Jiangxi Province. Lu Hongtao 陆洪涛 (from Tongshan, Jiangsu Province), the commander of Longdong, became the acting military governor of Gansu Province, while Ma Fuxiang 马福祥, a local powerful figure, vied for

542 *Shibao* (6 January 1921), third edition, domestic special telegram.

the position of military governor. Both sides appealed to the public using the language of ethnicity.[543] The slogan "Gansu people governing Gansu" therefore carried the connotations of ethnic contradictions that other provinces did not have. The struggle ended with a compromise. Lu Hongtao became the military governor of Gansu Province, Ma Fuxiang became the military commander of Suiyuan, and his nephew Ma Hongbin 马鸿宾 acted as his agent. Although Lu Hongtao was in office for several years, the potential for opposition within the Gansu Provincial Council never disappeared. In 1925, it was reported that the "Gansu Provincial Council asked the central government to follow the popular will and appoint Gansu personnel to govern Gansu."[544]

6. Shandong 山东: As in many other provinces, a campaign by Shandong local elites to expel a military governors from another province created a wave of public opinion based on the notion of "Shandong people governing Shandong." In December 1919, Premier Jin Yunpeng 靳云鹏 (from Zou County, Shandong Province), who belonged to the Anhui faction, supported the appointment of Tian Zhongyu 田中玉 as military governor of Shandong, and tried to dominate Shandong by controlling Tian Zhongyu. Tian was initially inclined toward the Anhui faction, but in the war between the Anhui faction and Zhili faction, he sat quietly off to the side and watched the fall of the Anhui faction. When most provinces were calling for "military-civilian separation," Tian Zhongyu drove out Governor Qi Yaoshan 齐耀珊 (from Changyi, Shandong Province) and became provincial governor himself. As a non-Shandong native, Tian Zhongyu's imperious actions inevitably brought him into conflict with local elites. Many Shandong elites organized a call for "expelling Tian Zhongyu and abolishing the military governor," and sent representatives to Beijing to submit their petition. Some even suggested inviting Wu Peifu 吴佩孚 to be the military governor of Shandong. Zhang Huaizhi 张怀芝, a native of Dong'e who used to be the military governor of Shandong, and Zhang Shuyuan 张树元, a native of Binzhou, were also important promoters of the movement. They were trying to drive Tian Zhongyu out and take the post of military governor for themselves. However, Tian Zhongyu attached himself to the Zhili faction and remained in office. Finally, in 1923, Tian Zhongyu's attempt to suppress a group of bandits led to a train hijacking by those bandits, who killed many foreigners on the train. Under pressure from the Great Powers, Tian was forced to take the blame and resign. Both of his successors, military governor Zheng Shiqi 郑士琦 and provincial governor Gong Jibing

543 For related cables, see Ding Mingjun 丁明俊, *Ma Fuxiang zhuan* 马福祥传 [*Biography of Ma Fuxiang*], (Yinchuan: Ningxia renmin chubanshe, 2001), 83.

544 *The Times* (17 September 1925), second edition.

龚积炳, were Anhui natives, and the appointed many of their townsmen to government positions. In April 1925, Shandong elites in Beijing submitted a petition to the Beiyang government, asking that Zheng and Gong be dismissed under the banner of "Shandong people governing Shandong."[545] Taking advantage of this slogan, Zhang Zuolin, the leader of the Fengtian faction, arranged for Zhang Zongchang 张宗昌, a Shandong native affiliated with the Fengtian faction, to take charge of the province's military, political affairs and civil affairs. Zhang Zongchang controlled Shandong until he was defeated by the Kuomintang Northern Expeditionary Army and left Shandong.

None of the afore-mentioned Provincial Monroe Doctrines, no matter how parochial, publicly called for secession from China. It can be seen that the tradition of China's "great unification" had deep politico-cultural roots and could not be shaken by a few decades of political turmoil. However, with the intervention of imperialist forces, a local Monroe Doctrine affiliated with Japanese imperialism in Northeast China rose to the political stage, and deserves additional discussion here.

In 1928, *New Beiping* 新北平, a tabloid newspaper in Beiping, published a comment titled "Manchurian Monroe Doctrine" (under the byline "Kuai"), which severely criticized the Tanaka Giichi Cabinet's policy on Northeast China, accusing the Japanese government of promoting a "Manchurian Monroe Doctrine" 满洲门罗主义. The substantial practice of the Manchurian Monroe Doctrine in Northeast China came to the forefront with the Mukden Incident in 1931. On November 5, 1931, Yu Chonghan 于冲汉, who served as staff for the security commander-in-chief of the three eastern provinces under Zhang Zuolin 张作霖 and Zhang Xueliang 张学良, put forward eight political proposals to Honjō Shigeru 本庄繁, the commander of the Kwantung Army at that time, including implementing the policy of protecting the hometown and the people, pursuing Monroe Doctrine in Northeast China, and replacing the Chinese army with the Japanese army.[546] According to the testimony of Kwantung Army staff officer Katakura Tadashi 片仓衷 to the International

545 "Lvjing luren daozhenggong zhi daqingyuan 旅京鲁人倒郑龚之大请愿 [The Great Petition of People Traveling to Beijing and Shandong to Pour Zheng Gong]," *Shenbao* (6 April 1925).

546 See Puppet Palace Exhibition Hall ed., *Weihuanggong chenlieguan nianjian* 伪皇宫陈列馆年鉴 [*Yearbook of Puppet Palace Exhibition Hall*], (Changchun: Puppet Palace Exhibition Hall, 1987), 84; Editorial Department of Changchun Literature and History Materials, *Changchun wenshi ziliao: Zong di 53 ji: Weimanzhouguo shisinian shihua* 长春文史资料·总第53辑·伪满洲国十四年史话 [*Changchun Literature and History Materials, Volume 53, History of the Puppet Manchukuo in the Fourteenth Year*], (Changchun Municipal Committee of Political Consultative Conference, 2002), 248.

Military Tribunal for the Far East after World War II, Yu Chonghan stated in his conversation with Honjō Shigeru (November 3, 1931): "The current situation has developed to such an extent that in order to protect and maintain security, people's well-being and the rule of law and order in Northeast China, this region should be separated from the Nanjing government to form a new independent country. To establish a new region in independent form in Northeast China, we should adopt the principle of no military training, that is, the principle of anti-militarization, as well as the principle of non-intimidation and non-aggression, and build a Monroe society on the basis of the above principles."[547] On November 10, the Department of Guidance for Manchurian Autonomy was established, and Yu Chonghan served as its head, responsible for publicizing Japanese "imperial rule" at the grassroots level.[548] After the establishment of the Manchukuo puppet state in 1932, Yu Chonghan was appointed first president of the Control Yuan.

The author who provides a systematic exposition of Manchuria Monroe Doctrine is Zheng Xiaoxu 郑孝胥, former Minister of Internal Affairs under Puyi. Zheng was of Han origin and served as Pu Yi's "Premier of State" after the establishment of Manchukuo. Zheng Xiaoxu's *A Brief History of the Founding of Manchuria* constructed a historical narrative with the aim of demonstrating that "Manchuria has been an independent country since ancient times." He also said that the founding of Manchukuo "followed the principle of the so-called Manchukuo Monroe Doctrine."[549] The essence of this doctrine was

---

547 Cheng Zhaoqi 程兆奇 et al. eds., Yang Xiaming 杨夏鸣 trans., *Yundong guoji junshi fating tingshen jilu: Zhongguo bufen: Qinzhan dongbei bianfang juzheng* 远东国际军事法庭庭审记录·中国部分·侵占东北辨方举证 [*Trial Records of the International Military Court of Yundong, Chinese Part, Evidence of the Defense of the Occupation of Northeast China*] (1), (Shanghai: Shanghai jiaotong daxue chubanshe, 2015), 143. In his testimony, Katakura explained Yu Chonghan's idea of "building a country on the basis of Monroe Doctrine": "According to Yu Chonghan's point of view, as long as a country can be established independently in Northeast China, a country like Switzerland can be established, which is not armed in principle, does not threaten other countries, and is not threatened by other countries. His views also include that a national defense army should be established to protect Northeast China. In this way, an army in the region can fight back against Japanese and Russian troops." Of course, here is Yu Chonghan's view before he joined the puppet Manchukuo. Ibid., 148.

548 Puppet Palace Exhibition Hall (n. 544), 84; Editorial Department of Changchun Literature and History Materials (n. 544), 248.

549 Zheng Xiaoxu 郑孝胥, Manzhou jianguo suyuan shilue 满洲建国溯源史略 [A Brief History of the Founding of Manchuria], in *Weimanzhouguo shisinian shihua* 伪满洲国十四年史话 [*History of the Puppet Manchukuo in the Fourteenth Year*] Volume 1 eds. Editorial Board of Puppet Manchukuo Historical Materials of Jilin Provincial Library (Beijing: National Library Document Microfilming Center, 2002): 480.

"Manchuria ruled by the people of Manchukuo ..." "Manchuria completely dominated by all ethnic groups living in Manchuria now."[550] What he meant by "the people of Manchukuo" or "the Manchurians" generally referred to all ethnic groups living in Manchuria, including Manchu, Han, Mongolian, Korean, Russian and Japanese. But if the Japanese were included among the "Manchurians," it was possible to disguise Tokyo's domination of Manchukuo as autonomous decision-making by Pu Yi's puppet government.

Zheng Xiaoxu's Manchurian Monroe Doctrine echoed Japan's Manchuria Monroe Doctrine. The third issue of *Jiuguo Weekly* in Shanghai in 1932 published a Chinese translation of Nakano Seigō's article "Japan and the Manchurian-Mongolian Monroe Doctrine." Nakano Seigō 中野正刚 said: "Japan has no rich resources of its own and is looking for a place for immigration. Now it is absolutely necessary to support Japanese forces in Manchuria and Mongolia, and foreign countries have no reason to interfere. The U.S. advocated Monroe Doctrine and established its influence in South American countries. Britain, on the other hand, forms a large circle of economic power with its vast and boundless colonies. France is also building its economic power circle on the European continent. Then what is wrong with the Japanese promotion of Monroe Doctrine in Manchuria and Mongolia?" "We think that if we don't resolutely adopt the policy of forbidding any third country from interfering with the Manchuria-Mongolian issue, the Manchuria-Mongolian policy will fail and there will be the possibility of being invaded."[551] This statement was a blatant appeal to Japan's colonial needs, and called on the Japanese government to "aid" the puppet Manchukuo and exclude interference from other countries. From this point of view, the Manchurian Monroe Doctrine was essentially an extension of Japan's Asiatic Monroe Doctrine, which was a brazen violation of China's territorial sovereignty.

3 The Decline of the Provincial Monroe Doctrine

The key turning point for the Provincial Monroe Doctrine, from the positive image of Wilson-style democratic autonomy to the negative image of separatism and resistance to national unification, came with the cooperation between the Kuomintang and the Communist Party of China in 1923.

550 Ibid., 464.

551 Zi Zheng 子正, "Guanyu riben de faxishite: Zhongye dachang manmeng menluozhuyi 关于日本的法西士特：中野大倡满蒙门罗主义 [About Fashite in Japan: Nakano advocates Manchu-Monro Doctrine]," *Jiuguozhoubao* 3 (1932), 23–25.

As I analyzed at the beginning of this chapter, Mao still supported the Provincial Monroe Doctrine in 1920 before he joined the Communist Party of China. Among the founders of the CPC, Li Dazhao's disenchantment with provincial autonomy happened much earlier. Li Dazhao was still in supportive of provincial autonomy in 1916. The Russian October Revolution brought Li Dazhao new inspiration concerning the future path of China. He enthusiastically supported the October Revolution, and found in the solidarity of the proletariat a new possibility for reintegrating the fragmented political situation in China. In July 1918, Li Dazhao published an article titled "Pan … sm's failure and Democracy's victory" in which he juxtaposed German militarism with the expansionism of Chinese provincial warlords, regarding both as symptoms of "Pan … ism." What, however, was the actual difference between the two phenomena? From Li Dazhao's perspective, imperialist expansion was based upon a strong state releasing its power over a large space, but China was so weak that its powerful men were unable to expand into the international arena. They could therefore only compete domestically and create conflict at the provincial level.[552] This analogy was very important. In 1917–1918, Li Dazhao also wrote a series of articles criticizing the Japanese Monroe Doctrine, which he also included in "Pan … ism." The Chinese warlords were merely working out the same logic on the provincial level. The antithesis of "pan … ism," according to Li Dazhao, was democracy, which had both political and the social-economic dimensions. The October Revolution represented the social-economic dimension of democracy. Li Dazhao enthusiastically supported the path of the October Revolution, and saw in the solidarity of the proletariat the possibility of genuine unification of China.

Li laid a foundation for the early organization of the Communist Party of China. The Second National Congress of the Communist Party of China was held in Shanghai from July 16–23, 1922. The congress produced "The Declaration of the Second National Congress of the Communist Party of China," which argued that "in the last decade, all political power has been completely divided and has fallen into the hands of military figures in various provinces. If one asks for further separation of powers, one could only call the province 'nation,' and military governors 'kings.'" The document held that "the principle of federalism

552 Li Dazhao 李大钊, "Pan … ism zhishibai yu Democracy zhishegnli Pan …… ism 之失败与 Democracy 之胜利 [The Failure of Pan …… ism and the Victory of Democracy]," in *Li Dazhao quanji* 李大钊全集 [*Complete Works of Li Dazhao*] (Volume II), eds. Zhu Wentong 朱文通 et al. (Shijiazhuang: *Hebei jiaoyu chubanshe*, 1999): 245.

cannot be adopted in all the provinces of China proper."[553] The CPC expressed a negative attitude toward the current situation of provincial autonomy. Li Dazhao met Sun Yat-sen in Shanghai soon after that, in August 1922. Both sides reached a consensus on opposing warlordism and unifying all of China.

What was Sun Yat-sen's experience with provincial autonomy? Before the 1911 Revolution, Sun supported the separation of provinces from the Qing Court for anti-Manchu purposes. After the 1911 Revolution, he gradually turned to the idea of county autonomy rather than provincial autonomy. In the early 1920s, he refrained from criticizing the United Provincial Autonomy Movement, since some provinces participating in the movement acknowledged his Guangdong government as the legitimate central government. However, in Sun's base area of Guangdong, the conflict between his Northern Expedition and Chen Jiongming's Guangdong Monroe Doctrine became increasingly intense. The two sides finally crossed swords in June 1922. This accelerated Sun's decision to completely break with the United Provincial Autonomy Movement. When he met Li Dazhao in August 1922, they had no difficulty in reaching a consensus concerning the Provincial Monroe Doctrine.

After Li Dazhao and Sun Yat-sen's meeting in Shanghai, the September 13 inaugural issue of the CPC Central Committee's *Xiangdao Weekly* 向导周刊 published party secretary Chen Duxiu's "United Province Autonomy and China's Political Situation," which argued that the essence of United Provincial Autonomy was "separatism by dividing the provinces" and "separatism by uniting military governors." Chen Duxiu proposed mobilizing democratic elements throughout the country to create powerful political parties in order to defeat warlords and build a unified national government with democratic politics.[554] Communist Party members soon participated in the reorganization of the KMT. In the "Manifesto of the First National Congress of the Chinese Nationalist Party" adopted in January 1924, we can see fierce criticism of the United Provincial Autonomy Movement: it was only pseudo-autonomy, which maintained the peace between small warlords seeking to defend their provinces and the big warlords who dominated the central government; genuine autonomy was unfeasible before the independence of China as a whole.[555]

553 Li Zhongjie and Duan Dongsheng 李忠杰、段东升 eds., *Zhongguo guochandang dierci quanguo daibiao dahui dang'an wenxian xuanbian* 中国共产党第二次全国代表大会档案文献选编 [*Selected Archives of the Second National Congress of the Communist Party of China*], (Beijing: Zhonggong dangshi chubanshe, 2014), 7.

554 Chen Duxiu 陈独秀, "Liansheng zizhi yu Zhongguo zhengxiang 联省自治与中国政象 [Union Province Autonomy and China's Political Image]," *Xiangdao* (September 1922).

555 Research Office of the Republic of China, Institute of Modern History, Chinese Academy of Social Sciences, et al. (n. 429), 116–117.

The consensus against the United Provincial Autonomy Movement was so strong that even after Chiang Kai-shek's military coup against the Communist Party and left wing of the Kuomintang in 1927, "Monroe Doctrine" remained a negative label in Chiang Kai-shek's language. In May 1927, Chiang Kai-shek and Hu Hanmin invited Tang Jiyao to Nanjing to discuss the establishment of the Nanjing Nationalist Government. The message said: "As a pillar of the country, you have great talent and great prestige among the people. We are confident that you wouldn't stick to the Monroe Doctrine, and will rise up with ardor in time, moving from love of the hometown to the love of the country."[556] Here, the term "Monroe Doctrine" referred to the mentality of focusing on one's province without interest in the overall national situation. The Kuomintang Archives in Wuhan registered a document on June 21, 1927, which was a letter from a student in Shanxi. The letter pointed out that Yan Xishan was shocked by the revolutionary wave, "so he gave up his Monroe Doctrine, which means the protection of the domain and the people, to cope with the upsurge of the revolution and maintain his home turf in Shanxi and Suiyuan."[557] In both of these historical documents, "Monroe Doctrine" is set against the cause of national reunification. The KMT official Xu Yongchang 徐永昌 wrote in his diary on April 21, 1949, that he witnessed Ma Hongkui 马鸿逵, longtime chairman of Ningxia Province, complaining to Bai Chongxi 白崇禧 that the relevant parties in the Kuomintang "provided supplies unfairly and even suspected Ma was following the Monroe Doctrine." Xu observed that Ma was very aggrieved, even bursting into tears.[558] It can be seen that the "Monroe Doctrine" was regarded as a very serious political label within the Kuomintang.

In the United Provincial Autonomy Movement, the meaning field for the slogan "X is X for the Xans" overlaps with that of "Monroe Doctrine." After the halo of the Monroe Doctrine faded, some local powers continued to use the slogan of "X is X for the Xans." In using the slogan, they weakened the connotations of excluding other provinces and the central government so as to avoid the label of Monroe Doctrine. For example, Xiong Shihui 熊式辉, who belonged to the New Zhengxue faction of the KMT, served as chairman of Jiangxi Province from 1931 to 1941. He published *A Decade of Government in Jiangxi* in 1941, including his own speech "The True Spirit of Jiangxi People Governing

556 "Jiang Zhongzheng yu Hu Hanmin dian Tang Jiyao laining gongdan dangguo daren 蒋中正与胡汉民电唐继尧来宁共担党国大人 [Jiang Zhongzheng and Hu Hanmin sent a telegram to Tang Jiyao to share the responsibility of the party and the country]." On May 16, 1927, Taipei Guoshiguan collected Jiang Zhongzheng's "President" cultural relics, revolutionary documents and Northern Expedition, 002-020100-00002-057.

557 Ibid. (n. 525).

558 Institute of Modern History, Academia Sinica (n. 527), 311.

Jiangxi" delivered to the Jiangxi Provincial Government on January 25, 1932, which stated: "The slogan 'Jiangxi people governing Jiangxi' does not simply mean the chairman and major members of the provincial government should be Jiangxi natives. It means that all Jiangxi people make a joint effort to govern Jiangxi. In other words, 30 million people should govern themselves. This is the true spirit of 'Jiangxi people governing Jiangxi.'"[559] However, before Xiong Shihui became chairman of Jiangxi Province, he appropriated the slogan of "Jiangxi people governing Jiangxi" to mobilize his allies to expel Lu Diping 鲁涤平, a Hunan native, from Jiangxi.[560] In other words, in practice, "Xans govern X" still had significant connotations of expelling the external forces of other provinces. The difference was that under the Kuomintang's "political tutelage" theory, it was no longer wise to include the central government among the "external forces." This prudent move could avoid the label of Monroe Doctrine.

After the break between the Kuomintang and the Communist Party in 1927, the Communist Party of China used "Monroe Doctrine" to refer to the closed-door behavior of the local warlords of the Kuomintang, but rarely used this term to refer to the similar phenomena within the Communist Party. The CPC's survival and development among the spheres of influence of various warlords relied on its ability to constantly break through existing boundaries and mobilize the people's power within the enemy's jurisdiction. Guerrilla warfare and mobile warfare across borders were in themselves a negation of the Monroe Doctrine of warlords. In order to maintain this ability to cross borders, the revolutionaries needed to overcome their own tendencies toward sectarianism and parochialism. In the revolutionary struggle, the Communist Party of China found new names for small factions within the party that closed their doors to their comrades: "mountain-strongholdism" 山头主义 or "sectarianism" 宗派主义.[561] In particular, "mountain-strongholdism," rooted in the

559 Editorial Board of "Ten Years of Jiangxi Administration," "Ganzheng shinian: Xiongzhuxi zhigan shizhounian jinian tekan 赣政十年：熊主席治赣十周年纪念特刊 [Ten Years of Jiangxi Administration: Special Issue on the Tenth Anniversary of President Xiong's Governance of Jiangxi]," in *Minguo zhenxi zhuankan tekan zengkan jinianhao huibian* 民国珍稀专刊特刊增刊纪念号汇编 [*Collection of Commemorative Numbers of Special Supplement of Rare Special Issue of the Republic of China*] (Volume 39), (Beijing: National Library Document Microfilming Center, 2010): 7.

560 Yao Ganlin 姚甘霖, "Tongzhi jiangxi shinian de Xiong Shihui 统治江西十年的熊式辉 [Xiong Shihui, who ruled Jiangxi for ten years]," in *Jiangxi wenshi ziliao xuanji* 江西文史资料选辑 [*Selected Works of Jiangxi Cultural and Historical Materials*] (Total No. 8 Series), eds. Jiangxi Provincial Committee of Chinese People's Political Consultative Conference (Culture and Historical Materials Press, 1982): 144.

561 Mao Zedong 毛泽东, "Zhengdun dangde zuofeng 整顿党的作风 [Rectifying the Party's Style] (February 1942)," in *Mao Zedong xuanji* 毛泽东选集 [*Selected Works of Mao Zedong*] (Volume III), (Beijing: Renmin chubanshe, 1991): 811–829.

experience of revolutionary parties engaged in guerrilla warfare in the mountainous regions, was a more vivid name for self-isolation and a contentment with semi-tranquility. When "mountain-strongholdism" or "sectarianism" could be used to address the problem sufficiently, it was unnecessary to use the label of Monroe Doctrine to describe the phenomenon within the party.[562]

However, the more negative image of the Monroe Doctrine was not only due to changes in China's domestic political situation, but was also closely related to Japan's abuse of Monroe Doctrine as a symbol. After the Mukden Incident in 1931, the Japanese government put increasing pressure on China by advocating the Asiatic Monroe Doctrine or Japanese Monroe Doctrine. As a result, it became increasingly difficult for the Monroe Doctrine to remain a positive phrase in Chinese. From 1931 until the victory of the War of Resistance against Japanese Invasion in 1945, Chinese newspapers and journals published many criticisms of the Japanese Monroe Doctrine. When the Chinese nation was at stake, the Provincial Monroe Doctrine openly espoused by warlords in various provinces became increasingly delegitimized.

For example, Yan Xishan's rule in Shanxi had long been referred to as Shanxi Monroe Doctrine. As summarized by Professor Wang Qisheng 王奇生, during the War of Resistance against Japanese Invasion, Yan Xishan "joined forces with Chiang Kai-shek against the Communist Party, or joined forces with the Communists against Chiang Kai-shek, or joined forces with Chiang and

---

562 There are two exceptions worth mentioning: (1) In 1929, Chen Duxiu tried to join the Trotskyist organization "Our Words School," which put forward conditions that Chen Duxiu could not accept. Therefore, Chen Duxiu, Peng Shuzhi and Yin Kuan set up their own small groups and condemned "Our Words School" for "Monroe Doctrine." Ji Gong 记工 ed., *Lishi nianjian* 1929 历史年鉴1929 [*Historical Yearbook 1929*], (Changchun; Jilin Literature and History Press, 2006), 171–172. Here, the two small groups in conflict are engaged in "non-organizational activities." (2) In June 1933, Fu Tian (a pseudonym of Kong Yuan), the representative of the Central Committee in the north, recommended the acting secretary of Hebei Provincial Party Committee in a letter to the Central Committee. When talking about Stingson (a pseudonym of Ruan Jinyun), then the organization minister of Hebei Provincial Party Committee, he said that the latter was weak and worked in Hebei. For a time, he held the attitude of "Monroe Doctrine" and only paid attention to part of his work, but paid little attention to the whole work. However, When referring to the Monroe Doctrine here, Fu Tian added brackets, which indicated: "His own words," which meant Ruan Jinyun's self-criticism. "Zhongyan zhubeifang daibiao Tian Fu zhizhongyangxin dishisanhao—Guanyu zhangjiakou shibian de bagao 中央驻北方代表田夫致中央信第十三号——关于张家口事变的报告 （一九三三年六月十八日）[Letter No. 13 from Fu Tian, Representative of the Central Committee in the North to the Central Committee-Report on Zhangjiakou Incident (18 June 1933)]," in *Zhonggong zhongyang beifangju wenjian huibian: 1933 nian–1934 nian* 中共中央北方局文件汇编：1933年 - 1934年 [*Collection of Documents of the Northern Bureau of the CPC Central Committee: 1933–1934*] (2), eds. Central Archives (Beijing: Central Archives, 1992): 114.

the Communists against Japan. He also planned to compromise with Japan in order to deal with the KMT and CPC. Basically he had no bottom line."[563] In *Generals' Talk on the War of Resistance against Japanese Invasion* published in 1938, Zhang Xiangshan 张香山 of the 129th Division of the Eighth Route Army criticized Yan Xishan's Shanxi Army for "failing not only militarily, but also politically. This failure originated from Yan Xishan's 'Monroe Doctrine,' which was manifested in the closed and conservative aspects of finance, transportation and personnel management, out of an unwillingness to mobilize the people to actively resist Japan."[564] A few months before the Shanxi Incident in 1939, Chiang Kai-shek also scolded Yan Xishan in his diary for "taking unification as the legacy of poison and misinterpreting the ideas of central government ..." "... His evilness is more despicable than that of the Communist Party, and his undermining of the Three People's Principles is unforgivable." On February 5, 1944, Chiang scolded Yan Xishan in his diary for plotting "surrender to the enemy and treason," which was "inconceivable."[565] After the Shanxi Incident in 1939, conflicts emerged in the anti-Japanese alliance between Yan Xishan and the CPC. In the late stage of the War of Resistance against Japanese Invasion, the song "Scolding Yan Xishan" created by Liu Wei 刘薇 and Tang He 唐诃 was popular in the Shanxi-Chahar-Hebei Border Region. The song included lyrics such as "paying lip service to defending the soil and fighting against Japan, while plotting the expansion of personal territory in his heart"; and "It is false to say he is allied to the Kuomintang and the Communist Party; it is true that he is allied to the Japanese devils."[566] *Jin-Ji Daily* 晋冀日报 also published a report stating that when Yan Xishan attacked the liberated areas at the end of 1945, members of the Children Corp captured by Yan Jun sang the song "Scolding Yan Xishan" before they were executed.[567]

Against the background of the War of Resistance against Japanese Invasion, what worried many commentators was not only the Monroe Doctrine at the

563 Wang Qisheng 王奇生, "Duozhong zhegnzhi liliangjian de boyi: yi 1935–1945 niande Yan Xishan weige'an 多种政治力量间的博弈:以1935－1945年的阎锡山为个案 [Game between Various Political Forces: Taking Yan Xishan from 1935 to 1945 as a Case]," *Jianghuai wenshi* 5 (2018).

564 Zhang Yuntao 张云涛 ed., *Quanguo jiangling kangritan* 全国将领抗日谈 [*National Generals' Talk on Anti-Japanese War*], (Shanghai: Huaguang chubanshe, 1938), 81.

565 The above statement in Chiang Kai-shek's diary is quoted from Wang (n. 562).

566 Wang Ruipu 王瑞璞 et al. eds., *Kangri zhanzheng gequ jicheng: Jinhanji: Jinjiluyu* 抗日战争歌曲集成·晋罕冀·晋冀鲁豫 [*War of Resistance against Japan Songs Integration Jin Han Ji Jin Ji Lu Yu*] (Volume 2), (Beijing: Zhongguo wenlian chubanshe, 2005), 80–81.

567 Tang Ke 唐诃, *Tang He sanwenji—Yiwei yinyuejia de zuji* 唐诃散文集———位音乐家的足迹 [*Tang He's Prose Collection: A Musician's Footprint*], (Jinan: Huanghe chubanshe, 2001), 126.

provincial level, but also the Monroe Doctrine at the sub-provincial levels. Xiao Qian 萧乾's *Dark Side of Lingdong* criticized all kinds of gaffes by Kuomintang officials in the Chaozhou and Shantou area during the War of Resistance against Japanese Invasion. It specifically mentioned that Liang, a county magistrate in Jieyang, not only imposed exorbitant taxes and miscellaneous taxes on ordinary people, but also adopted Monroe Doctrine and refused to cooperate with the commanding committee of the People's Anti-Japanese Self-defense Regiment in the 8th District of Guangdong Province, refused to employ women cadres trained in the 8th District, and so on.[568] In July 1939, a report by the Youth Work Committee of the Shaanxi Provincial Committee of the Communist Party of China referred to the situation in the Sanyuan Minzhi School, regarding it as "an organization of the Anti-Japanese Association, but following the Monroe Doctrine. Students from other schools cannot easily enter the door, and students at school are often under surveillance."[569] The Anti-Japanese Association was also called "the Kuomintang Association of Anti-Enemy Comrades," which was a national united front organization developed in the anti-Japanese base areas under the leadership of the Communist Party of China, possessing armed national self-defense forces. However, some grass-roots organizations within this association advocated the "third road," and were in conflict with the Communist Party. Consequently, the association was dissolved in 1942.[570] The report of the Youth Work Committee of the Shaanxi Provincial Party Committee reflected concerns about the increasingly closed-off grassroots organizations in this association.

During the War of Resistance against Japanese Invasion, it was very common for Kuomintang factions to guard against each other, and some Kuomintang cadres also labeled these phenomena as "Monroe Doctrine." He Zhen 何震, the last Kuomintang mayor of Fuzhou, recalled a spy faction in Fujian during the War of Resistance against Japanese Invasion in the article "A Brief Account of the Spy Faction in Fujian," saying that the navy stationed in Fujian pursued the Monroe Doctrine in order to maintain internal consistency, and it

---

568 Xiao Qian 萧乾, *Xiao Qian wenji* 萧乾文集 [*Selected Works of Xiao Qian*] (Volume 2), (Chengdu: Sichuan renmin chubanshe, 1983), 93.

569 Central Archives and Shaanxi Provincial Archives eds., *Shanxi geming lishi wenjian huiji–1939 nian* 陕西革命历史文件汇集·1939年 [*Collection of Historical Documents of Shaanxi Revolution in 1939*] (II), (Internal Materials of Central Archives and Shaanxi Provincial Archives, 1992), 484.

570 Party History Research Office of Shandong Provincial Committee of the Communist Party of China and Party History Society of Shandong Province eds., *Shandong dangshi ziliao wenku* 山东党史资料文库 [*Shandong Party History Database*] (Volume 19), (Jinan: Shandong renmin chubanshe, 2015), 205–206.

was difficult for outsiders to infiltrate. Someone in the military system once entered the fleet headquarters as a secretary and was discovered and kicked out.[571] Yuan Yansha 袁雁沙, then chief of the second section of the Political Department of the Fifth War Zone, said in his memoir *Chiang Kai-Shek and the Guangxi Faction's Infighting in the Political Work of the Fifth War Zone* that because Li Zongren 李宗仁 commanded not only his own army, but also a certain number of miscellaneous troops, "it was not easy for the New Guangxi Army to continue to implement Monroe Doctrine in their political work."[572] Through clever personnel arrangements, Li Zongren maintained his leadership of political work in the war zone while maintaining a show of nominal respect toward the people sent by the Kuomintang Central Committee.

The historical data recorded above during the War of Resistance against Japanese Invasion show a cross-party consensus: In the face of Japan's aggressive Asiatic Monroe Doctrine, the excessive consideration of narrow local interests and small group interests in the practice of Monroe Doctrine by provinces or even lower-level units only served the aggressors' ambitions. In this context, it was difficult for any province's Monroe Doctrine to be recognized as legitimate by the mainstream public opinion. The War of Resistance against Japanese Invasion greatly enhanced the national identity, and created the psychological conditions for a complete fading out of Provincial Monroe Doctrine in Mainland China.

4 Concluding Remarks

Throughout human history, whenever there has been the practice of delimiting exclusive space, it has been possible to produce discourse expressing

571 He Zhen 何震, "Lueji fujian de tewu paixi 略记福建的特务派系 [A Brief Account of the Secret Service Faction in Fujian]," in *Fujian wenshi ziliao—di 28 ji: CC, zhongtong zaimin neimu jishi* 福建文史资料·第28辑：CC、中统在闽内幕纪实 [*Fujian Literature and History Materials No. 28: CC, The Insider Documentary of the Central Committee in Fujian*], eds Literature and History Materials Committee of Fujian Provincial Committee of CPPCC (Fuzhou: Literature and History Materials Committee of Fujian Provincial Committee of CPPCC, 1992): 201.

572 Yuan Yansha 袁雁沙, "Jiang Gui zai diwu zhanqu jundui zhenggong fangmian de mingzheng andou 蒋桂在第五战区军队政工方面的明争暗斗 [Jiang Gui's infighting in military political work in the Fifth Theater]," in *Guangxi wenshi ziliao—di 30 ji: Xinguixi jishi* 广西文史资料·第30辑：新桂系纪实 [*Guangxi Literature and History Materials No. 30: Documentary of New Guangxi System* (CIMC)], eds. Guangxi Literature and History Materials Committee of Guangxi Zhuang Autonomous Region Committee of CPPCC (Nanning: Guangxi Zhuang Autonomous Region Committee of CPPCC, 1990): 259.

consciousness of exclusive space. The Monroe Doctrine discourse originating in the United States is only one of thousands of spatial political discourses in history. Starting in the nineteenth century, its appropriation by various political forces led to a sudden surge in the international influence of Monroe Doctrine discourse, which then spread throughout the world. Behind this dissemination process was the development of U.S. regional hegemony in the Western Hemisphere into global hegemony. The "presence" of the United States in various regions (at least as a potential audience) motivated cultural and political elites in these regions to "translate" the local demands of spatial politics into symbols of the Monroe Doctrine, so as to obtain better expressive effect in a space with a (potential) U.S. audience.

As the U.S. sought to establish colonial rule in the Philippines at the end of the nineteenth century, Chinese elites travelling in Japan absorbed the Monroe Doctrine as promoted and transformed by Japan, and then developed an anti-Manchu "Provincial Monroe Doctrine" discourse, which Ou Jujia pioneered in his *New Guangdong*. When the Revolution of 1911 ended in compromise, anti-Manchu discourse faded from the historical stage, but the discourse of Provincial Monroe Doctrine did not end. In the early Republic of China, the discourse of Monroe Doctrine was used as self-defense by local powerful factions in their confrontation with the central government, while a new interpretation of Monroe Doctrine by the Wilson Doctrine gave Provincial Monroe Doctrine a strong connotation of "democratic autonomy." When Mao Zedong supported the Hunan Monroe Doctrine in 1920, he emphasized the connotations of democracy and autonomy contained in the Monroe Doctrine. When domestic newspapers used the term "Monroe Doctrine" to describe the initiatives of local power factions that did not support civilian political participation in the sense of opposition to imperialism, this phrase maintained its association with "peace" and "local autonomy" without losing its positive connotations. However, as the Kuomintang and Communist Party sought to unify the entire country through revolution in the 1920s, the phrase "Monroe Doctrine" became increasingly associated with warlord separatism, closing-off and resistance to unification.

The transfer of Monroe Doctrine discourse from the supranational level to the subnational level involved an important "intermediate link": Under the influence of Japan's Great Asianism, Chinese elites in Japan in the late Qing Dynasty discovered an infectious sentence pattern for the Monroe Doctrine: "X is X for Xans." This sentence could be applied to different levels of political space, whether supranational, national or subnational. Through this sentence, political discourse at various levels gained the potential for mutual infection. However, the sentence pattern itself was only a tool, and the more important question is: Why were people motivated to use this sentence pattern so frequently? This can be traced back to the overall crisis of political order that China encountered at the end of the nineteenth century. After the Sino-Japanese War of 1894–1895, the Eastern and Western powers competed with China and East Asia, and China's Reform Movement of 1898 failed. For sensitive Chinese intellectuals at that time, the main question regarding the national order, the supranational regional order or the subnational provincial order was: Who is the master of this space? Furthermore, what degree of autonomy should be guaranteed? Both questions retained a high degree of uncertainty.

During this comprehensive reflection on spatial order at various levels, modern historical actors engaged in a theoretical summation and reflection on the application of Monroe Doctrine at both the supranational and subnational levels. In the article "Pan … ism's failure and the Victory of Democracy," published in July 1918, Li Dazhao explained Japan's Great Asianism and the Provincial Monroe Doctrine of Chinese warlords in conjunction with "Pan … ism": "Those who hold this doctrine only want to satisfy their own desires, and they want to force others by coercion and make them bend." During the First World War, the constitution order of China was divided by two governments in the North and South, each claiming itself to be the only legitimate central government, and warlords allied with them attacking each other. Li Dazhao perceived a "Pan-X doctrine" of infighting, which he differentiated from the expansionism of the great powers: "The 'Pan-X doctrine' of foreign powers develops externally; China's 'Pan-X doctrine' is to divide ourselves. Therefore, the 'Pan-X doctrine' of others is for magnification, while our country's 'Pan-X doctrine' is a 'minifying doctrine.'" The reason is that as a weak country, Chinese are unable to expand externally, so their 'contentious nature' can only be vented internally, and conflicts can only occur at the subnational provincial level. Li Dazhao argued that Yuan ShihKai's self-claimed monarchism and the warlordism of provincial military governors embodied this kind of minifying doctrine.[573]

In his article, Li Dazhao did not explicitly refer to the warlords' delineation and competition for spheres of influence as "Provincial Monroe Doctrine." However, as early as December 1912, Li Dazhao and his colleagues from the Beiyang Law and Politics Society linked Japan's Great Asianism with Monroe Doctrine in their edited volume *Refutation of the Destiny of China's Division*: "In recent years, Japanese people are advocating Asiatic Monroe Doctrine and Great Asianism. If you listen to what they say, you may think that they are

573 Li (n. 550), 245.

friends, but if you look into their hearts, you see they are enemies. This doctrine is a pretext for Japan's attempt to dominate East Asia."[574] From 1917 to 1918, Li Dazhao wrote many articles and continued to criticize Japan's Asian Monroe Doctrine and Far East Monroe Doctrine.[575] Li Dazhao's analogy between Japan's Great Asianism and the Chinese warlords' sphere of influence mentality was only a step away from referring to the Chinese warlord's sphere of influence mentality as a kind of Monroe Doctrine. Although Li Dazhao criticized the Provincial Monroe Doctrine of warlords during this period, there was still some hope for China's re-integration through federalism.[576] However, with the development of the United Provincial Autonomy Movement, Li increasingly perceived that local warlords and bureaucrats were resisting substantive unity under the slogan of federalism, and that those who actually wished to promote democratic autonomy at the provincial level while also promoting substantive unity throughout the country had no room to express their ideals. Li Dazhao and Sun Yat-sen therefore joined forces in August 1922, when they met in Shanghai and reached a consensus on opposing warlordism and unifying the entire country.

Li Dazhao was arrested by Zhang Zuolin on April 6, 1927. On that day, his last article was published in the 193rd issue of *Guide Weekly*, the official newspaper of the Central Committee of the Communist Party of China. "The Recent Political Situation in the North" (published under the pen name "Lie Wu" 列武) included the comment that "the military rule of the Fengtian faction always adheres to Monroe Doctrine, and no outsiders are allowed to participate."[577] Li Dazhao was executed on April 28, strangled by the Monroe Doctrine of the warlords that he had attacked. However, the new political party he had helped to create continued to promote social revolution in order to overcome the two Monroe Doctrines that he opposed. In this sense, we can say that the Chinese revolution after the First World War was closely related to

574 Li Dazhao 李大钊, "<Zhina fenge zhi yunming> boyi《支那分割之运命》驳议 [Refutation of the Destiny of zhina's Division]," in *Li Dazhao quanji* 李大钊全集 [*Complete Works of Li Dazhao*] (Volume II), eds. Zhu Wentong 朱文通 et al. (Shijiazhuang: *Hebei jiaoyu chubanshe*, 1999): 479.

575 Li Dazhao 李大钊, "Xin zhonghua minzu zhuyi 新中华民族主义 [New China Nationalism]," in *Li Dazhao quanji* 李大钊全集 [*Complete Works of Li Dazhao*] (Volume II), eds. Zhu Wentong 朱文通 et al. (Shijiazhuang: *Hebei jiaoyu chubanshe*, 1999): 281–286; "Jidong menluo zhuyi 极东们罗主义 [Extreme Eastern Romanticism]," in *Complete Works of Li Dazhao* (Volume I): 290.

576 Li Dazhao 李大钊, "Shengzhi yu xianfa 省制与宪法 [Provincial System and Constitution]," in *Li Dazhao quanji* 李大钊全集 [*Complete Works of Li Dazhao*] (Volume II), eds. Zhu Wentong 朱文通 et al. (Shijiazhuang: *Hebei jiaoyu chubanshe*, 1999): 211–227.

577 Li, Feng, and Zhou (n. 516), 71.

the discourse of Monroe Doctrine, which resisted Japanese regional hegemony under the banner of Asian Monroe Doctrine (or East Asian Monroe Doctrine) at the supranational level, and overcame the Provincial Monroe Doctrine of the warlords at the sub-national level for the overall reconstruction of the political, social and legal order. Although the Monroe Doctrine originated from the other side of the world and was a purely American specialty, it crossed the ocean, and after constant reinterpretation, finally became profoundly involved in the process of China's rebirth in the 20th century.

CHAPTER 5

The Disenchantment of the Asiatic Monroe Doctrine Discourse

> Asian brass, Asian brass
> After the drum beats, we should call the heart that dances in the dark the moon
> And the moon is mainly made up of you
>
> HAIZI, Asian Brass[578]

As a policy, the Asian Monroe Doctrine ended along with the Second World War. However, the attitude of China's cultural/political elites towards the Japanese Monroe Doctrine had changed from positive to negative long before then. Relating the spread of the Monroe Doctrine in China requires tracing the Chinese cultural/political elites' evolving understanding of Japan.

At the turn of the nineteenth century, both reformists and revolutionaries initially placed their hopes in the Japanese government and civil forces, and communicated with those who used the Asiatic Monroe Doctrine discourse. This situation originated with the Japanese government's policy towards China after the Sino-Japanese War. Japan had been under great pressure from the European and American powers since the Triple Intervention, so "discourse on the 'integrity' of China" was very popular in Japan for a time. The Japanese government was also actively investing in the future by vigorously absorbing Chinese students and sending people to China to lobby Chinese political and academic figures. In 1898, Tatung Translation Press, which was controlled by the reformists, published Tarui Tōkichi's *Theory of the Federation of Great East*, which had been published in Japan in 1893. Kang Youwei advocated "alliance with Japan" in 1897–1898, and even proposed that China, Japan, Britain and the U.S. should "unite as a federation."[579] After the failure of the Hundred Days Reform, Kang, Liang and others went into exile, and Japan became their key

578 Haizi 海子, *Haizi de shi* 海子的诗 [*Poems of Haizi*], (Nanchang: Jiangxi renmin chubanshe, 2017), 1.
579 Mao (n. 295), 387.

 DOI:10.1163/9789004746237_007

stronghold. At the same time, anti-Manchurian revolutionaries were also seeking the support of the Japanese government and people. As mentioned above, the anti-Manchu slogan "China for the Chinese" originated with Chinese elites in Japan, and was influenced by the American Monroe Doctrine as translated by Japan and by the resulting Japanese Monroe Doctrine.

However, as the situation progressed, the attitudes of representatives of China's intellectual and public opinion circles towards the Asiatic Monroe Doctrine was constantly divided. Among the Chinese intellectuals in Japan, Kang Youwei was probably one of the first to break away from Asiatic Monroe Doctrine. After the failure of the Hundred Days Reform, he went into exile in Japan and imitated Shen Baoxu's "appeal to the Qin court" in hopes of obtaining the support of the Japanese government to rescue Emperor Guangxu and continue to promote reform. In the process of seeking help, Kang Youwei also resorted to Japanese Asianism discourse. However, the Japanese government was afraid of the reaction of the European and American powers, and the Qing government also exerted pressure on the Japanese government to restrict the political activities of Kang et al. in Japan. After the Japanese government put pressure on Kang Youwei, he "voluntarily" left Japan for Canada in March 1899. For Kang Youwei, it was a rather dark experience. Before that, Kang's writings had held up Japan's Meiji Reform as an example; after that, Japan's status plummeted in his opinion. At the same time, Kang Youwei's North American-based Royalist Party relied on donations from overseas Chinese and did not try to obtain support from the Japanese government or Japanese individuals, and this financial independence largely explains why Kang was not greatly motivated to appeal to the Japanese government and public with Asianist discourse.[580]

580 At the beginning of the 20th century, Kang Youwei traveled around the world, and then set the German Second Reich under the leadership of Wilhelm II as a model of China. In the fragment of Kang Youwei's *Ta Tung Book*, published in 1913 in the journal *Bu Ren*, Kang Youwei even predicted that Germany would defeat Britain and unify Europe: "The weak will be destroyed in a hundred years, Sweden, Denmark, the Netherlands and Switzerland will merge with Germany. Spain and Portugal will merge with France at the beginning, and then will merge with Britain. However, Britain will change internally or lost in the war with Germany." Kang Youwei 康有为, *Datongshu* 大同书 [*Ta Tung Book*], in *Kang Youwei quanji* 康有为全集 [*Complete Works of Kang Youwei*] (Volume 5), eds. Jiang Yihua and Zhang Ronghua 姜义华、周荣华 (Beijing: Renmin daxue chubanshe, 2007): 132. It is worth mentioning that this text was not found in the manuscript of *Ta Tung Book* in the earlier period, so it is highly probable that Kang Youwei had made a new judgment on Germany by traveling Europe, and added this text when he published it. During World War I, Kang Youwei also opposed China's accession to the Allies to declare war on Germany. In 1917, he supported the restoration of Zhang Xun and the international support behind Zhang Xun came from Germany. Kang Youwei's apartment in Qingdao,

However, many modern Chinese cultural and political elites either lived in Japan or arrived there after Kang Youwei's departure. Their relationship with Japan's Asiatic Monroe Doctrine was more complicated, and their break with Asiatic Monroe Doctrine discourse was more tortuous. This chapter will focus on representative figures in Japanese Monroe Doctrine: Liang Qichao, the representative of constitutionalism and nationalism; Sun Yat-sen, the leader of the revolutionary group in the late Qing Dynasty and later the leader of China's Kuomintang; Chiang Kai-Shek, who gained control of the Kuomintang after Sun Yat-sen; and Li Dazhao, one of the founders of the Communist Party of China. This chapter will also discuss how the Warring States Strategy school, the members of which studied mainly in Europe and the U.S. rather than in Japan, regarded the Japanese Monroe Doctrine and the trend of world order, and how their discourse of "the Reemergence of the Warring States Period" gained acclaim among many members of the Youth Party, a "third power" separate from the KMT and CPC. We will see that Liang Qichao, the Youth Party and many nationalists in the Warring States Strategy school expected to replace the Japanese Asiatic Monroe Doctrine with an Asian order dominated by China. However, in Li Dazhao we can see the genuine transcendence of Monroe Doctrine discourse at that time—not the replacement of one regional hegemony with another, but reflection on the logic of hegemony itself. Outlining the full range of this thinking requires going back to the historical context and reviewing the statements of these thinkers.

1 Liang Qichao: Leader of the Disenchantment

Unlike Kang Youwei's "voluntary" departure under pressure from the Japanese government, Liang Qichao soon found that he could quickly understand and absorb Western knowledge by virtue of Japanese translations of Western learning, so he stayed in Japan for a long time and returned to China after the 1911 Revolution. Liang Qichao was influenced by the discourse of the Japanese Monroe Doctrine, but at the beginning of the twentieth century, he perceived its aggressive motivations and advocated the restoration of China's status as "leader of Asia" through self-improvement. In his subsequent political career, Liang Qichao had both pro-Japanese and anti-Japanese moments. Both were oriented by his calculation of political interest, and held little illusion concerning the Japanese Monroe Doctrine.

"Tianyou Garden," was originally the residence of the adjutant of the German Jiao'ao Governor.

In the early stage after his arrival Japan in 1898, Liang Qichao still held great expectations for Japan. His words echoed Japan's Asianism. When Liang Qichao founded *Qingyi Bao* (China Discussion) in December of that year, the four tenets stated in his "Xu Li" 叙例 (Foreword) were as follows: "First, to maintain discussion by the righteous literati of China and to stimulate the uprightness of the people; second, to increase the knowledge of the Chinese; third, to communicate the voices of China and Japan and improve their friendship; fourth, to develop East Asian learning in order to preserve Asian quintessence." He also called for "we four hundred million compatriots to jointly learn from it; we yellow people who hope to pursue the cause of Asian autonomy in the twentieth century to jointly support it."[581] Liang Qichao's words here strongly echoed the Asianism prevailing in Japan at that time. In the review article "On the Benefits of Learning Japanese," Liang Qichao discussed the significance of learning Japanese in this way: "Japan and China are interdependent. We must cooperate with each other to protect the independence of the yellow race and to stop European powers from expanding eastward. In the future, Japan and China will become a union. The interflow of language is the first essence of the alliance. Japanese scholars should therefore make learning Chinese their first priority, and Chinese scholars should make learning Japanese their first priority."[582] This passage expressed more Japanese Asianism.

However, by 1899, the tone of Liang Qichao's commentaries in *Qingyi Bao* had changed. This was most obvious in his article "On China's Strength for Independence and Japan's East Asia Policy" (论中国独立之实力与日本东方政策), in which Liang pointed out major blind spots in the Japanese discourse of "protecting Asian independence" and "following the balance of power of European states." He argued that neither discourse acknowledged the factors contributing to China's potential for self-protection, including the inclination toward unity in the Chinese race, geography and religion, the wisdom of Emperor Guangxu, the development of civil self-government, and the large number of overseas Chinese. If Japan decided to divide up China along with the European powers and the U.S., it would inevitably bring disaster upon itself. However, in Liang Qichao's opinion, Japan's policy of "preserving China" by making friends with Empress Dowager Cixi was also counterproductive.[583] At that time, Liang Qichao expected to achieve China's self-improvement by supporting Guangxu and implementing constitutional monarchy through bottom-up political mobilization. In his article "Preserving China" 保全支那,

581 Zhang (n. 167), 168.
582 Ibid., 324.
583 Ibid., 316–317.

Liang Qichao pointed out more directly: "The European and Japanese always claim to protect China, but this is the last thing I want to hear. If China needs to be preserved by others, she cannot be preserved; if China can be preserved, she does not need to rely on others. Those who say they want to protect others are violating others' liberty; those who expect others to protect them are giving up their liberty."[584] In this article, Liang Qichao applied the European liberalism he had learned through Japanese translation to the analysis of Japanese Monroe Doctrine.

In 1900, China was invaded by the Eight-Power Allied Forces and was on the verge of being divided up. In his commentary "On the Correct Treatment of China by the Great Powers Today" (论今日各国待中国之善法), Liang Qichao commented on several possible ways for the Great Powers to treat China. He pointed out that joint rule such as that by Britain and France in Egypt would not work in China, as the Great Powers would struggle with each other rather than coordinate with each other. Partition such as that of Poland by Prussia, Austria and Russia in the eighteenth century would encounter fierce resistance from the Chinese people. Liang Qichao not only observed the resistance of the Chinese people in the Boxer Movement, but also the Philippine revolution and the Boer War, which encouraged him to believe that resistance by weak and small nationalities had hope for success. As for the future, Liang Qichao affirmed the significance of the U.S. Open Door Policy to "preserve" China's land and autonomy, and said that "… Britain is the most advanced country in the world, Japan is our eastern brother, and its intentions towards China are similar to those of the U.S.. If the U.S. is willing to do this work, then Britain and Japan will follow."[585] This was the hope that the U.S., Japan and the United Kingdom would contain other powers from carving up China so as to maintain China's territorial integrity and political autonomy.

If "On the Correct Treatment of China by the Great Powers Today" was still full of wishful thinking toward the American Open Door Policy, Liang Qichao's 1901 essay "On the New Methods of Destroying the Country" (灭国新法论) went further by pointing out that even the Open Door Policy could be regarded as a new method for destroying the country: "Taking the whole country as a trading port amounts to taking the whole country as a colony."[586] Therefore, Japan's discourse on the "integrity" of China meant the restriction and deprivation of China's liberty, and the U.S. Open Door Policy was nothing but an instrument of imperialism.

---

584 Ibid., 358.
585 Ibid., 433–434.
586 Ibid., 474.

Liang Qichao's exile in Japan coincided with the U.S. taking the Philippines from Spain after the Spanish-American War. In the Asianist discourse atmosphere of Japan, Liang Qichao linked the Filipino's struggle for independence with Asian identity. Liang praised the Philippines for its resistance to Spain and the U.S. in his 1902 article "On the Implications of the U.S.-Philippines War and the Boer War to China" (论美菲律英杜之战事关系于中国). He argued that the Philippines was "the pioneer of advocating independence in Asia, and the beginning of yellow people's pursuit of civil rights!" If the Filipinos won, "it would cheer the yellow race and make the white race lose heart." Liang Qichao emphasized in particular that the grandmother of the leader of the Philippines independence movement was of Chinese origin, and many of his subordinates were also Chinese. If the Philippines became independent, Japan, the Philippines and China could support each other in the West Pacific and "work together to resist the European Powers expanding eastward."[587] Liang's discourse of "the rivalry between the yellow race and white race" reflected the significant influence of Japan's intellectual atmosphere at that time.

However, Liang Qichao did not accept the emphasis in Japanese Monroe Doctrine discourse on Japan's leading position in the "the struggle between the yellow race and white race." We gain a glimpse of his views on Asia from the article "On the General Trend of Asian Geography," which he wrote in the same year. In this article, Liang Qichao divided Asia into four parts: Siberia, China, India and Iran. The China section included countries such as China, Japan, Korea, Annam (Vietnam), Siam (Thailand), Myanmar, etc., populated by the "superior yellow race," as opposed to the "inferior yellow race" in Siberia. India was inhabited by the Caucasian race, while Iran was a mix of yellow and Caucasian races.[588] Obviously, Liang Qichao regarded China rather than Japan as the center of the world of the so-called "yellow race." Liang Qichao also argued: "God has high hopes for the Chinese, and allowed them experience countless difficulties and obstacles in order to teach them the lessons of their predecessors."[589] In his essay "On the General Trends of China's Geography" (中国地理大势论) written during the same period, he even more explicitly declared: "Asia is the leader of the whole earth; and China is the leader of Asia."[590]

The Russo-Japanese War in 1904 was an important moment for the surge in Japanese discourse on "the rivalry between the yellow race and white race," and exerted great influence on public opinion in China. At this time, however,

587 Ibid., 949.
588 Ibid., 923.
589 Ibid., 923.
590 Ibid., 926.

Liang Qichao wrote "Brief History of the Destruction of Korea" (朝鲜亡国史略),[591] which showed him maintaining a certain distance from the discourse of "rivalry between the yellow race and white race" in Japan. After Ōkuma Shigenobu delivered a speech on "Ōkumaism" at the founding meeting of the Qing-Korea Association of Waseda University, Liang Qichao quickly responded on October 23, 1904, by writing an article in *Xin Min Cong Bao* 新民丛报 that stated: "Okuma's opposition to the partition theory and his proposal for preservation could be dated to ten years ago. From what we Chinese have suffered, being partitioned and being preserved are equally humiliating, and there is no choice between the two."

Here, Liang Qichao reiterated exactly what he put forward in the article "Preserving China" (保全支那) by criticizing Okuma's exposition of "preserving China," but he suddenly changed his tone: "However, Okuma claimed that China can't be divided, which makes people exultated. He said that a state can perish by itself, but not through others, which is thought-provoking." Liang found some valuable insights in the "preservation theory" that he disagreed with. First, China could not be divided. Second, a country's demise was mainly due to internal and not external causes. Liang Qichao thought this could promote self-reflection among the Chinese: "Therefore, for ordinary Chinese people, it is a good suggestion." Liang Qichao generally affirmed the Okuma's thesis: "His theory, which rejects the concept of a sphere of influence, can be characterized as independent and fearless; his emphasis on shared ethnicity and teachings can be seen as valuing ancestral heritage. Japanese scholars have for a long time not considered themselves to belong to the same ethnic group as Chinese. I take no pride in flattering Japan; why should Japan keep us at a distance and treat us as a disgrace? Okuma is a respectable man."[592]

Therefore, in just a few years, Liang Qichao completed an extremely important turning point. Facing Japan's Asianism discourse, Liang Qichao agreed with the historical connection that emphasized "same language and same race," but emphasized that it was China, not Japan, that had played the role of "suzerain of Asia"; he agreed that China and Japan needed to support each other to resist the European and American powers at that moment, but opposed the "East Asian leader" posture toward China and Korea by Japanese Monroe Doctrine theorists, opposed Japan's "preserve China" theory, and advocated that China achieve self-preservation through self-reliance and self-strengthening. Liang Qichao underwent a cognitive transformation as well: from depending on

---

591 Ibid., 1537–1544.

592 Liang Qichao 梁启超, "Suowei dawei zhuyi 所谓大隈主义 [The so-called Okuma Doctrine]," *Xinmin congbao*, 57 (21 November 1904).

the United States' Open Door Policy for China's preservation, to recognizing that the Open Door Policy was merely a "new method for the destruction of a country." In the context of subsequent changes in the international situation in East Asia, when many people tried to use the United States Open Door Policy to restrict Japan's Asian Monroe Doctrine, Liang Qichao remained vigilant against both.

Liang Qichao returned to China in 1912 and organized the Progressive Party to compete with the Kuomintang in 1913. In 1915, Japan's Okuma Cabinet forced Yuan Shikai's government to accept its Twenty-one Demands. Liang Qichao wrote a commentary on Japanese oppression in the form of retelling a dialogue. He said that he had argued with people who doubted Japan's intentions: "The Japanese have declared many times that they will preserve the integrity of China, and do they have a reason to break their promise?" However, critics refuted this argument by citing how Japan declared its intentions to preserve the integrity of Korea, but then eventually annexed Korea. "I didn't know how to respond."[593] Under pressure, Yuan Shikai's government finally accepted Japan's Twenty-one Demands, and Liang Qichao expressed great indignation at the Japanese government, saying that "Japan is the Russia of the past."[594] This not only meant that Japan was as aggressive as Russia, but also that in terms of civilizational hierarchy, Japan's claim to be more civilized than Russia since the Russo-Japanese War was simply untenable.

But this did not mean that Liang Qichao had completely broken with the Japanese government. Soon, in response to Yuan Shikai's move to become emperor, Liang Qichao published his essay "The Strange So-called National Body Issue." After that, he traveled from Beijing to Shanghai, Hong Kong and Vietnam, and then re-entered Yunnan from Guangxi to meet with Cai E and launch the National Protection Movement. Along the way, he received support from Japanese officials and civilians. Based on Liang Qichao's memories in his later years, Japanese scholar Naoki Hazama 狭间直树 said that Liang Qichao reflected on why the Japanese helped him during the National Protection Movement and saw through Japan's true intentions. "He felt horror and disgust, and began to be vigilant," thus establishing a stable view of Japan.[595] However, this argument ignored the possibility of Liang Qichao whitewashing

593 Liang Qichao 梁启超, "Zhongri zuijin jiaoshe pingyi 中日最近交涉平议 [The Recent Negotiation between China and Japan]," in Zhang (n. 167): 2760.

594 Liang Qichao 梁启超, "Zaijinggao waijiao dangju 再警告外交当局 [Warn the Diplomatic Authorities Again]," in Zhang (n. 167): 2770.

595 Naoki Hazama, Gao Yingying 高莹莹 trans., *Dongya jindai wenmingshi shangde Liang Qichao* 东亚近代文明史上的梁启超 [*Liang Qichao in the Modern Civilization History of East Asia*], (Shanghai: Shanghai renmin chubanshe, 2016), 120.

himself in retrospect, especially by ignoring his pro-Japanese policy after the National Protection Movement.

In 1916, Yuan Shikai failed in his attempt to become emperor and announced the restoration of the republic. He soon fell ill and died. Li Yuanhong 黎元洪 became President, but Prime Minister Duan Qirui 段祺瑞 held the real power in the Beijing government. Liang Qichao became close to the pro-Japanese Duan Qirui. According to the recollections of Kamezo Nishihara 西原亀三, who vigorously promoted the Nishihara Loan in 1917, after arriving in Beijing on February 16, 1917, he "held talks with senior advisers such as Cao Rulin, Liang Qichao and Wang Daxie for several days, and visited Premier Duan."[596] Beijing's declaration of war against Germany triggered the "dispute between the President and the Premiere," which led to the Zhang Xun Restoration in July. After quelling the Zhang Xun Restoration, Duan Qirui reorganized the cabinet, with Liang Qichao as Minister of Finance. Nishihara Kamezo recalls that he was unwell on July 11–12 and was eager to return home, "but Minister of Finance Liang Qichao repeatedly asked him to stay and negotiate on China's financial issues. Liang proposed a loan request. Over the next ten days, he discussed the resumption of loans from the Bank of Communications, arranging a Bank of China loan and Fengtian loan, etc."[597] As Minister of Finance, Liang Qichao supported Duan Qirui in accepting the Nishihara Loan from the Japanese government, participating in World War I and training Chinese troops to seek military unification of the country. Some of the policies he implemented actually consolidated Japan's dominant position in China after the Twenty-one Demands. After the United States and Japan signed the Lansing-Ishii Agreement on November 2, Zeng Qi 曾琦 wrote a letter to Liang Qichao, urging him to retreat: "You cannot save the country, but instead you and your comrades are labeled as traitors. You should wake up from your foolish dream of the future."[598]

In addition, after the Zhang Xun Restoration, Liang Qichao strongly advocated convening a Provisional Senate to formulate a new constitution rather than restoring the original Provisional Constitution.[599] Duan Qirui's government accepted Liang Qichao's idea and refused to restore the Provisional

596 Wang Yunsheng 王芸生 ed., *Liushinianlai Zhongguo yu Riben* 六十年来中国与日本 [*China and Japan in the Past 60 Years*] (Volume 7), (Beijing: Shenghuo, Dushu, Xinzhi sanlian shudian, 1981), 201.

597 Ibid., 212.

598 Ding Wenjiang and Zhao Fengtian 丁文江、赵丰田 eds., *Liang Qichao nianpu changbian* 梁启超年谱长编 [*Long Chronicle of Liang Qichao*], (Shanghai: Shanghai renmin chubanshe, 1983), 853.

599 Ibid., 831–832.

Constitution, which led to a split in the constitutional order of the Republic of China. Sun Yat-sen went to South China and launched a Movement to Protect the Constitution under the banner of defending the Provisional Constitution.

Liang Qichao expected that his Yan Jiu Xi ("the research faction," whose core members included Tang Hualong, Zhang Dongsun, Lin Changmin, Lan Gongwu, etc.) would become the largest party in the newly convened congress, and he that this would enable him to serve as Prime Minister. However, after the political struggles in the early Republic of China, the Beiyang warlords had become more adept at playing the game of constitutional politics. In 1918, the Anfu faction dominated the elections for congress, and Liang Qichao's Yan Jiu Xi was marginalized. This created tensions in the relationship between Liang Qichao and the Beiyang Anhui faction.

The end of World War I brought new expectations to Liang Qichao. At the end of 1918, Liang Qichao, Ding Wenjiang, Zhang Junmai, Xu Xinliu, Jiang Baili, Liu Chongjie and Yang Weixin sailed to Europe on the Japanese ship Yokohama, aiming to play a role in the post-war peace negotiations. At the same time, the Yan Jiu Xi also enhanced its profile in China. On January 18, 1919, the Paris Peace Conference began in Versailles, and the negotiations continued until June 28, when the Versailles Peace Treaty was signed. Liang Qichao and others arrived in London on February 11. On February 16, the National Diplomatic Association initiated by the Yan Jiu Xi was established in Xiong Xiling's apartment, and Liang Qichao was elected a director in absentia. On February 18, Liang Qichao went to Paris to observe the Paris Peace Conference. He remained in France until he left for England on June 7.

In the process of observing the peace conference, Liang Qichao kept sending back messages to his colleagues in the Yan Jiu Xi such as Lin Changmin 林长民 (then the purser of the Foreign Affairs Committee of the Office of President, Beiyang Government, and director of the National Foreign Affairs Association), and widely disseminated them through Yan Jiu Xi-controlled media. Liang Qichao paid close attention to negotiations on the Shandong issue. In a telegram to Lin Changmin and others in mid-March, he had attacked Zhang Zongxiang, Cao Rulin and others in the Anhui faction.[600] Before long, after learning about the decision of the Paris Peace Conference on the Shandong issue, Liang Qichao sent a telegram from Paris to Lin Changmin and others. Lin Changmin published "Diplomatic Alert to the People" in the *Morning Post*

600 The Compilation Office of Modern History Materials, Institute of Modern History, Chinese Academy of Social Sciences eds., *Miji lucun (jindaishi ziliao zhuankan)* 秘笈录存（近代史资料专刊） [*Secret Records (Special Issue of Modern History Materials)*], (Beijing: Zhongguo shehuikexue chubanshe, 1984), 133.

on May 2, which had a great impact in China. Two days later, the May Fourth Movement broke out, and the masses demanded the punishment of Cao Rulin, Zhang Zongxiang, Lu Zongyu and others. This was due to the public opinion efforts of Liang Qichao, Lin Changmin and others. This movement struck a heavy blow to the pro-Japanese Anhui faction, leading to the emergence of the Beiyang clique's Zhili faction.

On June 3, 1919, Lin Changmin published "A Letter to the Japanese" in *Shen Bao*, refuting Japan's recent claims in five aspects. The last aspect was Japan's Asiatic Monroe Doctrine: "Japan advocates the distinction between the yellow race and the white race, as well as the boundary between Europe, America and we in Asia; the United States has the Monroe Doctrine, and we in Asia should also follow this doctrine. Asian issues should be decided by our Asian countries, not by other countries. China and Japan's issues should be decided by the Chinese and Japanese, not by other peoples." Lin Changmin pointed out that all these statements sounded very good, but Japan's actual behavior was to constantly encroach on Asian countries and humiliate countries of "the same race": "When there is an opportunity, they will try to advance; when they are unable to do so, they will bring in powerful neighbors from different continents to enhance their interests and consolidate their position." This was a stigmatization of the Monroe Doctrine.[601] As for the argument that the Sino-Japanese issue should be determined by China and Japan themselves, Lin Changmin argued that it was just a superficial statement. What was the explanation for Japan signing secret treaties with Britain, France, Italy, the United States and other countries to deal with China's interests? Lin Changmin rebutted Japan's claim of "self-preservationism of the same continent and fraternity of the same race" by citing the Twenty-one Demands imposed on China by Japan in 1915.

These points were probably the result of discussions with Liang Qichao. Liang Qichao met Lin Changmin when the latter was studying abroad. In the early years of the Republic of China, they cooperated to establish the Progressive Party 进步党, which evolved into the Yan Jiu Xi 研究系. They maintained close cooperation from then on. In April 1919, Liang Qichao telegraphed to Lin Changmin: "All my speeches, writings, and interviews with dignitaries follow your instructions."[602]

Liang Qichao paid close attention to the U.S. and Japanese Monroe Doctrine from the perspective of his *Records of My European Travels*, which was written

601 The Compilation Office of Modern History Materials, Institute of Modern History, Chinese Academy of Social Sciences eds., *Wusi aiguo yundong* 五四爱国运动 [*The May 4th Patriotic Movement*] (1), (Beijing: Zhishi chanquan chubanshe, 2013), 336–340.

602 *Morning News* 129 (23 April 1919).

late in the journey and was first published in Shanghai's *Shishi Xinbao* 时事新报 in March 1920. This was probably the last time that Liang Qichao focused on the U.S. and Japanese Monroe Doctrine. In "Europe Before and After the War," written early in the journey, Liang Qichao summed up many great historical turning points brought about by the war, one of which was U.S. participation in the war: "Who would dare to say that the United States, which tightly shuts its doors and talks about the Monroe Doctrine at home, would become so popular and meddle in the affairs of people across the sea."[603]

The Monroe Doctrine was the focus of Liang Qichao's discussion in the chapter "The Review of League of Nations" written late in his journey through Europe. He discussed Wilson's struggle with Congress after he returned from the Paris Peace Conference: "It turns out that Americans have a traditional idea of history. They are afraid that Europeans will interfere in American affairs. So the Monroe doctrine has become an invisible golden rule." Republicans were deeply resentful of Wilson and used their opposition to the League of Nations to force Wilson to compromise and add the ideas of the Monroe Doctrine to Article 21 of the League of Nations Covenant. Liang Qichao commented: "This makes the covenant look like a weird mixture of things."[604] Liang Qichao believed that the reason why the world wanted to establish this grand alliance was that "the former partial alliances (such as the Entente and the central powers) are actually the original motivating force for disturbing the peace." In order to eliminate these partial alliances, it was necessary to make a grand alliance of all countries. Wilson had emphasized this in his previous speeches, but he ultimately added the Monroe Doctrine clause to the Covenant of the League of Nations: "It is a contradiction to recognize that there is an alliance in the alliance." Liang Qichao thought that this article was the most fragmenting one. It introduced the Monroe Doctrine in a general way and disturbed other international agreements and declarations. In fact, it violated the fundamental spirit of the League. At the same time, this article aroused the dissatisfaction of other powers. Britain and Japan took advantage of the situation and demanded maintaining the Anglo-Japanese alliance. Japan even advocated invoking the Monroe Doctrine to assert its special status in China, but the result was "the same old tricks from before the war."[605]

During World War I, the relationship between the U.S. and Mexico underwent fluctuations. Wilson's government launched the Pershing Expedition to Mexico in 1916. On July 24, 1916, the "Zimmerman Secret Telegram" sent by

603 Zhang (n. 167), 2969.
604 Ibid., 3035.
605 Ibid., 3040–3041.

Germany to the Mexican government to propose an alliance against the U.S. was intercepted and made public. Although the Mexican government denied the alliance with Germany, the relationship between the U.S. and Mexico remained cold. Mexico was dissatisfied with the provision in Article 21 of the Covenant of the League of Nations on the Monroe Doctrine, and Wilson opposed the inclusion of Mexico as a founding member of the League of Nations at the Paris Peace Conference.[606] Liang Qichao noticed that the League of Nations did not extend an invitation to Mexico, and he expressed his "utter puzzlement" about this: "Some newspaper people said that because the U.S. and Mexico are hostile to each other, the U.S. rejected her. Indeed, the U.S. is too mean. As Mexico was already in an isolated situation, its president made a speech in Congress (in September last year) to declare, 'As for the organization and operation of the organs of the League of Nations, Mexico will not join in until all races are completely equal.' He also said, 'The Monroe Doctrine is clearly recognized in the covenant, which infringes on Mexico's sovereignty. Mexico cannot recognize it.' Some people say that these words were manipulated by the Japanese behind the scenes. I dare not say that they are definitely right, but the old saying is good that 'a dam worth thousands of pieces of gold can be breached by an ant hole.' It is uncertain whether the League of Nations will be damaged in the future due to the U.S.-Mexico issue."[607]

The League of Nations Covenant stipulated that the United States, Britain, France, Italy and Japan were permanent members, and there were four other non-permanent members. Liang Qichao complained that Asia was not adequately represented in the Council of the League of Nations, with only Japan as a member. "If we say that we rely on Japan to represent Asia, this is no different from recognizing Japan's Asian Monroe Doctrine. This alone is enough to trigger another world war."[608] Liang Qichao's solution was clear. He thought that since even Spain could be a (non-permanent) Council member, China's degree of political progress was not far behind that of Spain, and China should strive to become a member of the Council of League of Nations. This reminds us of his claim in his 1902 "On the General Tide of China's Geography" that "Asia is the suzerain of the whole earth; and China is the suzerain of Asia."[609]

Starting in 1916, Liang Qichao's political stance underwent a reversal from pro-Japanese to anti-Japanese. The main reason for this reversal was not a

606 Philip Marshall Brown, "Mexico and the Monroe Doctrine," *The American Journal of International Law*, Vol. 26, No. 1 (January, 1932), 117–121.
607 Zhang (n. 167), 3036.
608 Ibid., 3037.
609 Ibid., 926.

change in Liang Qichao's understanding of Japan's strategic intentions, but rather because of profound changes in China's domestic politics. As early as the beginning of the twentieth century, Liang Qichao had already seen covert aggressive intentions in Japan's Asiatic Monroe Doctrine and regarded it, along with the United States Open Door Policy, as a "new way to destroy a country." For Liang Qichao, who was adept at gaining advantages from different sides, being pro-Japanese or pro-American in specific foreign policies became a strategic issue based on calculated interest rather than a question of belief, emotion or even identity.

2 Sun Yat-sen: Financial Autonomy and Discursive Autonomy

After the Sino-Japanese War of 1894–1895, the Japanese government was eager to be recognized as a "first-class nation" by the Western powers and canceled its consular jurisdiction, but at the same time it was worried about its own destruction through the Western powers' partitioning of China. Therefore, in terms of foreign policy, the Japanese government paid close attention to trends among the European and American powers and made sure not to violate the general trend, while at the same time giving limited support to Asianist civil movements. In 1898, Konoe Atsumaro, the Speaker of the House of Lords, became president of the Association for the Unification of East Asian Languages 東亜同文会, which was a manifestation of this trend.

In the late nineteenth and early twentieth centuries, Japan became a gathering place for revolutionary patriots from various Asian countries. From the anti-Manchu revolution to the Third Revolution against Yuan Shikai, Sun Yat-sen was able to obtain a degree of resource support from the Japanese government or public. The practical consequence of this resource connection was that Sun often responded positively to Japan's Asianism in his own discourse. After Yuan Shikai failed to become emperor and passed away, the Japanese government supported Duan Qirui as the new head of the Beijing government. As Sun's resource connections with Japan weakened, he gradually moved away from the Asianism discourse led by Japan and turned to a more autonomous interpretation.

During the Sino-Japanese War, Sun Yat-sen had a talk with Japanese businessman Umeya Shōkichi 梅屋莊吉 in Hong Kong in February 1895. He pointed out that China was in danger of being divided up by the Western European colonial powers, and all Asian countries might become slaves of Western Europe. "Unfortunately, there is a war between China and Japan, but we must unite. We should extricate China from the crisis of colonization. This is the first step in defending Asia. In order to save China, my comrades and I are preparing to launch a revolution to overthrow the Qing Dynasty."[610] Umeya Shokichi was moved by Sun's claims, and through his intervention, Sun Yat-sen met in March with Nakagawa Kōjirō 中川恒次郎, the Japanese consul in Hong Kong, hoping that he would support Sun's Guangzhou Uprising. The Japanese government took a conservative stand on this matter, but Umeya Shokichi raised funds and purchased weapons for Sun Yat-sen through personal channels.

Sun's Guangzhou Uprising plan soon failed, and he went into exile in Japan in November 1895. While in Japan, Sun was in contact with Ōkuma Shigenobu 大隈重信, Oishi Masami 大石正己, Ozaki Yukio 尾崎行雄, Soejima Taneomi 副島種臣, Inukai Tsuyoshi 犬养毅, Tōyama Mitsuru 頭山満, Miyazaki Torazo 宮崎寅藏, Hirayama Shū 平山周, Uchida Ryohei 内田良平, Hiraoka Kōtarō 平岡浩太郎, Akiyama Sadasuke 秋山定辅, Nakano Tokujirō 中野徳次郎, Suzuki Goro 铃木五郎, Yasukawa Keiichirō 安川敬一郎, Inuzuka Shintarō 犬塚信太郎, Yamada Yoshimasa 山田良政, Kuhara Fusanosuke 久原房之助, Yamada Junzaburō 山田純三郎, Kikuchi Ryoichi 菊池良一, Kayano Nagatomo 萱野長知, Soejima Yoshikazu 副岛义一, Terao Toru 寺尾亨 and other Japanese elites, remarking that "people with lofty ideals have given so much support to the Chinese revolution."[611] Correspondingly, Sun Yat-sen's discourse at that time responded positively to Japanese Asianism. For example, in written correspondence with Miyazaki Tozo 宮崎寅藏 and Hirayama Shū 平山周 in mid-to-late August 1897, Sun emphasized "wiping out the humiliation of East Asia and the yellow race" through the Chinese Revolution.[612] In correspondence with Miyazaki Torazo 宮崎寅藏 in August 1898, he agreed with Miyazaki that "China and Japan should unite as the leaders of Asia … to stop the West from aggrandizing in the East," and in regarded Russia as the enemy.[613] In a discussion with Zhang Taiyan 章太炎 in the spring 1902 over where China should establish its capital, he showed a strong sense of Asianism: "If we focus on the central part of China, we should establish the capital in Wuchang; if we focus on the

610 The Literature and History Research Committee of Guangdong Provincial Political Consultative Conference eds., *Sun Yat-sen yu xinhai geming shiliao zhuanji* 孙中山与辛亥革命史料专辑 [*Special Collection of Historical Materials of Sun Yat-Sen and the Revolution of 1911*], (Guangzhou: Guangdong renmin chubanshe, 1981), 259–270.

611 Research Office of the Republic of China, Institute of Modern History, Chinese Academy of Social Sciences, eds., *Complete Works of Sun Yat-Sen* (Volume 6), (Beijing: Zhonghua shuju, 1986), 232–233.

612 *Complete Works of Sun Yat-Sen* (Volume 1), 174, 216, 243.

613 Ibid., 181–182.

frontier of China, we should establish the capital in Xi'an; and if we focus on the whole continent, we should establish the capital in Ili."[614]

On August 20, 1905, the Revolutionary Alliance led by Sun Yat-sen held its inaugural meeting at the residence of the Japanese industrialist Sakamoto Kinya 坂本金弥 (member of the House of Representatives, and member of the Association for the Unification of East Asian Languages), who was from southern Akasaka District in Tokyo. Umeya Shōkichi 梅屋莊吉 established a China Revolutionary Alliance Support Office to raise funds in Japan to support the activities of the Revolutionary Alliance. Miyazaki Tozo 宮崎寅蔵, Hirayama Shū 平山周, Kayano Nagatomo 萱野長知, Wada Saburo 和田三郎, Ike Kyōkichi 池亨吉, Kita Ikki 北一輝 and others joined the Revolutionary Alliance and participated in Sun Yat-sen's revolutionary cause. Uchida Ryohei 内田良平, Hirayama Shū 平山周, and Kita Ikki 北一輝 were members of the Kokuryūkai 黒龍会 that coveted Northeast China. At that time, the revolutionary discourse of the Revolutionary Alliance was influenced by both the traditional discourse of "distinction between Yi and Xia" and the nationalist discourse that emphasized the sovereignty of a single ethnic group. It focused on "anti-Manchuism" and called for the establishment of a Han Chinese republic. In terms of territorial imagination, it focused on the so-called eighteen provinces of so-called "China proper," while viewing Japan as a restraining force on Russian influence. At that time, many Asianists in Japan advocated "preserving China," but the China they were trying to preserve was the so-called "China proper," so their theory of "preserving China" could coexist with their aspirations in Northeast China. The strong presence of Russian forces in Northeast China provided a common enemy for the Revolutionary Alliance and Japan's Asianists.

Sun Yat-sen further developed his ideas of Asian revolution in Japan. When the Filipino people raised troops to oppose the U.S. aggression in 1899, the Japanese military was determined to aid the Philippines, but the Ministry of Foreign Affairs resolutely opposed it. At that time, Sun planned to take members of the Hsing Chung Hui to help the Philippine Revolution, and once they succeeded, Sun then could launch a revolution in China with the help of the Filipino people.[615] Chen Shaobai 陈少白 said that Sun's goal was to "make the Philippines independent first, and then use the remaining strength to help the Chinese revolution succeed, to lay the foundation for the Asian Alliance, and to resist the powers that ostensibly advocate fraternity but are

614 Ibid., 215.

615 Duan Yunzhang 段云章 ed., *Sun Wen yu riben shishi biannian* 孙文与日本史事编年 [*Chronicle of Sun Wen and Japanese History*] (updated edition), (Guangzhou: Guangdong renmin chubanshe, 2011), 51–52, 68–70.

actually inhumane, and expel them from Asia."[616] Through his relationships in the Japanese military, Sun helped Filipino revolutionaries purchase and transport ordnance, and Japanese who supported Sun gave their lives in the process. According to Pensi, an independent in the Philippines, Sun eagerly supported the East Asian Youth Association organized by students from China, Korea, Japan, India, Philippines, Siam and other Asian countries in Tokyo.[617] Statistics from the Japanese Metropolitan Police Department, which monitored Sun Yat-sen's activities in Japan at the time, showed that Sun Yat-sen met with Indian revolutionaries twenty-nine times during the period from 1914 to 1915 alone.[618]

However, it was difficult for the Japanese government to publicly support Sun. First, it could not ignore pressure from the Qing government, and second, after the establishment of the Anglo-Japanese alliance in 1902, Japan was even more cautious about Sun Yat-sen's launching of a revolution in southern China, which was close to the British sphere of influence. The Japanese government closely monitored Sun's activities in Japan lest they harm British interests. In 1900, the Japanese cabinet at one point ordered Japanese people not to participate in the Chinese revolution, and the Governor-General of Taiwan under Japanese rule expelled Sun from the country.[619] In 1907, the Japanese government gave Sun a severance payment as a "gift to leave the country." When Sun passed through Japan in 1910, the Ministry of Foreign Affairs and the Military Ministry had a disagreement over whether to allow Sun to stay. In the end, the Military Ministry's opinion prevailed, and Sun had a short stay in Japan.

Compared with Zhang Taiyan's Asian discourse, Sun Yat-sen's discourse in the Revolutionary Alliance was more expedient and flexible. Zhang Taiyan published the article "Asians Should Be Interdependent on Each Other" in *Shi Wu Bao* in 1897, advocating solidarity with Japan and rejecting Russia to achieve "peace and prosperity in Asia."[620] Zhang Taiyan's observations on the circumstances in East Asia in 1899 still regarded Germany and Russia as the greatest threats, so he believed that China could unite Japan, Britain and the U.S. to contain Germany and Russia. This judgment was not fundamentally

616 Ibid., 59.

617 Ibid., 75.

618 Yu Xintun, Wang Zhensuo, 俞辛焞、王振锁 et al. eds., Sun Yat-sen zairi huodong milu (1913 nian 8 yue–1916 nian 4 yue) 孙中山在日活动密录（1913年8月 – 1916年4月）[*A Secret Record of Sun Yat-Sen's Activities in Japan (August 1913 ~ April 1916)*], (Tianjin: Nankai daxue chubanshe, 1990).

619 Duan (n. 614), 101.

620 *Complete Works of Zhang Taiyan, Supplement to Records of Taiyan Literature (1)* (n. 317), 341, 4–6.

different from that of Kang et al. at the time. He even thought that the U.S. occupation of the Philippines would bring more advantages than disadvantages for East Asia, by helping the U.S. play a role in balancing the European powers.[621] The performance of the Qing government during the invasion of China by the Eight-Power Allied Army in 1900 caused a great shock to Zhang Taiyan. His position changed from promoting reform of the Qing government to calling for an anti-Manchu revolution. In 1906, Zhang Taiyan joined the Revolutionary Alliance and once served as the editor-in-chief of *Min Bao*. When *Min Bao* was in financial difficulties and could not get funding from Sun Yat-sen, Zhang Taiyan thought of sending Tao Chengzhang to raise money from overseas Chinese in Southeast Asia, rather than from the governments of foreign powers.

In 1907, Zhang Taiyan joined with Japanese and Indian patriots in initiating preparations for the establishment of the Asian Friendship Association. The Charter of the Asian Friendship Association drafted by Zhang Taiyan emphasized "Asian Harmony" with China and India as the main axis, as well as resistance to imperialism, but did not mention Japan at all. Furthermore, Zhang Taiyan wrote several articles criticizing Japan's invasion of Korea. Indeed, he didn't seek revolutionary funding from the Japanese government at all.

In contrast, Sun Yat-sen went to all sides to raise funds for the revolution, not only trying to gain support from the Japanese government and the private sector, but also trying to cooperate with revolutionaries in the Philippines, India and other places, leading to fluctuations in his Asianism discourse. When facing potential Japanese collaborators, his Asianism discourse would emphasize Japan's exemplary role, in hopes that the Japanese government and private sector would support his revolution. At the same time, he would inevitably acquiesce to certain vested interests in Japan and ignore certain acts of aggression. When facing revolutionaries in the Philippines, India and so on, Sun would emphasize the need for weak and small nations to unite against oppressors, but rarely criticized Japan as an imperialist power. In a conversation with a Japanese reporter in early March 1911, Sun Yat-sen also directly used the term "Asiatic Monroe Doctrine." He strongly condemned the Canadian government's policy of discriminating against the Asian diasporas, and declared that "he actively supports the plan of certain Japanese politicians to convene a conference of Asian countries to establish an alliance of Asian countries, and to call on Japan to lead Asian countries to oppose Britain, the U.S., France, Germany and Russia." He pointed out: "Only when a revolution occurs in China

621 Ibid., 126–127.

and India wakes up from its deep sleep can Asian countries unite and implement Asiatic Monroe Doctrine."[622]

After the Wuchang Uprising broke out in October 1911, the great powers headed by Britain coordinated with each other to maintain "financial neutrality" with China, making loans to neither the Qing government nor the revolutionary party. Sun received news of the outbreak of the Wuchang Uprising in Denver, Colorado, and immediately contacted the governments of the great powers in an attempt to borrow loans for the Revolutionary Party. However, the U.S., Britain and France all rejected Sun's loan request. When Sun returned to China in December, he did not bring back any money from the foreign powers for the Revolutionary Party in Nanjing. Due to an adjustment in Japan's foreign policy, the Nanjing Provisional Government obtained a small amount of loans from Japan at the beginning of 1912, but Britain quickly stopped Japan's financial support to the revolutionaries. In the end, Yuan Shikai, supported by the great powers, harvested the fruits of the revolution, rising from prime minister of the Qing court to interim president of the Republic of China.[623]

In September 1912, Yuan Shikai appointed Sun Yat-sen to supervise the establishment of national railways. Because Russia supported the independence of Outer Mongolia during the Revolution of 1911, the Chinese government and public felt deeply threatened by Russia. Sun advocated that Yuan Shikai's government should adopt a "pro-Japan" policy, and Yuan Shikai agreed that Sun could visit Japan in his personal capacity. While the first National Assembly election was still underway, Sun traveled to Japan in February 1913 to promote his "pro-Japan" policy and raised funds for China's railway construction. From February to March, Sun Yat-sen delivered many speeches in Japan with a strong Asianist tone:

- In a speech at the welcome meeting of the Association for the Unification of Asian Languages in Japan on February 15, Sun Yat-sen pointed out that China and Turkey had both undergone revolutions in recent years, but that China had not fallen into a tragic situation like Turkey. The reason was that China had a strong neighbor like Japan serving as backup. Sun Yat-sen reiterated the Japanese slogan "Asia for the Asians" and said that "Asian people should have the obligation to maintain peace in Asia. However, China now lacks the strength to maintain it, so Japan has a great responsibility." Japan was the "strongest country" in Asia, and China was the "biggest country" in the East. By supporting each other, the two countries

622 Wang Gengxiong 王耿雄 et al. ed., *Sun Yat-senji waiji* 孙中山集外集 [*Sun Yat-Sen's Collection*] (Volume 1), (Shanghai: Shanghai renmin chubanshe, 1990), 150.

623 See Zhang (n. 332).

could maintain peace not only in the East, but also in the world.[624] In a speech at the welcome meeting of the Japanese-Chinese student group in Japan on February 22, Sun also proposed to students studying in Japan: "Your vocation is to protect the reputation of East Asia, to maintain the power of East Asia, to make sure that alien powers will not encroach on East Asia."[625]

- In his speech at the Chinese Students Welcome Conference in Tokyo on February 23, Sun Yat-sen pointed out: "At this moment, two of the five continents, Australia and Africa, are controlled by white people. The responsibility for preserving the Asian continent should belong to our yellow people." He also thanked Japan on behalf of the Revolutionaries: "Had it not been for Japan, the future of East Asia would have been completely dark. With the help of Japan, our revolutionary cause in East Asia has been successful. For the success of China's revolution, we cannot but thank Japan." Finally, he called on Chinese and Japanese students to work together: "The Asian population, which accounts for two-thirds of the entire earth, is now partly under the sphere of influence of the Europeans. If China and Japan work together, our power will expand, and it will not be difficult to create a Great Asia and restore the glorious history of the past. We could make the world peaceful, we could make great harmony for humanity, and we could bring everyone the rights of equality and liberty."[626] At the Osaka welcome party on March 10, Sun Yat-sen said, "I hope that from now on, we will jointly defend against the invasion of European powers and make sure that the Orient is for the Orientals."[627]
- Sun Yat-sen also said in his speech at the Overseas Chinese dinner party organized by the Chinese Consulate in Nagasaki on March 22: "With regard to China's future, some people have advocated that we rely on the aid of the U.S.. However, China cannot rely on the U.S. Monroe Doctrine. Does the U.S. have the power to control the destiny of China?" Sun contended that

624 Sun Yat-Sen 孙中山, "Zai Riben dongya tongwenhui huanyinghui de yanshuo 在日本东亚同文会欢迎会的演说 [Speech at the Welcome Meeting of East Asian Commonwealth Association in Japan] (February 15, 1913)," in *Complete Works of Sun Yat-Sen* (Volume III), (Beijing: Zhonghua shuju, 1982): 15–16.

625 Sun Yat-Sen 孙中山, "Riben rihua xueshegntuan huanyinghui shangde yanshuo 日本日华同学团欢迎会上的演说 [Speech at the Welcome Meeting of Japan-China Student Group]," in *Complete Works of Sun Yat-Sen* (Volume III): 21.

626 Sun Yat-Sen 孙中山, "Zai dongjing Zhongguo liuxuesheng huanyinghui shangde yanshuo 在东京中国留学生欢迎会上的演说 [Speech at the Welcome Conference for Chinese Students in Tokyo] (February 23rd, 1913)," in *Complete Works of Sun Yat-Sen* (Volume III): 26–27.

627 *Complete Works of Sun Yat-Sen* (Volume III), 41.

"only Japan has the power to destroy the future of China."[628] These remarks raised doubts in the U.S. government and public opinion. The China-based English-language newspaper *China Press* 大陆报, sponsored by the Americans, published quite negative comments on Sun Yat-sen's relationship with Japan.[629]

When China's first National Assembly election ended in March 1913, the Kuomintang became the largest party in Congress. Song Jiaoren 宋教仁 was elated with the KMT's success and prepared to go north to form a cabinet. The assassination of Song in Shanghai on March 20 aroused the anger of the revolutionary camp against the Beiyang government. Sun Yat-sen returned to Shanghai on March 27, and convened a meeting at Huang Xing 黄兴's apartment that night. Sun advocated preemptive strikes against Yuan Shikai by force. He proposed a "quick battle" with the "help of Japan," but the majority opinion represented by Huang Xing was to resolve the matter by "legal methods."[630] From April 26 to 27, the Yuan government officially signed the "Chinese Government Rehabilitation Loan Contract" to borrow a total of 25 million pounds from the five great powers: Britain, France, Germany, Russia and Japan. Yuan soon obtained loans from foreign powers to strengthen his troops. On May 17, Sun sent a letter to the Japanese veteran Inoue Kaoru 井上馨 about the case of Song Jiaoren, hoping that the Japanese government would put forward new conditions for Yuan Shikai's "rehabilitation loan" to prohibit the use of the loan for military purposes. Sun believed that one of the crimes of Yuan Shikai's government was colluding with the Russians, and that the government "will rely on the power of Europe to reject our interests and friends."[631] Obviously, Sun was appealing to the mental framework of Japan's Greater Asianism.

The Second Revolution broke out in South China in July 1913, but was quickly suppressed by the Beiyang government. On August 7, 1913, the *New York Times* reported that Sun had fled to Taiwan on a Japanese ship after the failure of the Second Revolution. The subtitle particularly emphasized that it was a

628 Sun Yat-Sen 孙中山, "Zai changqi Zhongguo lingshiguan huaqiao wancanhui de yanshuo 在长崎中国领事馆华侨晚餐会的演说 [Speech at the Overseas Chinese Dinner at the Chinese Consulate in Nagasaki] (March 22, 1913)," in *Complete Works of Sun Yat-Sen* (Volume III): 50.

629 Yang Fan and Jiang Pei 杨帆、江沛, "<Niuyue shibao> shiyezhongde Sun Yat-sen 《纽约时报》视野中的孙中山 [Sun Yat-Sen from The New York Times's perspective] (1896–1925)," *Nanjing shehui kexue* 7 (2016).

630 Liu Yangyang 刘泱泱 ed., *Huang Xi ji* 黄兴集 [*Works of Huang Xing*], (Changsha: Hunan renmin chubanshe, 2008), 760.

631 *Complete Works of Sun Yat-Sen* (Volume III), 61.

Japanese ship.[632] On August 9, Sun arrived in Kobe, Japan, and soon moved to Tokyo to continue plotting against Yuan. After the failure of the Second Revolution, Sun hoped to win the support of Japan to launch the Third Revolution. On May 11, 1914, Sun wrote a letter to Japanese Prime Minister Ōkuma Shigenobu 大隈重信, saying that "today's Japan should help China reform and resolve the crisis in East Asia; and China will repay Japan by opening its market." Sun hoped Okuma's cabinet would help the revolutionaries.[633] On June 22, the first meeting of the Revolutionary Party of China was held in Tokyo. Ju Zheng 居正 was appointed commander of the Northeast Army of the Revolutionary Army of China, with his headquarters located in Qingdao, Shandong, which the Japanese had recently taken from Germany. In order to weaken Yuan Shikai's power, in addition to supporting Sun's Third Revolution, Japan also supported other anti-Yuan forces, including the Royalist Party in the Northeast and the National Protection Army led by Cai E in the Southwest.[634]

After the fall of Yuan Shikai in 1916, Li Yuanhong 黎元洪 succeeded him as president, and Duan Qirui served as prime minister. Duan Qirui had a better relationship with Japan. Japan had previously tried its best to oppose China's accession to the Allied Powers during the Yuan Shikai period, but now it had adjusted its strategy and provided loans to the Beiyang government to encourage its participation in the First World War under the leadership of Japan. The Duan Qirui government could use Japanese loans to train troops in the name of participating in the First World War and weaken the revolutionaries and local powers. Sun Yat-sen called the Beijing National Assembly and then British Prime Minister Lloyd George to firmly oppose China's participation in the war.[635] In March–April 1917, Sun Yat-sen was in contact with Hubert Knipping, the German consul general in Shanghai, and the German side was preparing to join forces with Sun to overthrow Duan Qirui's government and provide the necessary funding. In June 1917, the "dispute between the Office of the President and the State Council" on the issue of participating in the war became intense. Zhang Xun entered Beijing on June 14 to "mediate" and grasp the opportunity to prepare for restoration. On June 27, Sun Yat-sen provided

632 "Dr. Sun Yat-Sen Flees From China," *New York Times* (7 August 1913), 4.

633 Sun Yat-Sen 孙中山, "Zhi daweizhongxin han 致大隈重信函 [A Letter to Ōkuma] (May 11, 1914)," in *Complete Works of Sun Yat-Sen* (Volume III): 84–87.

634 Cheng Honglei 承红磊 "Riben yu huguo zhanzheng qijian de nanbei tuoxie 日本与护国战争期间的南北妥协 [Japan and the North-South Compromise during the Protect Republic War]," *Lishi yanjiu* 3 (2020).

635 Jin Guangyao and Wang Jianlang 金光耀、王建朗 eds., *Beiyang shiqi de Zhongguo waijiao* 北洋时期的中国外交 [*China's Diplomacy in Beiyang Period*], (Shanghai: Fudan University Press, 2006), 18.

Navy commander Cheng Biguang with 300,000 *yuan* of the funds obtained from the German side to overthrow Duan Qirui's government, hoping that Cheng would send the naval fleet south.[636] In the same month, Sun Yat-sen sent a letter to the new Japanese Prime Minister Masatake Terauchi to congratulate him for forming a cabinet, saying that "Peace in East Asia and the future development of China and Japan must be truly supported by the two countries."[637] However, the Japanese government that supported Duan Qirui could not provide assistance to Sun Yat-sen, who was "trying to overthrow Duan Qirui's government."

On July 1, Zhang Xun announced the "restoration" of Puyi to the throne, but this attempt was soon wiped out by the army mobilized by Duan Qirui. The Republic was restored, but once again faced the choice of legal system. Duan Qirui advocated a new constitution and refused to restore the 1912 Provisional Constitution. Sun continued to promote the cause of "overthrowing the Duan Qirui government" and launched the Constitution Protection Movement in Guangzhou, and Cheng Biguang responded to Sun's call for protecting the constitution by leading some naval vessels to the south. On July 31, Sun said in a talk with reporters from Guangzhou newspapers that the South would not yield to the North's pursuit of a "pseudo-republic": "For example, Japan is the stronger country in Asia, but the Chinese will never voluntarily merge with Japan."[638]

Germany's funding to Sun was not a free gift. The Germans expected Sun's government to remain neutral in World War I and refrain from joining the Entente. However, the military government in Guangzhou was under great pressure from the Entente. On August 25, 1917, Sun telegraphed Japanese Prime Minister Masatake Terauchi 寺内正毅, Foreign Minister Motono Ichiro 本野一郎, Inukai Tsuyoshi 犬養毅, Tōyama Mitsuru 頭山満 and others, hoping that Japan would give support to the Constitution Protection Movement led by him. In the letter, Sun reviewed the Republican revolution he had led before, explaining that its goal was to "seek permanent peace and happiness for Chinese people, and progress and development for Asian nations." The revolutionaries had carried forward the "spirit of patriotism and the love for the continent," so that "not only Chinese helped us, people from friendly

636 Li Jikui 李吉奎, *Sun Yat-sen yanjiu conglu* 孙中山研究丛录 [*A Collection of Sun Yat-Sen Studies*], (Guangzhou: Fudan daxue chubanshe, 2014), 112.

637 Sun Yat-Sen 孙中山, "Zhi riben shouxiang sineizhengyi han 致日本首相寺内正毅函 [Letter to Japanese Prime Minister Masatake Terauchi]," in *Complete Works of Sun Yat-Sen* (Volume IV): 108.

638 *Complete Works of Sun Yat-Sen* (Volume IV), 127–128.

countries also expressed their sympathy," with the result that the revolutionaries had finally succeeded.[639] In a conversation on September 15 with Kawakami Kiyoshi 河上清, a Japanese political commentator living in the U.S., Sun argued that if Germany was defeated in World War I, the result would be to strengthen British control over Asia, which would be of no benefit to Asia. "Japan, as a recognized leader of Asia, should not be with them [referring to Duan Qirui, Feng Guozhang and others in the Beiyang government] to take risks for the white people."[640]

On September 22, Dai Jitao 戴季陶 brought back news from Japan, saying that the Japanese side asked the military government protecting the constitution to declare war on Germany, and that it would provide financial assistance after that. Based on this expectation, the military government in Guangzhou declared war on Germany and Austria on September 26. However, Guangzhou's expected financial assistance from Japan soon fell through, and the Japanese government's support for Duan Qirui's government continued unabated. On November 20, 1917, Sun telegraphed Masatake Terauchi 寺内正毅 and other senior Japanese government officials to thank Japan for its support for the Chinese revolution. He said that he'd heard that Duan Qirui had recently borrowed tens of millions of dollars from Japan to train troops in the name of participating in World War I, and he hoped that the Japanese government would not accept Duan Qirui's request.[641] Of course, this proposal was rejected by the Japanese government. Between the two opposing governments, the Japanese government obviously preferred the Northern government. In a telegraph to Tang Jiyao 唐继尧 on November 29, Sun said that "declaring war on Germany was a big mistake."[642]

Japan's official support for the Beiyang government increasingly pushed a distressed Sun Yat-sen to seek new international allies. In November 1917, the Bolshevik Revolution broke out in Russia and the Soviet regime was established. During a conversation at a Guangzhou police banquet on January 28, 1918, Sun stated: "If the present revolutionary government in Russia can be consolidated, then we could hope that they will thrive."[643] In May 1918, Sun conceived of a bold plan in which China would withdraw from World War I and form an alliance with Soviet Russia and Germany. Sun even sent Cao Yabo 曹亚伯, Counselor of his Grand Marshal's Office, to Berlin to lobby the German

639 Ibid., 134.
640 Duan (n. 614), 548.
641 *Complete Works of Sun Yat-Sen* (Volume IV), 243.
642 Ibid., 254.
643 Ibid., 320.

government, hoping that Germany and Soviet Russia could unite with him to overthrow the Duan Qirui government. But by then, Germany had been defeated and had lost its diplomatic autonomy, so Sun's idea failed.[644]

During the Paris Peace Conference in January 1919, Liang Qichao and others kept sending back reports from Paris on the progress of negotiations on the Shandong issue. Within the Beiyang Clique, there was strong dissatisfaction with the pro-Japanese Anfu faction headed by Duan Qirui. The increasingly anti-Japanese atmosphere in China also fortified Sun Yat-sen's anti-Japanese sentiment. After Japan slaughtered more than 10,000 Korean demonstrators in Seoul on April 5, 1919, Sun Yat-sen gave a statement to Japanese journalist Oe Taku, condemning Japan's aggression against Korea: "The Japanese are not Asians; those who invade us Asians like the Europeans can't be Asians!" Sun Yat-sen demanded that Japan resolve the Shandong issue, and at the same time raised the Manchuria issue, which he had seldom mentioned before, while also clearly supporting Korean "national self-determination." In Sun's new exposition, the enemies of the "Asian peoples" were no longer the "white people" in general, but the Anglo-Saxon nations specifically. Russia was excluded from this list of enemies.[645]

After the May Fourth Movement broke out, Sun Yat-sen expressed his support for it. On May 8, his followers Zhang Ji 张继, He Tianjiong 何天炯 and Dai Jitao 戴季陶 published "Report to Japanese Nationals," which condemned Japan's expansionistic policy and aggression against Taiwan Province, Manchuria, Mongolia, Korea and mainland China.[646] Sun Yat-sen made his critical attitude towards Japan more explicit in a June 24, 1919, interview with a reporter from Japan's Asahi Shimbun 朝日新闻. Sun stated, "In recent years, every time the Japanese government helps our bureaucrats, it frustrates the pro-democratic party, which inevitably hurts." Sun compared the Kuomintang to Japan's Meiji reformers fifty years ago. The KMT regarded Japan as a model for transforming China and wanted to maintain friendship with Japan. "However, Japanese militarists have acted on their imperialist ambitions and have forgotten the reformers, treating China as the easiest state to invade and developing its

644 Unpublished political archives of the German Ministry of Foreign Affairs, China 7, BD.11–12, A53674 Hintzean A.A. Berlin, 1. Dezemember.1918. Quoted from Li Guoqi 李国祁, "Deguo dang'anzhong youguan Zhongguo canjia diyici shijie dazhan de jixiang jizai 德国档案中有关中国参加第一次世界大战的几项记载 [Several Records of China's Participation in the First World War in German Archives]," in *Minguo shilunji* 民国史论集 [*On the History of the Republic of China*], (Taipei: Nantian shuju, 1990): 321–323.

645 Duan (n. 614), 596–597.

646 Ibid., 598.

aggressive policy towards her."[647] In the interview, Sun also responded to the question raised by Japan's ruling and opposition parties: Why did Chinese people resent Japan more than the European powers and the U.S.? Sun pointed out that this was similar to a younger brother who teamed up with thieves to rob his eldest brother's house, but then blamed his eldest brother for hating him more than those thieves.

In the interview, Sun Yat-sen further expressed his dissatisfaction with Japan's seizure of Shandong. He pointed out that when Japan captured Qingdao, it announced that it would return Qingdao to China. When China participated in World War I, Japan signed a secret agreement with European powers instead, intending to inherit Germany's rights in Shandong. Japan induced China to participate in World War I, but then tried to seize Shandong. This was like foreign capitalists in Macau luring Chinese labors to go abroad and "trafficking them overseas like piglets."[648] Sun stressed that Japan must return Shandong to China. In Europe, even Denmark, a neutral state, gained the territory seized by Germany in the 1860s. China made great contributions to the First World War, but could not recover its own territory. This situation could not be justified. Sun said, "If noble-minded patriots really consider Japan's friendship with China as being of the same culture and the same race, they should urge the Japanese government to reflect on its actions and change its basic policy."[649]

In remarks to a reporter from the *North China Daily News* 字林西报 in Shanghai on June 11, 1920, Sun Yat-sen strongly opposing renewal of the Anglo-Japanese alliance, arguing that it meant that the British supported Japanese aggression against China. Sun also commented that since the Anglo-Japanese alliance had eliminated Tsarist Russia, the further expansion of Japan in the Pacific Ocean would have an impact on British colonies.[650] On June 29, Sun sent a letter to Tanaka Giichi 田中义一, Minister of the Imperial Japanese Army, accusing the Japanese government of "helping the reactionary party to eliminate democracy" and arguing that if Japan did not change its course, "the ill feelings of Chinese people will grow deeper, grievance will be generated, and Chinese may boycott Japanese goods." He hoped that Japan would "change its former policy in view of major world trends and the security of East Asia."[651] In a letter to Miyazaki Torazo 宫崎寅藏 on October 5, he said

647 Sun Yat-Sen 孙中山, "Da riben chaori xinwen jizhewen 答日本朝日新闻记者问 [Answering the reporter of Asahi Shimbun in Japan]," in *Complete Works of Sun Yat-Sen* (Volume V): 72.

648 Ibid.

649 Ibid., 74.

650 Duan (n. 614), 613.

651 *Complete Works of Sun Yat-Sen* (Volume V), 259.

that invasions by white people had decreased recently, and the greatest worry was the policy of Japanese warlords. If Japan's policy remained unchanged, "then we have no choice but to be pro-British and pro-American in order to repel Japan. The only one who should be blamed is Japan."[652] In a conversation with Miyazaki Torazo 宮崎寅蔵 and Kayano Nagatomo 萱野長知 on March 12, 1921, Sun talked about the Japanese authorities regarding him as pro-American and pro-British. Sun pointed out that this was only the wishful thinking of the Japanese authorities.[653]

During this period, Sun constantly criticized the Beiyang government and Japan. In a letter to the Soviet-Russian Foreign People's Committee on August 28, 1921, Sun asserted that "Beijing is actually the tool of Tokyo on all major policy issues related to Japan's vital interests."[654] In a conversation with an American reporter from *Dalu Bao* in mid-November, he said that he was not attacking the North, because the people in the North agreed with his claim: "We only want to overthrow the Chinese government manipulated by Japan today."[655] In a conversation with a *Washington Post* reporter in mid-April 1922, Sun announced that the purpose of his government's Northern Expedition was "not the people of northern China, but Japan and the Japanese puppet government in the north." He said that the traitorous government in the north sold China's rights to Japan, so that Japan could take advantage of China's products and population to promote imperialism, thus endangering peace in the Pacific area. Sun asserted: "The country that can maintain peace in the Pacific is not Britain, but China. If we save ourselves today, we can save the world from the harm of Japanese coercion."[656]

But this didn't mean that Sun placed no hopes in Japan at all. On November 16, 1923, after learning that his friend Inukai Tsuyoshi was appointed Minister of Posts and Telecommunications and Minister of Education of Yamamoto Gonnohyo's Cabinet, Sun was very excited and wrote a long letter to Inukai Tsuyoshi, pointing out that Russia and Germany were oppressed in Europe, while China and India were oppressed in Asia. Britain and France were oppressors in Europe and Asia, and the U.S. would not stand on the side of the oppressed in any case. Sun hoped that Inukai Tsuyoshi would play a role in the new Japanese cabinet and urged Japan to give up imitating European

652 Duan (n. 614), 618.
653 *Complete Works of Dr. Sun Yat-Sen* (Volume V), 482.
654 Duan (n. 614), 631.
655 Ibid., 636.
656 *Complete Works of Sun Yat-Sen* (Volume VI), 101.

imperialism, to truly support Asia and to stand on the side of the oppressed.[657] In fact, just two months earlier, even Li Dazhao had been discussing the relationship between China, Japan and Russia. Focusing on the Tokyo earthquake that occurred on September 1, Li Dazhou believed that the goodwill expressed by China after the earthquake might bring Japan closer to China, and suggested that China should welcome Japan to "join the nations against imperialism."[658]

In November 1924, Duan Qirui invited Sun to negotiate a North-South peace plan with the Beiyang government via Japan. Sun tried to communicate an idea to the Japanese government and people: In order to establish an alliance between China, Japan and Soviet Russia, Japan should support China's efforts to oppose unequal treaties and unite with China in opposing Western imperialism. In a conversation with Nagasaki journalists on November 23, Sun accused Japan of gaining strength after the Meiji Restoration and forgetting the failure of the Chinese revolution. By contrast, "the recently successful Russian revolution has not forgotten the failure of the Chinese revolution, so Chinese nationals and Russian nationals have become increasingly friendly because of the struggle of the revolution."[659] In a conversation with Nagasaki's guests on the same day, Sun asserted that "China will never expect any assistance from friendly countries, and will use its national strength to deal with the current situation." China and Japan could imagine establishing some kind of economic alliance in the future, but if Japan wanted such an opportunity, it needed to support China's campaign to abolish unequal treaties.[660]

In a conversation with Takagi 高木, a reporter with Japan's *Chūgai Shōgyō Shinpō* 中外商業新報 on November 24–26, Sun Yat-sen pointed out that "all the citizens of both countries should unite, fight for the Oriental nations, and more broadly for all the oppressed nations in the world, to gain equality. It is wrong to talk about friendship between the two countries without this purpose. If Japanese people don't change their perception of Japan as one of the great powers, they will not be able to conceive of true Sino-Japanese friendship."[661]

On November 28, 1924, Sun Yat-sen gave a speech on the theme of "Great Asianism" to a welcoming party held by five groups, including the *Kōbe Shōgyō Kaigisho* 神戸商業会議所.[662] In his speech, Sun pointed out that Asia was "the birthplace of the most ancient cultures," and had gradually declined only in

657 Duan (n. 614), 658–659.

658 Editorial Committee, *Li Dazhao nianpu* 李大钊年谱 [*Li Dazhao's Chronicle*], (Lanzhou: Gansu renmin chubanshe, 1984), 176.

659 *Complete Works of Sun Yat-Sen* (Volume XI), 364–365.

660 Ibid., 371.

661 Ibid., 392–393.

662 Ibid., 401.

the last few hundred years. The success of the Meiji Restoration and Japan's victory over Russia in 1905 had greatly encouraged the Asian nations. National independence movements had taken place in Egypt, Persia, Turkey, Arabia and India, and ties among Asian nationalities were being strengthened. Sun further referred to Western culture as hegemonic culture, and Eastern culture as kingly culture, and cited the example of the China-centered tributary system to demonstrate this kingly culture, highlighting the case of Nepal coming to China to pay tribute in the first year of the Republic of China. Sun pointed out: "We are now in this new world. What should we use as the basis for creating our Greater Asianism? We should use our inherent culture as the foundation. We must rely on morality, benevolence and justice, and benevolence and morality are the good foundation of our Great Asianism. We have this good foundation, and we also need to learn European science, revitalize our industry and improve our weapons. However, we must not learn from Europe by eliminating other countries and oppressing other nations. We learn in order to defend ourselves."[663]

Sun Yat-sen called on Asian nations to unite on the basis of benevolence, justice and morality to overthrow the Western imperialists who oppressed them. But he also believed that there was an anomaly in the West, which was Soviet Russia, which by following the imperial way was an appropriate candidate for solidarity with Asian countries. As early as mid-November 1922, when Sun Yat-sen had a conversation with a reporter from Jiji Press of Japan, he said that Russians were also Asians: "In their veins, the blood of Asians flows." He advocated that Japan and Russia should jointly oppose Anglo-Saxon aggression.[664] But in his Great Asianism remarks, the focus was no longer on the racial affiliation of the Russians, but rather on the ideas they pursued. At the end of his speech, Sun Yat-sen stated his own expectations for Japan: "You Japanese have not only gained the hegemonic culture of Europe and America, but also the essence of Asian imperial culture. From now on, the future of world culture depends on whether you Japanese people choose hegemonic culture or imperial culture."

In his speech at a welcoming banquet by various groups in Kobe on the same day, Sun Yat-sen gave another example to illustrate Sino-Japanese relations: China was not an independent country, but was like a "servant" with more than a dozen masters; Japan wanted to make friends with China, but while walking along the road, it kept bumping into China's first master, second master and third master. At this time, China was supposed to bring umbrellas

663 Ibid., 407.
664 Duan (n. 614), 645.

to these masters. Even if Japan wanted to invite China to dinner, it would not be possible. Therefore, if Japan really hoped for friendship between China and Japan, it needed to support China's campaign to abolish unequal treaties and free China from the domination of more than a dozen masters. Only then could China truly become brothers with Japan.[665]

The Great Asianism speech in 1924 clearly showed the different intentions of Sun Yat-sen's Great Asianism and the mainstream Japanese Asiatic Monroe Doctrine. However, in the context of Japanese people's resentment of the new U.S. law restricting Japanese immigration at that time, Japanese newspapers highlighted Sun Yat-sen's emphasis on "Sino-Japanese Friendship." Few analyzed the difference between his claim and the Asiatic Monroe Doctrine advocated by mainstream Japan.[666] After Sun Yat-sen's death, his speech was appropriated by Japanese politicians. Ishiwara Kanji 石原莞爾, who planned the Mukden Incident, promoted the East Asia Alliance movement in the 1930s. In 1939, Japan also organized the East Asia Alliance Association, advocating the formation of the East Asia Alliance between Japan, Manchuria and China to build a new East Asian order. Japan's East Asian Alliance theory referred to Western culture as hegemonic culture and Eastern culture as imperial culture. When demonstrating that China and Japan shared a common imperial culture, it commented: "Although Sun Wen's thought is not clear, it contains imperial thought and Great Asianism."[667]

The Japanese also used Great Asianism in making contact with the powerful anti-Chiang factions in Southwestern China. In February 1936, Matsui Iwane 松井石根 went to Guangdong and Guangxi to contact Southwestern dignitaries. As spiritual leader of the anti-Chiang forces in the Southwest, Hu Hanmin 胡汉民 published an article in *Three Principles of the People Monthly*, Volume 7, Issue 3, and disclosed part of the transcript of the meeting with Japanese warlord Matsui Iwane in Guangzhou on February 21, 1936. Hu Hanmin made it clear that Sun Yat-sen's Great Asianism was very different from Japan's Great Asiatic Monroe Doctrine. Hu criticized Japan's military and political policies as "effective in implementation, but lack of long-term planning. It won't take long for the Far East to become a mess that cannot be dealt with. So-called Asianism will backfire." Hu Hanmin declared, "I am an Asianist, and at the same time anti-Japanese," hoping that Matsui, who advocated Great Asianism, would correct the mistakes of the past and put Japanese politics back on the

665 *Complete Works of Sun Yat-Sen* (Volume XI), 412–413.

666 Duan (n. 614), 707–708.

667 Nakayama Masaru 中山優:『新秩序の東洋的性格』[The Oriental Character of the New Order],『東亜聯盟』[East Asia League, No. 1, 1939].

right track.[668] However, although the Southwest anti-Chiang forces took the stand of being both "anti-Japanese" and "anti-Chiang" and also "suppressing the Communists," they always wanted to use Japanese policies to weaken Chiang. In addition to the constraints on their power, their criticism of Japan's Great Asianism was to a large extent mere posturing without real action.

When Wang Jingwei established a puppet government in Nanjing in 1940, he claimed to carry on Sun Yat-sen's Asianism, and founded magazines such as *Great Asianism* 大亚洲主义 and *Great Asianism and the East Asian Alliance* 大亚洲主义与东亚联盟 to demonstrate a consistency between Sun's ideas and Japan's Asianist policies.[669] This completely abandoned the "anti-imperialist" thinking of Sun Yat-sen in his later years, and conflated the anti-imperialist Great Asianism of Sun Yat-sen with the Great Asianism of Japanese militarism. Sun Yat-sen rejected Japan's Asiatic Monroe Doctrine in his later years, but many of the Revolutionary Alliance/KMT elites who followed him were inextricably linked with Japanese militarism in their beliefs or interests. Against the backdrop of invasive Japanese militarism, it was not easy to eradicate Asian Monroe Doctrine discourse.

3 Chiang Kai-shek: between the US and Japan Monroe Doctrines

After the death of Sun Yat-sen in Beijing on March 12, 1925, fierce conflict broke out in the Kuomintang around the issue of succession. It was not until the death of Hu Hanmin 胡汉民 in 1936 that Chiang Kai-shek actually consolidated

668 Hu Hanmin 胡汉民, "Dayaxiya zhuyi yu kangri—Yu Songjing dajiang zhi tanhua 大亚细亚主义与抗日——与松井大将之谈话 [Great Asianism and Anti-Japanese War—A Talk with General Matsui]," in *Hu Hanmin xianshegn yijiao jilu* 胡汉民先生遗教辑录 [*A Collection of the Legacy of Mr. Hu Hanmin*], eds. Southwest Executive Department of the Central Executive Committee of the Kuomintang, quoted from Jiang Yongjing 蒋永敬, *Hu Hanmin xiansheng nianpu* 胡汉民先生年谱 [*Chronicle of Mr. Hu Hanmin*], (Taipei: Central Party History Committee of the Kuomintang, 1978): 543–544. However, according to Matsui's diary, the focus of Hu Fang's attention was to hope that the Japanese side would come up with a substantial policy toward Chiang Kai-shek. To the Japanese side's proposal of Greater Asianism, Hu Fang's response was that China had had its own Greater Asianism since the Sun Wen era, which did not contradict the Japanese side's views. Matsui Iwane 松井石根,『松井石根大将の陣中日誌』[War Journal of General Matsui Iwane], (Fuyo Shobō, 1985), 277.

669 Wang Jingwei 汪精卫, "Zhongri guojiao tiaozheng yu dongya lianmeng 中日国交调整与东亚联盟 [China-Japan Diplomatic Relations Adjustment and East Asian Association]," *East Asian Association* (reprint edition), Volume III, No. 1, Special issue, (Tokyo, 1996), 7.

his leadership in the Kuomintang.[670] So, how did Chiang Kai-shek view the American Monroe Doctrine and the Japanese Monroe Doctrine? Judging from Chiang's written records, he realized very early that both were manifestations of imperialism. However, in order to obtain American aid during World War II, Chiang deliberately distinguished between the American Monroe Doctrine and the Japanese Monroe Doctrine, thus reversing some of his earlier statements in terms of discourse.

Chiang Kai-shek went to Japan to study for the first time in April 1906 and enrolled at a school in Tokyo to study Japanese. Since self-funded students could not study military affairs, Chiang returned to China that year and entered the Baoding Military Academy. At the end of 1907, he qualified to study abroad at the public expense and went to study at the Tokyo Shinbu Gakkō, a preparatory school of the Japanese Army Academy. After graduating in 1910, he entered the 19th Regiment of the Field Artillery of the 13th Division of the Imperial Army as a non-commissioned officer candidate for internship. After the Wuchang Uprising broke out in October 1911, Chiang returned to China to participate in the Revolution of 1911 under the pretext of personal leave. After Chiang assassinated Tao Chengzhang 陶成章, leader of the Restoration Society, in Shanghai in 1912, he fled to Japan. However, because he had violated Japanese military discipline in the previous year, he could no longer study military affairs. He could only learn German first in hopes of studying in Germany later. During this period, Chiang Kai-shek founded a magazine called *Jun Sheng* (The Voice of the Army) in Tokyo, and wrote introductions titled "The Management of Military and Political Affairs after the Revolutionary War," "The Unification of Military Academy," "The Fundamental Settlement of the Mongolia-Tibet Issue," "The Controversy of the March to Mongolia" and "The Effects of The Balkan War on China's Diplomacy with the Powers." In one of his introductions for *Jun Sheng*, Chiang analyzed the international situation at that time as follows:

> The only land along the Pacific coast that is the focus of competition among all nations is our Chinese land. Why? Since the Americas are protected by the Monroe Doctrine of the United States, no other country dares to covet them. Australia is within the sphere of influence of Britain,

670 See Jin Yilin 金以林, *Kuomintang gaoceng de paixi zhengzhi: Chiang Kai-shek "zuigao lingxiu" diwei shi ruhe quelide* 国民党高层的派系政治：蒋介石"最高领袖"地位是如何确立的 [*Factional Politics at the Top of the Kuomintang: How Chiang Kai-shek's "supreme leader" Status was Established*], (Beijing: Shehui kexue wenxian chubanshe, 2009).

> and the British flag points to it, which intimidates others. The southern tip of Africa has been seized by Britain, and Morocco, Algeria, Abyssinia and other northern regions are the territories of France and Italy. As for Asia Minor and northern India, they are of little value, and the great powers are playing the long game. Those who are hawkish and eagle-eyed, advocating partition, and seeking to satisfy their desires by dividing the benefits among the powers, have long since ceased to reserve any room for the Chinese people in their vision of the world![671]

Here, Chiang Kai-shek 蒋介石 understood the U.S. Monroe Doctrine as an hegemonic proposition to establish a sphere of influence. Chiang understood how the Revolution of 1911 was situated in the "rivalry of nations" (an expression that Kang Youwei also liked to use), believing that the Revolution was "ostensibly domestic, but essentially serving an external agenda," because the despotic imperial regime "took all-under-heaven as the private property of the emperor" and was incompetent to deal with the great powers. He held that the Revolution's overthrow of imperial order provided the necessary conditions for China's revival.[672]

In 1913, Chiang Kai-shek took part in the Second Revolution against Yuan Shikai in China. After failing, he went to Japan again. The adjustment of Sun Yat-sen's political discourse also profoundly influenced Chiang's political discourse. After Sun's death, Chiang Kai-shek took on the appearance of a Kuomintang leftist, so that the Soviet representatives at one point pinned their hopes of restraining the KMT's rightists on Chiang Kai-shek. After being frustrated in inner-party struggle, Chiang Kai-shek went to Japan again in 1927, turning to the Cabinet of Tanaka Giichi and receiving the promise of Japan's support. However, the Jinan Massacre and Huanggutun Incident created by young Japanese officers in 1928 made cooperation between Chiang Kai-shek and the Tanaka cabinet unsustainable.

After the Mukden Incident in 1931, Japan's expansion in Northeast China triggered a diplomatic counterpunch from the U.S. This led to comparisons between the U.S. Monroe Doctrine and Japanese Monroe Doctrine in Chinese domestic newspapers. Lin Shaochang's article in the *South China Review*

---

671 Chiang Kai-shek 蒋介石, "Fakanci 发刊词 [An Introduction]," *Junsheng* 1 (1912); Qin Xiaoyi 秦孝仪 ed., *Zongtong jianggong sixiang yanlun zongji* 总统蒋公思想言论总集 [*A Collection of President Jiang's Thoughts and Remarks*] (Vol. 35), (Taipei: Party History Committee of the Central Committee of the Chinese Nationalist Party, 1984), 2–3.

672 Ibid.

published on October 17, 1931, pointed out that unlike the Monroe Doctrine implemented by the U.S. in the Americas, Japan's Asiatic Monroe Doctrine had never promoted, assisted or protected the political independence of any Asian country or nation. Of course, Lin Shaochang's article also stated that since Theodore Roosevelt, the Monroe Doctrine in the U.S. had changed from conservative to offensive, and the scope of encroachment had expanded from the Western Hemisphere to Europe and Asia. It was far larger than Japan's Monroe Doctrine in coverage, but its degree of encroachment was not as outrageous as Japan's. Lin Shaochang advocated a "genuine" Asiatic Monroe Doctrine for the benefit of Asia and even all mankind, and called for China to be the leader of this Asiatic Monroe Doctrine.[673]

In early 1932, *Shen Bao* Monthly published the commentary "Asiatic Monroe Doctrine and U.S. Monroe Doctrine" under the byline Bai Ying, which commenting on a diplomatic note by U.S. Secretary of State Henry Lewis Stimson on January 7 about not recognizing Japan's international territorial changes imposed by force. The article stated: "Imperialists always use the Monroe Doctrine as the signboard for obtaining colonies exclusively, and Open-Door Doctrine as a banner for invading other places. The conflict between Japan and the U.S. was a contest for Asia under the banner of the Monroe Doctrine. It was fundamentally 'the Monroe Doctrine against the Monroe Doctrine.'"[674] These two articles were quite typical of a batch of comments comparing the Monroe Doctrines of Japan and the U.S. that emerged at that time; i.e., the Monroe Doctrines of Japan and the U.S. were both expressions of imperialism, and the difference between them was only in degree.

As is well known, in March 1931, Chiang Kai-shek put Hu Hanmin under arrest in Tangshan, a suburb of Nanjing, which stirred an outcry among the KMT's anti-Chiang forces urging him to "go into exile." In the following period, Chiang Kai-shek focused on maintaining his political position in the KMT, while externally he emphasized relying on the League of Nations, Britain and the U.S. to contain Japan. In particular, he emphasized that Japan's Asiatic Monroe Doctrine should be countered by the Open Door Policy of the Nine-Power Treaty. However, after the Japanese occupied the northeast, they advanced on North China. Chiang Kai-shek pointed out the Japanese threat in various talks and speeches, and revealed the deception of the Japanese Monroe Doctrine,

673 Lin Shaochang 林绍昌, "Yazhou de menluo zhuyi 亚洲的门罗主义 [Monroe Doctrine in Asia]," *Nanhua pinglun*, Volume 1, No. 22 (1931).

674 Bai Ying 百英, "Yazhou meiluo zhuyi yu meizhou menluo zhuyi 亚洲门罗主义与美洲门罗主义 [Asiatic Monroe Doctrine and American Monroe Doctrine]," *Shenbao yuekan* Volume 1, No. 1 (1932).

but also emphasized that the Japanese Monroe Doctrine violated the interests of the European and American powers, and would trigger a strong rebound by the European and American powers. Chiang's emphasis on the prospect of Western intervention was meant to echo his own policy of "pacifying the interior before resisting foreign aggression."

On January 23, 1933, Chiang Kai-shek noted in his talk with Zhang Xueliang 张学良 in Nanjing: "The real enemy of Japan is the U.S. If Japan engages in large-scale combat with us, they will miss the real target and lose the war even if they seem to be wining. This is their greatest weakness, so we are determined to engage in protracted warfare with them." The next day, he said: "When Japanese power expands to North Manchuria, it borders Russia with a long frontier line, and its strength is not enough to handle it. This is another weaknesses of Japan." His talk on January 25 directly referred to the Monroe Doctrine: "Japan is arrogant, unaware that it has become an enemy of all the other countries in the world, and still pretends to be the center of Asia and imitate the U.S. Monroe Doctrine, going against the trend of times regardless of the limitations of its own status and the current situation. Will it not perish eventually?"[675] This comparison was to treat the Monroe Doctrines of both Japan and the U.S. as pretexts for regional domination. Chiang made no moral distinction between them.

On March 5, 1934, Chiang Kai-shek delivered a speech at his official residence in Beitan, Nanchang 南昌北坛官邸, analyzing the situation in East Asia and discussing China's strategy. He pointed out that two forces were currently competing in East Asia to invade China. The forces represented by Britain and the U.S. advocated "open doors, equal opportunities" and "balance of power for the equal sharing of interests." Japan and Russia, on the other hand, used the Monroe Doctrine or World Revolution as slogans with the intent "to dominate China exclusively by monopolizing the benefits." The former aimed to maintain the status quo, while the latter aimed to break the status quo and "use every opportunity to invade China militarily and politically at any time to achieve the goal of swallowing up China." Comparing the two evils, Chiang Kai-shek advocated using Britain and the U.S. to contain Japan and Russia.[676]

On April 23, 1934, Chiang Kai-shek once again expressed his views on the situation in Nanchang: "It is expected that Japan has plans against us to a) implement the requirements of the Twenty-one Demands; b) oppose all actions of white people to help China; c) take military action at any time." The next day, he said: "Japan prevented the League of Nations from helping China

675 Qin (n. 670), 367.
676 Ibid., 95.

to eliminate its threat. It will never stop. And Japan's ambition to fight with the whole world in order to accomplish the East Asia Monroe Doctrine will not change."[677]

Chiang Kai-shek believed that Sino-Japanese relations were intensifying after the "Amo Statement" issued by Amo Eiji, intelligence chief of the Japanese Foreign Ministry. In December 1934, *Foreign Affairs Review* 外交评论 published the article "Enemy? Friend? A Review of Sino-Japanese Relations" under the byline Xu Daolin 徐道邻. It was actually dictated by Chiang Kai-shek and recorded by Chen Bulei 陈布雷. This article criticized Japan's Asiatic Monroe Doctrine for failing to distinguish between Asia in 1935 and the U.S. in 1823. In 1823, Britain, France and other powers "had no significant or profound interest in the Americas." Furthermore, at that time, transportation methods were backward. The U.S. was therefore able to use the slogan "America for the Americans" to achieve the domination of the American continents by a single country. Chiang Kai-shek then pointed out, "But in fact, the U.S. has to abandon its Monroe Doctrine policy now," referring to the Good Neighbor Policy promoted by President Franklin Roosevelt. Japan advocated the Asiatic Monroe Doctrine to repel European and American forces with the slogan "East Asia for the East Asians." "Not only the U.S. and Russia are already hostile to Japan, but all European powers are hostile to Japan, and in particular, British interests are in deep conflict with those of Japan." Chiang Kai-shek made the point that Japan's strength was the result of Britain's "cultivation," and that proclaiming itself master of East Asia would eventually lead to Japan's isolation.[678]

On January 16, 1936, Chiang Kai-shek delivered a speech at the Nanjing Lizhi Society 励志社 to principals and representatives of all schools above the secondary level. Part of his speech expressed his views on Sino-Japanese relations. Chiang Kai-shek talked about white race's discrimination against the yellow race before the Meiji Restoration. He argued that the success of the Meiji Restoration changed the white race's attitude toward the yellow race from contempt to fear, but racial stereotypes remained. However, the Japanese preceded the whites in attacking China, a nation of the same race. This move further aroused the whites' fear of Japan. In Chiang Kai-shek's analysis, Britain had been jealous of Russia and Germany and allied with Japan before the First World War, and that had contributed to Japan's rise in power, but after the First World War, Britain was challenged by Japan, so tensions between Britain and Japan had increased. The U.S. tried to use Japan to contain Russia before the Russo-Japanese War, but after Japan defeated Russia, it

677 Ibid., 316.
678 Ibid., 160.

took the opportunity of World War I to grow in strength and invaded the four Northeastern provinces of China through the Mukden Incident, "openly advocating the so-called East Asian Monroe Doctrine in order to repel European and U.S. power in East Asia, and especially to prevent American capital and commodities from entering Manchuria, which dealt a major blow to the development of American commerce in the Far East and the entire Pacific region." Chiang Kai-shek emphasized that both Britain and the U.S. were currently very displeased with Japan, but their conflict with each other prevented them from jointly sanctioning Japan.[679]

Facing internal and external pressure after the Xi'an Incident in December 1936, Chiang Kai-shek finally made up his mind to end the civil war and fight Japan. On July 7, 1937, the Japanese imperialists launched a full-scale invasion of China. The Nationalist Government in Nanjing organized resistance while vigorously seeking support from Britain and the U.S. The launch of the Battle of Shanghai came from a strong motivation to win international support, but Britain and the U.S. stood off to the side for a long time.

In his opening remarks at the Seventh Plenum of the Fifth Central Committee of the Kuomintang on July 1, 1940, Chiang Kai-shek analyzed the world situation. He pointed out that in the past ten days, Japan had advocated "the independence of East Asian" and declared that it would announce its so-called East Asian Monroe Doctrine, but had not issued any official diplomatic statement out of fear over the international situation. "Although Japan wants to declare its so-called East Asian Monroe Doctrine as a precursor to its Southward invasion, its illusion will never be made a reality." The reasons lay in the surveillance of the U.S., the indifference of Germany, the might of the Soviet Union, and China's persistent war of resistance. "It wants to use the East Asian Monroe Doctrine as a talisman of aggression today, but that is obviously nonsense!"[680]

Chiang Kai-shek then went on to analyze the essence of Japan's East Asian Monroe Doctrine, in particular distinguishing between the Japanese Monroe Doctrine and the U.S. Monroe Doctrine: "Japan has long been rattling out its argument of the East Asian Monroe Doctrine, especially in recent days. Of course its main intention is to appropriate familiar words that have been used elsewhere in the world and use them to deceive the world and to suppress the opposition of the European and American powers, especially the U.S., to prevent European and American presence in the Far East and their handling of Far East issues. It believed that by changing some words, it could realize

679 Ibid., 109–110.

680 Ibid., 375.

its long fantasized plot of 'establishing a new East Asian order' that the world opposed, but had no idea that the success of the U.S. Monroe Doctrine was due to the specific era and environment at that time, as well as the spirit and characteristics of the doctrine advocated by U.S. President Monroe, which suited the needs of independent and free nations in the Americas."

Chiang Kai-shek believed that "the implementation of Monroe Doctrine is by no means the result of U.S. military aggression, nor can it succeed with a single declaration." Japan's implementation of East Asian Monroe Doctrine was overestimated. First, Japan's national strength was far inferior to that of the U.S.; second, "The U.S. advocates the Monroe Doctrine based on the principle of equality and freedom. The U.S. has been advocating the Monroe Doctrine for a century. Dozens of countries in the Americas are still independent and equal, and can coexist and prosper together. Only the Monroe Doctrine advocated by the U.S. has a spirit that can be endorsed by other countries in the Americas!" Given that the rise of Japan had led to the destruction of Korea, the invasion of China, and Japan being hated by Asian nations, Chiang asked, "What qualifies Japan to talk about 'East Asian independence' today?" Finally, Chiang Kai-shek pointed out that only a large country like China was qualified as a pillar of peace in East Asia and a guarantor of order in the Far East.[681] Chiang Kai-shek requested that the Kuomintang center its foreign policy on the Nine-Power Treaty, maintaining the status quo, ensuring the integrity of territorial sovereignty and administration, and rebuilding peace in East Asia.[682]

At the Seventh Plenum of the Fifth Central Committee of the Kuomintang on July 5, Chiang Kai-shek delivered a "General Review of Current Diplomacy," saying that "Japan's ambitions to conquer China and implement East Asian Monroe Doctrine have been crushed by our three-year war of resistance." The policy of conquering Annan was only used to console domestic warmongers.[683] However, on July 6, Roosevelt's press secretary issued a statement stating that all three continents could implement their own Monroe Doctrine. Chiang Kai-shek was very surprised by this and commented: "This statement is exceptional! But it is all for Germany." On July 9, Chiang Kai-shek carefully studied the U.S. views on Asiatic Monroe Doctrine and commented: "It intends to deal with Annan issues together with Asian countries and doesn't recognize the Japanese occupation alone."[684]

681 Ibid., 374–376.

682 Li Yong and Zhang Zhongtian 李勇、张仲田 eds., *Chiang Kai-shek nianpu* 蒋介石年谱 [*Chronicles of Chiang Kai-shek*], (Beijing: Zhonggong dangshi chubanshe, 1995), 282.

683 Qin (n. 670), 383–384.

684 Huang Zijin and Pan Guangzhe 黄自进、潘光哲 eds., *Chiang Kai-shek zongtong wuji* 蒋介石总统五记 [*The Five Chapters of President Jiang*] (1), (Taipei: Guoshiguan, 2011), 728–729.

On July 12, Chiang Kai-shek revised his closing speech for the Seventh Plenum of the Fifth Central Committee and made a self-evaluation in his diary: "Although this article focuses on criticizing the Asiatic Monroe Doctrine, the main point is to make the enemy feel that the bombing of Chongqing is ineffective."[685] In his closing speech for the plenum, Chiang Kai-shek once again emphasized Japan's East Asian Monroe Doctrine since the Mukden Incident, pointing out that Japan used the pretext of the U.S. having the Monroe Doctrine to justify pursuing a similar doctrine: "Its intention is nothing more than eliminating Europe and the U.S. as obstacles to its invasion of China and plundering of Asia, especially the U.S., which promotes 'non-recognition' and 'adherence to the Nine-Power Treaty.'" Chiang Kai-shek once again emphasized that the spirit of the Monroe Doctrine pursued by the U.S. was very different from the spirit of Japan's East Asian Monroe Doctrine and pointed out that Asia was a region related to both the Eastern and Western Hemispheres, from Soviet Russia in the north to the Pacific and Indian Oceans. However, Japan had no foundation for "being the master of Asia" and advocating Asiatic Monroe Doctrine, whether in terms of cultural morality or strength.

Next, Chiang Kai-shek interpreted the statement made by President Roosevelt's press secretary on July 6. He believed that the statement that "the U.S. government hopes and believes that it should be realized that the Monroe Doctrine should be implemented in all continents" should not be interpreted as Japan understood it. The original intention was in fact that "the U.S. government would like to see both Europe and Asia adopt the Monroe Doctrine, and the interpretation and application of this Monroe Doctrine should be as same as what has been applied in the Americas," based on "mutual assistance, self-defense, equality and independence." The core of this remark was how to deal with the possessions of the defeated European countries in America, while in Asia, it was intended to oppose Japan's occupation of other countries by force. In particular, it was proposed that "the East Asian countries should use the method of collective consultation to resolve the issue of ownership of French Annan." The intention of this sentence was not to advocate that Japan alone using force to dominate Annan, but to insist on the U.S. proposal of respecting the independence of countries and "opening the door of the Far East." The recent expansion of U.S. armaments was to a large extent also aimed at the situation in the Pacific and Asia.[686]

---

685 Ibid., 157.

686 Qin (n. 670), 393–396. What can be compared here is the judgment of the Central Committee of the Communist Party of China on the same information. On August 2, 1940, *The Secretariat of the Central Committee of the Communist Party of China on the Current International Situation and Our Party's Propaganda Policy* pointed out: "Everything in the

We can see that Chiang Kai-shek's description and evaluation of the American Monroe Doctrine in his speech delivered to the Seventh Plenum of the Fifth Central Committee of the Kuomintang in 1940 was different from that expressed in his 1934 article "Enemy? Friends? A Review of Sino-Japanese Relations." If the 1934 article regarded the U.S. Monroe Doctrine as an expansion strategy for the U.S., the speech in 1940 leveled considerable praise at the U.S. Monroe Doctrine. We do not know if Chiang Kai-shek had read the emphasis on differences between the American Monroe Doctrine and Japan's Asiatic Monroe Doctrine by officials and advisers of the Far East Department of the U.S. State Department during that same period. But regardless of whether he had read those words or not, the changes in his discourse obviously had political rhetoric in mind. We should here introduce the historical background: One of the hot topics discussed at the Seventh Plenum was whether the Nationalist Government should unite diplomatically with Germany.

During the plenary discussion on July 2, 1940, Foreign Minister Wang Chonghui 王宠惠 reported that Japan had forced the French government to close down the Yunnan-Vietnam Railway and had compelled Britain to terminate China's external communication channels through Hong Kong and Myanmar. Sun Ke 孙科 argued that with Germany winning, Britain was bound to fail in Europe, and China should "unite with Germany" 联德. This idea was also endorsed by Bai Chongxi 白崇禧. At that time, the call to "unite with Germany" was very loud within the Kuomintang, and some people even proposed supporting Myanmar's resistance to Britain in order to gain Germany's favor. Chiang Kai-shek didn't object to uniting with Germany, but only emphasized maintaining good relations with foreign powers to isolate Japan. On July 8, Chiang Kai-shek emphasized "striving for self-improvement" in his closing remarks and expressed his observation of Hitler's "success due to his own struggle."[687] After the plenum session, Chiang Kai-shek pursued a policy of secretly strengthening Sino-German relations.

However, the road of uniting with Germany was not smooth. On September 27, 1940, Germany, Italy and Japan signed an economic and military

---

U.S. is actively against the German, Italian and Japanese front. He announced the Monroe Doctrine in Asia in early July to prevent Japan from joining the German-Italian front. And he won't want this Monroe doctrine after Konoe Fumimaro come to power. The old tune of 'Open Door' and 'Aid China' will be repeated again." Institute of Journalism, Chinese Academy of Social Sciences eds., *Zhongguo gongchandang xinwen gongzuo wenjian huibian* 中国共产党新闻工作文件汇编 [*The News Document Compilation of the Communist Party of China*] (Volume I: 1921–1949), (Beijing: Xinhua chubanshe, 1980), 93–94.

687 Rong Mengyuan 荣孟源 ed., *Zhongguo Kuomintang lici daibiao dahui ji zhongyangquanhui ziliao* 中国国民党历次代表大会及中央全会资料 [*Materials of Chinese Nationalist Party Congresses and Central Plenary Sessions*] (II), (Beijing: Guangming ribao, 1985), 635.

alliance, and the Great East Asian New Order advocated by Japan won the support of Germany and Italy. Only then did pro-German sentiment within the Kuomintang gradually decline, and the significance of the U.S. become more explicit. On January 13, 1941, Chiang Kai-shek reviewed the previous year's debate over the diplomatic line in his diary: "In June and July of last year, when Britain and France suffered a fiasco and Germany won a major victory, the confidential secretary of the U.S. President issued a statement that Europe and Asia could establish their own respective Monroe Doctrines. At that time, almost all members of the party central committee advocated that we should unite with Germany, while Sun Zhesheng 孙哲生 and Bai Jiansheng 白健生 (here Chiang Kai-shek is referring to Sun Ke and Bai Chongxi—editor's note) were especially radical, having always considered American diplomacy unreliable. If I hadn't insisted on it at that time, but followed what Jiansheng said and chose to unite with Germany and oppose the U.S., then Britain and the U.S. would not only have been unwilling to cooperate with me today, but would have united with Japan to harm me. I would be in a very disadvantageous position! Looking back at it now, what they said was as naive as ever. I am really worried about the future of our country!"[688]

However, Chiang Kai-shek's words here were somewhat self-vindicating. At the Seventh Plenum of the Fifth Central Committee, Chiang Kai-shek did not debate the pro-German faction, and he pursued a foreign policy of further contact with Germany after the plenum. He was cautiously moving toward strengthening diplomatic relationship with Germany, but as his pace was slow, he did not appear to be pursuing a line of "opposing the U.S. and uniting with Germany" that might arouse the suspicion of other powers.

To sum up, starting in the early 1930s, Chiang Kai-shek tried to contain Japan's ambition of Asiatic Monroe Doctrine by appealing to the Nine-Power Treaty, the Pact of Paris and the League of Nations led by Britain and France. This was essentially a "balance of power" strategy. Even at the Seventh Plenum of the Fifth Central Committee of the Kuomintang, Chiang Kai-shek still openly insisted on the idea of forming strong alliances with all Western powers to contain Japan, and of trying to win over both the U.S. and Germany. Judging from Chiang Kai-shek's earlier expositions, he was fully aware that the U.S. Monroe Doctrine was essentially imperialism, but in order to win over the U.S., he did not hesitate to adopt new expositions to distinguish the U.S. Monroe Doctrine from the Japanese Asiatic Monroe Doctrine.

688 Huang and Pan (n. 683), 757–758.

4 Warring-States Strategists: the Prospect of Great Powerism

During the War of Resistance against Japanese Invasion, a school of nationalist thought, the Warring States Strategy school, emerged in the Kuomintang-controlled areas. Its ideas were published in the semi-monthly magazine *Warring States Policy* and the supplement of *Ta Kung Pao* (Chongqing edition), and it was named after what at that time was considered "a repetition of the Warring States era." Representative figures of the Warring States Strategy school included Lei Haizong, Lin Tongji, Chen Quan, He Yongji, He Lin, etc. Its members had studied mainly in Europe and America but not Japan, so their knowledge framework was different from that of the large number of senior Kuomintang elites who had studied in Japan, especially in advocating German thinkers such as Nietzsche and Spengler.

As representatives of the Warring States Policy school, Lin Tongji and Lei Haizong creatively combined Spengler's historical view of cultural form with China's own historical vision to create a unique historical view. They compared the history of Europe before the French Revolution to the Spring and Autumn Period, and regarded the history after the French Revolution as similar to the period from the Spring and Autumn Period to the Warring States Period. The First World War marked the complete entry into the Warring States Period, and many features of the Second World War, in which China was now immersed, could also be explained by the Warring States Period. When the first issue of *Warring States Policy* was published on April 1, 1940, Lin Tongji's *The Repetition of the Warring States Period* was also published. Among the domestic political forces, the China Youth Party showed the greatest interest in this thinking. In 1936, party member Chen Qitian[689] proposed a "Repetition of Warring States Period Theory," which was supported by Chang Naihui, Huang Xinzhou, Jiang Yungang and others in the party, but the social response was tepid. The emergence of the Warring States Strategy school boosted the spirits of advocates of "Repetition of Warring States Period Theory" in the China Youth Party, and Chang Naihui and Zeng Qi both published positive commentaries.[690]

689 What is worth mentioning here is Chen Qitian's view on the "Monroe Doctrine," "The so-called Monroe Doctrine is also known as nationalism." Chen Qitian 陈启天, "Guojia zhuyi yu Zhongguo qiantu 国家主义与中国前途 [Nationalism and China's Future]," in *Guojia zhuyi lunwenji* 国家主义论文集 [*Selected Works of Nationalism*] (3rd edition), ed. Shaonian zhongguo xuehui 少年中国学会 (Shanghai: Zhonghua shuju, 1925): 46.

690 See Sang Bing and Guan Xiaohong 桑兵、关晓红 eds., *Jindai Zhongguo xueshu liupai yanjiu* 近代中国学术流派研究 [*A Study of Modern Chinese Academic Schools*], (Beijing: Shenghuo, Dushu, Xinzhi sanlian shudian, 2007), 541–543.

One month after the Seventh Plenum of the Fifth Kuomintang Central Committee was held, on August 1, 1940, the Japanese government announced its Outline of Basic National Policy, in which Foreign Minister Matsuoka Yosuke trumpeted the Greater East Asia Co-Prosperity Sphere. Against this background, on August 15, Hong Siqi published "Interpretation of Great Politics" in *Warring States Policy*, pointing out that "the ironclad facts of the past two decades have proved the fiasco of international idealism. We have to admit that we have gone the wrong way, and the only way to save the nation from now on is to implement the big politics of international struggle." According to Hong Siqi, so-called "great politics" referred to the struggle between countries. "Its methods are war and diplomacy, and its law is Macht Politik." It was called "great" because it was "super-factional, super-class, super-provincial; it is struggle politics with the nation as the unit and the world as the stage."[691] The word "great" could be considered the response of the Warring States Strategy school to the various Provincial Monroe Doctrines in China, and it could also be considered a response to the civil war between the Kuomintang and the Communist Party before the War of Resistance against Japanese Invasion.

Hong Siqi pointed out that the immediate goal of "great politics" was to defeat the Japanese aggressors, but the future goal was to make Asia peaceful: "The responsibility of stabilizing East Asia should belong to China, not Japan, because we are superior to Japan in talent, attitude towards others and history." China needed to build a strong army and gain assistance from the Soviet Union and the U.S. to destroy Japan's control of Chinese territory, so that China could become a first-class world power within ten years. Peace of Asia would bring stability and prosperity to China. Hong Siqi added: "This is not to say that China wants to implement imperialism. What China needs is collective security and prosperity in Asia. And China doesn't need aggression. As long as we are strong, the old vassals will naturally join the Asian Federation led by China, and an independent and free India will automatically cooperate with China on an equal basis. We also don't need to attack British colonies in Asia. They will very likely become independent after the decisive battle in Europe."[692]

In the same issue of *Warring States Policy*, He Yongxi published the article "The Fight between Dragon and Tiger," at the end of which he also remarked on the Nazi Germany's plan for European unification: "The Nazis have advocated creating a federation of European continent, with the exception of the Soviet Union and the British Empire. Judged from historical rule of evolution, this kind of endeavor is inevitable. Europe has become a cultural region, but it

691 Cao and Guo (n. 78), 358.

692 Ibid., 359.

has not yet become a political region. Will the latter be achieved by Hitler?"[693] As mentioned earlier, during the same period, there was discussion within the Kuomintang over whether to "unite with Germany." The Warring States Strategy school made extensive use of German theoretical resources in their articles, which easily gave people the impression of being "pro-German" in foreign policy, and it did attract such criticism at the time.[694] However, in 1940, most authors in the Warring States Strategy school focused on the situation in East Asia, hoping that the U.S., neutral at that time, would abandon its appeasement policy towards Japan and involve itself in the war.

In September 1940, He Yongji published a commentary entitled "Gentleman's Diplomacy—Words without Hands-on" in *Warring States Policy*, criticizing the U.S. policy towards Japan: "After Hitler's victory in Europe, the colonies belonging to the Netherlands, France and Belgium in the two hemispheres will be a problem, and the Monroe Doctrine will encounter an experiment unprecedented in the past hundred years." He Yongxi mentioned the declaration made by Stephen Early, Roosevelt's press secretary on July 6, 1940, and summarized the following points of the declaration: 1) The U.S. was not prepared to send troops to fight in the war; 2) the possesions of the three countries in the Western Hemisphere should be managed through joint negotiation by twenty-one countries in the Western Hemisphere; 3) if the U.S. Monroe Doctrine was extended, then possesions in the Far East (the declaration clearly stated Vietnam) should also be handled through consultation among Asian countries. He Yongji noted that in July 1940, the U.S. convened the Pan-American Conference for consultation and reached the following consensus: 1) The possesions of the defeated European countries in the Americas should be jointly managed by the a committee organized by U.S., Cuba and Panama; 2) this kind of management was not meant to be a permanent cession, but supervision of possessions that could still be returned to their original owners after the war; 3) during the joint management period, all local taxes should be used to serve the local area, and any shortage should be filled by the three co-managing countries.

However, He Yongji only noticed the declaration made by Roosevelt's press secretary on July 6, while failing to notice the new statement made by U.S. Secretary of State Cordell Hull on July 8. Hull criticized the misinterpretation of the Monroe Doctrine in some parts of the world, and contended that the Monroe Doctrine was only a collective defense policy, which did not imply U.S. hegemony. It was different from military occupation and complete economic

693 Ibid., 288.

694 Sang and Guan (n. 689), 529–617.

and political control in these places.[695] In fact, this was a "fire-fighting" exercise by the White House following Early's statement.

In December 1940, He Yongji wrote "The U.S. Should Declare War Immediately," which from the geopolitical perspective played up the threat of South America to the U.S. He Yongji pointed out that in terms of race, culture, trade and geography, South America was closer to Europe than to North America, especially in cultural psychology. "Some countries in South America hate the aggressiveness of Big Brother through the Monroe Doctrine, and lean toward Europe above political sentiment."[696] The Axis powers had great influence in Brazil, Argentina, Chile and Peru. He Yongji predicted that if the Axis powers won the European battlefield, within two years, "Americas will face challenges to the Monroe Doctrine; if you want to fight at that time, you will have three enemies and no friends around you," and the U.S. might repeat the mistakes made by Britain at the Munich Conference.[697]

In "Gentleman's Diplomacy—Words without Hands-on," He Yongji was actually accusing America's diplomatic posturing of not being helpful to China. With the U.S. joining the Pacific War at the end of 1941, the situation in World War II shifted in favor of China. In June 1942, Lin Tongji wrote an article predicting the future trend of world order: "No matter which side wins this war, the result will not be the unification of the world, but the birth of two or three superpowers. These two or three superpowers are overwhelming 'great powers,' which will actually determine the future of human destiny. With cooperation, there must be a kind of 'Great Powerism.'" Theoretically, these two or three powerful countries would be granted recognized status and privileges. This actually meant that the European Federation or Asian Federation envisioned by He Yongji and Hong Siqi would essentially be dominated by several super-countries. Lin Tongji pointed out that the question was whether this Great Powerism "takes the form of Hitler and Tojo's brutal style, or a Duke Huan of Qi style of enlightened leadership—we can also call it Roosevelt's style." In his view, if Germany and Japan won, nationalism would gradually die out; but if the U.S. won, "nationalism can achieve a new way to coexist with Great Powerism."[698]

695 Wilcox (n. 387), 452.

696 Zhang Changshan 张昌山 ed., Zhanguocepai wencun 战国策派文存 [*The Literature of the Warring States Policy School*] (part two), (Kunming: Yunnan renmin chubanshe 云南人民出版社, 2013), 472.

697 Ibid., 476.

698 Cao and Guo (n. 87), 149.

The theorists of the Warring States Strategy school mainly mentioned the Monroe Doctrine in their comments on American and Japanese policies, but did not regard it as the core concept of their own analysis of Chinese history and current politics. However, in the course of world history they conceived, regional integration and regional hegemony were the inevitable results of the Warring States period, whether or not the "Great Powerism" for regional hegemony is expressed through the symbol of the Monroe Doctrine. This reminds us of Kang Youwei's vision at the beginning of the twentieth century—that the U.S. would unify America, Europe would be unified by Germany, and Asia would complete its own regional integration under the leadership of China and finally proceed towards "great harmony."[699] Unlike Kang Youwei's assumption, the Warring States Strategy school adopted Spengler's view of historical cycles. Every vivacious culture (*Kultur*) would eventually become a decayed civilization through historical evolution, after which a new historical cycle would begin. Therefore, the unification of the world did not mean the end of history. But for Kang Youwei, *Ta tung* or "the great unity" really meant the end of history.

5 Li Dazhao: Criticism of the Monroe Doctrine towards the Future

Finally, we will discuss Li Dazhao, one of the founders of the Communist Party of China (CPC). If we say that many political elites of the Revolutionary Alliance–Kuomintang went through a complicated process to break away from Japanese Monroe Doctrine discourse because of the complicated relationship between their revolutionary course and Japan, Li Dazhao began to criticize Japan's Great Asianism before studying in Japan, and revealed the deception contained in its discourse.

In 1912, the Japanese author Nakajima Tan published *The Fate of the Division of China*, saying that China was not qualified as a republic, and could only be divided into pieces. This aroused great indignation from Li Dazhao, then one of the editors of the Beiyang Law and Politics Society (the student group of the Beiyang Law and Politics Special School). Li Dazhao and his colleagues in the Beiyang Law and Politics Society edited *Refutation of the Destiny China's Division*, which was published in December 1912. In this paper, Li Dazhao and

699 Kang (n. 579), 132.

his colleagues refuted Nakajima in the form of comments head notes, and interlinear notes, and in particular pointed out, "In recent years, Japanese people are advocating the Asiatic Monroe Doctrine and Great Asianism. If you listen to what they say, you may think that they are our friends, but if you look into their hearts, you see they are enemies. This doctrine is a pretext for Japan's attempt to dominate East Asia."[700] This commentary laid the intellectual foundation for Li Dazhao's continuous criticism of Japan's Great Asianism. At the end of the year, Li Dazhao joined the Chinese Socialist Party launched by Chen Yilong and others. He became the head of the Tianjin branch of the party in February 1913.

In 1913, twenty-four-year-old Li Dazhao received financial support from the Progressive Party led by Liang Qichao and Tang Hualong to study in Japan, where he entered the political department of Waseda University in Tokyo. At Waseda University, Li Dazhao was influenced by Abe Isoo, who co-sponsored the Japanese Social Democratic Party with Kōtoku Shūsui.[701] He also approached Zhang Shizhao, who published the monthly journal *Jia Yin* while participating in the Second Revolution against Yuan Shikai (the Progressive Party took a pro-Yuan position). Just as Japan proposed to impose Twenty-one Demands on the Beiyang government in 1915, Li Dazhao joined protests by Chinese students studying in Japan. Before long, Yuan Shikai proclaimed himself emperor, and the National Protection Movement broke out. In May 1916, Li Dazhao dropped out of school, returned to China and joined the anti-Yuan struggle.

We can compare Li Dazhao's experience with that of Chen Duxiu, another party founder. Chen Duxiu went to Japan three times in 1901, 1907 and 1908 for carrying out the anti-Manchu revolution. However, Chen Duxiu did not join the Revolutionary Alliance, but became a member of the Asian Friendship Association initiated by Zhang Taiyan, Japanese socialist Kōtoku Shūsui and the Indians Borohan and Pausch. As mentioned above, the idea of Asian Friendship Association was quite different from mainstream Asianism in Japan for being very vigilant against Japanese imperialism. Li Dazhao was influenced by anarchism and socialism before studying in Japan and had become immune to the Japanese Monroe Doctrine by editing "Refutation of the Fate of the

700 Zhu Wentong 朱文通 et al. eds., *Li Dazhao quanji* 李大钊全集 [*Complete Works of Li Dazhao*] (Volume 1), (Shijiazhuang: *Hebei jiaoyu chubanshe*, 1999), 479.

701 Zhu Wentong 朱文通, "Li Dazhao shehui zhuyi sixiang fazhan licheng xintan 李大钊社会主义思想发展历程新探 [A New Probe into the Development Course of Li Dazhao's Socialist Thought]," *Hebei xuekan* 1 (2007).

Division of China." The experience of studying at Waseda University further strengthened his critical view of Japanese Monroe Doctrine.

After Li Dazhao returned to China in 1916, he once again approached the Progressive Party apparatus led by Liang Qichao. Although Li Dazhao had criticized the Progressive Party's pro-Yuan stance during his stay in Japan, after Yuan Shikai proclaimed himself emperor, Liang Qichao and others took an anti-Yuan stance and won back Li Dazhao's favor. Li Dazhao served as director of the editorial department of *Chen Zhong Bao*, a party newspaper under the leadership of Liang Qichao, but soon broke away from Liang's faction because of their different stands. In January 1918, Li Dazhao succeeded Zhang Shizhao as curator of the Peking University Library, and became a professor in July 1920.

On February 19, 1917, Li Dazhao published "The Nationalism of New China" in *Jia Yin*, in which he referred to the Monroe Doctrine of the U.S., the Anglo-Saxon Doctrine of Britain, the Slavic Doctrine of Russia and Serbia, the Germanic Doctrine of Germany and Asiatic Doctrine of Japan as "nationalist movements." The article said, "Although there is Asianism in Japan, I don't know its purpose." However, "if they want to conquer the Asian nation by Asianism without awakening the New China and the flourishing of new Chinese nationalism, they will never succeed." When the Republic of China was founded, there were still five major ethnic groups. Now the cultures of the five ethnic groups were becoming increasingly consistent. "All peoples who belong to the Republic of China are the new Chinese nation," giving birth to "New Chinese Nationalism." "New Chinese nationalism can actually be carried forward in East Asia, and then Great Asianism can shine in the world."[702]

On February 21, 1917, Li Dazhao published "The Monroe Doctrine in Far East" in *Jia Yin*. The article started by introducing the opposition between the U.S. Monroe Doctrine and the Holy Alliance, and then turned to Chinese affairs. Li Dazhao pointed out that in recent decades, the main reason for maintaining peace in the Far East was the existence of the Open Door Policy and Equal Opportunity. "Now, suddenly, there is a power that wants to make a Monroe Doctrine Declaration in East Asia. Does it run counter to the Open Door and Equal Opportunity Doctrine? Can the world's great problems be determined by a country's declaration when the European war has not yet ended? Will the country that made the declaration have the determination and strength to see it through to the end? After the end of the European War, will this declaration bring the threat of a world war?"[703]

702 Zhu (n. 699), 281–286.

703 Ibid., 290.

In April, Li Dazhao published "Great Asianism," which made a more thorough critique of the Japanese Monroe Doctrine. Firstly, the article reviewed the paper "What is Great Asianism" published by *Chūōkōron* in Tokyo, Japan. This paper criticized Western civilization as a predatory civilization. As the yellow race, Asians should unite and "reject the whites" in order to "exclude non-Asian forces from Asia, and make Asia for the Asians." This paper called for changing Japan's policy based on the Anglo-Japanese alliance "as the Far East's watchdog for Britain," and liaising with China and India to promote Asianism. Li Dazhao severely criticized this, saying that Japan's Asianism was essentially "concealing its imperialism and hegemonic policy in the Far East, forbidding the plundering of other states so that they themselves can plunder, refusing the bullying others so that they themselves can bully, with the result that white people will be jealous, and ultimately all of Asia will be blamed." Li Dazhao believed that true Asianism "should be based on the reconstruction of China, the revival of the Chinese nation." Japan should recognize that China was "the pillar of the overall situation in Asia." When China was invaded by foreign forces, it should not help those outsiders, but "support each other with friendship based on being of the same continent and the same race." In the end, Li Dazhao believed that European and American powers should abandon racial prejudice and avoid the "yellow-white war" to bring about "harmony between the Eastern and Western races."[704]

In the article "The Failure of Pan … ism and the Victory of Democracy" published in July 1918, Li Dazhao deepened his criticism of Great Asianism, putting Japan's Asianism in the category of "Pan … ism": "Those who hold this doctrine only want to satisfy their own desires, and they want to force others by coercion and make them bend." Li Dazhao similarly analyzed the root cause of the outbreak of World War I: "Anyone who can exist in the universe must have his own realm of freedom, keeping it in harmony with the outside world or opposing each other, and trying to coexist with each other. If there is someone who doesn't show sympathy and tries to invade others, one side could initially be huge, powerful and lucky, and the other side small, weak and devastated, and the side that is lucky and happy may think that he deserves it. However, the other side that suffers from endless trouble and pains will summon all its strength and seek revenge. This kind of psychology will easily become its backbone and be irrepressible. People want to be powerful, and weaker people who believe in 'Pan … ism' may fight with them, However, if two men ride a horse, one must sit behind. The result is a lose-lose situation."[705]

704 Ibid., 106–108.
705 Li (n. 550), 245.

Here, Li Dazhao depicted a "zero-sum game" scenario: Some forces were too inflated and invaded the space of others, which was bound to cause a rebound by the other party. Those engaging in expansionism inspired joint resistance by the weak or the envy of other expansionists, which would inevitably lead to conflict. Although this mainly explained the defeat of Germany in the European War, it was also aimed at the Japanese Monroe Doctrine to a certain extent. In an article in January 1923, Li Dazhao further added: "The spirit rooted in despotism and imperialism is often embodied as 'Pan ... ism.'"[706]

More importantly, Li Dazhao also tried to use this principle to explain warlord separatism and conflict in China. During the First World War, the Republic of China was divided, with the North and South confronting each other and warlords attacking each other. In Li Dazhao's view, this was a kind of "Pan ... ism" of internal strife. Li Dazhao explained the difference between this doctrine and the expansionism of the great powers: "... the 'Pan ... ism' of others is to expand their power and develop externally; our country's 'Pan ... ism' is to invade each other and divide China. Therefore, the 'Pan ... ism' of others is the doctrine of expansion, and the 'Pan ... ism' of our country is the doctrine of contraction." The reason was that as a weak country, China's citizens were unable to expand abroad and could only vent their "contentious nature" internally. Moreover, China's "Pan ... ism" had the feature that the scope of its expansion was never too large, and the center of that scope was never too small, so it could be reduced to the selfishness of one single person. Li Dazhao's criticized Yuan Shikai's Hong Xian monarchy and the despotism of the provincial governors at that time as the expansion of the selfishness of one person.[707]

Therefore, the article "The Failure of Pan ... ism and the Victory of Democracy" not only commented on various Monroe Doctrines in the world, but also criticized the phenomenon of conflicting provinces in China. Li Dazhao did not refer to this phenomenon as Monroe Doctrine, but as explained above, some people were referring to this phenomenon as "Monroe Doctrine" in newspapers as early as 1917. With the rise of the United Provincial Autonomy Movement in 1920, Monroe Doctrine discourse flourished. As a leading figure in public opinion circles, Li Dazhao would not have been unfamiliar with this discourse.

On New Year's Day 1919, Li Dazhao published "Great Asianism and Neo-Asianism," further criticizing Japan's Great Asianism and naming the

706 Zhu Wentong 朱文通 et al. eds., *Li Dazhao quanji* 李大钊全集 [*Complete Works of Li Dazhao*] (Volume IV), (Shijiazhuang: *Hebei jiaoyu chubanshe*, 1999), 154.

707 Zhu Wentong 朱文通 et al. eds., *Li Dazhao quanji* 李大钊全集 [*Complete Works of Li Dazhao*] (Volume II), (Shijiazhuang: *Hebei jiaoyu chubanshe*, 1999), 245.

alternative proposition "Neo-Asianism." The beginning of the article named the Japanese authors who advocate Great Asianism, including Takebe Tongo, Otani Kozui, Tokutomi Soho, Kodera Kenkichi, etc. Li Dazhao pointed out, "China can only be maintained by the balance of power among the great powers." In order to monopolize China, Japan had to eliminate these forces, so it invented Great Asianism, which was ostensibly "affectionate words for the same language and the same race" but with evil intentions behind it. Fundamentally speaking, Great Asianism was just another name for Great Japanism. It was the Japanese who used the Asiatic Monroe Doctrine to stop the Europeans and Americans and turned Asia into Japan's Asia. "In this way, this Great Asianism is not a doctrine for peace, but a doctrine for invasion; not a doctrine for national self-determination, but a doctrine for imperialism that gobbles up weak nations; not a doctrine for Asian Democracy, but for militarism in Japan. It's not an organization adapted to the organizing of the world but a seed to destroy the organization of the world."[708] Japan's advocacy of Asianism would not only arouse the discontent of weak countries and small countries in Asia, but also attract the envy of European and American powers, which made it a suicidal policy.

In "Great Asianism and Neo-Asianism," Li Dazhao imagined that the world would eventually move towards a major alliance. Before that, there would be continent-wide federations in America and Europe, and a similar organization should be set up in Asia to advocate a kind of "Neo-Asianism" to replace the "Great Asianism" advocated by some Japanese. This neo-Asianism was also different from the Asianism advocated by Ukita Kazutami based on the Sino-Japanese alliance. Instead, it was based on the liberation and self-determination of all nationalities in Asia, who would then form a great alliance, "juxtaposed with the European Federation and the American Federation, thus jointly completing the world federation and benefiting the happiness of mankind."[709] Here, the Asian Federation was neither an essentialist "Asian Unity" (Okakura Tenshin) culture, nor a permanent regional organization, but a transitional step towards equality and unity for all mankind.

6 Concluding Remarks

Following the Meiji Restoration, Japan became the birthplace of much of modern China's thought. Under pressure from European and American powers

708 Ibid., 269.
709 Ibid., 270.

after the Sino-Japanese War of 1894–1895, The Meiji government focused on attracting Chinese students and influencing Chinese cultural and political elites in Japan. As a result, the late Qing Dynasty's cultural and political elites in Japan, whether reformers or anti-Manchu revolutionaries, were greatly influenced by Japanese ideological trends. Japan's political and academic circles combined the Monroe Doctrine with Japanese Asianism to form Japanese Monroe Doctrine, which inspired China's anti-Manchu nationalism (including anti-Manchu provincial independence), and some revolutionaries hoped for financial assistance from the Japanese government and people. They therefore responded positively to Japanese Monroe Doctrine discourse.

However, as the situation developed, tension between Japan's foreign policy and Asianism discourse increasingly came to the fore. Chinese political elites who tried to get support from the Japanese government and private sector with the help of the Asianism discourse also suffered repeated setbacks, resulting in disenchantment with Asiatic Monroe Doctrine discourse. This chapter discusses how the various factions and political elites in Japan discarded the Japanese Monroe Doctrine discourse:

– After failing to obtain help from Japan in 1898, Kang Youwei quickly distanced himself from Japanese Monroe Doctrine discourse, while Liang Qichao realized the substance of Japanese Monroe Doctrine discourse by reading the discussion on imperialism in Japanese at the turn of the century and making a field trip to the U.S. in 1903.

- As the leader of the revolutionary group, Sun Yat-sen had long faced the problem of an unstable financial foundation. Hoping for support from Japan, he frequently appealed to Japanese Monroe Doctrine. However, after Yuan Shikai's death, the Japanese government supported the Beiyang government rather than the government led by Sun Yat-sen, who then began to distance himself from the Japanese Monroe Doctrine in his discourse. After the May Fourth Movement in 1919, Sun became a more determined critic of Japanese imperialism.
- Chiang Kai-shek also sought the Japan government's support in his early years. However, after the Mukden Incident, he became much more critical of Japanese Monroe Doctrine, emphasizing that it endangered the interests of European nations and the U.S. and was bound to be resisted by all nations. However, in terms of policy, he still employed the Nine-Power Treaty and Kellogg-Briand Pact to curtail Japanese aggression against China, and pursued the policy of "pacifying the interior before resisting foreign aggression." It was not until the Xi'an Incident that he decided to end the civil war and join forces with the CPC against Japan. When hard pressed by Japan, Chiang

Kai-shek further attempted to strengthen his relations with the U.S. by deliberately distinguishing between the U.S. Monroe Doctrine and the Japanese Monroe Doctrine, praising the former and denouncing the latter.

- During the War of Resistance Against Japanese Invasion, the Warring States Strategy School learned from Spengler's Morphology of Cultures and referred to the current era as a Warring States Period. The school envisaged the rise of a number of great powers in various regions, which would implement some form of Monroe Doctrine and finally move towards world unification. Hong Siqi also hoped that China could integrate former tributary vassal states by building an "Asian Federation."
- Among the above mentioned elites of all political orientations, the most amazing was Li Dazhao. Before studying in Japan in 1913, Li Dazhao had been "immune" to Japanese Monroe Doctrine. In 1912, Li Dazhao was in close contact with Chinese socialists such as Jiang Kanghu and Chen Yilong, who were influenced by Japanese anarchism and socialism. One of his important ideological sources was Kōtoku Shūsui. In 1907, Zhang Taiyan and Kōtoku Shūsui joined to launch the Asian Friendship Association, and advocated an Asianism in which weak and small nationalities united for self-liberation. This incident had an impact on Chen Duxiu. Li Dazhao, who was studying in Japan, was influenced by Abe Isoo, a close friend of Kōtoku Shūsui.[710] We can see that Japan's anarchist-socialist ideological trend in the early twentieth century provided important ideological resources for rethinking Japan's regional hegemonism.

After Li Dazhao and Chen Duxiu met at Peking University, they ultimately accepted Marxism-Leninism and jointly founded the Communist Party of China (CPC) in 1921. As is well known, Leninism's criticism of imperialism was extremely thorough, and its support for weak nations resisting imperialism was also extremely thorough. Compared with Lenin, Wilson's nationalism could not eradicate racism and imperialism. In the face of Lenin's Imperialism, even the original U.S. Monroe Doctrine could hardly enjoy a moral advantage, much less its parody by the Japanese right wing. Lenin's theory and practice contributed to the great transformation of Dr. Sun Yat-sen's Asianism discourse—in Sun's Great Asianism speech in 1924, Asia was no longer defined by the Japanese right wing's concept of the "yellow race," and the key to defining "Asia" was not its natural attributes but whether the principle it pursued was "kingly" or "hegemonic." The tributary system in the East was regarded as

710 Zhu (n. 700).

a model of the kingly way, and Russia, although long regarded as "white," was now regarded as demonstrating the kingly way.

Compared with Sun Yat-sen, what Li Dazhao initiated was a tradition with more historical significance for the future. Neo-Asianism was the negation of the "sphere of influence" thinking contained in Japan's Great Asianism, and it did not revive the ancient Asian tributary system. Instead, it called on all nationalities in Asia to refute imperialism-colonialism and unite on an equal footing on the basis of self-liberation. The purpose of this alliance was not to construct a collective and exclusive sphere of influence and set a closed boundary, but rather to keep vigilance against all forms of imperialism. The liberation of Asia was part of the liberation of the whole world and was associated with the liberation of other regions.

At the beginning of the twentieth century, Kang Youwei had envisaged that the U.S. would unify America, Germany would unify Europe, China would unify Asia, and the three regions would eventually move towards *Ta Tung* or "great harmony." However, Kang Youwei envisaged a hegemonic regional integration model, in which a leading country would unify Germany in a way similar to Prussia and establish a regional federation that was not substantially equal, and would first achieve a "canceling" of states within the regional scope. Under this logic, the colonies of the great powers did not need to undergo a process of independence and then union; rather, as a part of the suzerain, they would be directly integrated into the new regional federation.[711] Compared with Kang Youwei, Li Dazhao's plan supported the liberation of colonies, while more explicitly rejecting the logic of hegemonic integration.

The path envisioned by Kang Youwei did not become a historical reality. During the First World War, European powers weakened each other in the process of killing each other, and the October Revolution brought Russia a revolutionary regime that supported the independence of vast colonies and semi-colonial nations. The rising U.S. had stepped beyond the Western Hemisphere and constantly intervened in Eurasian affairs. It also greatly impacted the domination of European powers over colonies and semi-colonies. This weakened the position of "the center of Europe," and the "civilization hierarchy theory" jointly maintained by European powers in the nineteenth century lost its prestige to a great extent. The independence and self-liberation movements of vast colonial and semi-colonial nations and countries were like sparks that caught fire and stoked each other.

711 Kang (n. 579), 132.

In the twentieth century, it was the common cause of anti-imperialism and anti-colonization that led various regions to support each other and form the concepts and recognition of "people of Asia, Africa and Latin America" and even "people of the world." In this sense, Li Dazhao's call for Neo-Asianism was the forerunner of the slogans "Great Unity of the People of Asia, Africa and Latin America" and "Long live the great unity of the people of the world" at Tiananmen Gate. The political subject of "people of the world" was not exclusive to any specific region, but was based on the global political space. It did not refer to politics based on "spheres of influence." It was not a politics of concert of global capital for profit maximization, but a politics based on labor and sociability, a politics strongly oriented toward the future.

Currently, the unipolar hegemonic system is experiencing its decay, and multi-polarization is emerging as an ever more evident development trajectory. This implies that numerous regions across the globe might attain a greater degree of autonomy than in the past. Yet, this autonomy also harbors the potential for regional hegemonism and the fragmentation of the global order. Against this background, can we re-imagine the unified power of "the people of the world"? What prospect can we outline through the discourse of the Community of a Shared Future for Mankind? Can the current global mode of production and relations of production support our imagination of "people of the world" and "Community of Shared Future for Mankind"? Discussions on the Monroe Doctrine will continue, but new issues are slowly rising to the surface.

Bibliography

Literature in Chinese

Anderson, Perry, Li Yan 李岩 trans., *Meiguo waijiao zhence jiqi zhinang* 美国外交政策及其智囊 [*American Foreign Policy and Its Think Tanks*], (Beijing: Jincheng chubanshe 金城出版社, 2017).

Cao Yinglong and Guo Na 曹颖龙、郭娜, *Zhanguo cepai* 战国策派 [*The School of the Warring States Strategies*], (Changchun: Changchun chubanshe 长春出版社, 2013).

Changchun wenshi ziliao bianjibu 长春文史资料编辑部, Changchun wenshi ziliao: Zong di 53 ji: Wei Manzhouguo Shisi Nian Shihua 长春文史资料·总第53辑·伪满洲国十四年史话 [*Changchun Historical Materials: Volume 53: A Brief History of the Puppet Manchukuo*], (Changchun: Changchunshi zhengxie wenshi he xuexi weiyuanhui 长春市政协文史和学习委员会, 2002).

Chen Yong 陈勇, *Minguo shijia yu shixue 1912–1949: Minguo shijia yu shixue guoji xueshu yantaohui lunwenji* 民国史家与史学1912 - 1949：民国史家与史学国际学术研讨会论文集 [*Historians and Historiography of the Republic of China, 1912–1949: Proceedings of the International Academic Symposium on Historians and Historiography of the Republic of China*], (Shanghai: Shanghai daxue chubanshe 上海大学出版社, 2014).

Cheng Zhaoqi 程兆奇, *Yundong guoji junshi fating tingshen jilu Zhongguo bufen Qinzhan dongbei bianfang juzheng* 运东国际军事法庭庭审记录·中国部分·侵占东北辨方举证（上）[*Records of the Trials of the International Military Tribunal for the Far East: Chinese Section—Evidence Presented by the Defense in the Occupation of Northeast China*] (Volume One), (Shanghai: Shanghai jiaotong daxue chubanshe 上海交通大学出版社, 2015).

Deng Shusheng 邓蜀生, *Woodrow Wilson*, (Shanghai: Shanghai renmin chubanshe 上海人民出版社, 1982).

Ding Wenjiang and Zhao Fengtian 丁文江、赵丰田, *Liang Qichao nianpu changbian* 梁启超年谱长编 [*Chronological Biography of Liang Qichao*], (Shanghai: Shanghai renmin chubanshe 上海人民出版社, 1983).

Duan Yunzhang 段云章, *Sun Wen yu riben shishi biannian* 孙文与日本史事编年 [*Chronology of Sun Yat-sen and Japanese Historical Events*] (Revised Edition), (Guangzhou: Guangdong renmin chubanshe 广东人民出版社, 2011).

Duan Yunzhang and Ni Junming 段云章、倪俊明, *Chen Jiongming ji* 陈炯明集 [*The Collected Works of Chen jiongming*], (Guangzhou: Zhongshan daxue chubanshe 中山大学出版社, 2007).

Gao Hongzhi 高鸿志, *Wilson yu beiyang junfa zhengfu* 威尔逊与北洋军阀政府 [*Wilson and the Beiyang Warlord Government*], (Beijing: Renmin chubanshe 人民出版社, 2015).

Gilbert, Felix, *Xiandai ouzhou shi* 现代欧洲史 [*Modern European History*], (Beijing: Zhongxin chubanshe 中信出版社, 2016).

Gong Gujin and Yun Xiu 龚古今、恽修, *Diyici shijie dazhan yilai diguo zhuyi qinhua wenjian xuanzhuan* 第一次世界大战以来帝国主义侵华文件选辑 [*Selections of Imperialism's Documents on the Invasion of China Since World War 1*], (Beijing: Shenghuo, Dushu, Xinzhi sanlian shudian 生活·读书·新知三联书店, 1958).

Gu Yanwu 顾炎武, *Gu Tinglin shiwenji* 顾亭林诗文集 [*The Collected Poems and Writings of Gu Tinglin*], (Beijing: Zhonghua shuju 中华书局, 1983).

Guan Xiaohong 关晓虹, "Qingji waiguan gaizhi de 'difang' kunrao 清季外官改制的'地方'困扰 [The 'Local' Dilemma of the Reform of Foreign Officials in the Late Qing Dynasty]," *Jindaishi yanjiu* 近代史研究 5 (2010).

Guangdongsheng zhengxie wenshi ziliao yanjiu weiyuanhui 广东省政协文史资料研究委员会, *Sun Yat-sen yu xinhai geming shiliao zhuanji* 孙中山与辛亥革命史料专辑 [*Special Collection of Historical Materials on Sun Yat-sen and the Xinhai Revolution*], (Guangzhou: Guangdong renmin chubanshe 广东人民出版社, 1981).

Guangxi wuzhoushi zhengxie wenshi ziliao weiyuanhui and cangwuxian zhengxie wenshi ziliao weiyuanhui 广西梧州市政协文史资料委员会、苍梧县政协文史资料委员会, *Wuzhou wenshi ziliao di 15 ji: Li jishen minzhu sixiang yanjiu* 梧州文史资料第15辑：李济深民主思想研究 [*Wuzhou Historical Materials Volume 15: Research on Li jishen's Democratic Thought*], (Wuzhou: Zhongguo renmin zhengzhi xieshang huiyi wuzhoushi weiyuanhui wenshi ziliaozu 中国人民政治协商会议梧州市委员会文史资料组, 1991).

Guojia dang'an ju mingqing dang'an guan 国家档案局明清档案馆, *Wuxu bianfa dang'an shiliao* 戊戌变法档案史料 [*Documents on the Hundred Days' Reform*], (Beijing: Zhonghua shuju 中华书局, 1958).

Han Li 韩莉, *Xinwaijiao·Jiushijie: Woodrow Wilson yu guoji lianmeng* 新外交·旧世界：伍德罗·威尔逊与国际联盟 [*New Diplomacy, Old World: Woodrow Wilson and the League of Nations*], (Beijing: Tongxin chubanshe 同心出版社, 2002).

Huang Xingtiao 黄兴涛, *Chongsu zhonghua* 重塑中华 [*Reshaping China*], (Beijing: Beijing shifan daxue chubanshe 北京师范大学出版社, 2017).

Huang Xingtao 黄兴涛, "Gainianshi fangfa yu zhongguo jindaishi yanjiu 概念史方法与中国近代史研究 [Conceptual History Methodology and the Study of Modern Chinese History]," *Shixue yuekan* 史学月刊 9 (2012).

Huang Zijin and Pan Guangzhe 黄自进、潘光哲, *Jiang Zhongzheng zongtong wujiji · Kunmianji* (*Shang*) 蒋中正总统五记·困勉记（上）[*Five Records of President Chiang Ching-kuo: The Record of Difficulties* (*Volume One*)], (Taipei: Guoshiguan 国史馆, 2011).

Huang Zijin and Pan Guangzhe 黄自进、潘光哲, *Jiang Zhongzheng zongtong wuji·Xueji* 蒋中正总统五记·学记 [*Five Records of President Chiang Ching-kuo: The Record of Learning*], (Taipei: Guoshiguan 国史馆, 2011).

Hunansheng shehui kexueyuan 湖南省社会科学院, *Huang Xing ji* 黄兴集 [*The Collected Works of Huang Xing*], (Changsha: Hunan renmin chubanshe 湖南人民出版社, 2008).

Huntington, Samuel, Li Sheng 李晟 trans., *Junren yu guojia: Junzheng guanxi de lilun yu zhengzhi* 军人与国家：军政关系的理论与政治 [*The Soldier and the State: The Theory and Politics of Civil-Military Relations*], (Beijing: Zhongguo zhengfa daxue chubanshe 中国政法大学出版社, 2017).

Jiang Yihua and Zhang Ronghua 姜义华、张荣华, *Kang Youwei quanji* 康有为全集 [*The Complete Works of Kang Youwei*], (Beijing: Zhongguo renmin daxue chubanshe 中国人民大学出版社, 2007).

Jiang Yongjing 蒋永敬, *Hu Hanmin xiansheng nianpu* 胡汉民先生年谱 [*Chronology of Mr. Hu Hanmin*], (Taipei: Central Committee of the Kuomintang Party History Commission, 1978).

Jilinsheng tushuguan weimanzhouguo shiliao bianweihui 吉林省图书馆伪满洲国史料编委会, *Weimanzhouguo shiliao* (*Diyice*) 伪满洲国史料（第一册）[*Historical Materials of the Puppet Manchukuo* (*Volume One*)], (Beijing: Quanguo tushuguan wenxian suowei fuzhi zhongxin 全国图书馆文献缩微复制中心, 2002).

Jin Guangyao 金光耀, *Gu Weijun yu zhongguo waijiao* 顾维钧与中国外交 [*Gu Weijun and Chinese Diplomacy*], (Shanghai: Shanghai guji chubanshe 上海古籍出版社, 2001).

Kagan, Robert, Yuan Shengyu 袁胜育 et al. trans., *Weixian de guojia: Meiguo cong qiyuan dao ershi shijichu de shijie diwei* 危险的国家：美国从起源到20世纪初的世界地位 [*Dangerous Nation: America's Place in the World from Its Origins to the Early 20th Century*], (Beijing: Shehui kexue wenxian chubanshe 社会科学文献出版社, 2011).

Koichi Nomura and Zhang Xuefeng 张学锋 trans., *Jindai riben de zhongguo renshi: Zouxiang yazhou de hangzong* 近代日本的中国认识：走向亚洲的航踪 [*Modern Japan's Understanding of China: A Course Towards Asia*], (Beijing: Zhongyang bianyi chubanshe 中央编译出版社, 1999).

Li Dazhao nianpu bianxie zu 李大钊年谱编写组, *Li Dazhao nianpu* 李大钊年谱 [*Chronology of Li Dazhao*], (Lanzhou: Gansu renmin chubanshe 甘肃人民出版社, 1984).

Li Guoqi 李国祁, *Minguo shilunji* 民国史论集 [*Collected Essays on the History of the Republic of China*], (Taipei: Nantian shuju 南天书局, 1990).

Li Jihua, Feng Tiejin, and Zhou Fang 李继华、冯铁金、周芳, *Li Dazhao yiwen jizhu yu yanjiu* 李大钊轶文辑注与研究 [*Collected Essays and Studies on Li Dazhao*], (Beijing: Xianzhuang Shuju 线装书局, 2013).

Li Maosheng 李茂盛, *Minguo shanxishi* 民国山西史 [*History of Shanxi in the Republic of China*], (Taiyuan: Shanxi renmin chubanshe 山西人民出版社, 2011).

Li Shiyu 李世瑜, *Shehui lishixue wenji* 社会历史学文集 [*Collected Works of Social History*], (Tianjin: Tianjin guji chubanshe 古籍出版社, 2007).

Li Yeguang 李野光, *Huiteman mingzuo xinshi* 惠特曼名作欣赏 [*Appreciation of Whitman's Masterpieces*], (Beijing: Zhongguo heping chubanshe 中国和平出版社, 1995).

Li Yong and Zhang Zhongtian 李勇、张仲田, *Jiang Kai-shek nianpu* 蒋介石年谱 [*Chronology of Chiang Kai-shek*], (Beijing: Zhonggong dangshi chubanshe 中共党史出版社, 1995).

Li Yongsheng 李永胜, "1907–1908 nian Zhongdemei lianmeng wenti yanjiu 1907–1908 年中德美联盟问题研究 [Research on the Sino-German-American Alliance Issue (1907–1908)]," *Shijie Lishi* 世界历史 4 (2011).

Li Zhongjie and Duan Dongsheng 李忠杰、段东升, *Zhongguo gongchandang dierci quanguo daibia odahui dang'an wenjian xuanbian* 中国共产党第二次全国代表大会档案文献选编 [*Selected Documents of the Second National Congress of the Communist Party of China*], (Beijing: Zhonggong dangshi chubanshe 中共党史出版社, 2014).

Liu He 刘禾, *Shijie zhixu yu wenming dengdai* 世界秩序与文明等级 [*World Order and Civilizational Hierarchies*], (Beijing: Shenghuo, Dushu, Xinzhi sanlian shudian 生活·读书·新知三联书店, 2016).

Liu Jie 刘杰, *Chaoyue guojing de lishi renshi: Laizi riben xuezhe ji haiwai zhongguo xuezhe de shijiao* 超越国境的历史认识：来自日本学者及海外中国学者的视角 [*Understanding History Beyond Borders: Perspectives from Japanese Scholars and Overseas Sinologists*], (Beijing: Shehui kexue wenxian chubanshe 社会科学文献出版社, 2006).

Liu Jinzao 刘锦澡, *Qingchao wenxian tongkao* (*Yingyinben*) 清朝文献通考（影印本）[*Comprehensive Examination of Qing Dynasty Literature* (*Reprint*)], (Taipei: Xinxing shuju 新兴书局, 1963).

Liu Peng 刘朋, *Zhonggong dangshi koushu shilu* (*Diyijuan*) 中共党史口述实录（第1卷）[*Oral History of the Communist Party of China* (*Volume 1*)], (Beijing: Zhongguo guji chubanshe 中国古籍出版社, 2010).

Liu Qingbo 刘晴波, *Yang Du ji* 杨度集 [*The Collected Works of Yang Du*], (Changsha: Hunan renmin chubanshe 湖南人民出版社, 1986).

Liu Xiaofeng 刘小枫, "Ouzhou wenming de 'ziyou kongjian' yu xiandai zhongguo 欧洲文明的'自由空间'与现代中国 [The free space in European civilization and modern China]," in *Zhongguo zhengzhixue* 中国政治学 [*Chinese Political Science*], ed. Zhang Guangsheng (Beijing: Zhongguo shehuikexue chubanshe 中国社会科学出版社, 2018, No. 2).

Liu Xiaofeng and Wen Yuwei 刘小枫、温玉伟, *Schmitt yu posui shidai de shiren* 施米特与破碎时代的诗人 [*Schmitt and the Poets of the Broken Era*], (Shanghai: Huadong shifan daxue chubanshe 华东师范大学出版社, 2019).

Luo Chunpu 雒春普, *Yan Xishan zhuan* 阎锡山传 [*Biography of Yan Xishan*], (Taiyuan: Shanxi renmin chubanshe 山西人民出版社, 2004).

Ma Jianbiao 马建标, "Suzao jiushizhu: 'Yi zhan'qianhou 'weierxun zhuyi' zaizhongguo de chuanbo 塑造救世主：'一战'后期'威尔逊主义'在中国的传播 [Shaping a Savior: The Spread of Wilsonianism in China in the Later Stages of the First World War]," *Xueshu yuekan* 学术月刊 6 (2017).

Mao Haijian 茅海建, *Cong jiawu dao wuxu: Kang Youwei "wo shi" jianzhu* 从甲午到戊戌：康有为〈我史〉鉴注 [*From the jiawu War to the Wuxu Reform: Commentary on Kang Youwei's 'My History'*], (Beijing: Shenghuo, Dushu, Xinzhi sanlian shudian 生活·读书·新知三联书店, 2009).

Matsumoto Shigeharu, Cao Zhenxian, Shen Zhongqi 曹振威、沈中琦 et al. trans., *Shanghai shidai* 上海时代 [*The Shanghai Era*], (Shanghai: Shanghai shudian chubanshe 上海书店出版社, 2010).

Mi Rucheng 宓汝成, *Zhongguo tielu shi ziliao* (*Di'erce*) 中国铁路史资料（第2册）[*Materials on the History of Chinese Railways* (*Volume 2*)], (Beijing: Zhonghua shuju 中华书局, 1963).

Nanjing daxue malie zhuyi jiaoyanshi Wang Jingwei wenti yanjiuzu 南京大学马列主义教研室《汪精卫问题研究组》选编, *Wang Jingwei jituan maiguo toudi pipan ziliao xuanbian* 汪精卫集团卖国投敌批叛资料选编 [*Selected Materials on Wang jingwei's Collaboration and Treachery*], (Nanjing daxue xuebao bianjibu 南京大学学报编辑部, 1981).

Okamoto Sakan 冈本监辅, *Wanguo shiji* 万国史记 [*History of All Nations*], (Shanghai: Liuxian shuju 六先书局, 1897).

Pan Wu 潘武, *Zhonghua zhongxue lishi jiaokeshu benguo zhibu* (*Di'erce*) 中华中学历史教科书本国之部（第二册）[*Chinese Middle School History Textbook: National Volume* (*Volume 2*)], (Beijing: Zhonghua shuju 中华书局, 1913).

Qin Shan 秦珊, *Meiguo wei'erxun zhengfu duihua zhengce yanjiu* 美国威尔逊政府对华政策研究 [*Research on the Wilson Administration's Policy Towards China*], (Beijing: Zhongguo shehuikexue chubanshe 中国社会科学出版社, 2005).

Qin Xiaoyi 秦孝仪, *Zongtong jianggong sixiang yanlun zongji* (*Di shiqi juan*) 总统蒋公思想言论总集（第17卷）[*Collected Thoughts and Discourses of President jiang* (*Volume 17*)], (Taipei: Central Committee of the Kuomintang Party History Commission, 1984).

Qiu Tao and Zheng Kuangmin 邱涛、郑匡民, "Wuxu zhengbian qian de rizhong jiemeng huodong 戊戌政变前的日中结盟活动 [Sino-Japanese Alliance Activities Before the Wuxu Coup]," *Jindaishi yanjiu* 近代史研究 1 (2010).

Rao Huaimin 饶怀民, *Yang Yulin ji* 杨毓麟集 [*The Collected Works of Yang Yulin*], (Changsha: Yuelu shushe 岳麓书社, 2008).

Ren Liming 任李明, *Wei'erxun zhuyi yanjiu* 威尔逊主义研究 [*Research on Wilsonianism*], (Beijing: Zhongguo shehuikexue chubanshe 中国社会科学出版社, 2013).

Ruskola, Teemu, Wei Leijie 魏磊杰 trans., *Fazhi Dongfang Zhuyi* 法制东方主义 [*Legal Orientalism*], (Beijing: Zhongguo zhengfa daxue chubanshe 中国政法大学出版社, 2016).

Sakuma Naoki, *Dongya jindai wenmingshi shang de Liang Qichao* 东亚近代文明史上的梁启超 [*Liang Qichao in the History of Modern East Asian Civilization*], (Shanghai: Shanghai renmin chubanshe 上海人民出版社, 2016).

Sakuma Naoki, Zhang Wen 张雯 trans., *Riben zaoqi de yazhou zhuyi* 日本早期的亚洲主义 [*Early Asianism in Japan*], (Beijing: Peking University Press 北京大学出版社, 2016).

Sang Bing and Guan Xiaohong 桑兵、关晓红, *Xianyin houchuang yu bupo buli: Jindai zhongguo xueshu liupai yanjiu* 先因后创与不破不立：近代中国学术流派研究 [*Precedence and Innovation: Research on Modern Chinese Academic Schools*], (Beijing: Shenghuo, Dushu, Xinzhi sanlian shudian 生活·读书·新知三联书店, 2007).

Schmitt, Carl, Liu Feng 刘锋 trans., *Xianfa xueshuo* 宪法学说 [*Constitutional Theory*], (Shanghai: Shanghai renmin chubanshe 上海人民出版社, 2005).

Schmitt, Carl, Liu Zongkun 刘宗坤 et al. trans., *Schmitt wenji* (*diyijuan*) 施米特文集（第一卷）[*The Collected Works of Schmitt* (*Volume One*)], (Shanghai: Shanghai renmin chubanshe 上海人民出版社, 2004).

Schmitt, Carl, Liu Yi, and Zhang Chengguo 刘毅、张陈果 trans., *Dadi de fa* 大地的法 [*The Law of the Earth*], (Shanghai: Shanghai renmin chubanshe 上海人民出版社, 2017).

Schmitt, Carl, Zhu Yanbing 朱雁冰 trans., *Lunduan yu gainian* 论断与概念 [*Judgments and Concepts*], (Shanghai: Shanghai renmin chubanshe 上海人民出版社, 2006).

Seager, Robert, Liu Xuecheng 刘学成 et al. trans., *Mahan* 马汉 [*Mahan*], (Beijing: Jiefangjun chubanshe 解放军出版社, 1989).

Shanghai renmin chubanshe 上海人民出版社, *Zhang Taiyan quanji·Taiyan wenlu bupian* (*Shang*) 章太炎全集·太炎文录补编（上）[*The Complete Works of Zhang Taiyan: Supplement to the Writings of Taiyan* (*Volume 1*)], (Shanghai: Shanghai renmin chubanshe 上海人民出版社, 2017).

Shanghai renmin chubanshe 上海人民出版社, *Zhang Taiyan quanji·Shuxinji* (*Shang*) 章太炎全集·书信集（上）[*The Complete Works of Zhang Taiyan: Collected Letters* (*Volume 1*)], (Shanghai: Shanghai renmin chubanshe 上海人民出版社, 2017).

Shaonian zhongguo xuehui 少年中国学会, *Guojia zhuyi lunwenji* (*Disanban*) 国家主义论文集（第3版）[*Collection of Nationalist Essays* (*3rd Edition*)], (Shanghai: Zhonghua shuju 中华书局, 1925).

Shen Xiaomin 沈晓敏, *Chuchang yu qiubian: Qingmo minchu de zhejiang ziyiju he shengyihui* 处常与求变：清末民初的浙江咨议局和省议会 [*Continuity and Change: The Zhejiang Advisory Council and Provincial Assembly in the Late Qing and Early Republic*], (Beijing: Shenghuo, Dushu, Xinzhi sanlian shudian 生活·读书·新知三联书店, 2005).

Shijie Zhishi Chubanshe 世界知识出版社, *Guoji tiaoyue ji* (*1917–1923*) 国际条约集（1917 - 1923）[*Collection of International Treaties* (*1917–1923*)], (Beijing: Shijie zhishi chubanshe 世界知识出版社, 1961).

Sichuansheng Difangzhi Bianzuan Weiyuanhui 四川省地方志编纂委员会, *Sichuansheng zhi·Renwu zhi (Shang)* 四川省志·人物志（上）[*Chronicle of Sichuan Province: Biographies (Volume 1)*], (Chengdu: Sichuan renmin chubanshe 四川人民出版社, 2001).

Sichuansheng Wenshi yanjiuguan 四川省文史研究馆, *Sichuan junfa shiliao (Disanji)* 四川军阀史料（第三辑）[*Materials on the History of Sichuan Warlords (Volume 3)*], (Chengdu: Sichuan renmin chubanshe 四川人民出版社, 1985).

Spykman, Nicholas, Wang Shan, and Guo Xinyu 王珊、郭鑫雨 trans., *Shijie zhengzhi zhong de meiguo zhanlue* 世界政治中的美国战略 [*American Strategy in World Politics*], (Shanghai: Shanghai renmin chubanshe 上海人民出版社, 2018).

Spykman, Nicholas, Yu Haijie 俞海杰 trans., *Heping dilixue: Bianyuan didai de zhanlue* 和平地理学：边缘地带的战略 [*Geopolitics: Strategy of the Margins*], (Shanghai: Shanghai renmin chubanshe 上海人民出版社, 2016).

Sun Lulu and Zhang Yongle 孙璐璐、章永乐, "Cong bolan wenti fansi ka'er shimite de ouzhou guoji zhixu lunshu 从波兰问题反思卡尔·施米特的欧洲国际秩序论述 [Reflecting on Carl Schmitt's Discourse on European International Order from the Polish Issue]," *Ouzhou yanjiu* 欧洲研究 2 (2019).

Takenouchi Mitsuru, Cheng Ma 程麻 trans., *Zhongguo lishi yu shehui pinglun* 中国历史与社会评论 [*Comments on Chinese History and Society*], (Beijing: Zhongguo wenlian chubanshe 中国文联出版社, 2006).

Tang Zhijun 汤志钧, *Zhang Taiyan nianpu changbian* 章太炎年谱长编 [*Extended Chronology of Zhang Taiyan*], (Beijing: Zhonghua shuju 中华书局, 1979).

Tucker, Richard, Luo Jiong 罗炯 et al. trans., *Zhanzheng yu heping de quanli* 战争与和平的权利 [*The Rights of War and Peace*], (Nanjing: Yilin chubanshe 译林出版社, 2009).

Wang Gengxiong 王耿雄, *Sun Yat-sen ji waiji (Diyijuan)* 孙中山集外集 [*Collected Works of Sun Yat-sen (Volume 1)*], (Shanghai: Shanghai renmin chubanshe 上海人民出版社, 1990).

Wang Hui 汪晖, "Zhongguo jueqi de jingyan jiqi mianlin de tiaozhan 中国崛起的经验及其面临的挑战 [The Experience of China's Rise and the Challenges It Faces]," *Wenhua zongheng* 文化纵横 2 (2010).

Wang Shengzu 王绳祖, *Guoji guanxishi: Diwujuan (1929–1939 nian)* 国际关系史：第五卷（1929–1939年）[*History of International Relations: Volume 5 (1929–1939)*], (Beijing: Shijie zhishi chubanshe 世界知识出版社, 1995).

Wang Shengzu, He Chunchao, and Wu Shimin 王绳祖、何春超、吴世民, *Guoji guanxishi ziliao xuanbian: Shiqi shiji zhongye–1945* 国际关系史资料选编：17世纪中叶 – 1945 [*Selected Materials on the History of International Relations: Mid-17th Century to 1945*], (Beijing: Falü chubanshe 法律出版社, 1988).

Wang Xiaode 王晓德, *Mengxiang yu xianshi: Wei'erxun 'lixiang zhuyi' waijiao yanjiu* 梦想与现实：威尔逊"理想主义"外交研究 [*Dreams and Reality: Research on

Wilsonian 'Idealism' in Foreign Policy], (Beijing: Zhongguo shehuikexue chubanshe 中国社会科学出版社, 1995).

Wang Xuetai 王学泰, *Youmin wenhua yu zhongguo shehui* 游民文化与中国社会 [*Vagrant Culture and Chinese Society*], (Beijing: Tongxin chubanshe 同心出版社, 2007).

Wang Yunsheng 王芸生, *Liushi nianlai zhongguo yu riben* 六十年来中国与日本 [*China and Japan in the Last Sixty Years*], (Beijing: Shenghuo, Dushu, Xinzhi sanlian shudian 生活·读书·新知三联书店, 1981).

Watanabe Hiroshi and Qu Jianying 区建英 trans., *Dongya de wangquan yu sixiang* 东亚的王权与思想 [*Kingship and Thought in East Asia*], (Shanghai: Shanghai guji chubanshe 上海古籍出版社, 2016).

Weihuanggong chenlieguan 伪皇宫陈列馆, *Weihuanggong chenlieguan nianjian* 伪皇宫陈列馆年鉴 [*Yearbook of the Puppet Palace Museum*], (Changchun: Wei huanggong chenlieguan 伪皇宫陈列馆, 1987).

Wilson, Woodrow, Jiang Menglin 蒋梦麟 trans., *Meiguo weierxun zongtong canzhao yanshuo* 美国威尔逊总统参照演说 [*Reference Speeches by President Wilson of the United States*], (Shanghai: Commercial Press, 1919).

Xia Xinhua 夏新华, *Jindai zhongguo xianzheng licheng: Shiliao huicui* 近代中国宪政历程：史料荟萃 [*The Constitutional History of Modern China: A Collection of Historical Materials*], (Beijing: Zhongguo zhengfa daxue chubanshe 中国政法大学出版社, 2004).

Yang Du 杨度, *Kuangdai yicai* 旷代逸才 [*Exceptional Talent in the Era*], (Beijing: Dongfang chubanshe 东方出版社, 1998).

Yang Fan and Jiang Pei 杨帆、江沛, "'Niuyue shibao' shiye zhongde Sun Yat-sen (1896–1925) 《纽约时报》视野中的孙中山（1896 - 1925） [Sun Yat-sen in the Perspective of The New York Times (1896–1925)]," *Nanjing shehui kexue* 南京社会科学 7 (2016).

Yang Tianshi 杨天石, "Sun Yat-sen yu diyici shijie dazhan 孙中山与第一次世界大战 [Sun Yat-sen and the First World War]," *Jiangsu shifan daxue xuebao* (*Zhexue shehuikexue ban*) 江苏师范大学学报（哲学社会科学版） 5 (2018).

Yu Xintuan and Wang Zhensuo 俞辛焞、王振锁, *Sun Yat-sen zairi huodong milu* (*1913.8–1916.4*) 孙中山在日活动密录 （1913年8月 - 1916年4月）[*Confidential Records of Sun Yat-sen's Activities in Japan* (*August 1913–April 1916*)], (Tianjin: Nankai daxue chubanshe 南开大学出版社, 1990).

Yukio Hori and Xiong Dayun 熊达云 trans., *Zhanqian riben guojiazhuyi yundongshi* 战前日本国家主义运动史 [*History of Nationalism Movements in Pre-War Japan*], (Beijing: Shehui kexue wenxian chubanshe 社会科学文献出版社, 2010).

Zeng Yeying 曾业英, *Cai Songpo ji* 蔡松坡集 [*The Collected Works of Cai Songpo*], (Shanghai: Shanghai renmin chubanshe 上海人民出版社, 1984).

Zhang Pengzhou 张篷舟, *Zhongri guanxi wushinian dashiji: 1932–1982* (*Diyice*) 中日关系五十年大事记：1932 – 1982（第一册）[*Chronicle of Sino-Japanese Relations Over Fifty Years: 1932–1982* (*Volume 1*)], (Beijing: Wenhua yishu chubanshe 文化艺术出版社, 2006).

Zhang Pinxing 张品兴, *Liang Qichao quanji* 梁启超全集 [*The Complete Works of Liang Qichao*], (Beijing: Beijing chubanshe 北京出版社, 1999).

Zhang Shiming 张世明, *Kongjian, Falü yu xueshu huayu: Xifang bianjiang lilun jingdian wenxian* 空间、法律与学术话语：西方边疆理论经典文献 [*Space, Law, and Academic Discourse: Classic Western Frontier Theories*], (Harbin: Heilongjiang jiaoyu chubanshe 黑龙江教育出版社, 2014).

Zhang Yongle 章永乐, "'Daguo xietiao' yu 'Da tuoxie': Tiaoyue wangluo, yinhangtuan yu xinhai geming de lujing '大国协调' 与 '大妥协' ：条约网络、银行团与辛亥革命的路径 ['Great Power Coordination' and 'Great Compromise': Treaty Networks, Banking Groups, and the Path of the Xinhai Revolution]," *Xueshu yuekan* 学术月刊 10 (2018).

Zhang Zhan and Wang Renzhi 张枬、王忍之, *Xinhai geming qian shinian jian shilun xuanji* (*Diyijuan shangce*) 辛亥革命前十年间时论选集（第一卷上册）[*Selected Essays of the First Decade Before the Xinhai Revolution* (*Volume 1, Upper Volume*)], (Beijing: Shenghuo, Dushu, Xinzhi sanlian shudian 生活·读书·新知三联书店, 1960).

Zheng Dahua and Zou Xiaozhan 郑大华、邹小站, *Zhongguo jindaishi shang de minzuzhuyi—Di'erjie zhongguo jindai sixiangshi guoji xueshu yantaohui lunwenji* 中国近代史上的民族主义——第二届中国近代思想史国际学术研讨会论文集 [*Nationalism in Modern Chinese History—Proceedings of the Second International Academic Symposium on Modern Chinese Thought*], (Beijing: Shehuikexue wenxian chubanshe 社会科学文献出版社, 2006).

Zhonggong chongqing shiwei dangshi gongzuo weiyuanhui 中共重庆市委党史工作委员会, *Wusi yundong zai chongqing* 五四运动在重庆 [*The May Fourth Movement in Chongqing*], (1984, internal publication).

Zhonggong 'yida' huizhi jinianguan and Shanghai geming lishi bowuguan choubeichu 中共"一大"会址纪念馆、上海革命历史博物馆筹备处, *Shanghai gemingshi ziliao yu yanjiu* (*Disanji*) 上海革命史资料与研究（第三辑）[*Materials and Research on the History of the Shanghai Revolution* (*Volume 3*)], (Shanghai: Shanghai guji chubanshe 上海古籍出版社, 2003).

Zhonggong zhongyang ma, en, lie, si zhuanji bianyiju yanjiushi 中共中央马、恩、列、斯著作编译局研究室, *Wusi shiqi qikan jieshao* (*Disanji, Shangce*) 五四时期期刊介绍（第三辑，上册）[*Introduction to Periodicals During the May Fourth Period* (*Volume 3, Volume 1*)], (Beijing: Shenghuo, Dushu, Xinzhi sanlian shudian 生活·读书·新知三联书店, 1959).

Zhonggong zhongyang wenxian yanjiushi and Zhongyang dang'anguan 中共中央文献研究室、中央档案馆, *Jiandang yilai zhongyao wenxian xuanbian (1921–1949) (Dishice)* 建党以来重要文献选编（1921 - 1949）（第十册）[*Selected Important Documents Since the Founding of the Party (1921–1949) (Volume 10)*], (Beijing: Zhongyang wenxian chubanshe 中央文献出版社, 2011).

Zhongguo shehui kexueyuan jindaishi yanjiusuo jindaishi ziliao bianjibu 中国社会科学院近代史研究所《近代史资料》编辑部, *Jindaishi ziliao (Di 92 hao)* 近代史资料（第92号）[*Modern History Materials (Issue 92)*], (Beijing: Zhongguo shehui-kexue chubanshe 中国社会科学出版社, 2005).

Zhongguo shehui kexueyuan jindaishi yanjiusuo jindaishi ziliao bianyishi 中国社会科学院近代史研究所《近代史资料》编译室, *Miji lucun (Jindaishi ziliao zhuankan)* 秘笈录存（近代史资料专刊）[*Secret Record Storage (Special Edition on Modern History)*], (Beijing: Zhongguo shehuikexue chubanshe 中国社会科学出版社, 1984).

Zhongguo shehui kexueyuan jindaishi yanjiusuo jindaishi ziliao bianyishi 中国社会科学院近代史研究所《近代史资料》编译室, *Wusi aiguo yundong* 五四爱国运动 [*The May Fourth Patriotic Movement*], (Beijing: Zhishi chanquan chubanshe 知识产权出版社, 2013).

Zhongguo shehui kexueyuan jindaishi yanjiusuo zhonghua minguoshi yanjiushi 中国社会科学院近代史研究所中华民国史研究室, Sun Yat-sen quanji 孙中山全集 [The Complete Works of Sun Yat-sen], (Beijing: Zhonghua shuju 中华书局, 1982).

Zhongguo shehui kexueyuan xinwen yanjiusuo 中国社会科学院新闻研究所, *Zhongguo gongchandang xinwen gongzuo wenjian huibian (Shangjuan: 1921–1949)* 中国共产党新闻工作文件汇编（上卷：1921 - 1949）[*Compilation of CPC News Work Documents (Volume 1: 1921–1949)*], (Beijing: Xinhua chubanshe 新华出版社, 1980).

Zhongguo Shixuehui 中国史学会, *Zhongguo jindaishi ziliao congkan: Zhongri zhanzheng (Yi)* 中国近代史资料丛刊：中日战争（一）[*Collection of Modern Chinese Historical Materials: The Sino-Japanese War (Volume 1)*], (Shanghai: Shanghai renmin chubanshe 上海人民出版社, 1957).

Zhonghua minguo shishi jiyao bianji weiyuanhui 中华民国史事纪要编辑委员会, *Zhonghua minguo shishi jiyao (Chugao)·Zhonghua minguo shiyinian (1922) (Sizhiliu yuefen)* 中华民国史事纪要（初稿）·中华民国十一年（1922）（四至六月份）[*Chronicle of Events in the Republic of China (Draft)·The Eleventh Year of the Republic of China (1922) (April to June)*], (Taipei: Zhonghua minguo shiliao yanjiu zhongxin 中华民国史料研究中心, 1982).

Zhongyang dang'anguan, Zhongguo di'er lishi dang'anguan, and Jilinsheng shehui kexueyuan 中央档案馆、中国第二历史档案馆、吉林省社会科学院, *Huabei jingji lueduo* 华北经济掠夺 [*Economic Exploitation in North China*], (Beijing: Zhonghua shuju 中华书局, 2004).

Zhou Kaiqing 周开庆, *Minguo Liu Fucheng xiansheng xiang nianpu* 民国刘甫澄先生湘年谱 [*Chronology of Mr. Liu Fucheng in the Republic of China*], (Taipei: Taiwan shangwu yinshuguan gufen youxiangongsi 台湾商务印书馆股份有限公司, 1981).

Zhu Wentong 朱文通, *Li Dazhao quanji* 李大钊全集 [*The Complete Works of Li Dazhao*], (Shijiazhuang: Hebei jiaoyu chubanshe 河北教育出版社, 1999).

Zhu Wentong 朱文通, "Li Dazhao shehuizhuyi sixiang fazhan licheng xintan 李大钊社会主义思想发展历程新探 [New Exploration of the Development of Li Dazhao's Socialist Thought]," *Hebei xuekan* 河北学刊 1 (2007).

Literature in Other Languages

Adams, Charles Francis ed., *Memoires of John Quincy Adams, Comprising Portions of His Diary from 1795 to 1848*, Vol. 6, (Philadelphia: J.B. Lippincott & CO., 1875).

Akashi Kinji 明石欽司:「『大東亜国際法』理論–日本における近代国際法受容の帰結」[Theory of "Greater East Asian International Law"—The Consequences of Japan's Acceptance of Modern International Law], (『法学研究』Legal Studies, Vol. 82, No. 1, 2009).

Ambrosius, Lloyd E., *Woodrow Wilson and the American Diplomatic Tradition: The Treaty Fight in Perspective*, (Cambridge & New York: Cambridge University Press, 1987).

Amos S. Hershey, "The Calvo and Drago Doctrines, 1907," Articles by Maurer Faculty, (1961), URL: http://www.repository.law.indiana.edu/facpub/1961.

Anderson, Perry, *The H-Word: The Peripeteia of Hegemony*, (London: Verso, 2017).

Appleby, Joyce, and Terence Ball eds., *Jefferson: Political Writings*, (Cambridge: Cambridge University Press, 1999).

Armitage, David, *The Declaration of Independence: A Global History*, (Cambridge, Masssachussetts & London: Harvard University Press, 2008).

Balakrishnan, Gopal, *The Enemy: An Intellectual Portrait of Carl Schmitt*, (London: Verso, 2000).

Barton, Gregory A., *Informal Empire and the Rise of One World Culture*, (London: Palgrave Macmillan, 2014).

Bendersky, Joseph, *Carl Schmitt: Theorist for the Reich*, (Princeton: Princeton University Press, 1983).

Biography of Marquis Inoue Kaoru Editorial Committee 井上馨侯伝記編纂会 (ed.):『世外井上公伝』[Biography of Inoue Kaoru], (Tokyo: Hara Shobo, 1968).

Bluntschli, Kaspar, *Le Droit International Codifie*, trans. M.C. Lardy, (Paris: Guillaumin, 1870).

Bonn, M.J., "Germany and the Monroe Doctrine," *The Annals of the American Academy of Political and Social Science*, Vol. 66, *Preparedness and America's International Program* (July 1916), 102–105.

Boyle, Francis Anthony, *Foundations of World Order: The Legalist Approach to International Relations (1898–1922)*, (Durham & London: Duke University Press, 1999).

Bradley, James, *The Imperial Cruise: A Secret History of Empire and War*, (New York: Little, Brown and Company, 2009).

Burkman, Thomas W., *Japan and the League of Nations: Empire and World Order, 1914–1938*, (Honolulu: University of Hawaii Press, 2008).

Carnegie Endowment for International Peace. Division of Intercourse and Education eds., *American Foreign Policy: Based Upon Statements of Presidents and Secretaries of State of the United States and of Publicists of the American Republics*, (Washington D.C., 1920).

Carr, Edward Hallett, *Nationalism and After*, (London: Macmillan, 1945).

Cha, Changhoon, "China's Westward March: Strategic Views of One Belt, One Road," *The Korean Journal of International Studies*, Vol. 15, No. 3 (December 2017), 483–500.

Coudenhove-Kalergi, Richard N., *Crusade for Pan-Europe. Autobiography of A Man and A Movement*, (New York: G.P. Putnam's Sons, 1943).

Daitz, Werner, "Echte und unechte Großräume, 1941," in Lebensraum und gerechte Weltordung. Grundlagen einer Anti-Atlantikcharta. Ausgewählte Aufsätze von Werner Daitz, (Amsterdam: De Amsterdamsche Keurkamer, 1943).

Day, Richard B., *Leon Trotsky and the Politics of Economic Isolation*, (Cambridge & New York: Cambridge University Press, 1973).

Dickson, Paul, *Words from the White House: Words and Phrases Coined or Popularized by America's Presidents*, (New York: Walker Books, 2013).

"Dr. Sun Yat-Sen Flees From China," *New York Times* (7 August 1913).

Drago, Luis M., and H. Edward Nettles, "The Drago Doctrine in International Law and Politics," *The Hispanic American Historical Review*, Vol. 8, No. 2 (May 1928), 217.

Dugin, Alexander, *The Fourth Political Theory*, (London: Arktos, 2012).

East Asian Union, *East Asian Union (Reproduction Edition)*, Vol. 3, No. 1, Special Edition, (Tokyo: Kashiwa Shobō, 1996).

Editorial Bureau of Yomiuri Shimbun 読売新聞社編輯局 ed.,『支那事變實記』[A Chronicle of the China Incident], Vol. 3, (Hibonkaku, 1938).

Editorial Comment, "The Monroe Doctrine Again," *American Journal of International Law* 5 (1911), 729–735.

"Extension of the Monroe Doctrine," *The North China Daily News* 3 (27 December 1893).

Friedman, Thomas L., *The World Is Flat: A Brief History of the Twenty-first Century*, (New York: Farrar, Straus and Giroux, 2005).

Frye, Alton, *Nazi Germany and the American Hemisphere, 1933–1941*, (New Haven: Yale University Press, 1967).

Ginzburg, Carlo, Raymond Rosenthal trans., *Ecstasies: Deciphering the Witches' Sabbath*, (Chicago: University of Chicago Press, 1991).

Gruchmann, Lothar, *Nationalsozialistische Großraumordnung. Die Konstruktion einer "Deutschen Monroe-Doktrin,"* (Stuttgart: Deutsche Verlags-Anstalt, 1962).

Gruchmann, Lothar, *Nationalsozialistische Großraumordnung. Die Konstruktion einer "deutschen Monroe-Doktrin,"* (Stuttgart: Deutsche Verlags-. Anstalt, 1962).

Guinsberg, Thomas, *The Pursuit of Isolationism: In the United States Senate from Versailles to Pearl Harbor*, (New York: Garland Publishing, 1982).

Herrick, Samuel, "The Monroe Doctrine as a Principle of International Law," *4 Brief* 360 (1903).

Herriot, Édouard, Reginald J. Dingle trans., *The United States of Europe*, (New York: The Viking Press, 1930).

Hiden, John, *Germany and Europe 1919–1939*, (New York: Longman, 1977).

Hills, Jill, *The Struggle for Control of Global Communication, The Formative Century*, (Champaign, Illinois: University of Illinois Press, 2002).

Hitler, Adolf, *Der Führer antwortet Roosevelt. Reichstagsrede vom 28. April 1939*, (Munich: Zentralverlag der NSDAP, Franz Eher Nachfolger, 1939).

Hughes, Charles Evans, "Observations on the Monroe Doctrine," *9 A.B.A.J.* 559 (1923).

Hull, William, "The Monroe Doctrine: National or International," *Proceedings of the American Society of International Law at Its Annual Meeting (1907–1917)* 8 (22–25 April 1914), 155–170.

Ikeda Jugo 池田十吾,「石井·ランシング協定をめぐる日米関係(一)——中国に関する日米両国交換公文の成立過程から廃棄に至るまで」[U.S.-Japan Relations Regarding the Ishii-Lansing Agreement (1)—From the Establishment of the Japan-U.S. Exchange of Notes on China to its Termination], in『國士舘大學政經論叢』[Kokushikan University Political Science Review, Vol. 63, No. 4, 1988].

Ishii Kikujirō 石井菊次郎,『外交余録』[Diplomatic Commentaries], (Iwanami Shoten, 1930), 1930年.

Jackson, Steven F., "Does China Have a Monroe Doctrine? Evidence for Regional Exclusion," *Strategic Studies Quarterly*, Vol. 10, No. 4 (Winter 2016), 64–89.

Johnson, Keith, "Kerry Makes It Official: 'Era of Monroe Doctrine Is Over,'" *The Wall Street Journal* (November 18, 2013).

Kamishima Jiro 神島二郎 (ed.),『徳富蘇峰集』[Tokutomi Sohō Collection], (Chikuma Shobō, 1978).

Kaneko Kentarō 金子堅太郎, 東洋の平和はアジアモンロー主義にあり [Peace in the Orient lies in Asian Monroeism], (Kokikai, 1937).

Kazumin Uchida 浮田和民,『帝国主義と教育』【Imperialism and Education】, (Minyusha, 1901).

Kazumin Ukita 浮田和民:「新亜細亜主義——東洋モンロー主義の新解釋」[New Asianism—A New Interpretation of Oriental Monroe Docrine], Taiyo, Vol. 24, No. 9 (1918): 2–17.

Keio University 慶応義塾 (ed.),『福沢諭吉全集』第14巻[The Complete Works of Fukuzawa Yukichi, Vol. 14], (Tokyo: Iwanami Shoten, 1961).

Kenkichi Kodera 小寺謙吉,『大亜細亜主義論』[On Greater Asianism], (Tokyo Hobunkan, 1916).

Kennedy, Ross A. ed., *A Companion to Woodrow Wilson*, (Malden, Oxford & Chichester: John Wiley & Sons, Ltd, 2015).

Kita Ikki 北一輝,『支那革命外史』[Unofficial History of the Chinese Revolution], (Seiki Shobō, 1921).

Kita Tokichi 北昤吉,「誤解されたる亜細亜主義」[Misunderstood Asianism],『東方時論』[Oriental Journal, Vol. 2, No. 7, 1917].

Konoe Atsumaro 近衛篤麿,「同人種同盟附支那問題研究の必要」[The Necessity of Studying the Racial Alliance and the Chinese Problem],『太陽』[Taiyō], Vol. 4, No. 1, 1898.

Konoe Atsumaro Diary Publishing Committee 近衛篤麿日記刊行会 (ed.),『近衛篤麿日記』第2巻[Konoe Atsumaro Diary, Volume 2], (Kajima Institute Publishing, 1968).

Konoe Atsumaro Diary Publishing Committee 近衛篤麿日記刊行会 (ed.),『近衛篤麿日記 別巻 近衛篤麿日記付属文書』[Konoe Atsumaro Diary, Supplementary Volume: Documents Added to the Konoe Atsumaro Diary], (Kajima Institute Publishing, 1969).

Kusama Tokifuku, "Theory of Eastern and Western Connections," *Postal Newspaper News* (19 November 1879).

Laos, Nicolas, *The Metaphysics of World Order: A Synthesis of Philosophy, Theology, and Politics*, (Eugene, Oregon: Pickwick Publications, 2015).

Legg, Stephen ed., *Spatiality, Sovereignty and Carl Schmitt: Geographies of the Nomos*, (London & New York: Routledge, 2011).

Leonard, Mark, *What Does China Think?*, (London: Fourth Estate, 2008).

Levin, N. Gordon, *Woodrow Wilson and World Politics: America's Response to War and Revolution*, (New York: Oxford University Press, 1968).

Livingstone, Grace, *America's Backyard: The United States & Latin America from the Monroe Doctrine to the War on Terror*, (London & New York: Zed Books, 2009).

Lorimer, James, *The Institutes of the Law of Nations*, Vol. 1, (Edinburgh & London: William Blackwood and Sons, 1883).

Lovejoy, Arthur O., *The Great Chain of Being*, (Cambridge, MA: Harvard University Press, 1971).

Macris, Jefferey R., and Saul Kelly, *Imperial Crossroads: The Great Powers and the Persian Gulf*, (Annapolis: Naval Institute Press, 2012).

Manela, Erez, *The Wilsonian Moment: Self-Determination and the International Origins of Anticolonial Nationalism*, (New York: Oxford University Press, 2009).

Matsubara Kazuo 松原一雄,「リットン報告と日本モンロー主義」[The Lytton Report and the Japanese Monroe Doctrine],『東亜』(East Asia, Vol. 5, No. 11, 1932).

Matsushita, Masatoshi 松下正壽:『大東亜国際法の諸問題』[Problems of International Law in Greater East Asia], 日本法理研究会 [Japan Legal Principles Research Association, 1942].

Matsushita Masatoshi 松下正寿,『米洲広域国際法の基礎理念』[Fundamental principles of American Large-Space International Law] (有斐閣 Yuhikaku, 1942).

Meaney, Neville, *The Search for Security in the Pacific, 1901–1914*, (Sydney University Press, 2009).

Moore, John Bassett, "The Monroe Doctrine," *The Annals of the American Academy of Political and Social Science*, Vol. 96, The Place of the United States in a World Organization for the Maintenance of Peace (July 1921), 31–33.

Moyn, Samuel, and Andrew Sartori eds., *Global Intellectual History*, (New York: Columbia University Press, 2013).

Münkler, Herfried, *Macht in der Mitte: Die neuen Aufgaben Deutschlands in Europa*, (Hamburg: Edition Körber-Stiftung, 2015).

Murphy, Gretchen, *Hemispheric Imaginings: The Monroe Doctrine and Narratives of U.S. Empire*, (Durham & London: Duke University Press, 2005).

Nakayama Masaru 中山優「新秩序の東洋的性格」【The Oriental Character of the New Order】,『東亜連盟』The East Asian Union 1 (1939).

Neff, Stephen C., *War and the Law of Nations: A General History*, (New York: Cambridge University Press, 2005).

Odysseos, Louiza, and Fabio Petito, eds., *The International Political Thought of Carl Schmitt: Terror, Liberal War and the Crisis of Global Order*, (New York: Loutledge, 2007).

Ogata, Kohei 大形孝平 (ed.),『日本とインド』[Japan and India], (Sanseido, 1978).

Ōkawa Shūmei 大川周明,『大東亜秩序建設』[The Construction of East Asian Order], (Daiichi Shobō, 1943).

Ōkuma Shigenobu 大隈重信,『経世論』[Economic and Social Theory], (Fuzanbo, 1912).

Perkins, Dexter, *A History of the Monroe Doctrine*, (Boston: Little, Brown and Co., 1955).

Perkins, Dexter, *Monroe Doctrine, 1867–1907*, (Baltimore, Md: The Johns Hopkins University Press, 1937).

Perkins, Dexter, *The Monroe Doctrine, 1826–1867*, (Baltimore, Md: The Johns Hopkins University Press, 1933).

"Proposed Enlargement of the Monroe Doctrine," *The North China Daily News*. 3 (23 January 1896).

Rech, Walter, and Janis Grzybowski, "Between Regional Community and Global Society: Europe in the Shadow of Carl Schmitt and Kojève," *Journal of International Political Theory* 13 (2016), 148–149.

Reid, Whitelaw, "The Monroe Doctrine; The Polk Doctrine; Anarchism," *Yale L.J.* 13 (1903).

Roosevelt, Theodor, "The Monroe Doctrine," Speech at Chicago, Illinois (2 April 1903).

Root, Elihu, "The Declaration of the Rights and Duties of Nations Adopted by the American Institute of International Law," *The American Journal of International Law*, Vol. 10, No. 2 (April 1916), 211–221.

Root, Elihu, "The Real Monroe Doctrine," *The American Journal of International Law*, Vol. 8, No. 3 (July 1914), 427–442.

Rossi, Christopher, *Whiggish International Law: Elihu Root, the Monroe Doctrine, and International Law in the Americas*, (Leiden & Boston: Brill Nijhoff, 2019).

Scarfi, Juan Pablo, *The Hidden History of International law in the Americas: Empire and Legal Networks*, (Oxford & New York: Oxford University Press, 2017).

Schmitt, Carl, *Staat, Grossraum, Nomos: Arbeiten aus den Jahren 1916–1969*, (Berlin: Duncker & Humblot, 1995).

Schmitt, Carl, "The Order of the Great Space with the Intervention of External Domain Powers: a Contribution to the Concept of Empire in International Law," in *The State, the Great Space, and Law Essays: An Internal Set, 1916–1969*, (Berlin: Duncker & Humblot, 1995).

Schwarzenberger, Georg, *The Frontiers of International Law*, (London: Stevens and Sons, 1962).

Scott, J. ed., *The Hague Court Reports*, (New York: Oxford University Press, 1916).

Sexton, Jay, *The Monroe Doctrine: Empire and Nation in Nineteenth-Century America*, (New York: Hill and Wang, 2011).

Smith, Gaddis, *The Last Years of the Monroe Doctrine: 1945–1993*, (New York: Hill and Wang, 1994).

Stacey, Charles P., *The Military Problems of Canada*, (Toronto: Ryerson Press, 1940).

Tabata Shigejirō 田畑茂二郎,「東亜共栄圏国際法への道」[Toward a Path to International Law for the East Asia Co-Prosperity Sphere],『外交評論』[Diplomatic Review, Vol. 23, No. 1, 1943], 10–23.

Tabata Shigejirō 田畑茂二郎,「ナチス国際法学の轉開とその問題史的考察」【The Turning of Nazi International Jurisprudence and an Examination of the History of Its Problems】『外交時報』【Diplomatic Times, Vol. 107, No. 1, 1 July 1943】, 5–17.

Tabata Shigejirō 田畑茂二郎, :「東亜共栄圏国際法への道」【Toward a Path of International Law for the East Asian Co-Prosperity Sphere】,『外交評論』【Foreign Affairs Review, Vol. 23, No. 1 (1943)】, 10–23.

Tabata Shigejirō 田畑茂二郎,「ナチス国際法学の轉開とその問題史的考察」[The Development of Nazi International Law and a Historical Consideration of Its Problems],『外交時報』[Diplomatic Times, Vol. 107, No. 1, Issue No. 926, July 1, 1943], 5–17.

Tachisaku Taro 立作太郎,「英国の新モンロー主義の宣言及不戦条約の実効」[The Declaration of the British New Monroe Doctrine and the Effectiveness of the Non-War Treaty],『外交時報』[Diplomatic Times, Vol. 48 No. 12, (15 December 1928].

Taft, William, "The Duty of Americans in the Philippines," speech delivered by Taft before the Union Reading College in Manila (17 December 1903); reproduced in Official Gazette (Supplement) Vol. 1, No. 68 (23 December 1903).

Takeuchi Yoshimi 竹内好:『日本とアジア 竹内好評論集第3巻』[Japan and Asia: Takeuchi Yoshimi's Commentary, Vol. 3], (Chikuma Shobō, 1966).

Tanaka Masaaki 田中正明 (ed.),『松井石根大将の陣中日誌』[War Journal of General Matsui Iwane], (Tokyo: Fuyo Shobo, 1985).

Tatsusaku Taro 立作太郎,「英国の新モンロー主義の宣言及不戦条約の実効」[Britain's Declaration of the New Monroe Doctrine and the Effectiveness of the Kellogg-Briand Pact],『外交時報』[Diplomatic Times, Vol. 48, No. 12, Issue No. 577, December 15, 1928].

"The German Press and the Monroe Doctrine," *The North China Daily News* 3 (17 November 1896).

"The Monroe Doctrine," *The North China Daily News* 4 (13 December 1895).

"The Monroe Doctrine," *The North China Daily News* 4 (19 June 1900).

Tokifuku Kusama 草間時福:「東洋連横論」[On Inter-Oriental Union],『郵便報知新聞』[Yubin Hochi Shimbun], November 19, 1879.

Tsurumi Yusuke 鶴見祐輔,『後藤新平』第2巻 [Gotō Shinpei, Volume 2], (Keiso Shobō, 1965).

Ukita Kazutami 浮田和民,『帝国主義と教育』 [Imperialism and Education], (Minyusha, 1901).

Ullmann, Walter, "The Development of the Medieval Idea of Sovereignty," *English Historical Review* 64 (1949), 1–33.

United States Department of State, *Foreign Relations of United States*, (Washington: Government Printing Office, 1895).

Walther, Vogel, *Das Neue Europa und seine historisch-geographischen Grundlagen*, (Bonn: Schroeder, 1925).

Warf, Barney and Santa Arias eds., *The Spatial Turn: Interdisciplinary Perspectives*, (London & New York: Routeledge, 2009).

Waseda University Editorial Department 早稲田大学編輯部 (eds.),『大隈伯演説集』[Collected Speeches by Count Ōkuma], (Waseda University Press, 1907).

Washington, George, *Washington's Farewell Address to the People of the United States*, (Trenton: Printed by George Sherman, 1812).

Wilson, Woodrow, "An Address to a Joint Session of Congress," (Lecture, Washington, DC, 2 April 1917), in *The Papers of Woodrow Wilson*, Vol. 41, (Princeton: Princeton University Press, 1983): 525.

Wilson, Woodrow, "Peace without Victory," (Speech on 22 January 1917. 64th Cong., 23 Sess., Senate Document No. 685: "A League for Peace").

Wilson, Woodrow, "The Ideals of America," *Atlantic Monthly* 90 (December 1902), 721–734.

Wilson, Woodrow, *War and Peace: Presidential Messages, Addresses, and Public Papers (1917–1924)*, Vol. 2, (Honolulu: University Press of the Pacific, 2002).

Woolsey, T.S., "Drago and the Drago Doctrine," *The American Journal of International Law*, Vol. 15, No. 4 (July 1921), 558–559.

Yamaguchi Prefectural Education Association 山口県教育会 (ed.), 『吉田松陰全集』第4巻 [Complete Works of Yoshida Shōin, Vol. 4], (Iwanami Shoten, 1938).

Yasui Kaoru 安井郁,『歐洲広域国際法の基礎理念』[Fundamental principles of European Large-Space International Law] (有斐閣 Yuhikaku, 1942).

Yokota Kisaburō 横田喜三郎, 「アジア・モンロー主義批判」[Criticism of the Asian Monroe Doctrine]『中央公論』[Chūōkōron, July 1933], 92–104.

Yoshida Tomoaki 吉田鞆明 (ed.), 『巨人頭山満翁は語る』The Words of the Giant Tōyama Mitsuru, (Tokyo: Kansenso, 1939).

Yusuke Tsurumi 鶴見祐輔,『後藤新平』【Goto Shinpei】, Volume 2, (Jinko Shobo, 1965).

井上馨侯伝記編纂会『世外井上公伝（世外井上公传）』第5巻, 原書房, 1968年.

Index